A COMMENTARY ON
ROMANS

KREGEL EXEGETICAL LIBRARY

A COMMENTARY ON

ROMANS

JOHN D. HARVEY

Kregel
Academic

A Commentary on Romans

© 2019 by John D. Harvey

Published by Kregel Academic, an imprint of Kregel Publications, 2450 Oak Industrial Dr. NE, Grand Rapids, MI 49505-6020.

The English translations of the original Greek or Hebrew texts of the Bible are the author's own.

The Hebrew font used in this book is NewJerusalemU and the Greek font is GraecaU; both are available from www.linguisticsoftware.com/lgku.htm, +1-425-775-1130.

ISBN 978-0-8254-4210-0

Printed in the United States of America

19 20 21 22 23 / 5 4 3 2 1

To my wife, Anita,
who walks within our house
with the integrity of her heart
(Psalm 101:2b).

CONTENTS

PREFACE

Centuries ago, the author of Ecclesiastes wrote, "Of making many books there is no end, and much study is a weariness of the flesh" (Eccl. 12:12). A list of commentaries published in English since 1965 (below) supports the truth of the first half of that statement—at least as it applies to Paul's letter to the Romans—since that list includes eighty-one titles (and is, no doubt, still incomplete). As of this writing, the website www.bestcommentaries.com lists eleven additional commentaries on Romans scheduled for publication in 2019. Add monographs on Romans to the collection and it seems, indeed, that there is no end to making many books on Paul's best-known letter. Personally, though, I am less convinced by the second half of the Preacher's statement. Having invested the past seven years working on, first, an exegetical guide to Romans and, then, this commentary, I have found the process more energizing than wearying, perhaps because the Kregel Exegetical Library series provides the freedom to align this commentary with objectives close to my heart.

The 2017–2018 academic year is my twenty-seventh teaching at Columbia Biblical Seminary of Columbia International University. Following the trail blazed by my teachers and, then, my colleagues in biblical studies—particularly Terry Hulbert, Bill Larkin, and Alex Luc—our objective in teaching Hermeneutics, Greek, Hebrew, and English Bible book studies has always been to equip students to do their own exegetical work and reach their own conclusions. Only then should they turn to commentaries to validate and refine their own analysis. Further, our ultimate objective in exegesis has always been that students will communicate accurately the message of the text. In other words, the "deliverable" at the end of the process is a sermon or lesson outline, not an exegetical paper. Analysis of the Greek text is essential, but to be candid, despite our best intentions and fondest hopes, only a certain percentage of seminary graduates are going to maintain their Greek skills at the highest level.

So, the format and content of this commentary are geared to those ends and to that audience. This volume is not a technical commentary that is accessible only to scholars who live in the Greek language and the seminary library. Readers will not find a detailed history of the interpretation of Romans. They will not find extensive word studies that dive deeply into extrabiblical literature. They will not find closely argued discussions of the fine points of Greek verb tenses. They will not find technical analysis of textual variants. Those elements are present, but they are addressed briefly in footnotes. Active pastors, teachers, and students of the Bible tend to be interested in the answers to three basic questions: (1) What did the author say? (2) Why did he say it? (3) What should I do with it?

This commentary, then, seeks to answer those questions by focusing on explaining Paul's intended meaning, setting individual paragraphs of the letter in the context of Paul's overall argument and theology, and providing suggestions of how to appropriate each paragraph's significance for contemporary audiences. The expectation, of course, is not that readers will adopt this information in this commentary verbatim. Hopefully, though, they will be able to see how the material can be organized and will be challenged to develop their own exposition for their own situation. The section in the Introduction titled "Interpretive Approach and Commentary Organization" unpacks this approach more fully. The section on "Homiletical Considerations" uses Romans 1:8–12 to offer a very brief example.

—Columbia, SC
December 1, 2017

ABBREVIATIONS

Books of the Old Testament

Gen.	Genesis
Exod.	Exodus
Lev.	Leviticus
Num.	Numbers
Deut.	Deuteronomy
Josh.	Joshua
Judg.	Judges
Ruth	Ruth
1 Sam.	1 Samuel
2 Sam.	2 Samuel
1 Kings	1 Kings
2 Kings	2 Kings
1 Chron.	1 Chronicles
2 Chron.	2 Chronicles
Ezra	Ezra
Neh.	Nehemiah
Esther	Esther
Job	Job
Ps(s)	Psalms
Prov.	Proverbs
Eccl.	Ecclesiastes
Song	Song of Solomon
Isa.	Isaiah
Jer.	Jeremiah
Lam.	Lamentations
Ezek.	Ezekiel
Dan.	Daniel

Hos.	Hosea
Joel	Joel
Amos	Amos
Obad.	Obadiah
Jonah	Jonah
Mic.	Micah
Nah.	Nahum
Hab.	Habakkuk
Zeph.	Zephaniah
Hag.	Haggai
Zech.	Zechariah
Mal.	Malachi

Books of the New Testament

Matt.	Matthew
Mark	Mark
Luke	Luke
John	John
Acts	Acts
Rom.	Romans
1 Cor.	1 Corinthians
2 Cor.	2 Corinthians
Gal.	Galatians
Eph.	Ephesians
Phil.	Philippians
Col.	Colossians
1 Thess.	1 Thessalonians
2 Thess.	2 Thessalonians
1 Tim.	1 Timothy
2 Tim.	2 Timothy
Titus	Titus
Philem.	Philemon
Heb.	Hebrews
James	James
1 Peter	1 Peter
2 Peter	2 Peter
1 John	1 John
2 John	2 John
3 John	3 John
Jude	Jude
Rev.	Revelation

ABBREVIATIONS

General Abbreviations

ABD	D. N. Freedman, ed., *The Anchor Bible Dictionary*, 6 vols. New York: Doubleday, 1992.
BDAG	F. W. Danker, ed., *A Greek-English Lexicon of the New Testament and Other Early Christian Literature*. Chicago/London: University of Chicago Press, 2000. Based on W. Bauer's *Griechisch-deutsches Wörterbuch* (6th ed.) and on previous English ed. W. F. Arndt, F. W. Gingrich, and F. W. Danker.
BDF	F. Blass and A. Debrunner, *A Greek Grammar of the New Testament and Other Early Christian Literature*, ET and rev. by R. W. Funk. Chicago: University of Chicago Press, 1961.
CSB	Christian Study Bible (2017)
DNTB	C. A. Evans and S. E. Porter, eds., *Dictionary of New Testament Background*. Leicester / Downers Grove, IL: InterVarsity, 2000.
DPL	G. F. Hawthorne, R. P. Martin, and D. G. Reid, eds., *Dictionary of Paul and His Letters*. Downers Grove, IL: InterVarsity, 1993.
EDNT	H. Balz and G. Schneider, eds., *Exegetical Dictionary of the New Testament*, 3 vols. Grand Rapids: Eerdmans, 1990–93.
ESV	English Standard Version (2011)
GNB	Good News Bible (1976)
JBL	*Journal of Biblical Literature*
JETS	*Journal of the Evangelical Theological Society*
KJV	King James Version (1611)
LN	J. P. Louw and E. A. Nida, eds., *Greek-English Lexicon of the New Testament Based on Semantic Domains,* 2 vols. New York: United Bible Societies, 1988.
LXX	Septuagint
MT	Masoretic Text
NCV	New Century Version (1987)
NEB	New English Bible (1970)
NET	New English Translation (2005)
NIDNTT	C. Brown, ed., *The New International Dictionary of New Testament Theology*, 3 vols. Grand Rapids: Zondervan, 1975–78.
NIV	New International Version (2011)
NIRV	New International Readers Version

NLT	New Living Translation of the Bible (1996)
SJT	Scottish Journal of Theology
TDNT	*Theological Dictionary of the New Testament*
UBS[5]	B. Aland, K. Aland, J. Karavidopoulos, C. M. Martini, and B. M. Metzger, eds., *The Greek New Testament*, 5th rev. ed. Stuttgart: Deutsche Bibelgesellschaft; New York: United Bible Societies, 2014.

SELECTED BIBLIOGRAPHY

Key Resources: *The discussion in this commentary refers regularly to the following works.*

Cranfield, C. E. B. *A Critical and Exegetical Commentary on the Epistle to the Romans*. International Critical Commentary. 2 vols. Edinburgh: T&T Clark, 1980.

Dunn, J. D. G. *Romans*. Word Biblical Commentary. 2 vols. Waco, TX: Word, 1988.

Jewett, R. *Romans*. Hermeneia. Minneapolis: Fortress, 2007.

Longenecker, R. N. *The Epistle to the Romans*. New International Greek Testament Commentary. Grand Rapids: Eerdmans, 2016.

Moo, D. J. *The Epistle to the Romans*. New International Commentary on the New Testament. Grand Rapids: Eerdmans, 1996.

Schreiner, T. R. *Romans*. Baker Exegetical Commentary on the New Testament. Grand Rapids: Baker, 1998.

Commentaries in English published since 1965

Achtemeier, P. J. *Romans*. Atlanta: John Knox, 1985.

Andria, S. *Romans*. Nairobi: HippoBooks, 2011.

Barnett, P. *Romans: Revelation of God's Righteousness*. Fearn: Christian Focus, 2003.

Barrett, C. K. *A Commentary on the Epistle to the Romans*. 2nd ed. London: Black, 1991.

Bartlett, D. L. *Romans*. Louisville: Westminster/John Knox, 1995.

Barton, B. B. *Romans*. Wheaton, IL: Tyndale House, 1992.

Bence, C. L. *Romans: A Commentary for Bible Students*. Indianapolis: Wesleyan Publishing House, 1995.

Best, E. *The Letter of Paul to the Romans*. Cambridge: Cambridge University Press, 1967.

Bird, M. F. *Romans*. Grand Rapids: Zondervan, 2016.

Black, M. *Romans*. Grand Rapids: Eerdmans, 1973.

Boa, K. *Romans*. Nashville: Broadman and Holman, 2000.

Boice, J. M. *Romans: An Expositional Commentary*. 4 vols. Grand Rapids: Baker, 1991–1995.

Bray, G. L. *Romans*. Downers Grove, IL: InterVarsity, 2005.

Briscoe, D. S. *Romans*. Nashville: Nelson, 2003.

Bruce, F. F. *The Letter of Paul the Apostle to the Romans: An Introduction and Commentary*. 2nd ed. Grand Rapids: Eerdmans, 1984.

Byrne, B. *Romans*. Collegeville, MN: Glazier, 1996.

Cobb, J. B., Jr. and D. J. Lull. *Romans*. St. Louis: Chalice, 2005.

Custer, S. *The Righteousness of God: A Commentary on Romans*. Greenville, SC: Bob Jones University Press, 2007.

Dumbrell, W. J. *Romans: A New Covenant Commentary*. Eugene, OR: Wipf and Stock, 2005.

Edwards, J. R. *Romans*. Peabody, MA: Hendrickson, 1992.

Fitzmyer, J. A. *Romans: A New Translation with Introduction and Commentary*. New York: Doubleday, 1983.

Forlines, F. L. *Romans*. Nashville: Randall House, 1987.

Franzmann, M. H. *Romans: A Commentary*. St. Louis: Concordia, 1968.

Grayston, K. *The Epistle to the Romans*. Peterborough: Epworth, 1997.

Greathouse, W. M. *Romans*. Kansas City, MO: Beacon Hill Press of Kansas City, 1975.

Hahn, S. and C. Mitch. *The Letter of St. Paul to the Romans*. San Francisco: Ignatius, 2003.

Harrison, E. F. "Romans." In *The Expositor's Bible Commentary*, vol. 10. Grand Rapids: Zondervan, 1976.

Harrisville, R. *Romans*. Minneapolis: Augsburg, 1980.

Hendricksen, W. *Exposition of Paul's Epistle to the Romans*. 2 vols. Grand Rapids: Baker, 1980.

Hodges, Z. C. *Romans: Deliverance from Wrath*. Denton, TX: Grace Evangelical Society, 2013.

Hughes, R. K. *Romans: Righteousness from Heaven*. Wheaton, IL: Crossway, 1991.

Hultgren, A. J. *Paul's Letter to the Romans: A Commentary*. Grand Rapids: Eerdmans, 2011.

Johnson, A. F. *Romans: The Freedom Letter*. Rev. ed. 2 vols. Chicago: Moody, 1984, 1985.

Johnson, L. T. *Reading Romans: A Literary and Theological Commentary*. Macon, GA: Smyth & Helwys, 2001.

Karris, R. J. and D. Durkin. *Galatians and Romans*. Collegeville, MN: Liturgical, 2005.

Käsemann, E. *Commentary on Romans*. Translated and edited by G. W. Bromiley. Grand Rapids: Eerdmans, 1980.

Keck, L. E. *Romans*. Nashville: Abingdon, 2005.

Keener, C. S. *Romans: A New Covenant Commentary*. Eugene, OR: Cascade, 2009.

Kertelge, K. *The Epistle to the Romans*. Translated by F. McDonagh. New York: Herder & Herder, 1972.

Kruse, C. *Paul's Letter to the Romans*. Grand Rapids: Eerdmans, 2012.

Lyons, G. *Romans: A Commentary in the Wesleyan Tradition*. 2 vols. Kansas City, MO: Beacon Hill Press, 2008.

MacArthur, J. *Romans 1–8*. Chicago: Moody, 1991.

_____. *Romans 9–16*. Chicago: Moody, 1994.

_____. *Romans: Grace, Truth, and Redemption*. Nashville: Nelson, 2006.

Maly, E. H. *Romans*. Wilmington, DE: Glazier, 1979.

Matera, F. *Romans*. Grand Rapids: Baker, 2010.

Middendorf, M. P. *Romans*. 2 vols. St. Louis: Concordia, 2013.

Mohrlang, R. *Romans*. Carol Stream, IL: Tyndale House, 2007.

Moo, D. J. *Romans*. Grand Rapids: Zondervan, 2000.

_____. *Encountering the Book of Romans*. Grand Rapids: Baker, 2002.

Morgan, R. *Romans*. Sheffield: Sheffield Academic Press, 1995.

Morris, L. *The Epistle to the Romans*. Grand Rapids: Eerdmans, 1988.

Mounce, R. H. *Romans*. Nashville: Broadman & Holman, 1995.

Murray, J. *The Epistle to the Romans: The English Text with Introduction, Exposition, and Notes*. 2 vols. Grand Rapids: Eerdmans, 1959, 1965.

O'Neill, J. C. *Paul's Letter to the Romans*. Harmondsworth: Penguin, 1975.

Osborne, G. P. *Romans*. Downers Grove, IL: InterVarsity, 2003.

Panning, A. J. *Romans*. St. Louis: Concordia, 2004.

Pate, C. M. *Romans*. Grand Rapids: Baker, 2013.

Peterson, D. G. *Commentary on Romans*. Nashville: B&H, 2017.

Porter, S. E. *The Letter to the Romans: A Linguistic and Literary Commentary*. Sheffield: Sheffield Phoenix, 2015.

Robinson, J. A. T. *Wrestling with Romans*. Philadelphia: Westminster, 1979.

Ross, A. *Romans*. Louisville: Geneva, 1999.

Runge, S. E. *Romans*. Bellingham, WA: Lexham, 2014.

Seemuth, D. P. *Romans*. Nashville: Nelson, 2005.

Smart, J. *Doorway to a New Age: A Study of Paul's Letter to the Romans*. Philadelphia: Westminster, 1972.

Sproul, R. C. *Romans*. Wheaton, IL: Crossway, 2009.

Stott, J. R. W. *Romans: God's Good News for the World*. Downers Grove, IL: InterVarsity, 1994.

Stuhlmacher, P. *Paul's Letter to the Romans: A Commentary*. Translated by S. J. Hafemann. Louisville: Westminster/John Knox, 1994.

Talbert, C. H. *Romans*. Macon, GA: Smyth & Helwys, 2002.

Thistleton, A. C. *Discovering Romans*. Grand Rapids: Eerdmans, 2016.

Toews, J. E. *Romans*. Scottsdale, AZ: Herald, 2004.

Veerman, D. R. *Romans*. Carol Stream, IL: Tyndale House, 1992.

Witherington, B., III, with D. Hyatt. *Paul's Letter to the Romans: A Socio-Rhetorical Commentary*. Grand Rapids: Eerdmans, 2004.

Wright, N. T. "The Letter to the Romans: Introduction, Commentary, and Reflections." In *The New Interpreter's Bible*, vol. 10. Nashville: Abingdon, 1994–2004.

Zeisler, J. A. *Paul's Letter to the Romans*. Philadelphia: Trinity Press International, 1989.

Monographs

Becker, J. C. *Paul the Apostle: The Triumph of God in Life and Thought*. Philadelphia: Fortress, 1980.

Bultmann, R. *Theology of the New Testament*. Vol. 1. Translated by K. Grobel. New York: Scribner, 1951.

Davies, W. D. *Paul and Rabbinic Judaism: Some Rabbinic Elements in Paul's Theology*. London: SPCK, 1948.

Donfried, K. P. ed. *The Romans Debate*. Revised and expanded ed. Peabody, MA: Hendrickson, 1991.

Drane, J. W. *Paul: Libertine or Legalist?* London: SPCK, 1975.

Dunn, J. D. G. *The Theology of Paul the Apostle*. Grand Rapids: Eerdmans, 1998.

Ellis, E. E. *Paul's Use of the Old Testament*. Reprint ed. Grand Rapids: Baker, 1981.

SELECTED BIBLIOGRAPHY

Fee, G. D. *God's Empowering Presence: The Holy Spirit in the Letters of Paul*. Peabody, MA: Hendrickson, 1994.

_____. *Pauline Christology: An Exegetical-Theological Study*. Peabody, MA: Hendrickson, 2007.

Fowler, P. B. *The Structure of Romans: The Argument of Paul's Letter*. Minneapolis: Fortress, 2016.

Gamble, H. Jr. *The Textual History of the Letter to the Romans: A Study in Textual and Literary Criticism*. Grand Rapids: Eerdmans, 1977.

Gaston, J. *Paul and the Torah*. Vancouver: University of British Columbia Press, 1987.

Harvey, J. D. *Listening to the Text: Oral Patterning in Paul's Letters*. Grand Rapids: Baker, 1998.

_____. *Interpreting the Pauline Letters: An Exegetical Handbook*. Handbooks for New Testament Exegesis. Grand Rapids: Kregel, 2012.

_____. *Romans*. Exegetical Guide to the Greek New Testament. Nashville: B&H, 2016.

Hays, R. B. *The Faith of Jesus Christ: The Narrative Substructure of Galatians 3:1–4:11*. Second ed. Grand Rapids: Eerdmans, 2002.

Hübner, H. *Law in Paul's Thought*. Translated by J. C. G. Grieg. Edited by J. Riches. Edinburgh: T&T Clark, 1984.

Jervis, L. A. *The Purpose of Romans: A Comparative Letter Structure Investigation*. Sheffield: JSOT Press, 1991.

Longenecker, R. N. *Introducing Romans: Critical Issues in Paul's Most Famous Letter*. Grand Rapids: Eerdmans, 2011.

Räisänen, H. *Paul and the Law*. Tübingen: Mohr, 1983.

Ridderbos, H. *Paul: An Outline of His Theology*. Translated by J. R. deWitt. Grand Rapids: Eerdmans, 1975.

Sanders, E. P. *Paul and Palestinian Judaism: A Comparison of Patterns of Religion*. Philadelphia: Fortress, 1977.

Schoeps, H. J. *Paul: The Theology of the Apostle in Light of the Jewish Religious History*. Translated by H. Knight. Philadelphia: Westminster, 1961.

Schreiner, T. R. *Paul, Apostle of God's Glory in Christ: A Pauline Theology*. Downers Grove, IL: InterVarsity, 2001.

Stendahl, K. *Paul among Jews and Gentiles and Other Essays*. Philadelphia: Fortress, 1976.

Stowers, S. K. *The Diatribe and Paul's Letter to the Romans*. Chico, CA: Scholars, 1981.

Thielman, F. *From Plight to Solution: A Jewish Framework to Understanding Paul's View of the Law in Galatians and Romans*. Leiden: Brill, 1989.

Thompson, I. H. *Chiasmus in the Pauline Letters*. Sheffield: Sheffield Academic, 1995.

Waters, G. P. *Justification and the New Perspective on Paul: A Review and Response*. Phillipsburg, NJ: P&R, 2004.

Weima, J. A. D. *Neglected Endings: The Significance of the Pauline Letter Closings*. Sheffield: JSOT Press, 1994.

Westerholm, S. K. *Israel's Law and the Church's Faith: Paul and His Recent Interpreters*. Grand Rapids: Eerdmans, 1988.

Wright, N. T. *Paul in Fresh Perspective*. Minneapolis: Fortress, 2005.

Reference Works

Balz, H. and G. Schneider, eds., *Exegetical Dictionary of the New Testament*, 3 vols. Grand Rapids: Eerdmans, 1990–93.

Blass, F. and A. Debrunner. *A Greek Grammar of the New Testament and Other Early Christian Literature*, ed. and rev. by R. W. Funk. Chicago: University of Chicago Press, 1961.

Brown, C. ed., *The New International Dictionary of New Testament Theology*, 3 vols. Grand Rapids: Zondervan, 1975–78.

Danker, F. W., ed. *A Greek-English Lexicon of the New Testament and Other Early Christian Literature*. Chicago/London: University of Chicago Press, 2000. Based on W. Bauer's *Griechisch-deutsches Wörterbuch* (6th ed.) and on previous English ed. W. F. Arndt, F. W. Gingrich, and F. W. Danker.

Evans, C. A. and S. E. Porter, eds. *Dictionary of New Testament Background*. Leicester / Downers Grove, IL: InterVarsity, 2000.

Harris, M. J. *Prepositions and Theology in the Greek New Testament*. Grand Rapids: Zondervan, 2012.

Hawthorne, G. F., R. P. Martin, and D. G. Reid, eds. *Dictionary of Paul and His Letters*. Downers Grove, IL: InterVarsity, 1993.

Louw, J. P. and E. A. Nida, eds. *Greek-English Lexicon of the New Testament Based on Semantic Domains*. 2 vols. New York: United Bible Societies, 1988.

Metzger, B. M. *A Textual Commentary on the Greek New Testament*. New York: United Bible Societies, 1994, 2nd ed. based on UBS[4].

Robertson, A. T. *A Grammar of the Greek New Testament in the Light of Historical Research*, 4th ed. Nashville: Broadman, 1934.

Wallace, D. B. *Greek Grammar Beyond the Basics: An Exegetical Syntax of the New Testament*. Grand Rapids: Zondervan, 1996.

INTRODUCTION

THE INTERPRETATION AND INFLUENCE OF ROMANS

Paul's letter to the Romans has a long history of interpretation and influence. Cranfield provides a helpful history of exegesis through the 1960s.[1] Reasoner's more recent history of the interpretation of Romans identifies twelve "loci" in the letter and provides a diachronic summary of representative interpreters on each locus.[2] As Reasoner's work makes clear, a detailed summary of the history of interpretation would require a monograph and is beyond the scope of this commentary. Instead, seven interpreters will provide a representative overview.

Origen (185–254) wrote the first full-scale commentary on Romans and regarded the letter as the basis for building a theology and living a holy life. Later in the patristic period, Augustine (354–430) focused on the sinful state humankind inherits from Adam and the need for salvation each individual faces as a result of his sin. In the medieval period, Abelard (1079–1142) focused on how divine grace draws the elect individual into salvation, while Aquinas (1225–1274) underscored the role of Romans (and Paul's other letters) in building a systematic theology. During the Reformation, Luther (1483–1546) defined "God's righteousness" as the righteousness God bestows on the individual on the basis of grace through faith, and Calvin (1509–1564) emphasized the use of

---

1. Cranfield, *Romans, 30–44.*
2. M. Reasoner, *Romans in Full Circle: A History of Interpretation* (Louisville: Westminster John Knox, 2005). His analysis concludes that the interpretation of Romans has come "full circle" from Origen to contemporary narrative-based approaches.

Romans to promote holy living. In the modern period, Barth (1886–1968) found in Romans the sinner's absolute dependence on God and his grace.

It is difficult to improve on Bruce's succinct synopsis of the influence of Romans, as he highlights the letter's impact on four individuals.[3] While reading Romans 13:13–14, Augustine found the resolution to turn from a life of sin to a life dedicated to God. When he rightly understood Romans 1:16–17 and 3:21–28, Luther found the hermeneutical key to the Bible and life that launched the Protestant Reformation. It was in response to a reading of Luther's Preface to Romans that Wesley felt his heart "strangely warmed" resulting in the beginning of the eighteenth-century Evangelical Revival. In Romans, Barth discovered "the mighty voice of Paul" and the dynamic corrective to the failed optimism of liberal orthodoxy. Bruce concludes, "There is no telling what may happen when people begin to study the Epistle to the Romans. What happened to Augustine, Luther, Wesley, and Barth launched great spiritual movements which have left their mark on world history. But similar things have happened, much more frequently, to very ordinary people as the word of this Epistle came home to them with power."[4]

INTRODUCTORY MATTERS

Longenecker groups aspects of introductory matters into three categories: "matters largely uncontested" (authorship, occasion, date), "matters recently resolved" (integrity), and "matters extensively debated today" (addressees, purpose, epistolary genre, rhetorical genres, focus of presentation).[5] The following discussion follows that general sequence with a few additions (e.g., occasion, destination, setting).

Author, Occasion, Place of Origin, and Date

Romans has been accepted as Pauline since post-apostolic times (1 Clem 32.2; 35.5; 50.6; Polycarp 3.3; 4.1; 6.2; 10.1; Ignatius, Eph 19.3; Magn 6.2; 9.1; Trall 9.2; Smyr 1.1). Cranfield notes that Romans was listed as one of Paul's letters before the end of the second century and that "every extant early list of New Testament books includes it among his letters."[6] The testimony of this external evidence is seldom

---

3. F. F. Bruce, *The Epistle of Paul to the Romans*, reprint ed. (Grand Rapids: Eerdmans, 1982), 58–60.
4. Bruce, *The Epistle of Paul to the Romans*, 60.
5. Longenecker, *Romans*, 4–18.
6. Cranfield, *Romans*, 2. Cranfield's conclusion about Tertius's role in writing the letter is also helpful: "We conclude that Tertius either wrote the epistle

disputed, and five lines of internal evidence support it. First, the salutation identifies Paul as the author (1:1). Second, the author's background fits that of Paul (11:1; cf. 2 Cor. 11:22; Phil. 3:5). Third, the author's companions, travels, and ministry all fit the record of Paul's activities in Acts, especially his third missionary journey (15:14–33; 16:21–23; cf. Acts 18:23–20:7). Fourth, the language and style are similar to other letters ascribed to Paul. Fifth, the content of the letter reflects others ascribed to Paul.

The occasion for Paul's writing is clear from the opening and closing sections of the letter. In 1:8–15 he notes his longing to visit Rome "in order . . . [to] impart some spiritual gift" and "[to] be encouraged together with you." He repeats that desire in 15:23; 15:29; and 15:32. When he writes, he notes that he has completed his task of preaching the gospel "from Jerusalem and round about as far as Illyricum" (15:19). As a result, he hoped to be traveling and ministering in the western Mediterranean area (15:24, 28) after he had delivered the collection to the church in Jerusalem (15:25–26).[7] Those travels would give him the opportunity to fulfill his desire to visit Rome (15:24, 28). He wrote in anticipation of that visit.

Three internal statements point the way to determining the place of origin for the letter. First, the collection had been completed (15:25–29), and Paul was ready to leave for Jerusalem (15:25). Second, Timothy and Sopater were present with Paul when he wrote (16:23). Third, Gaius was Paul's host (16:23). These statements from Romans correlate with other New Testament evidence to suggest that Paul wrote the letter close to the end of his third missionary journey, most likely from Corinth. Acts places Paul in Achaia for three months before he traveled to Jerusalem (Acts 20:1–3). Timothy and Sopater accompanied Paul when he left Greece for Jerusalem to deliver the collection (Acts 20:4). Gaius was a member of the church in Corinth, where Paul baptized him and his household (1 Cor. 1:14).[8] Paul, therefore, most likely wrote Romans during his three-month stay in Corinth.

---

long-hand directly from Paul's dictation or else took it down first in short-hand, and . . . we may be confident that we have in the text which Tertius wrote the thought of Paul for all intents and purposes expressed as Paul himself expressed it" (ibid., 4).

7. See the discussion of the collection in the commentary section on 15:22–29.

8. Paul also commends Phoebe to the Romans. She was a member of the church in Cenchrea, one of the ports for Corinth and most likely carried the letter to Rome. See the commentary section on 16:1–2.

If Paul wrote from Corinth, it is possible to establish the date of writing with some degree of likelihood.[9] Gallio was proconsul in Achaia when Paul first visited Corinth (cf. Acts 18:12–17), and the dates of Gallio's service are commonly set at A.D. 50–52.[10] If Paul left Corinth in A.D. 52, visited Ephesus, Caesarea, Jerusalem, and Antioch, and traveled through Galatia and Phrygia (cf. Acts 18:18–23), he most likely began his extended ministry in Ephesus in A.D. 53.[11] Between two and three years of ministry in Ephesus plus travel through Macedonia and Achaia (cf. Acts 19:1–10; 20:1–2) place Paul's second visit to Corinth at A.D. 55–56 or A.D. 56–57. Paul's departure for Jerusalem after the Feast of Unleavened Bread (cf. Acts 20:4–6), therefore, makes early A.D. 56 or early A.D. 57 the most likely dates for the letter.

Integrity
Although a few scholars have proposed composite letter theories for Romans,[12] Schreiner notes that "these theories are quite arbitrary and have persuaded scarcely anyone."[13] Jewett is representative of scholars who have argued that Romans 16:17–20 is a non-Pauline interpolation because of its tone, style, and place between two sets of greetings (16:3–16; 16:21–23).[14] Paul includes closing advice in other letters (e.g., 2 Cor. 13:5–10; Eph. 6:10–20; Phil. 4:2–9; 1 Thess. 5:12–22), however. He also drafts brief paragraphs in his own hand (1 Cor. 16:21–24; Gal. 6:11–18; Col. 4:18; 2 Thess. 3:17). It is likely that Romans 16:17–20 reflects both practices.

The primary questions related to the letter's integrity focus on (1) where the letter originally ended, (2) whether chapter 16 might have been a separate document, and (3) whether the doxology (16:25–27) is original. Moo summarizes six major manuscript combinations.[15]

---

9. For an extended discussion of Pauline chronology, see J. D. Harvey, *Interpreting the Pauline Letters* (Grand Rapids: Kregel, 2012), 54–76.
10. See C. K. Barrett, *The Acts of the Apostles*, 2 vols. (Edinburgh: T&T Clark, 1998), 862–71.
11. See Cranfield, *Romans*, 14.
12. W. Schmithals, for example, has argued that the canonical version is actually a combination of two letters (*Der Römerbrief als historisches Problem,* Gütersloh: Gerd Mohn, 1975), while J. Kinoshita has argued for a combination of three sources ("Romans—Two Writings Combined: A New Interpretation of the Body of Romans," *NT* 7 [1965]: 258–77).
13. Schreiner, *Romans*, 5.
14. Jewett, *Romans*, 986–88.
15. Moo, *Romans*, 6.

```
1:1–16:23   +   16:25–27
1:1–14:23   +   16:25–27   +   15:1–16:23   +   16:25–27
1:1–14:23   +   16:25–27   +   15:1–16:24
1:1–16:24
1:1–14:23   +   16:24–27
1:1–15:33   +   16:25–27   +   16:1–23
```

In an attempt to explain these combinations, scholars have suggested three major solutions. Lake argued that an original circular letter consisted of chapters 1–14, and chapters 15–16 were added when the letter was subsequently sent to Rome.[16] Manson argued that chapters 1–15 were originally sent to Rome, and chapter 16 was added when the letter was subsequently sent to Ephesus.[17] Lightfoot argued that chapters 1–16 were originally sent to Rome, but chapters 15–16 were subsequently deleted to create a circular letter.[18]

The shortest extant version of the letter (1:1–14:23) is the result of Marcion's work (Origen, *Commentary on Romans* 10.43). Ending the letter with Paul's statement in 14:23 that "everything that is not from faith is sin" would have fit Marcion's theology well, and excising everything beyond that point would have allowed him to avoid the concentration of Old Testament quotations in 15:1–13. In fact, the argument of chapter 14 continues to 15:13, and the close relationship between 1:8–15 and 15:14–33 supports at least 1:1–15:33 as original.[19]

Although there is general scholarly agreement on the integrity of 1:1–15:33, there has been considerably more discussion of whether chapter 16 was originally part of the letter. The most frequent suggestion is that chapter 16 was a letter originally sent to the church in Ephesus.[20] Scholars offer four main lines of argument in support of 16:1–23 as a separate letter: (1) 1 Corinthians 16:19 places Priscilla

16. K. Lake, "The Epistle to the Romans," in *The Earlier Epistles of St. Paul: Their Motive and Origin*, 2nd ed. (London: Rivingtons, 1914), 324–413.
17. W. T. Manson, "St. Paul's Letter to the Romans—and Others," in *The Romans Debate*, ed. K. P. Donfried, rev. and exp. ed. (Peabody, MA: Hendrickson, 1991), 3–15.
18. J. B. Lightfoot, "The Structure and Destination of the Epistle to the Romans," in *Biblical Essays*, repr. ed. (Eugene, OR: Wipf & Stock, 2005), 287–320.
19. For a list of verbal parallels between 1:8–15 and 15:14–33, see J. D. Harvey, *Listening to the Text: Oral Patterning in Paul's Letters* (Grand Rapids: Baker, 1998), 138–39.
20. For a list of scholars arguing for a separate letter destined for Ephesus, see J. A. Fitzmyer, *Romans: A New Translation with Introduction and Commentary* (New York: Doubleday, 1993), 57.

and Aquila in Ephesus rather than in Rome; (2) Paul's description of Epaenetus as "the firstfruits of Asia" (16:5) supports an Ephesian destination; (3) the extended list of greetings from Paul (16:3–16) is unlikely in a letter to a congregation Paul had not visited; and (4) the prayer-wish of 15:33 ("The God of peace be with all of you. Amen.") is an appropriate conclusion for the letter. None of these arguments, however, is ultimately persuasive.

First, there is no reason to restrict Priscilla's and Aquila's movements to a single city. Acts 18:2, for example, places them in Corinth with the comment that they had "recently come from Italy," and it is possible that they had returned to Rome after Claudius's death. Similarly, there is no reason to restrict Epaenetus's movements to Asia. Describing him as "the firstfruits of Asia" speaks only to the circumstances of his conversion and would be at least as natural in a letter destined for a city outside Asia. Third, Paul's letter to the Colossians suggests that his practice was to send more greetings to churches he had not visited. The greetings, in fact, seem more appropriate to a church he had not visited (Rome) rather than to a church he had founded (Ephesus).[21] Finally, there is no precedent elsewhere in Paul's letters for a prayer-wish as the end of a letter. Jervis notes that of the five possible units in Pauline conclusions the prayer-wish most often begins the conclusion rather than ending it.[22] It seems likely, therefore, that at least 16:1–23 was the original letter closing and that the letter consisted of at least 1:1–16:23.[23]

Although the strongest manuscript evidence (א, A, B, D, 33) supports the omission of 16:24 and the inclusion of 16:25–27, Cranfield,[24] Dunn,[25] and others view the doxology as a later addition.[26] Jewett argues that 16:24 was the original ending and the doxology is a non-Pauline interpolation that developed in three stages from an original

---

21. For a concise discussion of the greetings, see Jewett, *Romans*, 9.
22. L. A. Jervis, *The Purpose of Romans: A Comparative Letter Structure Investigation* (Sheffield: Sheffield Academic, 1991), 132–57. The basic pattern is prayer-wish/greetings/grace-benediction (cf. 2 Cor. 13:11–13; 2 Thess. 3:16–18).
23. For a monograph-length analysis, see H. A. Gamble Jr., *The Textual History of the Letter to the Romans: A Study in Textual and Literary Criticism.* Grand Rapids: Eerdmans, 1977.
24. Cranfield, *Romans*, 6–9.
25. Dunn, *Romans*, 912–13.
26. Longenecker views the doxology as Pauline, either written earlier in his ministry or composed after he had dictated Romans at the request of associates living in Corinth (*Romans*, 1085).

Hellenistic Jewish version.[27] In addition to the manuscript support, however, the doxology aptly summarizes major themes in the letter, especially the themes of God and the gospel.[28] Elsewhere in the letter, Paul uses confessional/doxological statements to conclude major sections (e.g., 4:25; 8:31–39; 11:33–36; 15:13). As the introduction of Romans (1:1–7) is distinctive and considerably longer than those in Paul's other letters, so the conclusion (16:25–27) is also distinctive and longer.[29] Although Metzger gives the UBS[5] reading a {C} rating (476), including the doxology after 1:1–16:23 seems to be the preferred reading.

Destination and Setting

The omission in a few manuscripts of ἐν ῾Ρώμῃ from 1:7 and 1:15 (G, it[g], Origen) is clearly secondary and most likely the result of the letter circulating to churches in other locations. Few scholars contest that the letter's original destination was Rome, the largest city in the empire and the administrative center for the various provinces. By the first century, Rome's population had reached one million and included people of all socioeconomic levels from across the empire. Participation in religious ritual was a way of life and was closely connected to the government. Religion was generally considered a legal matter in which following rituals was a way of maintaining peace with the gods. Foreign religions were assimilated but tended to be viewed with suspicion. The following sections provide overviews of the historical, social, cultural, and religious settings in which Paul's Roman readers lived.

Historical Setting

In 31 B.C., Octavius consolidated Roman rule over the entire eastern Mediterranean, including Egypt, and began the era of *Pax Romana*. For bringing peace to the Roman world, the Senate proclaimed Octavius as the chief citizen (*princeps*) of the republic and gave him the name Augustus ("venerable"). Under that name, he ruled Rome until A.D. 14 (cf. Luke 2:1), rebuilding temples and public buildings, reviving religion, and settling the borders of the empire.

Roman writers characterized the two-and-a-half centuries that began with Octavius's reign as a time of internal stability, material

---

27. Jewett, *Romans*, 998–1005. He suggests that the doxology was added after 14:23 when Marcion shortened the letter.
28. See the commentary section on 16:25–27.
29. Moo notes that it seems unlikely that Paul would choose to end the letter in 16:23 with "Quartus, our brother" (*Romans*, 936n2).

prosperity, and administrative efficiency. Greek was widely spoken in the eastern empire; a system of permanent roads facilitated freedom of movement; an official postal system facilitated imperial communication; and a legal system provided generally consistent rules that applied to Roman citizens, colonies, and governors' courts.

Tiberius (A.D. 14–37) succeeded Octavius but was more reclusive and chose to rule from Capri rather than Rome during his final ten years. Gaius Caligula (A.D. 37–41) promised reforms. Instead, he centralized power, depleted the imperial wealth, and revived the ruler cult until members of his personal guard assassinated him. Claudius (A.D. 41–54) stabilized imperial control and opposed religious proselytizing.[30]

Nero succeeded Claudius in A.D. 54 and ruled for fourteen years before committing suicide. His reign consisted of two distinct periods. When he took power, Nero promised to restore the role of the Senate and to rule following the principles of Augustus. From A.D. 54 until A.D. 62 he delegated the administration of the empire to others, and the provinces experienced sound government and good order. During the second half of his rule, however, Nero engaged in the activities for which he is best known. He revived the law of treason and turned the principate into a tyranny. He ignored the provinces and squandered imperial wealth on games and theaters. He initiated active persecution of Christians after the fire of A.D. 64, and tradition holds that Nero ordered the execution of both Peter and Paul during his final years.[31]

Since Paul wrote to the Romans during the earlier period of Nero's reign, his positive statements about governing authorities (e.g., Rom. 13:1–7) might well reflect the favorable circumstances in the provinces during those years. A generally positive view of the imperial authorities might also explain Paul's willingness to appeal to Caesar (Acts 25:6–12) as well as the tradition that he was released after appearing before the imperial tribunal. On the other hand, Nero's character and personal habits were never far below the surface and might, in part, lie behind Paul's denunciation of Gentile sin (e.g., Rom. 1:18–32).

Social Setting [32]

An individual's place in society was primarily a matter of birth and legal status. Jewett suggests that the usual estimate of the population across the empire was one-third slave, one-third freed slave, and

---

30. The preceding information also appears in Harvey, *Pauline Letters*, 122.
31. See M. T. Griffin, "Nero," in *ABD* 4.1076–81.
32. See D. J. Tidball, "Social Setting of Mission Churches," in *DPL*, 883–92.

one-third free born.[33] Households were the primary social unit and functioned as inclusive networks that crossed both Jewish and Gentile social lines. A household consisted of the principal family, slaves, tenants, friends, business partners, and clients. It functioned hierarchically under the authority and patronage of the family's father. Either the leading member(s) of the household made decisions for the group, or the group made decisions corporately. As Paul's greeting list suggests (Rom. 16:3–16), households constituted the basic congregations of the larger church in a metropolitan area such as Rome.

In addition to the household, the synagogue played an important role in the growth of the early church in general and the church in Rome in particular. If the church in Rome was planted by Jewish pilgrims who had been present at Pentecost, the synagogues served as natural venues for the initial introduction of Christianity into the city as well as a natural network for its growth. As a sect within an established religion, Christianity also benefited from the legal protection granted to Judaism. The Jewish origin of the church in Rome and the Jewish-Christian minority in the church when Paul wrote help explain his frequent appeals to the Old Testament (e.g., Rom. 15:1–13), the audience's familiarity with the Mosaic law (e.g., Rom. 7:1–12), and his extended discussion of Israel's place in salvation history (Rom. 9:1–11:32).

Cultural Setting

Lendon argues that "Honour was a filter through which the whole world was viewed, a deep structure of the Graeco-Roman mind . . . . Everything, every person, could be valued in terms of honour."[34] Building on Lendon's work, Jewett suggests that the emperor stood at the peak of a "pyramid of honor," and all other nonslaves were in competition for superiority and public honor.[35] The Romans claimed that they, their rulers, and their culture were superior in virtue, justice, and piety. Individuals who were successful were accorded "glory," and "boasting" in accomplishments was expected. Key terms related to honor and shame occur repeatedly throughout Paul's letter, including glory (e.g., Rom. 1:18–23; 2:7–10; 8:18–25), boasting (e.g., Rom. 3:27–30; 5:1–11; 15:17–21), honor (e.g., Rom. 2:7–10; 13:1–7), and shame (e.g., Rom. 1:16; 5:5; 6:21; 9:38; 10:11).

---

33. Jewett, *Romans*, 52.
34. J. E. Lendon, *Empire of Honour: The Art of Government in the Roman World* (Oxford: Clarendon, 1997), 73.
35. See Jewett, *Romans*, 49–51.

Religious Setting[36]

By the time Paul wrote to the Romans, at least four major religious influences were present throughout the empire. Greek religion existed in a variety of cult centers and focused on the observance of traditional rituals. The gods were considered the guardians of the moral order, and the object of religious ritual was to secure favorable status in this world and in the underworld. The Hellenistic religions of Asia Minor included mystery religions and ruler cults. The mystery religions offered preparation for a blissful afterlife (Eleusis) and preparation for astral salvation (Mithra). The ruler cults bestowed divine honors on rulers in the hope of influencing the internal affairs of individual city-states.

Traditional Roman religion emphasized peace with the gods. Offering sacrifices, praying, and fulfilling vows and oaths were intended to insure harmonious relations with the gods as the basis for prosperity and success. The imperial cult added elements of the Hellenistic ruler cults to traditional Roman religion. Imperial propaganda celebrated Octavius and his successors as the guarantors of peace and tranquility for the empire. The emperors received divine honors and, in return, professed respect for traditional Roman piety, sought to rule righteously, and promised to bring peace to the empire. Those concerns for righteousness (e.g., Rom. 1:16–17) and peace (e.g., Rom. 5:1–5) echo language Paul uses throughout the letter.

Audience and Purpose

As early as 139 B.C., Rome had a Jewish population of at least 40,000. Both Julius Caesar (49–44 B.C.) and Octavius (27 B.C.–A.D. 14) declared Judaism a legal religion. Although Tiberius expelled all Jews from the city in A.D. 19 as the result of a public scandal related to a donation to the temple in Jerusalem, they subsequently returned in substantial numbers. Jews from Rome were present at Pentecost (cf. Acts 2:10), and those pilgrims most likely carried the gospel back to Italy with them. The original church in Rome, therefore, was planted by and consisted of predominantly Jewish background believers.[37]

By A.D. 41, Jews had returned to Rome in such numbers that Claudius restricted them from gathering together (Dio Cassius, *Roman History* 40.6). In A.D. 49, he expelled all Jews from the city. The reported reason was that they were rioting "at the instigation of

---

36. See D. E. Aune, "Religions, Greco-Roman," in *DPL*, 286–96.
37. Moo addresses the tradition that the church in Rome was planted by either Peter or Peter and Paul together (*Romans*, 4).

Chrestus" (Seutonius, *Claudius* 25.4), which probably reflects growing Christian presence in the synagogues of Rome. Since Claudius's decree also affected Jewish Christians (cf. Acts 18:2), the composition of the Roman church became decidedly Gentile. Although Jews began returning after Claudius's death in A.D. 54, they were in the minority by the time Paul wrote his letter.[38]

Jewett estimates that by the time Paul wrote, there were several thousand Christians in Rome meeting in dozens of groups of twenty to forty individuals.[39] The greetings at the end of the letter (16:3–16) point to a cosmopolitan audience as would be expected in the capital of the empire. Of the twenty-six individuals addressed, six have Jewish backgrounds, while twenty have Gentile backgrounds. Nine appear to have been freedmen or freedwomen, while seventeen appear to have been slaves. Places of origin included Persia, Asia, Palestine, and Italy. Believers gathered in groups consisting of household slaves (16:10, 11) and in tenement churches without patrons (16:14, 15). Priscilla and Aquila were of high enough social status both to serve as patrons of a house church (16:5) and to have had business concerns in Corinth (Acts 18:1–4), Ephesus (18:24–28), and Rome.

Indicators from the letter suggest that Paul's audience included both Jewish and Gentile Christians. On the one hand, Paul associates his readers with those who knew the Mosaic law well (6:14–15; 7:1–4), he addresses "the Jew" directly (2:17), he identifies Abraham as "our forefather according to the flesh" (4:1), and he identifies "kinsmen" among those he greets (16:3, 7, 11). On the other hand, the epistolary sections include the readers among the Gentiles to whom Paul ministered (1:1–17; 15:14–16:27), and he addresses himself to "you Gentiles" (11:13–24). It is probably best, therefore, to conclude that Paul wrote to a collection of mixed congregations that included both Jewish and Gentile Christians. It is likely that the latter group comprised the majority and might possibly be identified with "we who are strong" (15:1), while the former group was in the minority and might possibly be identified with "[those who are] weak in faith" (14:1).

Because Paul does not state his purpose in writing, extensive discussion of that purpose has ensued. Jervis notes that the primary reason for the discussion resides in the tension between the occasional nature of the letter opening and closing (letter genre) and the systematic theological presentation of the letter body (content). Her

---

38. The preceding information also appears in Harvey, *Pauline Letters*, 124, 128.

39. Jewett, *Romans*, 62.

helpful overview groups proposed solutions into three main categories.[40] "Theological" solutions emphasize the way in which Paul sets out his gospel, suggesting that his purpose was either to expound his theology in a general way or to present his case in anticipation of his visit to Jerusalem. "Missiological" solutions emphasize Paul's concern to extend his missionary work, suggesting that his purpose was either to respond to negative reports about his preaching and practices or to seek support for his future ministry in Spain. "Pastoral" solutions emphasize the way in which Paul seeks to address issues within the Roman congregations, suggesting that his purpose was either to correct errors of doctrine or to correct errors of behavior.

Rather than trying to identify a single purpose for the letter, it is probably better to think of a "cluster" of purposes that address multiple concerns.[41] Theologically, Paul sought to clarify the nature of his "gospel to the Gentiles." Missiologically, he sought to elicit support for his proposed work in Spain. Pastorally, he sought to alleviate Jew-Gentile tensions within the congregations in Rome. Moo adds to this cluster of purposes the reminder that beyond dealing with immediate concerns related to the congregations in Rome, "these issues are ultimately those of the church—and the world—of all ages."[42] In that regard, therefore, we also need to embrace Paul's gospel and its implications for righteous living, emulate Paul's passion for preaching the gospel where Christ has not yet been named, and exercise discernment in applying Paul's guidelines for accepting others whose positions on nonessentials differ from our own.

Epistolary Genre and Structure

The opening and closing of Romans clearly establish it as a New Testament letter. Weima has identified three broad categories of Greco-Roman letters: literary, official, and private, with the third category further divided into family letters, letters of petition, letters of introduction, and business letters.[43] Paul's letters are probably closest to the family letter type. Although his letters were occasional documents and

---

40. Jervis, *Purpose of Romans*, 14–28. Jervis's own conclusion falls in the "theological" category (ibid., 163–64). Jewett provides a different summary, while advocating strongly for the "missiological" solution (*Romans*, 80–91).
41. Although Jewett disagrees (*Romans*, 80), Cranfield (*Romans*, 23–24), Dunn (*Romans*, lvii), Moo (*Romans*, 20), and Schreiner (*Romans*, 19) all take similar positions.
42. Moo, *Romans*, 22.
43. J. A. D. Weima, "Greco-Roman Letters," in *DNTB*, 640–44.

not intended for formal publication, it is clear that Paul intended them to be read in public settings (1 Thess. 5:27) and to be circulated among the churches he planted (Col. 4:16).[44]

Doty was one of the first to set out the general form used in Greek letters as Introduction (sender, addressees, greetings, health wish), Body, and Conclusion (greetings, wishes, final greeting or prayer sentence).[45] More recently, Klauck has proposed a more detailed form.[46]

Letter Opening
    Prescript (sender, addressee, greeting)
    Proem (prayer-wish, thanksgiving, remembrance before gods, joy expression)

Letter Body
    Body-opening (disclosure, request, recommendation of self or others)
    Body-middle (information, appeal, instructions, exhortation, request)
    Body-closing (possible request or exhortation, travel and visitation plans)

Letter Closing
    Epilogue (concluding exhortation, act of writing, possible visit)
    Postscript (greetings, wishes/farewell, autograph)

Although Paul's letters are considerably longer and more complex than extant papyrus letters, they follow the overall form set out above.[47] As was true with other first-century letters, Paul used certain epistolary conventions and formulaic language to introduce different portions of his letters. Noting significant clusters of such conventions and language can help establish the major contours of

---

44. For an overview of the context in which first-century letter writing and delivery took place, see Harvey, *Listening*, 35–55.
45. W. G. Doty, *Letters in Primitive Christianity* (Philadelphia: Fortress, 1973), 11–12.
46. H. J. Klauck, *Ancient Letters and the New Testament* (Waco, TX: Baylor University Press, 2006), 42.
47. For a comparison of the length of Paul's letters with the length of other Greco-Roman letters, see R. E. Richards, *Paul and First-Century Letter Writing: Secretaries, Composition, and Collection* (Downers Grove, IL: InterVarsity, 2004), 163.

Paul's letters in general and of Romans in particular.[48] Three such clusters occur in Romans.

1:1–13	Sender (1:1), recipients (1:7), greeting (1:7), thanksgiving (1:8), attestation (1:9), visit wish (1:10–11), disclosure formula (1:13)
11:25–12:3	Disclosure formula (11:25), doxology (11:33–36), request formula (12:1), verb of saying (12:3)
15:13–16:27	Prayer-wish (15:13), confidence formula (15:14), writing statement (15:15), visit wish (15:22), intention to visit (15:23–25), intention to visit (15:28–29), request formula (15:30), prayer-wish (15:33), grace benediction (16:20), greetings (16:21–23), doxology (16:25–27)

The first cluster coincides with the letter opening. The second marks a major turning point within the letter body. The third coincides with the letter closing. This analysis establishes the overall structure of Romans. [49]

Letter opening (1:1–17)
   Salutation (1:1–7)
   Thanksgiving (1:8–12)
   Occasion for writing (1:13–15)
   Thesis (1:16–17)

Letter body (1:18–15:13)
   First section: Theological (1:18–11:36)
   Second section: Practical (12:1–15:13)

Letter closing (15:14–16:27)
   Apostolic apologia (15:14–21)[50]

---

48. See also the discussions in Harvey, *Listening*, 120–21 and Harvey, *Pauline Letters*, 30–31.
49. "Pure" epistolary analysis would include both 1:13–17 (body-opening) and 15:14–33 (body-closing) in the body. In order to highlight both the epistolary frame of Romans and the systematic argument of the body, however, this analysis includes them as parts of the letter opening and closing, respectively.
50. See Harvey, *Pauline Letters*, 37.

Apostolic parousia (15:22–29)[51]
Request for prayer (15:30–33)
Letter of commendation (16:1–2)
First greeting list (16:3–16)
Closing advice (16:17–20)
Second greeting list (16:21–23)
Doxology (16:25–27)

The letter body is considerably longer and more complex than extant papyrus letters. Apart from the two sections identified above, the structure of the body is best analyzed on the basis of Paul's argument. The outline of the letter set out in this commentary, therefore, is informed by both epistolary and content analysis.

Comparative Letter Structure

Because it is often helpful to compare parallel sections of Paul's letters, the following tables set out four standard epistolary sections as they occur in the thirteen letters ascribed to Paul: salutation, thanksgiving, apostolic parousia, and closing.[52]

Salutation Sections in Paul's Letters

	Sender(s)		Recipients	Greeting
Romans 1:1–7	1:1–6		1:7a	1:7b
1 Corinthians 1:1–3	1:1	(with Sosthenes)	1:2	1:3
2 Corinthians 1:1–2	1:1a	(with Timothy)	1:1b	1:2
Galatians 1:1–5	1:1–2	(with all the brethren)	1:2	1:3–5
Ephesians 1:1–2	1:1a		1:1b	1:2
Philippians 1:1–2	1:1a	(with Timothy)	1:1b	1:2

---

51. Harvey, *Pauline Letters*, 36. See also R. W. Funk, "The Apostolic 'Parousia': Form and Significance," in *Christian History and Interpretation: Studies Presented to John Knox*, eds. W. R. Farmer, C. F. D. Moule, and R. R. Niebuhr (Cambridge: Cambridge University Press, 1967), 249–68.
52. A similar comparative table related to the apostolic apologia appears in the Theology and Appropriation section of 15:14–21. Weima provides a monograph-length comparative study of epistolary elements in Paul's letters in *Paul the Ancient Letter Writer: An Introduction to Epistolary Analysis* (Grand Rapids: Baker, 2016).

	Sender(s)		Recipients	Greeting
Colossians 1:1–2	1:1	(with Timothy)	1:2a	1:2b
1 Thessalonians 1:1	1:1a	(with Silvanus and Timothy)	1:1b	1:1c
2 Thessalonians 1:1–2	1:1a	(with Silvanus and Timothy)	1:1b	1:2
1 Timothy 1:1–2	1:1		1:2a	1:2b
2 Timothy 1:1–2	1:1		1:2a	1:2b
Titus 1:1–4	1:1–3		1:4a	1:4b
Philemon 1–3	1		2	3

The salutation in Romans is considerably longer than in other letters. It expands Paul's self-identification and highlights his status as an apostle. The key emphases are (a) Paul (1:1, 5), who is separated for the gospel and an apostle to the Gentiles, (b) the gospel (1:2), which concerns Jesus, is promised by the prophets, and is recorded in the Old Testament, and (c) Jesus (1:3–4), who is the Davidic Messiah, the Son of God, and our Lord.

Thanksgiving Sections in Paul's Letters

	Statement of Thanksgiving	Manner of Thanksgiving	Cause of Thanksgiving	Explanation	Prayer Report
Romans 1:8–12	1:8a	1:8b	1:8c	1:11–12	1:9–10
1 Corinthians 1:4–9	1:4a	--	1:4b–5	1:6–8	1:9
2 Corinthians 1:3–7	Blessing Section				
Galatians 1:6–10	Rebuke Section				

	Statement of Thanks-giving	Manner of Thanks-giving	Cause of Thanks-giving	Explanation	Prayer Report
Ephesians 1:15–23	1:16a	--	1:15	1:19b–23	1:16b–19a
Philippians 1:3–11	1:3a	1:3b–4	1:5–6	1:7–8	1:9–11
Colossians 1:3–23	1:3a	--	1:4	1:5–8, 13–23	1:3b, 9–12
1 Thessalonians 1:2–10	1:2a	1:2b	1:2c–5	1:6–10	--
2 Thessalonians 1:3–12	1:3a	1:3b	1:3c	1:4–10	1:11–12
1 Timothy (none)	--	--	--	--	--
2 Timothy 1:3–5	1:3a	1:3b	1:5	1:4	1:3c
Titus (none)	--	--	--	--	--
Philemon 4–7	4a	4b	5	7	6

The thanksgiving section of Romans is also longer than usual. It follows the most common form in Paul's letters and serves two of four common purposes.[53] It serves an epistolary purpose by introducing the theme of faith that is proclaimed in the whole world (1:8), and it serves a pastoral purpose by introducing Paul's concern to establish the Romans in their faith (1:11) and his hope that they will encourage him in return (1:12).

---

53. A thanksgiving section can introduce main themes in the letter (epistolary purpose), express concern for the readers (pastoral purpose), recall previous teaching (didactic purpose), and/or indicate areas for growth (paraenetic purpose). See Harvey, *Pauline Letters*, 35.

Apostolic Parousia Sections in Paul's Letters[54]

	Writing Unit	Emissary Unit		Visit Unit
Romans 15:22–29	(15:14–21)	--		15:22–29
1 Corinthians 4:14–21	4:14–16	4:17	(Timothy)	4:18–21
2 Corinthians 13:1–10	13:10	--		13:1–9
Galatians 4:19–20	--	--		4:19–20
Ephesians 6:21–22	--	6:21–22 (Tychicus)		--
Philippians 2:19–24	--	2:19–23 (Timothy)		2:24
Colossians 4:7–9	--	4:7–9	(Tychicus)	--
1 Thessalonians 2:17–3:10	--	3:1–8	(Timothy)	2:17–20; 3:9–10
2 Thessalonians (none)	--	--		--
1 Timothy 3:14–15	3:15	--		3:14
2 Timothy 4:9–18	--	--		Timothy to visit Paul
Titus 3:12–14	--	3:12	(Artemas or Tychicus)	Titus to visit Paul
Philemon 21–22	21	--		22

---

54. Jervis identifies 15:14–33 as the apostolic parousia for Romans, although verses 14–21 are more accurately the apostolic apologia (*Purpose of Romans*, 111). She also includes verses 30–33 as a "special unit," although it is better understood as a stand-alone prayer request section. She analyzes the prayer request section of 1 Thessalonians 3:11–13 as another special unit; the Christ hymn of 1 Timothy 3:16 would be a third such unit. Each has been excluded from this table. Jervis does not include 2 Corinthians, Ephesians, Colossians, 1 Timothy, 2 Timothy, or Titus in her analysis.

Paul uses the three elements of the apostolic parousia to address different issues. The writing unit emphasizes his authority to write. The emissary unit emphasizes the credentials of the individual(s) who carry the letter. The visit unit emphasizes Paul's intention or desire to visit. The fact that only the visit unit appears in Romans reinforces the importance he places on visiting Rome as he pursues his plan to shift the focus of his ministry from the eastern half of the empire to the western half.

Closing Sections in Paul's Letters

	Peace Wish	Closing Advice	Greetings	Autograph	Benediction
Romans 16:3–27	(15:33)	16:17–20a	16:3–16, 21–23	--	16:20b–27
1 Corinthians 16:13–24	--	16:13–18	16:19–20	16:21–22	16:23–24
2 Corinthians 13:11–14	--	13:11	13:12–13	--	13:14
Galatians 6:11–18	--	--	--	6:11–17	6:18
Ephesians 6:23–24	6:23	--	--	--	6:24
Philippians 4:8–9, 21–23	4:9b	4:8–9a	4:21–22	--	4:23
Colossians 4:10–18	--	4:16–17	4:10–15	4:18a	4:18b
1 Thessalonians 5:23–28	5:23	5:24–25, 27	5:26	--	5:28
2 Thessalonians 3:16–18	3:16	--	--	3:17	3:18
1 Timothy 6:20–21	--	6:20–21a	--	--	6:21b
2 Timothy 4:19–21	--	--	4:19–21a	--	4:22b
Titus 3:15	--	--	3:15a	--	3:15b
Philemon 23–25	--	--	23–24	19–22	25

Paul used the closings of his letters to develop and maintain his relationship with the recipients. The extended greeting sections in Romans serve at least two purposes. They introduce Paul as someone who is associated with individuals who were already well-known to the congregations in Rome. They also emphasize the inclusiveness (all ethnic backgrounds and socioeconomic levels) and the extensiveness (at least four different provinces) of Paul's ministry.

Rhetorical Considerations

There is a range of views on how best to use rhetorical categories in analyzing Paul's letters. Perhaps they are most helpful at the "middle" level in analyzing individual passages within the letter.[55] At the "macro" level, however, two issues have generated the most scholarly discussion: the type of persuasion Paul uses and the arrangement of his argument.

Classical rhetoric included three genres or types of persuasion: forensic, deliberative, and epideictic. The following table compares those types of persuasion with regard to their occasion, time, purpose, and topic.

Genre	Occasion	Time	Purpose	Topic
Forensic	Judicial	Past	Accuse/defend	What is just
Deliberative	Legislative	Future	Persuade/dissuade	What is worthy
Epideictic	Ceremonial	Present	Praise/blame	What is honorable

Jewett rejects the forensic and deliberative genres that have most often been proposed and argues that Romans is best understood as epideictic rhetoric, in particular an ambassador's speech.[56] Longenecker, however, suggests that protreptic rhetoric is a more appropriate understanding for three of the major sections on the letter (1:16–4:25; 5:1–8:39; 12:1–15:13).[57] Protreptic rhetoric is a word or message of exhortation that seeks to win converts and attract to a certain way of life. Yet another suggestion is that the primary rhetorical style used in Romans is the diatribe.[58] Although multiple sections of the letter

---

55. See Harvey, *Pauline Letters*, 41–43.
56. Jewett, *Romans*, 42–46.
57. Longenecker, *Romans*, 15. His suggestion that 9:1–11:36 is characterized by "Jewish remnant theology rhetoric" is not especially persuasive.
58. S. K. Stowers, *The Diatribe and Paul's Letter to the Romans* (Chico, CA: Scholars, 1981).

use a diatribal style,[59] characterizing the entire letter as a diatribe seems remote. The mixed results of these analyses appear to support Schreiner's conclusion: "Even if Paul uses a certain rhetorical category, he does not follow the form rigidly."[60]

As far as arrangement is concerned, Jewett suggests a five-part rhetorical arrangement that includes four proofs:[61]

Exordium (Introduction)	1:1–12
Narratio (Statement of Facts)	1:13–15
Propositio (Basic Contention)	1:16–17
Probatio (Proof)	1:18–15:13
First Proof (1:18–4:25)	
Second Proof (5:1–8:39)	
Third Proof (9:1–11:36)	
Fourth Proof (12:1–15:13)	
Peroratio (Conclusion)	15:14–16:24

Jewett argues that the categories used in epistolary analysis are products of modern scholarship, while the categories used in rhetorical analysis are preferable because they date from classical times. It is worth noting, however, that the resulting divisions within the text are virtually identical.

Theological Framework and Topics

Although there are multiple approaches to exploring the theology of Romans, this section will consider the letter from two perspectives: the basic framework of Paul's theology and the major topics of Paul's argument.

The Framework of Paul's Theology

Two verses capture the central focus of Paul's theology. Second Corinthians 5:17 highlights the change that takes place when a person responds to the gospel in repentance and faith: "If any man is in Christ, he is a new creature; the old things passed away; behold, new things have come." Colossians 1:13 makes it clear the change is the result solely of God's work: "For he delivered us from the domain of darkness, and transferred us to the kingdom of his beloved son." Both verses

---

59. Those sections include Romans 2:1–16; 3:1–20, 27–31; 4:1–12; 6:1–14, 15–23; 9:19–29; 9:30–10:4; 11:1–10, 11–24; 13:1–7.
60. Schreiner, *Romans*, 24.
61. Jewett, *Romans*, 29–30.

reflect the basic framework of Paul's theology. For Paul, there are two spheres of existence, and every person is in one of them. He refers to those spheres interchangeably as being "in Adam" and "in Christ" (e.g., 1 Cor. 15:21–22) or as "the old man" and "the new man" (e.g., Eph. 4:23–24; Col. 3:10–11). Contrasting pairs such as these occur repeatedly throughout Paul's letters, and Romans is no exception, as chapters 5 through 8 make clear.

	In Adam	In Christ
5:9; 5:1	Wrath of God	Peace with God
5:16, 18	Condemnation	Justification
5:17; 6:21, 23; 8:13	Death	Life
5:17	Death reigns	Grace and righteousness reign
5:19	Many made sinners	Many made righteous
5:21	Sin reigns in death	Grace reigns to life
6:14	Under law	Under grace
6:17–19	Slaves of sin/impurity	Slaves of righteousness/God
6:19	Lawlessness	Sanctification
6:20, 22	Free in regard to righteousness	Freed from sin
7:6	Oldness of letter	Newness of life
5:3–5; 7:14–20	Living in futility of the flesh	Living in hope of glory
7:24–25	"Wretched man that I am!"	"Thanks be to God!"
8:2	Law of sin and death	Law of the Spirit of life
8:5–9, 13	Living according to the flesh	Living according to the Spirit
8:15	Spirit of slavery	Spirit of adoption
8:21	Slavery of corruption	Freedom of glory

Christ's work makes it possible for God to transfer a person from being "in Adam" to being "in Christ." Ephesians 2:8–9 captures the dynamics concisely: "For by grace you have been saved through faith; and that not of yourselves, it is the gift of God; not as a result of works, that no one should boast." God is the agent who saves us; grace is the basis on which he acts;[62] and faith is the means by which we respond to the gospel Paul preaches. This basic idea of transfer ("saved by grace through faith") from one sphere of existence ("in Adam") to the other ("in Christ") provides the overall framework for Paul's presentation of his gospel in Romans.

The two spheres are explicit in Romans 5:12–21, where Paul unfolds the typological relationship between Adam and Christ. After he explains Adam's role in salvation history (5:12–14), Paul sets out three key differences between Adam and Christ (5:15–17) and concludes with parallel explanations of how Adam's disobedience and Christ's obedience inaugurate the two spheres in which all human beings exist (5:18–21).[63]

	Adam	Christ
Nature of act	Disobedience	Obedience
Immediate effect	Condemnation	Justification
Resulting status	Sinners	Righteous
Ultimate effect	Sin reigns in death	Grace reigns in life

Romans 1:18–3:20 sets out in detail both the sinfulness of Gentile and Jew and the condemnation that places them under God's wrath as a result of being in Adam. Romans 3:21–31 establishes the fact that the transfer to being in Christ occurs on the basis of grace through faith alone, while Romans 4:1–25 makes it clear that works, religious ritual, and law-keeping play no role in that transfer. Romans 5:1–11 summarizes the benefits that accrue to those who are in Christ and highlights the "upward spiral" of perseverance ⇨ proven character ⇨ hope (5:3–5) that contrasts sharply with the subsequent "downward spiral" of sinful passions ⇨ sinful acts ⇨ death (7:5).

Romans 6:1–23 calls those who are now in Christ to live accordingly because they are both dead to sin and alive to God (6:1–14) and freed from sin and enslaved to God (6:15–23). Romans 7:1–25 highlights the futility

---

62. See Wallace, *Greek Grammar Beyond the Basics* (Grand Rapids: Zondervan, 1996), 167–68.
63. For the following table, see Harvey, *Pauline Letters*, 181.

of trying to live out this new status by relying on the law, while Romans 8:1–39 explains that when this new status is lived out in the power of the Holy Spirit (8:1–30), the result is total victory (8:31–39). Finally, Romans 12:1–15:13 provides practical instruction for day-to-day living in Christ.

The Topics of Paul's Argument

Moo suggests that only a theme as broad as "the gospel" can "encompass the diverse topics in Romans."[64] The noun εὐαγγέλιον (1:1, 9, 16; 15:16, 19, 20; 16:25) and the verb εὐαγγελίζω (1:15; 15:20) occur multiple times in the letter opening (1:1–17) and closing (15:14–16:27), and the gospel is the subject of the letter's thematic statement (1:16–17). That thematic statement also includes four topics that relate directly to the major sections of Paul's argument: God's righteousness, power, plan, and people.

The gospel is **the revelation of God's righteousness** ("the righteousness of God is being revealed"). It is possible to understand the phrase "the righteousness of God" in three ways: (1) "the righteousness God possesses" (possessive genitive), (2) "the righteous actions God performs" (subjective genitive), or (3) "the righteousness God bestows" (genitive of source). A combination of the second and third is probably the best option: "God's righteous act that results in a righteous life." The topic of God's righteousness is central to Romans 1:18–4:25. In that section, Paul makes it clear that God reveals his righteousness against ungodliness (1:18–3:20), apart from law (3:21–31), and in response to faith (4:1–25).

The gospel is **the demonstration of God's power** ("the power of God for salvation"). The phrase "the power of God" describes "the power God exercises" (subjective genitive), specifically the effectiveness of that power in bringing about salvation.[65] The topic of God's saving power is central to Romans 5:1–8:39. In those chapters, Paul sets out multiple plights from which God's power delivers us: divine wrath (5:1–11), Adam's condemnation (5:12–21), sin's dominion (6:1–23), the law's futility (7:1–25), living according to the flesh (8:1–30), and any imaginable source of opposition (8:31–39).

The gospel is **the fulfillment of God's plan** ("to the Jew first, then to the Gentile"). Paul's concern for the priority of the Jewish people in

---

64. Moo, *Romans*, 30.
65. God's power is a recurring theme in Paul's letters (Rom. 1:20; 9:17; 1 Cor. 1:18, 24; 2:5; 6:14; 2 Cor. 4:7; 6:7; 13:4; 2 Tim. 1:8). For Paul, salvation refers to spiritual deliverance (Rom. 10:1, 10; 11:11; 13:11; 2 Cor. 1:16; 6:2; 7:10; Eph. 1:13; Phil. 1:19, 28; 2:12; 1 Thess. 5:8–9; 2 Thess. 2:13; 2 Tim. 2:10; 3:15).

God's plan (1:16; cf. 2:9–10) echoes Jesus's approach (e.g., Matt. 10:5–6; 15:21–28) and reflects his own ministry practice (e.g., Acts 13:44–52). It also raises the question of how to understand Israel's lack of responsiveness to the gospel. The topic of God's plan for redemptive history is the focus of Romans 9:1–11:36. In that section, Paul explains God's sovereign working (9:1–29), Israel's current unresponsiveness (9:30–10:21), and the role that unresponsiveness plays in God's plan to show mercy to all (11:1–36).

The gospel leads to **the transformation of God's people** ("the righteous one will live by faith"). Paul's quotation of Habakkuk 2:4 can be understood as either "the one who is righteous by faith will live" (forensic sense) or "the one who is righteous will live by faith" (transformative sense). While chapters 1–8 address the former, the transformative aspect is the focus of Romans 12:1–15:13. In the latter section, Paul describes the way in which the gospel should transform the way God's people relate to him (12:1–2), serve and love one another (12:3–9; 13:8–10), relate to others (12:10–21), relate to authority (13:1–7), approach each day (13:11–14), and exercise the liberty they have in Christ (14:1–15:13).

Paul's Use of the Old Testament

Silva writes, "Hardly a paragraph in the Pauline corpus fails to reflect the influence of the Old Testament on the apostle's language and thought."[66] The Index of Quotations in UBS[5] lists sixty verses in Romans that incorporate direct quotations of the Old Testament. Four of those verses involve combined citations, for a total of sixty-four occurrences. The Index of Allusions and Parallels in UBS[5] lists an additional eighty-eight verses from the letter. Half of the quotations (32) occur in chapters 9–11; sixteen occur in chapters 1–4; three occur in chapters 5–8; and thirteen occur in chapters 12–16. Twenty-five quotations are from the Law (nine from Genesis, eight from Deuteronomy); twenty-four are from the Prophets (nineteen from Isaiah); and fifteen are from the Writings (thirteen from Psalms). The latter distribution suggests that Paul was intent on demonstrating that the entire Old Testament supported the gospel he preached. Within the letter, Paul uses Old Testament quotations almost exclusively as proofs to support his argumentation.[67]

The distribution of Old Testament quotations within the letter is distinctive and aligns with key word groups as the following table shows.

---

66. M. Silva, "Old Testament in Paul," in *DPL*, 634.
67. Old Testament quotations fill four basic functions in the New Testament. In Romans, the distribution is proof (56), analogy (4), application (4), and fulfillment (0).

	Chapters 1–4	Chapters 5–8	Chapters 9–11	Chapters 12–16
Old Testament Quotations	16	3	32	13
δικαιοσύνη/δικαιόω	29	19	13	1
πίστις/πιστεύω	33	3	14	10
ζωή/ζάω	2	24	2	6
πνεῦμα	3	24	1	7
χάρις	5	10	5	5

Longenecker suggests that the distribution of Old Testament quotations, on the one hand, reflects gospel proclamation Paul held in common with Jewish-Christian believers (1:18–4:25; 9:1–11:36), and, on the other hand, reflects the basic features of the gospel as Paul contextualized them in the Gentile mission (5:1–8:39).[68] Regardless of whether Longenecker's proposed sources are on target, it is worth noting that Paul's argument in chapters 1–4 and 9–11 tends to be traditional, judicial, and messianic, while his argument in chapters 5–8 tends to be personal, relational, and participatory.

Of the sixty-four direct quotations in Romans, Paul follows the LXX forty-six times; he follows the MT four times; and he differs from both the LXX and the MT fourteen times.[69] Although he demonstrates a clear preference for the LXX and sometimes departs from whatever source he uses, it is wise to avoid attempting to establish a pattern that Paul follows absolutely. Each occurrence should be investigated separately. Silva, however, provides a helpful summary of principles that appear to have guided Paul in his use of the Old Testament: (1) the text carries divine authority; (2) the text's historical meaning must be respected; (3) the text is applicable to the contemporary situation at hand; (4) literary associations within the Old Testament can add to the persuasive power of the text; and (5) the redemptive-historical context of the text is christological.[70]

---

68. Longenecker, *Romans*, 542 and 547.
69. These figures use the categories Silva proposes ("Old Testament," 630–32), but they have been adjusted slightly to reflect the total number of quotations listed by UBS[5]. The number of LXX quotations (46) combines passages where LXX and MT agree (24) with passages where LXX is clearly the source (22).
70. "Old Testament," 642.

The New Perspective on Paul and Related Interpretive Issues

The "new perspective on Paul" describes a movement in scholarship that proposes an alternative understanding of Paul's emphasis in Romans and Galatians.[71] The traditional perspective (sometimes labeled "Lutheran orthodoxy") is that Paul was arguing against a Pharisaic Jewish legalism that advocated observance of the law as a means of establishing a right relationship with God—in other words, that salvation could be earned through the merit of good works. Advocates of this view point to passages such as Romans 4:1–8, where Paul makes it clear that Abraham was justified (counted righteous) by faith alone apart from works.[72] Paul's primary focus, therefore, is on justification, and he develops topics such as sanctification, the role of the law, the work of the Holy Spirit, and God's plan for Israel in relation to that focus.

Some scholars trace the beginning of the new perspective to Davies's work on the Jewish sources of Paul's thought;[73] others point to Stendahl's focus on the Jew/Gentile question.[74] Sanders's work *Paul and Palestinian Judaism*, however, gave the discussion particular impetus.[75] Sanders argues that Second Temple Judaism was characterized not by legalism but, rather, by *nomism*. That is, Israel was already in a covenantal relationship with God, and obeying the law was their means of maintaining and expressing that relationship.[76] Paul was so deeply affected by his conversion experience that he subsequently found fault with Judaism because it did not recognize the importance of faith in Christ and because it continued to view Gentiles as outside the community of God's people. Judaism is not wrong because it advocated a pattern of legalistic works-righteousness; Judaism is wrong because "it is not Christianity."[77]

---

71. Guy Prentiss Waters provides a detailed history and critique from a Reformed perspective in *Justification and the New Perspective on Paul: A Review and Response* (Phillipsburg, NJ: P&R, 2004).

72. Outside Romans, see also Galatians 3:1–14 and, in particular, Philippians 3:9, where Paul rejects "a righteousness of my own derived from the Law" in favor of "that which is through faith in Christ, the righteousness that comes from God on the basis of faith."

73. W. D. Davies, *Paul and Rabbinic Judaism* (London: SPCK, 1948).

74. K. Stendahl, *Paul Among Jews and Gentiles and Other Essays* (Philadelphia: Fortress, 1976).

75. E. P. Sanders, *Paul and Palestinian Judaism* (Philadelphia: Fortress, 1977).

76. The idea is frequently described as "covenantal nomism" in order to highlight the connection to God's covenant with Israel. Longenecker suggests "reacting nomism" as a contrast to "acting legalism" (*Romans*, 364–65).

77. Sanders, *Palestinian Judaism*, 552.

Although Sanders sees Paul's thought as somewhat incoherent, and contradictory, Dunn sees the religious pattern of covenantal nomism as the key that unlocks a consistent understanding of Paul and his attitude toward Judaism.[78] The law is an expression of Israel's distinctiveness that serves to distinguish the Jews from lawless sinners. In the Second Temple period, the Jews placed particular focus on circumcision, food laws, and the Sabbath, which became identity markers and sources of ethnic pride. It was necessary, therefore, for Gentiles to adopt the practices of Jewish piety in order to become members of the covenant. Judaism is not wrong because it advocated a pattern of legalistic works-righteousness; Judaism is wrong because of its attitude of ethnic pride.

Wright also finds consistency in Paul's thought, but for him the key is the narrative dimension of the new perspective.[79] For Wright, the narrative substructure of Paul's thought focuses on God's righteousness, which Wright prefers to understand as God's faithful covenant justice. God established his covenant with Israel and gave them the law to mark them as his people. They were to play a central role in solving the problem of evil and in bringing saving order to the world, but they failed in that role. In order to be both faithful to his covenant and just in his dealings, God sent his Messiah, who faithfully fulfilled God's plan and redefined God's people around Messiah and the Spirit. Both Jew and Gentile are now welcome as members of God's renewed covenant on equal terms with the new covenant signs of faith and the Spirit. Judaism is not wrong because it advocated a pattern of legalistic works-righteousness; Judaism is wrong because it appeals to possession of the law to legitimate Israel's covenant status. The law neither guarantees Israel's current place in the covenant nor excludes it from a future place in the covenant.

Each of these views on the new perspective is helpful. Sanders's work provides a reminder that Second Temple Judaism was not monolithic and highlights the radical change that takes place when an individual responds to Christ in faith. Dunn's work provides a reminder to seek coherence in biblical revelation and highlights the danger of ethnic or religious pride. Wright's work provides a reminder of the continuity of God's redemptive plan and highlights the centrality of

---

78. Dunn, *Romans*, lxiv–lxxii.
79. N. T. Wright, *Paul in Fresh Perspective* (Minneapolis: Fortress, 2005). Wright traces the narrative dimension to R. B. Hays's work, *The Faith of Jesus Christ: The Narrative Substructure of Galatians 3:1–4:11*, 2nd ed. (Grand Rapids: Eerdmans, 2002).

faith, Christ, and the Spirit in defining the people of God. The potential danger lies in minimizing the traditional perspective, replacing it entirely with one of the new perspectives, or allowing it to override the insights of the other perspectives altogether. Commentators might decide that one emphasis is primary, but they cannot ignore the evidence that informs the other emphases.

Not surprisingly, discussion of the new perspective has raised related interpretive issues in Pauline studies. Three of the most prominent are (1) the interpretation of "faithfulness of/faith in Jesus Christ" (πίστις Ἰησοῦ Χριστοῦ), (2) the interpretation of "works of law" (ἔργα νόμου), and (3) the proper understanding of Paul's teaching on the law. The following sections summarize each issue briefly.

Faithfulness of / Faith in Jesus Christ

The Greek phrase πίστις Ἰησοῦ Χριστοῦ or its equivalent occurs six times in Paul's letters (Rom. 3:22; Gal. 2:16 [2 x]; 3:22; Eph. 3:12; Phil. 3:9). The interpretive question is whether the genitive is better understood as a subjective genitive ("faithfulness of Jesus Christ") or an objective genitive ("faith in Jesus Christ").[80] The primary evidence and arguments offered in support of the subjective genitive are: (1) when πίστις occurs with a genitive of person, the faith involved is the faith/faithfulness the individual possesses and/or exercises (e.g., Rom. 3:3; 4:12, 16); (2) the phrase that follows in 3:22—εἰς πάντας τοὺς πιστεύοντας—renders an objective genitive redundant; (3) the phrase διὰ τῆς πίστεως in 3:25 occurs in the context of Christ's work rather than the believer's response; (4) the use of the personal name alone in 3:26 (τὸν ἐκ πίστεως Ἰησοῦ) points to Jesus's "faithfulness." In response to the latter three arguments, the overall context of 3:21–4:25 focuses on the faith men and women exercise in God and/or Christ. Elsewhere in the New Testament, the objective genitive with πίστις is clearly intended (Mark 11:22; Acts 3:16; James 2:1). Other nouns occur in similar constructions where an objective genitive is the natural understanding.[81] The value of this particular discussion is the focus it places on both Christ's active obedience in perfectly obeying the law ("faithfulness of Christ") and his passive obedience in paying the penalty for

80. Longenecker, Wright, and Wallace adopt the subjective genitive interpretative, while Cranfield, Dunn, Jewett, Moo, and Schreiner adopt the objective genitive interpretative.
81. For example, τῆς ἐλπίδος τοῦ κυρίου ἡμῶν Ἰησοῦ Χριστοῦ ("hope in our Lord Jesus Christ") in 1 Thessalonians 1:3 and τῆς γνώσεως Χριστοῦ Ἰησοῦ τοῦ κυρίου μου ("the knowledge of Jesus Christ my Lord") in Philippians 3:8.

sin and, so, becoming the object of faith ("faith in Christ").[82] It is interesting to consider is whether Wallace's category of "plenary genitive" (*both* subjective *and* objective) might apply to this phrase.[83]

Works of Law

The Greek phrase ἔργα νόμου or its equivalent occurs eight times in Paul's letters (Rom. 3:20, 28; Gal. 2:16 [3 x]; 3:2, 5, 10). Scholarly discussion of this phrase began well before (and apart from) the advent of the new perspective. For example, Bultmann argued that any attempt to achieve salvation by keeping the law was, in itself, idolatry and, therefore, a sin.[84] More recently, Jewett has argued that any traditional system that seeks to achieve honor or avoid shame is sinful and should be abandoned.[85] Gaston argues for a subjective genitive understanding in which any works produced by the law are inherently sinful.[86] An objective genitive understanding is more common in which "works of law" describes deeds required/commanded by the law. The issue then becomes whether Dunn's understanding of specific works of law as identity markers should be preferred over the more traditional understanding of attempting to establish a relationship with God by observing the Mosaic law. The following considerations support the traditional understanding: (1) the overall argument of 1:18–4:25 is that law and circumcision will not protect the Jews from wrath; (2) the Jews are judged for failing to keep the law (2:1–3, 8–9, 12, 21–24, 25, 27); (3) judgment falls on all because of their sinful acts (3:9–18); (4) the use of "works" in 4:1–8 carries a general sense that suggests the whole law rather than specific "identity markers."

Paul and the Law

Sanders's work on the view of the law in Palestinian Judaism re-energized the discussion of Paul and the law by adding a new approach.

---

82. See the discussion of 4:24–25.
83. Wallace, *Grammar*, 119–21. Wallace's analysis is that in most cases the subjective notion produces the objective notion. In this instance, the result would be that the faithfulness of Christ produces the individual's faith in Christ. Another understanding would be that the individual's faith is in Christ's faithfulness.
84. R. Bultmann, *Theology of the New Testament*, vol. 1, trans. K. Grobel (New York: Scribner, 1951).
85. Jewett, *Romans*, 266.
86. L. Gaston, *Paul and the Torah* (Vancouver: University of British Columbia Press, 1987).

Historically, studies had focused on Paul's teaching regarding the law as a consistent response to Jewish beliefs. Schoeps, for example, argued that Paul's teaching represents a logical development of the Jewish belief that the law ceased when the messianic age began.[87] Cranfield represented the traditional position that Paul's teaching is a polemic against the legalistic works-righteousness of Judaism. Nevertheless, the law remains in effect as a moral guide for believers.[88]

At about the same time Sanders wrote, two scholars suggested that Paul's teaching on the law in Romans reflected a development in his thinking in response to ministry circumstances. Drane argued that Romans represents a balanced position between the more "libertine" position of Galatians and the more "legalistic" ethical position of 1 Corinthians.[89] Hübner suggested that Paul had a discussion with James after writing Galatians, and that discussion caused Paul to rethink his theology. Romans reflects Paul's more fully developed position.[90]

Sanders's own conclusion was that Paul's teaching on the law is inherently contradictory, because Paul approaches the issue from the starting point of salvation through Christ alone (divine solution) rather than from humankind's need (human plight). As a result, the tension between his "learned" and "revealed" convictions about the law lead to contradictions when Paul addresses different questions.[91] Six years later, Räisänen argued that the Jew-Gentile conflict forced Paul into the radical position of arguing that a divine institution had been abolished through what God has done in Christ. The arguments of "Paul the theologian," therefore, do not correspond to the thoughts of "Paul the man."[92]

Two slightly later scholars renewed the argument for consistency in Paul's teaching on the law, albeit with different emphases than either Schoeps or Cranfield. Westerholm provides a helpful review of scholarly discussions of Paul and the law and, then, offers his own conclusions. He argues that the issue with the law was never Jewish self-righteous boasting or a rabbinic tradition of salvation by works. Paul's starting point is the offer of the gospel about Jesus, the crucified Messiah. The law promises life on the condition of perfect obedience,

---

87. H. J. Schoeps, *Paul: The Theology of the Apostle in Light of the Jewish Religious History*, trans. H. Knight (Philadelphia: Westminster, 1961).

88. C. E. B. Cranfield, "St. Paul and the Law," *SJT* 17 (1964): 43–68.

89. J. W. Drane, *Paul: Libertine or Legalist?* (London: SPCK, 1975).

90. H. Hübner, *Law in Paul's Thought*, trans. J. C. G. Greig (Edinburgh: T&T Clark, 1984).

91. Sanders, *Paul and Palestinian Judaism*.

92. H. Räisänen, *Paul and the Law* (Tübingen: Mohr, 1983).

but it also threatens death for disobedience. Justification by grace through faith in Christ demonstrates the failure of the law and the inadequacy of human righteousness.[93] Thielman argues that, in contrast to Sanders, the framework of plight to solution was common in Second Temple Judaism. Humankind's plight lies in the reality that the law is impossible to obey, and disobedience results in wrath. Paul was not criticizing the practice of doing the law but the *failure* to do it. Messiah inaugurated the eschatological age in which it is now possible to obey the law by walking in the Spirit.[94]

To anticipate the discussion in the commentary proper, a few summary comments about Paul's (internally consistent) teaching on the law in Romans are in order. From Paul's perspective, the law is holy, just, good, and spiritual. It promises life for perfect obedience and was intended to result in life. Because the law also brings a knowledge of sin, however, it makes individuals accountable before God. The law itself is not sin, but indwelling sin uses the law as an occasion to provoke sinful acts. Consequently, the law can never be a means by which any individual is declared righteous. Because Christ fulfilled the righteous requirement of the law, however, his death and resurrection (as one entity) ends the law's role as an administrative system for relating to God. Nevertheless, as individuals walk according to the Spirit, they fulfill the intent of the law. Paul can affirm, therefore, that his gospel establishes the law as God's revelation that brings the knowledge of sin, as God's requirement that he fulfills in Christ, and as God's expression of his moral norms for living.

Interpretive Approach and Commentary Organization

The basic approach behind this commentary has been set out in *Interpreting the Pauline Letters: An Exegetical Handbook* (Kregel, 2012). That approach views the twin tasks of exegesis and exposition as essential to handling Scripture appropriately. In the case of Paul's letters, understanding the first-century message (exegesis) without considering how to appropriate and communicate that message in the twenty-first century truncates the process. Similarly, trying to appropriate and communicate the message (exposition) without understanding it also

---

93. S. Westerholm, *Israel's Law and the Church's Faith: Paul and His Recent Interpreters* (Grand Rapids: Eerdmans, 1988). Westerholm also concludes that the law's failure was part of God's plan.
94. F. Thielman, *From Plight to Solution: A Jewish Framework to Understanding Paul's View of the Law in Galatians and Romans* (Leiden: Brill, 1989).

truncates the process. In other words, Scripture is intended to change lives, and the whole point of studying it is to be able to apply its life-changing message to yourself and communicate it to others.

The process of taking a passage from text to sermon outline or teaching plan involves three basic tasks, each with a number of elements. **Examination** is the preparatory work of establishing what the text is and what it says. The task of examination includes textual criticism and translation. **Exegesis** is the analytical work of interpreting the first-century message. The task of exegesis includes historical analysis (introductory matters, historical-cultural-religious details), literary analysis (context, genre, structure, syntax, rhetoric, word study), and theological analysis (analogy of Scripture; analogy of faith). **Exposition** is the synthetic work of moving the passage's message into the world of the contemporary audience. The task of exposition includes first-century synthesis (basic message, shared need), twenty-first-century appropriation (connect, correct, commend), and homiletical packaging (objective, take-home truth)

Each section in this commentary rests on the careful application of these three tasks. Presenting the detailed findings in that form, however, would be less helpful to readers who are preparing to preach or teach Paul's letter to the Romans. For that reason, the discussion of each passage will be organized under five headings.

Text and Translation

The translation of each passage seeks to remain as close as possible to the Greek grammar, syntax, and word order. Clarifying words are kept to a minimum and italicized; interpretive decisions are discussed in footnotes. Discussion of significant textual variants is also provided in footnotes. For a detailed discussion of textual, grammatical, syntactical, and lexical issues, see *Romans* (Exegetical Guide to the Greek New Testament; B&H, 2017).

Context and Structure

Since understanding the place of any given passage in Paul's overall argument is crucial to its interpretation, each passage is set in the letter's outline. Similarly, understanding the passage's relationship to the genre of New Testament letters and/or any subgenres present in the passage is important. Those considerations are addressed in this section as well.

Basic Message and Exegetical Outline

The basic message is a one-sentence summary of the passage. That summary is followed by an outline that seeks to capture the structure, grammar, syntax, and rhetoric of the passage. The outline forms the basis for a detailed explanation of the passage.

Explanation of the Text

The explanation of the text follows the main points in the exegetical outline. It moves verse-by-verse through the passage and explains significant points of historical background, grammar, syntax, rhetorical features, and word study. Technical terms and Greek words are provided in parentheses to facilitate readability. Rather than setting out all the interpretive options in the commentary proper, the body of this section seeks to provide a coherent explanation of the passage. Footnotes cover the discussion of details as necessary.

Theology and Appropriation

Each passage is set in the theological context of Romans and of Paul's theology as a whole. In addition to a discussion of the analogies of Scripture (biblical theology) and/or faith (systematic theology), this section seeks to move the message of the passage into the world of the contemporary audience. It sets out the primary purpose and shared need of the passage. It also includes ways in which the passage might connect with an audience, correct wrong beliefs or attitudes, and commend positive beliefs and actions. Finally, it suggests an objective for communicating the message of the passage to others.

Homiletical Considerations

The primary purpose of this commentary is to help readers understand and communicate accurately Paul's message in the letter. To the latter end, the discussion of each text section includes a one-sentence summary of the passage, an exegetical outline, suggestions for connecting the passage to contemporary audiences, and a suggested objective for communicating the passage. The art of communicating the text properly belongs to the discipline of homiletics, and a full discussion of sermon preparation and delivery would involve a separate volume. It might be helpful, however, to provide a sample of one process for moving from exegesis to sermon, using Romans 1:8–12 as an example. The process includes six steps:

1. Identify the sentences in the Greek text.
2. Write an English summary of each Greek sentence.
3. Write a one-sentence summary of the passage's basic message.
4. Write an objective for the sermon.

5. Write a concise "sermon in a sentence."
6. Write a homiletical outline that frames the sermon.

Step 1: Identify the sentences in the Greek text.

The punctuation of the UBS[5] text of Romans 1:8–12 shows that the paragraph consists of three sentences (with the main verbal ideas underlined):

1:8   πρῶτον μὲν <u>εὐχαριστῶ τῷ θεῷ μου</u> διὰ Ἰησοῦ Χριστοῦ περὶ πάντων ὑμῶν, ὅτι ἡ πίστις ὑμῶν καταγγέλλεται ἐν ὅλῳ τῷ κόσμῳ.

1:9–10   μάρτυς γάρ μού ἐστιν ὁ θεός, ᾧ λατρεύω ἐν τῷ πνεύματί μου ἐν τῷ εὐαγγελίῳ τοῦ υἱοῦ αὐτοῦ, ὡς ἀδιαλείπτως <u>μνείαν ὑμῶν ποιοῦμαι</u> πάντοτε ἐπὶ τῶν προσευχῶν μου, δεόμενος εἴ πως ἤδη ποτὲ εὐοδωθήσομαι ἐν τῷ θελήματι τοῦ θεοῦ ἐλθεῖν πρὸς ὑμᾶς.

1:11–12   <u>ἐπιποθῶ γὰρ ἰδεῖν ὑμᾶς</u>, ἵνα τι μεταδῶ χάρισμα ὑμῖν πνευματικὸν εἰς τὸ στηριχθῆναι ὑμᾶς, τοῦτο δέ ἐστιν συμπαρακληθῆναι ἐν ὑμῖν διὰ τῆς ἐν ἀλλήλοις πίστεως ὑμῶν τε καὶ ἐμοῦ.

Step 2: Write an English summary of each Greek sentence.

Writing an English summary of each Greek sentence in the paragraph establishes the main points for an exegetical outline.

A. Paul thanks God for the Romans (1:8).
B. Paul prays for the Romans (1:9–10).
C. Paul longs to see the Romans (1:11–12).

The details of each sentence can then serve as subpoints in the outline.

A. Paul thanks God for the Romans (1:8).
    1. Because their faith is proclaimed in the whole world (1:8b)
B. Paul prays for the Romans (1:9–10).
    1. As God bears witness (1:9)
    2. To be granted a good journey to visit them (1:10b)
C. Paul longs to see the Romans (1:11–12).
    1. In order to share a spiritual benefit (1:11b)
    2. In order to be mutually encouraged (1:12)

Step 3: Write a one-sentence summary of the passage's basic message.

One approach to summarizing a passage's basic message is to follow Robinson's method for articulating the "big idea."[95] He suggests asking two questions: (1) "What is the author talking about?" and (2) "What is the author saying about what he is talking about?" The answer to the second question should reflect the main points in the exegetical outline. Together the answers to these questions comprise a single sentence that captures the basic message of the passage. Asking these questions of Romans 1:8–12 leads to the following basic message:

> What is the author talking about?
> Paul's pastoral concern for his Roman readers.
> What is the author saying about what he is talking about?
> He thanks God for them, prays for them, and expresses his longing to see them.

> Basic message:
> Paul shares his pastoral concern for his Roman readers by thanking God for them, praying for them, and expressing his longing to see them.

Step 4: Write an objective for the sermon.

A sermon that is true to the text of Scripture and true to the intent of Scripture will include both truth and application. A sermon objective envisions the action the hearers will take in response to the truth of the passage. One helpful pattern for writing an objective is:

> I want my listeners to understand _____[truth]_____,
> so that they will _____[action]_____.

For Romans 1:8–12, a possible sermon objective might be:

> I want my listeners to understand the spiritual bond that exists between believers, so that they will take practical steps to care for others in the church.

Step 5: Write a concise "sermon in a sentence."

To help listeners remember the central point of the sermon, it is

---

95. H. W. Robinson, *Expository Preaching: The Development and Delivery of Expository Messages*, 2nd ed (Grand Rapids: Eerdmans, 2001).

useful to craft a succinct memorable sentence they can "take home" with them.[96] Something like "Being there shows you care" might work for Romans 1:8–12.

Step 6: Write a homiletical outline that frames the sermon.

There are two basic ways to structure a sermon outline: deductively and inductively. A deductive sermon begins with a proposition and "proves" that proposition by presenting evidence in support of it. Deductive sermons move from general truth to specific instances. In contrast, an inductive sermon moves from specific instances to a general truth. It leads the listener through the evidence to arrive at a proposition, often by asking questions.[97]

Deductive Sermon	Inductive Sermon
Introduction	Introduction
Proposition	Point 1
Point 1	Point 2
Point 2	Point 3
Point 3	Proposition
Conclusion	Conclusion

Based on results from the first five steps, a deductive sermon outline for Romans 1:8–12 might be:

Proposition: Paul sets out three practices we should use to demonstrate our care for others.

Main Points:
   A. We should affirm them (1:8).
   B. We should pray for them (1:9–10).
   C. We should spend time with them (1:11–12).

---

96. D. R. Sunukjian suggests the label "take-home truth" (*Introduction to Biblical Preaching: Proclaiming the Truth with Clarity and Relevance* [Grand Rapids: Kregel, 2007], 136–41).

97. For a concise discussion of inductive sermons, see D. L. Hamilton, *Homiletical Handbook* (Nashville: Broadman and Holman, 1992), 97–103.

An inductive sermon outline for Romans 1:8–12 might be:

Thematic Question: What do we learn from Paul about demonstrating care for others?

Main Points (introduced as questions):
- A. What do we learn from verse 8?
  (We should affirm others.)
- B. What do we learn from verses 9–10?
  (We should pray for others.)
- C. What do we learn from verses 11–12?
  (We should spend time with others.)

Proposition: Paul's example gives us three practices we should use to demonstrate our care for others: affirming them, praying for them, and spending time with them.

Both types of sermons have advantages and disadvantages. The deductive approach has the advantage of alerting listeners to the central idea at the beginning of the sermon and leading them through the evidence to a clear destination. Some listeners, however, might lose interest in what they see as a dogmatic presentation of a preconceived conclusion. On the other hand, the inductive approach has the advantage of allowing listeners to interact mentally with the sermon and reach their own tentative conclusion. It also has the disadvantage that some listeners might become frustrated because they do not know the ultimate destination. Since congregations are comprised of men and women who hear and process truth differently, the wise communicator will incorporate both deductive and inductive approaches and will utilize a variety of sermon patterns.[98]

---

98. Harvey, *Pauline Letters*, 155.

LETTER OUTLINE

I. Letter Opening (1:1–17)
   A. Salutation (1:1–7)
   B. Thanksgiving (1:8–12)
   C. Occasion for Writing (1:13–15)
   D. Thesis (1:16–17)

II. Letter Body (1:18–15:13)
   A. The Gospel as the Revelation of God's Righteousness
      (1:18–4:25)
      1. The gospel reveals God's righteousness through wrath
         (1:18–3:20)
         a. Because humankind suppresses God's truth
            (1:18–23)
         b. Because the Gentiles practice unrighteousness
            (1:24–32)
         c. Because the moral person judges others (2:1–16)
         d. Because the Jews transgress the law (2:17–29)
         e. Because God always acts righteously (3:1–8)
         f. Because all are under sin (3:9–20)
      2. The gospel reveals God's righteousness apart from law
         (3:21–31)
         a. Through faith in Christ (3:21–26)
         b. Apart from works of law (3:27–31)
      3. The gospel reveals God's righteousness in response to
         faith (4:1–25)
         a. Apart from works or circumcision (4:1–12)
         b. Apart from law (4:13–25)

B. The Gospel as the Demonstration of God's Power
(5:1–8:39)
1. The gospel demonstrates God's power to save from
wrath (5:1–11)
2. The gospel demonstrates God's power to save from
condemnation (5:12–21)
3. The gospel demonstrates God's power to save from sin
(6:1–23)
a. Because we died with Christ (6:1–14)
b. Because we serve a new master (6:15–23)
4. The gospel demonstrates God's power to save from the
law (7:1–25)
a. Because dying with Christ brings release from the
law (7:1–6)
b. Because the law brings knowledge of sin (7:7–12)
c. Because sin uses the law to produce death (7:13–25)
5. The gospel demonstrates God's power to save from the
flesh (8:1–30)
a. Because the Spirit gives us life and assurance
(8:1–17)
b. Because the Spirit gives us hope of glory (8:18–30)
6. The gospel demonstrates God's power to save from all
opposition (8:31–39)
C. The Gospel as the Fulfillment of God's Plan (9:1–11:36)
1. Paul's concern for Israel (9:1–5)
2. The gospel fulfills God's plan to keep his word (9:6–29)
a. According to his calling (9:6–13)
b. Out of his mercy (9:14–18)
c. Under his authority (9:19–29)
3. The gospel fulfills God's plan to use Israel's unresponsiveness (9:30–10:21)
a. In pursuing a law of righteousness (9:30–10:4)
b. In failing to embrace righteousness by faith (10:5–13)
c. In failing to believe the gospel (10:14–21)
4. The gospel fulfills God's plan to show mercy to all
(11:1–32)
a. By preserving a Jewish remnant (11:1–10)
b. By bringing salvation to the Gentiles (11:11–16)
c. By demonstrating his kindness and severity
(11:17–24)
d. By restoring Israel (11:25–32)

5. Paul's doxology of praise to God for his working (11:33–36)
D. The Gospel as the Transformation of God's People (12:1–15:13)
    1. The gospel transforms the way God's people live their lives (12:1–13:14)
        a. As they pursue total transformation (12:1–2)
        b. As they exercise their spiritual gifts (12:3–8)
        c. As they overcome evil with good (12:9–21)
        d. As they are subject to authorities (13:1–7)
        e. As they love one another (13:8–10)
        f. As they wait for Jesus's return (13:11–14)
    2. The gospel transforms the way God's people exercise their liberty (14:1–15:13)
        a. By not despising one another (14:1–12)
        b. By not judging one another (14:13–23)
        c. By seeking to please one another (15:1–6)
        d. By accepting one another (15:7–13)

III. Letter Closing (15:14–16:27)
    A. Paul's Mission (15:14–21)
    B. Paul's Travel Plans (15:22–29)
    C. Paul's Prayer Request (15:30–33)
    D. Commendation of Phoebe (16:1–2)
    E. Greetings from Paul (16:3–16)
    F. Closing Advice (16:17–20)
    G. Greetings from Others (16:21–24)
    H. Doxology (16:25–27)

ROMANS 1:1–17
Letter Opening

Since John White's pioneering work on the body of New Testament letters, it has become common practice to limit the opening of Paul's letters to the salutation and thanksgiving sections and view the disclosure, request, or joy formula that characteristically follows the thanksgiving as the beginning of the body of the letter. Longenecker, for example, identifies 1:1–12 as the letter opening, with the disclosure formula in 1:13 marking the beginning of the letter body. Using such an approach, 1:13–15 serves as the body-opening, and 1:16–17 is part of the body-middle (1:16–15:13).

Rhetorical analysis takes a slightly different approach. Jewett, for example, identifies 1:1–12 as the *Exordium* (introduction), 1:13–15 as the *Narratio* (statement of facts), and 1:16–17 as the *Propositio* (thesis). The *Propositio* (proof of the thesis) encompasses 1:18–15:13, with 15:14–16:27 comprising the *Peroratio* (conclusion).

Given the connected nature of Paul's argument in 1:18–15:13 and the inherent unity of 1:1–17, it seems most natural to view the latter verses as the letter opening. There are four distinct sections within that opening: the salutation (1:1–7), the thanksgiving (1:8–12), the occasion for writing (1:13–15), and the thesis (1:16–17). In these opening sections, Paul seeks to establish his relationship with his readers so they will receive the information and instruction that form the letter body.

I. Letter Opening (1:1–17)
    A. Salutation (1:1–7)
    B. Thanksgiving (1:8–12)
    C. Occasion for Writing (1:13–15)
    D. Thesis (1:16–17)

ROMANS 1:1–7

Text and Translation

1 Paul, a slave of Christ Jesus,[1] called *to be* an apostle *who* has been set apart for the gospel of God,[2] **2** which he himself promised from the beginning through his prophets by means of the holy Scriptures[3] **3** concerning his Son,

> who came into being
>> out of the seed of David
>> according to the flesh,

4 and was appointed Son of God with power[4]
>> according to the Spirit of holiness
>> at the time of the resurrection[5] from the dead,

Jesus Christ our Lord, **5** through whom we received grace and apostleship for the obedience of faith[6] among all the Gentiles for the sake of his name, **6** among whom you also are called to belong to Jesus Christ,[7] **7** to all *those who* are in Rome[8] beloved by God, called to be saints, grace to you and peace from God our Father and the Lord Jesus Christ.

---

1. Although it is supported by fewer manuscripts, Χριστοῦ Ἰησοῦ (P¹⁰, B, 81) should be read instead of Ἰησοῦ Χριστοῦ (P²⁶, ℵ, A, D, 33) because it agrees with Paul's tendency to prefer the former (85 times) over the latter (25 times). The phrase is best understood as a title, "Messiah Jesus." The genitive of Χριστοῦ Ἰησοῦ is both possessive and objective.
2. Θεοῦ is both a genitive of source and an objective genitive.
3. The prepositional phrase ἐν γραφαῖς ἁγίαις is instrumental.
4. BDAG notes that ἐν δυνάμει designates state or condition and suggests the translation "clothed with power" (327b).
5. Ἐξ ἀναστάσεως describes temporal sequence (cf. Schreiner, *Romans*, 44).
6. The genitive in the phrase ὑπακοὴν πίστεως is best understood as a "plenary genitive" (both subjective and objective) with the idea "obedience to the call of faith (the gospel) that results in a lifestyle of faithful obedience" (cf. Harvey, *Romans*, 11). Εἰς + accusative denotes purpose/goal.
7. Ἰησοῦ Χριστοῦ is a possessive genitive. Longenecker notes that God the Father always issues a divine call (*Romans*, 68).
8. Ἐν Ῥώμῃ has solid manuscript support (𝔓10, 𝔓26, ℵ, A, B, C, D, 33). Its omission in a few manuscripts is most likely the result of attempts to show the general applicability of the letter (cf. Metzger, *Textual Commentary*, 446).

Context and Structure

I. Letter Opening (1:1–17)
   A. **Salutation (1:1–7)**
   B. Thanksgiving (1:8–12)
   C. Occasion for Writing (1:13–15)
   D. Thesis (1:16–17)

Paul opens his letter with the standard salutation of "A (writer) to B (recipient), greeting." He expands the writer section to introduce himself as well as the gospel he preaches (1:1–6). The recipient section includes a double description of the Romans (1:7a). The greeting of "grace . . . and peace" incorporates both Greek and Hebrew concepts (1:7b).

Basic Message and Exegetical Outline

Messiah Jesus is the source of Paul's apostleship, the focus of the gospel, and the one who calls the Romans into relationship with God the Father.

The Centrality of Messiah Jesus (1:1–7)
1. Jesus is the source of Paul's apostleship (1:1, 5)
   a. Called and set apart for the gospel (1:1)
   b. Given grace to minister among the Gentiles for God's glory (1:5)
2. Jesus is the focus of the gospel (1:2–4)
   a. As promised Davidic ruler (1:3)
   b. As exalted Davidic king (1:4a)
   c. As Messiah and Lord (1:4b)
3. Jesus is the one who calls the Romans into relationship with the Father (1:6–7)
   a. Called to be Christ's (1:6)
   b. Loved by God (1:7b)
   c. Called to be holy (1:7c)
   d. Given grace and peace (1:7d)

Explanation of the Text

1. Jesus is the source of Paul's apostleship (1:1, 5).

Following the salutation form common to first-century letters, Paul begins with his name as the writer. Roman citizens had tripartite names (e.g., Gaius Titius Justus; cf. 16:23) consisting of a personal name (*praenomen*), a clan name (*nomen*), and a family name (*cognomen*). Since he was a Roman citizen (Acts 16:37; 22:25–29), Paul (*Paulos*) was the apostle's official *cognomen*, while Saul (*Saulos*; cf. Acts 13:9) was an unofficial Semitic version. Writing to a majority Gentile church, Paul naturally uses the official form. He then adds three descriptors to that initial self-identification.

"Slave" (δοῦλος) describes one who was subject to a superior and suggests both total ownership and total obedience (cf. Phil. 1:1; Titus 1:1). The one to whom Paul belongs as well as the one he obeys is "Messiah Jesus."[9] "Called *to be* an apostle" (κλητὸς ἀπόστολος) describes a divine summons to service. "Apostle" is the most common self-designation in Paul's letters (e.g., 1 Cor. 1:1; 2 Cor. 1:1; Gal. 1:1). Although he was not one of the original Twelve, Paul claimed equal authority with that group as one who saw Christ after his resurrection (1 Cor. 9:1), received his commission directly from Christ (Gal. 1:1), and had his ministry validated by the signs and wonders of an apostle (2 Cor. 12:12). "Set apart" (ἀφορίζω) describes Paul as designated for a special and holy task (cf. Num. 8:11); in this case, his task is proclaiming the gospel that originates with and is about God.

More specifically (v. 5), the apostleship Paul received from Christ encompasses four aspects. First, its inherent *nature* is one of grace (χάριν); that is, it is a gift given to Paul so that he might accomplish the task assigned to him (cf. 15:15–16; Eph. 3:7–8). Second, his apostleship has as its *goal* "the obedience of faith" (εἰς ὑποκοὴν πίστεως); this phrase includes both an initial faith response to the message of the gospel and a subsequent walk of faithful obedience to God. Third, the *scope* of this apostleship is "among all the Gentiles" (ἐν πᾶσιν τοῖς ἔθνεσιν) and, so, includes the congregations in Rome. Fourth, the *motivation* behind Paul's apostleship is the name of Messiah Jesus (ὑπὲρ τοῦ ὀνόματος αὐτοῦ); that is, the impetus that drives his ministry is a desire to promote Christ's reputation and glory.

2. Jesus is the focus of the gospel (1:2–4).

A relative clause (v. 2) further describes the gospel God had promised from the beginning (προεπηγγείλατο). He "pre-promised" this gospel through his Old Testament prophets; they recorded it in "the holy Scriptures" (cf. 15:15; 16:26; 1 Cor. 15:3–4); and it focuses on "his son" (v. 3a). Paul calls Jesus "son" (υἱός) seven times in Romans (1:3, 4, 9; 5:10; 8:3, 29, 32) and ten times in his other letters. The

---

9. Jewett suggests that the entire phrase "slave of Christ Jesus" sets out Paul's "ambassadorial title," providing "proper credentials as an agent of Christ Jesus" (*Romans*, 100).

predominant use in these occurrences (12 x) highlights the close relationship between the Father and the Son ("his son"/"his own son"/"his beloved son"). A series of three parallel genitive constructions provides an extended description of this Son.

First, the Son is the fulfillment of the Davidic promise (cf. 2 Sam. 7:12–16). In his humanity (κὰτα σάρκα) Jesus's origin (τοῦ γενομένου) is from the line of David (ἐκ σπέρματος Δαυίδ). In this context "flesh" indicates human descent (4:1; 9:3, 5) rather than human nature that is hostile to God (8:4, 5, 12, 13). Jesus, therefore, is the promised ruler who would come from David's line (cf. Isa. 11:1–5; Jer. 23:5–6; Mic. 5:2).

Second, the Son is the exalted Davidic king (cf. Ps. 2:6–9). At the time of Jesus's resurrection (ἐξ ἀναστάσεως νεκρῶν), the Holy Spirit (κατὰ πνεῦμα ἁγιωσύνης) appointed Jesus (τοῦ ὁρισθέντος) as the authoritative Son of God (υἱοῦ θεοῦ ἐν δυνάμει). Since "spirit of holiness" is a literal translation of the Hebrew *ruach qodesh* (Ps. 51:13; Isa. 63:10–11), that phrase is best understood as a reference to the Holy Spirit. The phrase "with power" is best taken with Son of God as highlighting the power inherent in Jesus's enthronement as king. "Appointed" does not imply the bestowing of an entirely new status but, rather, the elevation to an exalted level of a status already possessed.[10] Jesus, therefore, is the exalted, authoritative Son of God (cf. 2 Cor. 1:19; Gal. 2:20; Eph. 4:13; 1 Thess. 1:10).

Third, the Son is Messiah and Lord. Although Paul used "Christ Jesus" (85), "Jesus Christ" (25 x), "Christ" (250+x), and "Jesus" (35 x) interchangeably, it is likely that Christ (Χριστός) carried the titular nuance of "Messiah" for him.[11] That nuance seems probable both here and in verse 1. Paul calls Jesus "Lord" (κύριος) over 200 times and most likely is influenced by the LXX, which used that Greek word to translate the divine name. Jesus, therefore, is both the anointed Messiah and the only Lord worthy of receiving glory and worship.[12]

3. Jesus is the one who calls the Romans into relationship with the Father (1:6–7).

Among the Gentiles whom Paul was called to serve (v. 5) are the believers in Rome (τοῖς οὖσιν ἐν Ῥώμῃ). Adding "all" (πᾶσιν) at the beginning of the recipient section, however, makes it clear that Paul is writing to both Gentile and Jewish Christians. Three qualifying phrases describe the readers. They are "called to belong to Jesus

---

10. See Moo for a helpful explanation (*Romans*, 47–49).
11. See Longenecker's discussion (*Romans*, 52–53).
12. The article with κυρίου is *par excellence*.

Christ" (κλητοὶ Ἰησοῦ Χριστοῦ). As God has called Paul to be an apostle (v. 1), so he has called the Romans to be Christ's special possession. They are "beloved by God" (ἀγαπητοῖς θεοῦ). The breadth and depth of God's love for them is demonstrated by Christ's death on their behalf (5:5–8; cf. 8:31–39). They are "called to be saints" (κλητοῖς ἁγίοις). As "saints," they are holy ones who have been specially chosen and set apart for God (Exod. 13:12; 20:8; Lev. 8:11–12; Deut. 10:8).

"Greetings" (χαίρειν) was the conventional opening wish in first-century letters. Paul replaced that single word with "grace" (χάρις) and added "peace" (εἰρήνη). The resulting combination incorporates both the Greek concept of divinely bestowed favor and the Hebrew concept of divinely bestowed well-being (*shalom*). Both gifts have their source in the Father and the Son. "Father" was Jesus's own way of addressing God (cf. Matt. 6:9; Luke 11:2).

Theology and Appropriation

A salutation opens each of Paul's letters.[13] At ninety-three words, the salutation of Romans is by far the longest.[14] It is twenty-four percent longer than the next longest salutation (Galatians at 75 words) and nearly five times longer than the shortest (1 Thessalonians at 19 words). The expansions Paul includes are informative and focus on his ministry as an apostle (1:1, 5), the nature of the gospel he preaches (1:2–4), and the status of his Roman readers (1:6–7). Paul subsequently develops each of these topics in the remainder of the letter. Paul returns to the details of his apostolic ministry in 15:14–33.[15] The gospel is, of course, the major topic for the body of the letter (1:18–15:13).[16] Relationships among the Roman believers come to the fore in 14:1–15:13.

Not surprisingly, Paul draws attention to the gospel. In particular, he focuses on the gospel as the Old Testament promise that has been fulfilled in Christ. The Old Testament unfolded that promise in a series of biblical covenants, three of which provide background for what Paul

---

13. The salutations in Paul's other letters are 1 Corinthians 1:1–3; 2 Corinthians 1:1 –2; Galatians 1:1–5; Ephesians 1:1–2; Philippians 1:1–2; Colossians 1:1–2; 1 Thessalonians 1:1; 2 Thessalonians 1:1–2; 1 Timothy 1:1–2; 2 Timothy 1:1–2; Titus 1:1–4; Philemon 1–3;

14. Klauck notes that it is the longest salutation found in Greek antiquity (H. J, Klauck, *Ancient Letters in the New Testament* [Waco, TX: Baylor University Press, 2006], 20, 302).

15. See the discussion at that point for a list of parallels (cf., Dunn, *Romans*, 857).

16. Longenecker suggests 5:1–8:39 in particular (*Romans*, 117–18).

writes in his salutation. The promise of a human seed who would counteract the effects of Adam's sin (Gen. 3:15) lies behind the messianic
hope that runs throughout the passage (cf. 5:12–21). The promise that
all the nations of the earth would be blessed in Abraham (Gen. 12:3) is
the bedrock on which Paul's ministry among all the Gentiles rests (cf.
4:1–25). The promise that God would raise up David's seed, establish
the throne of his kingdom forever, and relate to him as a father relates
to a son (2 Sam. 7:12–15) is the basis for Paul's description of Jesus as
the promised Davidic ruler and the exalted Son of God. This good news
of promise has been part of God's plan from the beginning.

Paul's briefer description of the Romans also has Old Testament
roots. They are called by God, set apart by God, and loved by God. Just
as Israel was God's special possession among all the peoples (Exod. 19:5),
so God calls the Romans to belong to Jesus Christ. Just as God set Israel
apart as his people and called them to be holy as he is holy (Lev. 20:26),
so God sets the Romans apart to be holy. Just as Israel was the object of
God's special, enduring, and undeserved love (Deut. 7:6–8), so God dearly
loves the Romans. Who they are in Christ should affect the way they
think about themselves and the way in which they relate to one another.

Helping the Romans understand the nature of the gospel and who
they are in Christ enables Paul to achieve his primary purpose of establishing common ground. If they understand what they have in common
with Paul, they are more likely to see how his apostolic ministry fits into
what God is doing to fulfill what the Old Testament "pre-promised." We
share with the original audience the need to realize the rich blessings we
have in common with others who have responded to the gospel in faith.
If we realize what we have in common with other believers, we will view
them in light of those blessings and will seek to understand how God is
working in and through them to accomplish his purposes.

The idea of promise offers a possible point of connection, because
everyone can relate to the hope inherent in a promise, the disappointment we experience when a promise fails to materialize, and the joy
when a promise is realized. This passage corrects the ideas that Jesus
is just another religious teacher or that the gospel offers just one more
religious system. Not only is Jesus the fulfillment of the Old Testament
promises, he is the exalted Son of God; the gospel offers a life of promise
made possible by the God who keeps his promises. The passage also
commends appropriation of the blessings available through a relationship with Jesus Christ. The objective in communicating this passage
should be to help others understand the rich community of faith the
gospel creates so that they will take steps to deepen their relationships
with other members of that community.

ROMANS 1:8–12

Text and Translation

8 First of all[1] I am indeed[2] giving thanks to my God through Jesus Christ concerning all of you,[3] because your faith is being proclaimed in the whole world. **9** For God is my witness—whom I worship with my spirit[4] in the gospel about his son[5]—that[6] I myself am constantly making[7] mention about you,[8] **10** always at the time of my prayers[9] while pleading[10] if somehow now at last I will be granted a good journey by the will of God to come to you. **11** For I am longing to see you, in order that I might share a certain spiritual gift with you in order for you to be strengthened, **12** that is, to be encouraged together among you through our[11] mutual faith, both yours and mine.

Context and Structure

I. Letter Opening (1:1–17)
   A. Salutation (1:1–7)
   B. **Thanksgiving (1:8–12)**
   C. Occasion for Writing (1:13–15)
   D. Thesis (1:16–17)

With the exception of 2 Corinthians, Galatians, 1 Timothy, and Titus, Paul's letters include a thanksgiving that serves one or more of four purposes: to introduce main themes of the letter (epistolary), to express concern for his readers (pastoral), to recall previous teaching (didactic), and to indicate possible areas for growth (paraenetic). In this letter he includes a thanksgiving proper (1:8) and a prayer report

---

1. Πρῶτον marks the first item in a sequence.
2. Μέν is emphatic.
3. Περί + genitive denotes reference.
4. Schreiner suggests that ἐν τῷ πνεύματί μου denotes "wholehearted service with all [Paul's] being" (*Romans*, 51).
5. Τοῦ υἱοῦ αὐτοῦ is an objective genitive.
6. Ὡς functions as a discourse marker equivalent to ὅτι ("that").
7. Ποιοῦμαι is a customary present and an indirect middle.
8. Ὑμῶν is an objective genitive.
9. Ἐπί + genitive is temporal, denoting a period of time.
10. Δεόμενος is an adverbial participle of time; the present tense is iterative.
11. The definite article functions as a possessive pronoun.

(1:9–12). The prayer report consists of an expression of prayer (1:9), the content of Paul's prayer for the Romans (1:10), and the reason for his prayer (1:11–12).

Basic Message and Exegetical Outline

Paul expresses pastoral concern for his Roman readers by thanking God for them, praying for them, and expressing his longing to see them.

Paul's Concern for the Romans (1:8–12)
1. Paul thanks God for the Romans (1:8)
2. Paul prays for the Romans (1:9–10)
   a. As God bears witness (1:9)
   b. To be granted a good journey to visit them (1:10)
3. Paul longs to see the Romans (1:11–12)
   a. In order to share a spiritual benefit (1:11)
   b. In order to be mutually encouraged (1:12)

Explanation of the Text

1. Paul thanks God for the Romans (1:8).

A first-century letter commonly included a "proem" as part of its opening.[12] Such an introductory section might consist of a prayer wish, a thanksgiving, a remembrance before the gods, or a joy expression. Paul most frequently incorporates a thanksgiving, as is true in the case of Romans.[13] Paul also writes "I am giving thanks to my God" (εὐχαριστῶ τῷ θεῷ μου) in 1 Corinthians 1:4 and Philippians 1:3. The present tense highlights the fact that Paul prays regularly for the Romans;[14] "my God" points to devotion and service rather than to possession or ownership. Jesus Christ is the agent through whom Paul gives thanks (διά Ἰησοῦ Χριστοῦ). He more commonly follows the expression of thanks with an adverbial phrase of time (e.g., Col. 1:3; 1 Thess. 1:2), but here, the reference to Christ reinforces the apostolic authority with which he intercedes for the Romans. The phrase "concerning all of you" (περὶ πάντων ὑμῶν) makes it clear that Paul's thanksgiving includes all the believers in Rome. Their faith (ἡ πίστις ὑμῶν) is the reason for his thanksgiving, because others

---

12. The term is Klauck's (*Ancient Letters*, 13).
13. The other thanksgiving sections in Paul's letters are 1 Corinthians 1:4–9; Ephesians 1:15–23; Philippians 1:3–11; Colossians 1:3–23; 1 Thessalonians 1:2–10; 2 Thessalonians 1:3–12; 2 Timothy 1:3–5; Philemon 4–7.
14. A customary present.

repeatedly proclaim (καταγγέλλεται)[15] both their initial response of faith and their faithful lifestyle (cf. 1:5) in the whole world (ἐν ὅλῳ τῷ κόσμῳ). The latter phrase most likely refers to the churches Paul has planted, specifically churches in the area from Jerusalem to Illyricum (cf. 15:19). It also reinforces the scope of Paul's apostolic ministry.

2. Paul prays for the Romans (1:9–10).

Not only does Paul give thanks for the Romans, he also prays for them. A witness formula (μάρτυς μού ἐστιν ὁ θεός) attests to the truthfulness of what he is about to write—in fact, God testifies on Paul's behalf (cf. 1 Thess. 2:5, 10). The thought of God's unreserved support for him and his ministry leads Paul to insert a parenthetical statement about his own wholehearted devotion to God. "Worship" (λατρεύω) includes the act of carrying out religious service, in this case service to the one true God.[16] The manner by which Paul carries out this service is "with my spirit" (ἐν τῷ πνεύματι), a phrase that is best understood as referring to Paul's own spirit and pointing to the entirety of his being. The sphere in which Paul carries out his service is the gospel about God's son (ἐν τῷ εὐαγγελίῳ τοῦ υἱοῦ αὐτοῦ). This phrase includes the second reference to the gospel (cf. 1:1) and the third reference to Jesus as son (cf. 1:3, 4); both ideas are central to Paul's overall purpose in writing.

The activity to which God bears witness is Paul's ceaseless mention of the Romans (ἀδιαλείπτως μνείαν ὑμῶν ποιοῦμαι) every time he prays (πάντοτε ἐπὶ τῶν προσευχῶν μου). The present tense and middle voice of the verb (ποιοῦμαι) emphasize both his regular practice and his special interest in praying for them. Paul regularly specifies the content of what he "mentions" in prayer (cf. Eph. 1:16–17; Phil. 1:3–5; 1 Thess. 1:2–3; 2 Tim. 1:3–5; Philem. 4–6). In this instance, his request is that he might soon visit the Romans. His act of regular pleading (δεόμενος) involves "asking with a sense of urgency based on perceived need."[17] He asks hopefully (εἴ πως) because the timing now seems to be right (ἤδη ποτέ), a state of affairs he explains later in the letter (15:22–24). He makes it clear, however, that it is only by God's will (ἐν τῷ θελήματι τοῦ θεοῦ) that he will be granted a good journey (εὐοδωθήσομαι)[18] to Rome.

---

15. An iterative present.
16. The definite article in μού ὁ θεός is monadic.
17. LN 33.170.
18. Εὐοδόω can carry the figurative nuance of "to have things go well" (figurative), but it is better understood literally as "to grant a good journey" (cf. Tobit 5:16). The verb form is a future passive.

3. Paul longs to see the Romans (1:11–12).

The reason for Paul's prayer (γάρ) is his longing (ἐπιποθῶ) to meet his Roman readers (ἰδεῖν ὑμᾶς). The verb describes a strong desire with the implication of need.[19] Paul uses it elsewhere to describe his "ardent desire" to be present with his readers (cf. Rom. 15:23).[20] The purpose of Paul's visit is to share "a certain spiritual gift" (τι χάρισμα πνευματικόν) with them. The phrase does not refer to a specific gift from the list in 12:3–8 but, rather, to a more general spiritual benefit. Paul's indefinite language suggests either that he is hesitant to spell out explicitly what he wants to say at this point in the letter,[21] or more likely, that he expects to learn the specific need(s) the Romans have when he visits them.[22] The spiritual blessing Paul envisions sharing will produce a double benefit. First, the Romans will be strengthened (εἰς τὸ στηριχθῆναι ὑμᾶς); second, both he and they will be encouraged (συμπαρακληθῆναι). God is the ultimate agent in both actions,[23] but the means by which those actions will be accomplished is the mutual faith Paul and the Romans share (διὰ τῆς ἐν ἀλλήλοις πίστεως). The desired outcome can be achieved only if Paul is present among them (ἐν ὑμῖν) so that both they and he (ὑμῶν τε καὶ ἐμοῦ) are able to contribute to the interaction.

Theology and Appropriation

Paul commonly uses the thanksgiving section to reinforce main themes of the letter in which it occurs. His references to faith (1:8, 12), the gospel (1:9), and Jesus's sonship (1:9) all serve to accomplish that purpose in the thanksgiving of Romans. At the same time, this particular thanksgiving highlights both Paul's pastoral orientation and his pastoral concern for his readers. He is wholeheartedly devoted to carrying out the ministry God has given him (1:9a), and he is totally dependent on God for the outcome (1:10b). He thanks God for the Romans and their faith (1:8), and he prays regularly and earnestly for them (1:9b–10a). He longs to be with them because he is seriously committed to their spiritual growth (1:11–12).

---

19. BDAG 377c.
20. Jewett (*Romans*, 123) notes that Paul uses the term to describe both his own bonding with members of churches he had planted (e.g., Phil. 1:8; 2:26; 1 Thess. 3:6) and the solidarity he expects among believers who were not personally acquainted (2 Cor. 9:14).
21. Longenecker, *Romans*, 118.
22. Cranfield, *Romans*, 79.
23. Both infinitives are divine passives.

Paul's thanksgiving also teaches important truths about the fellowship of the church universal. Paul had neither planted the church in Rome, nor had he visited any of the congregations there. Yet he emphasizes his solidarity with them in three ways. First, the churches in every locale are founded on faith. The Romans' faith is the reason for Paul's thanksgiving (1:8), and the faith they share with him is an important means of spiritual encouragement (1:12). Second, the health of those churches is promoted by prayer. Paul prayed for the Romans consistently (1:9) and specifically (1:10). Third, those churches are strengthened through sharing in spiritual benefits. Paul's stated purposes in visiting Rome were to strengthen the believers there (1:11) and to be encouraged by them (1:12).

Paul's primary purpose in these verses is to communicate his spiritual concern and care for the believers in Rome. Although he has never met them, he knows about them, thanks God for them, prays for them, and longs to help them grow spiritually. As members of Christ's body and as members of the human race, we share with the Romans the need to be assured that someone knows us and cares about us. That knowledge gives us confidence and hope as we seek to live out the obedience of faith to which we have been called as followers of Christ.

Possible points of connection include the ideas of thanksgiving and longing to see others. Thanksgiving is a response to events and circumstances men and women experience at times other than a single Thursday in November. We have probably all experienced a longing to see a family member or a close friend from whom we have been separated for an extended time. This passage corrects the ideas that churches and individual believers exist and function in insolation from one another. Paul reminds us that there is an inherent bond among followers of Christ and that we should be intentional in seeking to strengthen that bond. The passage commends a willingness to be involved in the spiritual lives of other believers, whether in the local congregation of which we are members or in congregations around the world. The objective in communicating the message of this passage should be to help others understand the spiritual bond that exists among believers and congregations so that they will take practical steps to care for others and promote the fellowship of the church universal.

ROMANS 1:13–15

Text and Translation

13 Now I do not want[1] you to continue being ignorant,[2] brothers, that I myself frequently intended[3] to come to you—but[4] I was prevented until now—in order that I might have some fruit among you also,[5] just as even[6] among the rest of the Gentiles. **14** Both to Greek and to Barbarian, both to wise and to foolish, I am under obligation, **15** so,[7] my eagerness *is* to proclaim the gospel[8] also[9] to you *who are* in Rome.

Context and Structure

    I. Letter Opening (1:1–17)
        A. Salutation (1:1–7)
        B. Thanksgiving (1:8–12)
        C. **Occasion for Writing (1:13–15)**
        D. Thesis (1:16–17)

The disclosure formula in verse 13 ("I do not want you to continue being ignorant . . .") marks the beginning of the body-opening. The paragraph provides Paul's occasion for writing and consists of his plan to visit (1:13) and how the anticipated visit relates to his apostolic calling (1:14–15).

Basic Message and Exegetical Outline

Although Paul's intended visit to Rome has been circumstantially hindered, the nature of his apostolic calling makes him eager to preach the gospel there also.

---

1. Οὐ θέλω has far stronger manuscript support (ℵ, A, B, C, Dᶜ) than οὐκ οἴομαι (D*).
2. Ἀγνοεῖν is a progressive present.
3. Προεθέμην is an indirect middle.
4. Καί is adversative.
5. Καί is adjunctive.
6. Καί is ascensive.
7. Οὕτως is inferential (BDAG 742a).
8. Εὐαγγελίσασθαι is an epexegetical infinitive that explains Paul's eagerness.
9. Καί is adjunctive.

Paul's Planned Visit to Rome (1:13–15)
1. Paul's intention to visit (1:13)
   a. Often planned (1:13b)
   b. Circumstantially hindered (1:13c)
   c. With an eye to fruit (1:13d)
2. Paul's reason to visit (1:14–15)
   a. Obligated to all humankind (1:14)
   b. Eager to preach the gospel (1:15)

Explanation of the Text

1. Paul's intention to visit Rome (1:13).

"I do not want you to continue being ignorant" (οὐ θέλω ὑμᾶς ἀγνοεῖν) is a disclosure formula similar to those Paul uses elsewhere to introduce important information (e.g., 11:25; 1 Cor. 10:1; 12:1; 1 Thess. 4:13). Paul uses the direct address "brothers" (ἀδελφοί) at key turning points in Romans to emphasize the spiritual relationship he and his readers share (7:1; 8:12; 10:1; 11:25; 15:14; 16:17). He wants them to know that he has intended to visit Rome repeatedly in the past (πολλάκις), but he has been prevented until the time of writing (ἄχρι τοῦ δεῦρο). The verb "intended" (προεθέμην) stresses a clear sense of purpose on Paul's part, and the middle voice highlights his personal commitment to the plan. The aorist tense of the verb "hindered" (ἐκωλύθην) suggests that the hindrances Paul has encountered have ended.[10] Paul does not state the precise nature of those obstacles, but his comments later in the letter suggest that they related to his work in the eastern Mediterranean (15:22–24). His purpose in visiting Rome has always been to have some fruit (τινὰ καρπὸν σχῶ) among them as he has had among other Gentiles (καθώς καὶ ἐν τοῖς λοιποῖς ἔθνεσιν). In this context, the best understanding of "fruit" (καρπόν) is the result of ministry activity (cf. 15:28; Phil. 1:22; 4:17; Col. 1:6).[11] Paul's reference to "the rest of the Gentiles" (τοῖς λοιποῖς ἔθνεσιν) implies that he views the Romans as included within the scope of his apostolic ministry.

---

10. A consummative aorist.
11. Of the eighteen times Paul speaks of "fruit" in his letters, one refers to effectiveness (1 Cor. 14:14), two are literal (1 Cor. 9:17; 2 Tim. 2:6), ten refer to either positive or negative conduct (Rom. 6:21, 22; 7:4, 5; Gal. 5:22; Eph. 5:9, 11; Phil. 1:11; Col. 1:10; Titus 3:14), and five refer to the results of ministry.

2. Paul's reason to visit (1:14–15).

By omitting a connecting conjunction (asyndeton) and placing two sets of dative nouns at the beginning of the sentence, Paul emphasizes the all-inclusive scope of his ministry. From the perspective of culture, his ministry encompasses both Greeks and Barbarians. "To Greeks" ("Ἑλλήσιν) describes those who have come under the influence of Greco-Roman culture, while "to Barbarians" (βαρβάροις) describes those people groups who could not speak Greek or Latin and were, therefore, considered lacking in culture.[12] From the perspective of education, his ministry encompasses both the well educated and the poorly-educated. "To wise" (σοφοῖς) describes those who are intelligent and well educated, while "to foolish" (ἀνοήτοις) describes those who are unintelligent and dull-witted. The former were able to make a constructive contribution to society, while the latter were not. Paul saw himself as under spiritual obligation (ὀφειλέτης εἰμί) to all four groups—indeed, to all humankind.[13] It is this sense of spiritual indebtedness that fuels Paul's eagerness (τὸ κατ' ἐμὲ πρόθυμον) to visit Rome: he wants to preach the gospel to his Roman readers as well (καὶ ὑμῖν τοῖς ἐν Ῥώμῃ). To do so is his apostolic calling. Although "to preach the gospel" (εὐαγγελίσασθαι) can refer to the initial act of winning converts, in this context it refers to the act of challenging believers to live in a manner worthy of the gospel (cf. Phil. 1:27). The latter sense aligns well with Paul's previously-mentioned purpose for visiting Rome (1:11–12).

Theology and Appropriation

Paul was no stranger to changes in plans. The record of his ministry in Acts includes the redirection of his entire life on the road to Damascus (9:1–25), the change in his role from church-based teacher to itinerant church planter (13:1–4), the change in the makeup of his missionary team before his second round of travels (15:36–41), and the change in plans that led him to take the gospel into Europe (16:6–13). He also knew from his experience with the Corinthian church that changed plans could create misunderstanding and mistrust (2 Cor. 1:15–2:13). It was, perhaps, the latter experience that led Paul to explain to the Romans that his delay in visiting did not reflect either a change in his intention or a diminished desire to do so (1:10–15; 15:22–29). He also made it clear that the details and timing of his visit

---

12. Since some people groups in Spain would fall into the latter category, there might also be a geographical component pointing to both the eastern (Greeks) and the western (Barbarians) Mediterranean.
13. See 15:22–29 for another discussion of "indebtedness."

were entirely dependent on God's will (1:10; 15:32). His plans, and any changes to those plans, were in God's hands.

The New Testament speaks of "knowing" God's will only three times (Eph. 5:17; Col. 1:9; 4:12). In contrast, the idea of "doing" God's will occurs eleven times, most frequently in contexts related to obedience (e.g., Matt. 7:21; Eph. 6:6; 1 John 2:17). Verses that speak of the content of God's will highlight two main factors: salvation (John 6:39–40) and sanctification (1 Thess. 4:3). The Holy Spirit provides the wisdom and understanding we need for knowing God's will (Col. 1:9), and the purpose of knowing God's will is to walk in a manner that is pleasing to him (Col. 1:10). God makes his will known through Scripture and his works of providence. His providence is his sovereign supervision of his creatures and their actions that includes his sustaining care (Ps. 36:5–6) and his certain control (Isa. 46:10–11). He accomplishes his supervision through extraordinary and ordinary means. The most common extraordinary means are miracles (e.g., Josh. 10:12–14), although God works more frequently through ordinary means. Ordinary means include the laws and processes of nature (Ps. 148:8), the acts of free moral agents (Acts 3:13–16), human reason (Acts 6:2), inner checks and restraints (Acts 16:6–8), and outward circumstances (1 Cor. 16:9).

Paul's primary purpose for including 1:13–15 was to clarify how his often-delayed visit would help fulfill his apostolic calling. The Romans needed to understand that Paul was eager to visit Rome because he considered them to be within the scope of his apostolic ministry even though he had not planted any of the congregations there. They also needed to understand that previous delays had not diminished Paul's desire to spend time with them or had somehow signaled God's disapproval of his ministry. With the Romans we share the need to understand how hindrances and delays fit into God's sovereignty over ministry plans. Possible points of connection include the ideas of changed plans and obligation/indebtedness, since everyone has most likely experienced both. The passage corrects the idea that delay necessarily signifies rejection or negation. The fact that Paul's visit was delayed did not mean that he was not supposed to visit Rome. The passage also reminds us that our timing does not necessarily align with God's timing. It commends an attitude of eagerness and submission in seeking to fulfill the calling God has placed on our lives. The objective in communicating this passage should be to help others know how a clear sense of calling should inform their attitude toward the circumstances of ministry so that they will diligently pursue their calling despite obstacles, hindrances, and delays that might come their way.

ROMANS 1:16–17

Text and Translation

16 For I am not ashamed of the gospel, for it is the power from God[1] that results in[2] salvation to everyone who is believing,[3] both to Jew first and to Greek. **17** For by it[4] God's righteousness is being revealed[5] from beginning to end,[6] just as it has been written, "Now the righteous one because of faith[7] will live."[8]

Context and Structure

   I. Letter Opening (1:1–17)
      A. Salutation (1:1–7)
      B. Thanksgiving (1:8–12)
      C. Occasion for Writing (1:13–15)
      D. **Thesis (1:16–17)**

Paul continues the body-opening with a thesis statement that sets out the basic claim for the argument that follows and introduces four key themes that run throughout the letter: God's power that results in salvation (1:16b; cf. 5:1–8:39), God's plan that includes both Jew and Greek (1:16c; cf. 9:1–11:36), God's righteousness that is entirely by faith (1:17a; cf. 1:18–4:25), and God's people who live by faith (1:17b; cf. 12:1–15:13).

---

1. Θεοῦ is a genitive of source.
2. Εἰς + accusative denotes result.
3. Τῷ πιστεύοντι is a substantival participle; the progressive present highlights continuing belief (cf. Wallace, *Grammar*, 621n22).
4. Ἐν + dative denotes instrument.
5. Ἀποκαλύπτεται is a divine passive; the present tense is progressive.
6. GNB; literally "out of faith into faith."
7. The placement of the prepositional phrase allows it to modify both the substantival participle and the finite verb (cf. Dunn, *Romans*, 45).
8. Paul's omission of the pronouns present in the MT ("his [i.e., the righteous one's] faith") and the LXX ("my [i.e., God's] faith") places the emphasis on the centrality of faith alone and removes any ambiguity as to whether ἐκ πίστεως should be translated "because of faith" or "because of faithfulness." (See Jewett, *Romans*, 145.)

Basic Message and Exegetical Outline

Paul is eager to preach the gospel because it demonstrates God's power and reveals God's righteousness.

Paul's Confidence in the Gospel (1:16–17)
1. The gospel demonstrates God's power (1:16)
   a. Resulting in salvation (1:16b)
   b. To everyone who believes (1:16c)
2. The gospel reveals God's righteousness (1:17)
   a. Entirely by faith (1:17b)
   b. As affirmed by God's Word (1:17c)

Explanation of the Text

1. The gospel demonstrates God's power (1:16).

The prospect of preaching the gospel in Rome makes Paul eager to visit (1:13–15), although the explanation (γάρ) for his eagerness begins with a negative statement. "I am not ashamed of the gospel" (οὐ ἐπαισχύνομαι τὸ εὐαγγέλιον) is best understood as an oratorical means of introducing material the hearers might consider sensitive or problematic.[9] The two most plausible reasons the Romans might have had reservations about the gospel are that they viewed one or more aspects of Paul's preaching as shameful,[10] or that the very nature of the gospel carries with it a temptation to be ashamed.[11] The latter understanding seems more likely in light of other passages where Paul connects the potential for shame with suffering and imprisonment (e.g., Rom. 5:5; Phil. 1:20; 2 Tim. 1:8, 12, 16). Regardless, the notion that the gospel should not be a reason for shame is rooted both in Jesus's teaching (Mark 8:38) and in the Old Testament (Isa. 28:16; cf. Rom. 9:3; 10:11).

The reason (γάρ) for Paul's positive view of the gospel is simple but profound. The gospel demonstrates power that has its source in God (δύναμις θεοῦ) and results in salvation (εἰς σωτηρίαν). The idea of God's power occurs frequently in Paul's letters (e.g., Rom. 1:20; 1 Cor. 1:18; 2 Cor. 6:7; 2 Tim. 1:8), often referring to the power God demonstrated

---

9. See Jewett's discussion, which provides both other suggested explanations and extrabiblical background for this understanding (*Romans*, 136–37).
10. Longenecker defends this approach and offers several possible reasons the Romans might have viewed Paul's preaching as questionable (*Romans*, 161–63).
11. Murray is representative of this approach (*Romans*, 26).

in raising Christ (Rom. 1:4; 1 Cor. 6:14; 15:43; 2 Cor. 13:4; Phil. 3:10).[12] Paul always speaks of salvation as spiritual deliverance (e.g., Rom. 10:1, 10; 11:11), especially from final destruction (e.g., Rom. 5:9; 13:11). This power that results in salvation is available to everyone who responds to the gospel in faith. The participial phrase "to everyone who is believing" (παντὶ τῷ πιστεύοντι) highlights both the universal scope of Paul's gospel and the expectation of a life of continuing faith. "Both to Jew first and to Greek" ('Ιουδαίῳ τε πρῶτον καὶ "Ελληνι) reflects Paul's missionary practice of preaching to Jews first (e.g., Acts 13:44–48; 18:5–11), while underscoring the equality that exists between Jew and Greek (cf. 2:9–10; 10:12).

2. The gospel reveals God's righteousness (1:17).

The explanation (γάρ) for why the gospel is God's saving power resides in its revelatory role: it is the instrument by which (ἐν αὐτῷ) God reveals his righteousness. The verb Paul uses (ἀποκαλύπτεται) describes the activity of causing something to be fully known[13] and points to the unfolding of God's redemptive plan in human history.[14] The present tense highlights the continuing nature of the revelation; by using a divine passive, Paul keeps the focus on God's righteousness. The phrase "God's righteousness" (δικαιοσύνη θεοῦ) has been understood in multiple ways.[15] Is it the righteous character God possesses (possessive genitive), the righteous acts God performs (subjective genitive), or the righteous status God bestows (genitive of source)? Although Schreiner correctly notes that Paul's "righteousness" language (δικαιόω, δικαιοσύνη, δίκαιος) has different nuances at different points in the letter, he also suggests that it is a mistake to adopt an either-or approach in this verse.[16] For that reason, Stott's summary statement combining all three aspects is helpful: God's righteousness is his righteous act of bestowing on us righteous status that is his, not ours.[17]

According to Cranfield, the enigmatic combination "from faith to faith" (NASB, NET; literally "out of faith into faith") has been

---

12. Cranfield highlights three aspects of God's power: it is effective and active, it delivers us from wrath, and it reinstates us in glory (*Romans*, 89).
13. BDAG 112a.
14. See Moo, *Romans*, 69.
15. See the excurses in Moo (*Romans*, 79–90) and Longenecker (*Romans*, 168–76).
16. Schreiner, *Romans*, 66–67.
17. Cf. Stott, *Romans*, 64.

interpreted in at least twelve ways.[18] Silva's observation is helpful: the interpretation adding the least meaning to an ambiguous construction should be preferred.[19] If the two prepositional phrases denote source (ἐκ πίστεως) and destination (εἰς πίστιν), respectively, the combination means something like "from beginning to end" (GNB) or "from first to last" (NIV). That is, both an initial response of faith and a continuing life of faith are central to the gospel Paul preaches. Paul uses "faith" language (πιστεύω, πίστις) sixty-one times in Romans to speak of human faith (cf. 1:16), including both acceptance of truth (e.g., 4:3; 6:8; 10:9) and reliance upon truth (4:5; 9:33; 10:11). He supports his emphasis on faith by quoting Habakkuk 2:4 (cf. Gal. 3:11; Heb. 10:38). "Just as it has been written" (καθὼς γέγραπται) is Paul's favorite way of introducing Old Testament quotations (e.g., 2:24; 3:4, 10; 4:17).[20] "The righteous one" (ὁ δίκαιος) denotes status; "because of faith" (ἐκ πίστεως) denotes cause; "will live" (ζήσεται) denotes transcendent life that is both "now" and "not yet." First-century Jewish interpretive practices included the possibility that the prepositional phrase could modify both the subject ("the one who is righteous because of faith") and the verb ("will live because of faith"), which would again highlight the centrality of faith in both responding to and living out the gospel.

Theology and Appropriation

It is appropriate that Paul's thesis statement not only focuses on the primary theme of the letter (εὐαγγέλιον) but also includes significant ideas that run throughout it. The most prominent ideas are faith/believe (πίστις, πιστεύω), which occurs four times in these two verses and fifty-seven times elsewhere in the letter, and righteousness/justify (δικαιοσύνη, δίκαιος, δικαιόω), which occurs twice in these two verses and fifty-four times elsewhere in the letter. In addition to those ideas, salvation/save (σωτηρία, σῴζω) occurs twelve other times in the letter,[21] and power (δύναμις) occurs seven other times in the letter.[22] The revelatory aspect of the gospel (1:16) is another notable idea that Paul expresses with three different verbs: "reveal" (ἀποκαλύπτω in 1:18; 8:18),

---

18. Cranfield, *Romans*, 99–100.
19. M. Silva, *Biblical Words and Their Meaning: An Introduction to Lexical Semantics* (Grand Rapids: Eerdmans, 1983), 72.
20. The intensive perfect emphasizes the present results of God's past action. For that reason, English translations tend to translate the verb as "it is written."
21. Cf. 1:16; 5:9, 10; 8:24; 9:27; 10:1, 9, 10, 13; 11:11, 14, 24; 13:11.
22. Cf. 1:4, 16, 20; 8:38; 9:17; 15:13; 15:19 (2 x).

"make manifest" (φανερόω in 1:19; 3:21; 16:26), and "make known" (γνωρίζω in 9:22, 23; 16:26). Finally, the quotation of Habakkuk 2:4 is the first of sixty-four direct quotations in the letter, testifying to the continuity between Paul's gospel and Old Testament teaching.[23]

Paul's primary purpose in writing this brief paragraph is to explain his own personal commitment to and confidence in the gospel he preaches. His commitment and confidence rest on the settled conviction that the gospel demonstrates God's power, reveals God's righteousness, and aligns with Old Testament teaching. Neither his preaching of it nor any afflictions that might come his way because of it are a cause for shame. He is, instead, eager to share it with his Roman readers. With the Romans, we share the need to understanding that the gospel is, indeed, good news—from first to last. Possible points of connection include faith and shame; both are ideas to which believers and non-believers can relate. Paul's opening statement, in particular, corrects the idea that identifying with the gospel is something of which followers of Christ should be ashamed. As he notes in 1 Corinthians, the preaching of the cross (i.e., the gospel) stands totally at odds with qualities the world would consider worthy of honor and boasting: wisdom, cleverness, education, oratorical skill, miraculous signs, strength, and nobility. Although individuals without a relationship with Christ might view the gospel as a reason for shame, Paul views it as an opportunity to boast—not before God, but about God (1:18–31). The passage commends a faith response to the gospel on the basis of the power, salvation, righteousness, and life it offers. The objective in communicating this passage should be to help others know that the gospel is the source of divine salvation and life so that they will respond in faith, whether to an initial call to salvation or to a continuing call to obedient living.

---

23. See the discussion "Paul's Use of the Old Testament" in the Introduction.

ROMANS 1:18–4:25

The Gospel as the Revelation of God's Righteousness

The body of Romans consists of four major parts, each of which unpacks one of the four topics Paul includes in his thematic statement of 1:16–17. The central topic of Romans 1:18–4:25 is **the revelation of God's righteousness** in the gospel. Paul's argument makes it clear that God reveals his righteousness through wrath (1:18–3:20), apart from law (3:21–31), and in response to faith (4:1–25).

II. Letter Body (1:18–15:13)
- A. The Gospel as the Revelation of God's Righteousness (1:18–4:25)
  - 1. The gospel reveals God's righteousness through wrath (1:18–3:20)
    - a. Because humankind suppresses God's truth (1:18–23)
    - b. Because the Gentiles practice unrighteousness (1:24–32)
    - c. Because the moral person judges others (2:1–16)
    - d. Because the Jews transgress the law (2:17–29)
    - e. Because God always acts righteously (3:1–8)
    - f. Because all are under sin (3:9–20)
  - 2. The gospel reveals God's righteousness apart from law (3:21–31)
    - a. Through faith in Christ (3:21–26)
    - b. Apart from works of law (3:27–31)
  - 3. The gospel reveals God's righteousness in response to faith (4:1–25)
    - a. Apart from works or circumcision (4:1–12)
    - b. Apart from law (4:13–25)

ROMANS 1:18–23

Text and Translation

18 For God's wrath is being revealed[1] from heaven against all ungodliness and unrighteousness[2] committed by humans[3] *who are* suppressing[4] the truth by unrighteousness;[5] **19** for that which can be known with reference to God[6] is readily evident among them;[7] for God makes it evident to them. **20** For his unseen *attributes*—both his eternal power and divine nature[8]—are being clearly seen since the creation[9] of the world and are being understood[10] by means of the things that are being made[11] so that they are[12] without excuse; **21** for although they knew[13] God they did not glorify God or give thanks, but they were made futile[14] in their reasonings[15] and their senseless heart was made dark. **22** By stating with confidence[16] that they are wise, they were made foolish **23** and exchanged the glory of the incorruptible God for a copy of the image of corruptible humans and birds and four-footed animals and crawling animals.

---

1. Ἀποκαλύπτεται is a divine passive; the progressive present tense emphasizes continuing action.
2. Ἐπί + genitive designates the objects against which God's wrath is directed.
3. Ἀνθρώπων is a subjective genitive.
4. Τῶν . . . κατεχόντων is an adjectival participle modifying ἀνθρώπων.
5. Ἐν ἀδικια denotes means.
6. The genitive of τοῦ θεοῦ denotes reference.
7. Ἐν + dative is spatial.
8. The third line of the verse (ἥ τε ἀΐδιος αὐτοῦ δύναμις καὶ θειότης) stands in apposition to τὰ ἀόρατα and has been brought forward accordingly.
9. Ἀπό + genitive is temporal.
10. Νοούμενα is an adverbial participle of attendant circumstance.
11. Τοῖς ποιήμασιν is an instrumental dative.
12. Εἰς τὸ . . . εἶναι is adverbial of result.
13. Γνόντες is an adverbial participle of concession.
14. Both ἐματαιώθησαν and ἐσκοτίσθη are resultative aorists and divine passives. So also ἐμωράνθησαν in verse 22.
15. Ἐν τοῖς διαλογισμοῖς αὐτῶν is locative.
16. Φάσκοντες is an adverbial participle of means.

Context and Structure

II. Letter Body (1:18–15:13)
    A. The Gospel as the Revelation of God's Righteousness (1:18–4:25)
        1. The gospel reveals God's righteousness through wrath (1:18–3:20)
            a. **Because humankind suppresses God's truth (1:18–23)**
            b. Because the Gentiles practice unrighteousness (1:24–32)
            c. Because the moral person judges others (2:1–16)
            d. Because the Jews transgress the law (2:17–29)
            e. Because God always acts righteously (3:1–8)
            f. Because all are under sin (3:9–20)

Paul begins his argument in the letter body with a paragraph of three sentences. The first provides an explanation of why the righteous person must live by faith: humankind suppresses God's truth (1:18–19). The second explains how humankind suppresses that truth: they ignore God's self-revelation in creation (1:20–21). The third highlights the foolishness that results from humankind's self-proclaimed wisdom (1:22–23).

Basic Message and Exegetical Outline

God reveals his wrath against humankind because they suppress his truth, ignore his witness in creation, and discard his glory.

God Reveals His Wrath Against Humankind (1:18–23)
    1. Because humankind suppresses God's truth (1:18–19)
        a. Despite knowing about God (1:19a)
        b. Despite God making truth manifest (1:19b)
    2. Because humankind ignores God's power and nature (1:20–21)
        a. Although seeing it clearly in creation (1:20)
        b. Resulting in foolish thinking and darkened hearts (1:21)
    3. Because humankind discards God's glory (1:22–23)
        a. Although claiming to be wise (1:22)
        b. Exchanging incorruptible reality for copies of the corruptible (1:23)

Explanation of the Text

1. Because humankind suppresses God's truth (1:18–19).

Paul begins to explain (γάρ) why the righteous person must live by faith by echoing verse 17. "God's wrath" (ὀργή θεοῦ) is parallel to "God's righteousness," and describes both the action he takes (subjective genitive) and the judgment he bestows (genitive of source).[17] Similarly, "is being revealed" (ἀποκαλύπτεται) describes continuing action and, as a divine passive, keeps the focus on the subject. God's wrath is revealed from heaven (ἀπ' οὐρανοῦ)[18] and is directed against ungodliness and unrighteousness. "Ungodliness" (ἀσέβειαν) describes a lack of reverence for God and his majesty, while "unrighteousness" (ἀδικίαν) describes a lack of respect for his righteous order; the combination "all human irreligion and injustice" captures the idea well. Their unrighteous conduct (ἐν ἀδικίᾳ) is the means by which men and women consistently suppress (τῶν κατεχόντων) the ultimate truth about God (τὴν ἀλήθειαν).

The reason (διότι) Paul can claim humankind suppresses truth is that God has made truth so obvious they cannot miss it. Although finite human beings cannot know God directly, truth about him can be known (τὸ γνωστὸν τοῦ θεοῦ). That knowledge is readily evident (φανερόν) "in their midst and all around them"[19] (ἐν αυτοῖς), and it is readily evident because (γάρ) God makes it evident (ἐφανέρωσεν) to them (αὐτοῖς). Their willful suppression of what they know about God earns them his wrath rather than his righteousness.

2. Because humankind ignores God's power and nature (1:20–21).

Paul continues by explaining (γάρ) how humankind suppresses what they know about God. In particular, since the creation of the world (ἀπὸ κτίσεως κόσμου), every person who has ever lived knows that God is eternal (ἀΐδιος) and possesses both power (δύναμις) and a

---

17. "Wrath" (ἡ ὀργή, -ῆς) occurs eleven other times in Romans (2:5 [2 x], 8; 3:5; 4:15; 5:9; 9:22 [2 x]; 12:19; 13:4, 5) and describes God's indignation over injustice, cruelty, and corruption (cf. BDAG 720d).
18. "Heaven" (ὁ οὐρανός, -οῦ) occurs in the New Testament with three nuances: (1) the atmosphere that surrounds all created life (e.g., Matt. 6:26), (2) the stellar spaces occupied by the sun, moon, and stars (e.g., Matt. 24:29), and (3) the transcendent dwelling place that is the location of God's throne (e.g., Matt. 6:9). The third nuance applies in this verse and highlights the divine nature and source of the wrath.
19. Cranfield, *Romans*, 114.

nature that is intrinsic to deity (θειότης). Paul uses a play on words to declare that, although they are not subject to being seen directly (τὰ ἀόρατα), those attributes are clearly seen (καθορᾶται). More precisely, they are understood (νοούμενα) by means of the things God makes (τοῖς ποιήμασιν). As a result (εἰς τὸ εἶναι) no one can say he or she is without excuse (ἀναπολόγητους) because he or she lacks knowledge about God.

The problem is not a lack of knowledge—they know that the one true God exists (γνόντες τὸν θεόν).[20] Instead, the problem is the way in which humankind responds to the knowledge they possess. The proper response to God's eternal power and deity is to offer him glory and thanksgiving in a manner that correctly recognizes who he is (ὡς θεόν). Humankind does neither and, so, fails to enhance God's reputation (ἐδόξασαν) and fails to express appreciation for the blessings he gives them (ηὐχαρίστησαν). In strong contrast (οὐχ . . . ἀλλ') to the positive results a proper response to God would bring, ignoring his glory and blessing results in a radical distortion of human sensibilities: their reasoning processes (ἐν τοῖς διαλογισμοῖς αὐτῶν) are made futile (ἐματαιώθησαν), and their senseless hearts (ἡ ἀσύνετος αὐτῶν καρδία) are made dark (ἐσκοτίσθη).

3. Because humankind discards God's glory (1:22–23).

The absence of a connecting conjunction (asyndeton) sets off the third sentence of the paragraph and focuses attention on the failure to glorify God that Paul mentioned in verse 21. By claiming to be wise (φάσκοντες εἶναι σοφοί), humankind is made foolish (ἐμωράνθησαν). Paul notes that they not only make their claim, they assert it with confidence.[21] In so doing, they exchange (ἤλλαξαν)[22] the glory the incorruptible God possesses (τὴν δόξαν τοῦ ἀφθάρτου θεοῦ) for something far less glorious. The object for which they exchange God's glory is a copy (ὁμοιώματι) of an image (εἰκόνος) of things that are corruptible (φθαρτοῦ) and, therefore, possess no glory at all. Whereas God is impervious to death and decay, human beings (ἀνθρώπου), birds (πετεινῶν), four-footed animals (τετραπόδων), and reptiles (ἑρπετῶν) all experience decay and death. The four groups Paul includes encompass all created things (cf. Gen. 1:20–27) and anticipate the more specifically formulated charge in verse 25 that humankind "worshipped and served the creation rather than the one who created."

---

20. The article with θεόν is monadic, designating one of a kind.
21. BDAG 1050c.
22. See also the strengthened cognate verbs (μετήλλαξαν) in verses 25 and 26.

Theology and Appropriation

Paul's discussion of God's revealing his righteousness through wrath introduces the doctrine of general revelation and raises a missiological question related to that doctrine. Theologians generally view creation and conscience as two major sources of general revelation. While Paul touches on conscience in Romans 2:14–16, he incorporates creation into his argument in 1:19–20. From those verses, it is possible to draw four truths about God's self-revelation through creation. First, it is clear ("is readily evident . . . God makes it evident"). Second, it is constant ("since the creation of the world"). Third, it provides specific content ("his eternal power and divine nature"). Fourth, it has specific consequences ("so that they are without excuse"). General revelation through creation, therefore, carries three implications: (1) every human being knows that God exists, (2) every human being is responsible before God, and (3) every human being is under the sentence of God's wrath. The problem, of course, is not God's goodness in making himself known; the problem is humankind's hard-hearted refusal to accept what they know (1:20–23). It is only by God's grace that anyone responds to God's self-revelation.

The missiological question that arises is, "What about those who have never heard?" Paul answers that question in Romans 10:18, when he quotes Psalm 19:4 regarding the witness of creation: "Their voice has gone out into all the earth, and their words to the ends of the world." In one sense, there is no person who has failed to "hear" the truth that God exists. Is it enough, though, to believe that God exists? Paul answers that question in the preceding verse: "Faith comes from hearing, and hearing by the word about Christ" (Rom. 10:17). Hearing and responding to the gospel are essential for salvation. How, then, does God get the gospel to those individuals who, by his grace, respond to his self-revelation in creation? The experiences of the wise men (Matt. 2:1–12), the Ethiopian (Acts 8:26–40), and Cornelius (Acts 10:1–48) suggest a principle: As men and women respond to the light they have, God gives them more light until they have a personal encounter with Christ in the gospel. A further implication, therefore, can be drawn from the doctrine of general revelation: (4) every follower of Christ is responsible to carry the good news of the gospel to those men and women who are responding to the light God has graciously given them.

Paul's primary point in including this paragraph in his letter was to make it clear that the consistent human response to God's truth is to reject that truth. All human beings naturally know that God exists and is powerful; yet, they suppress, ignore, and discard that truth. We share with Paul's Roman readers the need to realize that we should expect those apart from Christ to struggle with understanding and accepting the truth of the gospel. They are predisposed to reject it. Such a realization will drive us to trust God for any progress we might see as men and women make their pilgrimage of responding to the light God has graciously given them.

The idea of anger/wrath would provide a point of connection, since no human being is exempt from the experiences of being angry and/or of being the object of someone else's anger. The passage corrects two common beliefs. The first is that human beings will respond positively on their own to divine truth. Paul makes it abundantly clear that expecting a positive response is unrealistic. The second is the agnostic belief that human beings cannot know whether God exists. The doctrine of general revelation that Paul uses as part of his argument in this paragraph clearly refutes such a belief. The passage commends a proper response of worship and thanksgiving to God's self-revelation in creation. The primary objective in communicating this passage should be to help others understand that the natural human response to God's truth is to distort it, so that they will filter their own responses through the proper grid of worship and thanksgiving.

ROMANS 1:24–32

Text and Translation

24 Therefore, God handed them over in the lusts of their hearts[1] to uncleanness[2] so that their bodies are being dishonored[3] among them;[4] **25** who exchanged the truth about God[5] for a lie and worshipped and served the creation[6] rather than the one *who* created,[7] who is blessed forever. Amen. **26** For this reason, God handed them over to dishonorable passions,[8] for their females exchanged the natural function for that which is contrary to nature.[9] **27** Likewise also[10] the males *who* abandoned[11] the natural use of the females were enflamed with their strong desire[12] toward one another, males with males so that they repeatedly commit what is disgraceful and receive[13] in themselves the penalty that is fitting for their error. **28** And because[14] they did not see fit to have God in their knowledge, God handed them over to an unfitting mind, to be committing[15] what is not fitting, **29** *as a result they* have been filled[16] with all unrighteousness, wickedness, covetousness, evil;[17] full of envy, murder, strife, deceit, meanness; gossips, **30** slanderers, haters of God, insolent, arrogant, boastful; inventors

---

1. Ἐν + dative denotes the state in which they exist.
2. Εἰς + accusative denotes the resulting punishment. So also verses 26 and 28.
3. Τοῦ ἀτιμάζεσθαι indicates result; the present tense is iterative; the voice is passive; τά σώματα αὐτῶν is the subject of the infinitive.
4. Ἐν αὐτοῖς denotes sphere of relationships ("among them").
5. Τοῦ θεοῦ is an objective genitive.
6. Τῇ κτίσει is a dative of direct object.
7. Τὸν κτίσαντα is a substantival participle.
8. Ἀτιμίας is an attributive genitive.
9. Παρά + accusative denotes opposition.
10. Καί is adjunctive.
11. Ἀφέντες is an adjectival participle modifying ἄρσενες.
12. Ἐν + dative denotes manner.
13. Κατεργαζόμενοι καί . . . ἀπολαμβάνοντες are adverbial participles of result.
14. Καθώς is causal (Robertson, *Grammar*, 968).
15. The present tense of ποεῖν is iterative.
16. Πεπληρωμένους stands in apposition to αὐτους and describes the resulting state (intensive perfect).
17. The order of πονηρία, πλεονεξία, κακία differs considerably in the textual tradition, and πορνεία is added in some variants. The differences are most likely the result of copying errors, either of sight or of hearing, and the

of evil, disobedient to parents; **31** without understanding, without faithfulness, without affection,[18] without mercy; **32** who—although they are knowing[19] God's righteous requirement, that the ones *who are* practicing such things are worthy of death—not only are doing[20] the same things but also are joining in approval of the ones who are practicing[21] *them.*

Context and Structure

II. Letter Body (1:18–15:13)
   A. The Gospel as the Revelation of God's Righteousness (1:18–4:25)
      1. The gospel reveals God's righteousness through wrath (1:18–3:20)
         a. Because humankind suppresses God's truth (1:18–23)
         b. **Because the Gentiles practice unrighteousness (1:24–32)**
         c. Because the moral person judges others (2:1–16)
         d. Because the Jews transgress the law (2:17–29)
         e. Because God always acts righteously (3:1–8)
         f. Because all are under sin (3:9–20)

The paragraph consists of three sentences, each introduced by "God handed them over" (παρέδωκεν αὐτοὺς ὁ θεὸς), that describe God's response to humankind's suppression of his truth (1:24–25; 1:26–27; 1:28–32). Verses 29–31 constitute an extended vice list describing acts that are "not fitting" (1:28), followed by a summary statement of indictment (1:32).

---

precise order is not exegetically significant. It is likely that Paul chose and grouped words by type of sin and by sound.

18. The addition of ἀσπόνδους in some manuscripts (א², C) is most likely an assimilation to 2 Timothy 3:3.
19. Ἐπιγνόντες is an adverbial participle of concession.
20. The present tenses of ποιοῦσιν and συνευδοκοῦσιν are iterative presents.
21. Τοῖς πράσσουσιν is a substantival participle; the present tense is iterative.

Basic Message and Exegetical Outline

Because humans suppress his truth, God delivers humankind to punishment that consists of perverted worship, perverted sex, and perverted conduct.

> God "Hands Over" Humankind (1:24–32)
> 1. God hands over to perverted worship (1:24–25)
>   a. In the lusts of their hearts (1:24a)
>   b. To uncleanness that dishonors their bodies (1:24b)
>   c. Because they exchange God's truth for a lie (1:25)
> 2. God hands over to perverted sex (1:26–27)
>   a. To dishonorable passions that exchange the natural for the unnatural (1:26)
>   b. Leading to shame and penalty (1:27)
> 3. God hands over to perverted conduct (1:28–32)
>   a. Because they do not recognize God (1:28a)
>   b. To unfit minds that do what is not fitting (1:28b–31)
>   c. Despite knowing they deserve death (1:32)

Explanation of the Text

1. God hands over to perverted worship (1:24–25).

The conclusion (διό) Paul draws from humankind's rejection of God's self-revelation in creation is that God responds by handing them over to punishment. This punishment is the visible evidence of God's revealed wrath, and Paul borrows a technical term from the Old Testament (παραδίδωμι) to describe God's act of delivering someone for punishment (e.g., Exod. 23:31; Deut. 7:23; Josh. 7:7; Judg. 2:14).[22] The declaration "God handed them over" (παρέδωκεν αὐτοὺς ὁ θεός) introduces each of the three sentences in the paragraph (1:24, 26, 28).

In verse 21, Paul described the state in which humankind exists because they suppress God's truth as characterized by futile reasonings and darkened hearts. Here, he uses the phrase "in the lusts of their hearts" (ἐν ταῖς ἐπιθυμίαος τῶν καρδιῶν αὐτῶν) to describe the same state and in so doing makes it clear that humankind is "already

---

22. Cranfield suggests that God's act of "handing over" is a deliberate forsaking in order to show mercy (*Romans*, 121). Moo notes that Paul also describes the corresponding human role in Ephesians 4:19, when he writes that "they handed themselves over" (ἑαυτοὺς παρέδωκαν) to sin (*Romans*, 111).

immersed in sin"[23] when God hands them over. The punishment to which he hands them over is "uncleanness" (εἰς ἀκαθαρσίαν)—a condition of moral corruption characterized by impurity and depravity—with the result that their bodies are regularly and consistently being dishonored (τοῦ ἀτιμάζεσθαι τὰ σώματα αὐτῶν) in the way they relate to one another (ἐν αὐτοῖς).

Paul has already mentioned the reason God hands over humankind in verse 23. He now develops that idea further. They begin by exchanging (μετήλλαξαν) the truth about the one true God (τὴν ἀλήθειαν τοῦ θεοῦ; cf. 1:20) for the lie of idolatry. "The lie" (ἐν τῷ ψεύδει) is the teaching that the focus of their worship should be on the creation (τῇ κτίσει) rather than on the One who did the creating (παρὰ τὸν κτίσαντα). Having adopted that lie, they give created beings and/or objects their reverential awe (ἐσεβάσθησαν) and render religious service to them (ἐλάτρευσαν). As a result, they fail to give God the eternal glory he deserves (ὅς ἐστιν εὐλογατὸς εἰς τοὺς αἰῶνας), the foundational sin Paul previously identified in verse 21.

2. God hands over to perverted sex (1:26–27).

Because of their idolatry (διὰ τοῦτο), God takes the second step in handing over humankind. Moo notes the Jewish teaching that connected idolatry with sexual immorality,[24] and Paul makes it clear that God's judicial act is the reason for the connection. The penalty for engaging in perverted worship is God's handing over to perverted sex that is driven by "dishonorable passions" (πάθη ἀτιμίας).[25] Paul describes these passions as contrary to nature (τὴν παρὰ θύσιν, 1:26b), disgraceful (τὴν ἀσχημοσύνην, 1:27b), in error (τῆς πλάνης, 1:27c), and expressed particularly in homosexual acts.

By using "females" (αἵ θήλειαι) and "males" (οἱ ἄρσενες) Paul stresses sexual distinction. The passions that result from God's handing them over lead both females and males to exchange (μετήλλαξαν) and abandon (ἀφέντες) natural intimacy (τὴν φυσικὴν χρῆσιν)[26] for intimacy that is contrary to nature (τὴν παρά φύσιν). "Natural" (φυσικός, -ή, -όν) describes something that is in accordance with the basic order of things in nature, while "nature" (φύσις) describes the established order

---

23. Moo, *Romans*, 110.
24. Moo, *Romans*, 113.
25. Jewett provides Greco-Roman background for the idea that "passion" (πάθος) describes an irrational, involuntary state that comes over a person, rules him or her, and must be rooted out (*Romans*, 172).
26. "Function" (ἡ χρῆσις, -εως) denotes intimate involvement with a person.

of things. The acts Paul describes, therefore, are in opposition to the intrinsic order of creation and, consequently, in opposition to God and his will.[27] The result of the strong desire (ἐν τῇ ὀρέξει) with which the individuals described are enflamed (ἐξεκαύθησαν) toward one another (εἰς ἀλλήλους) is the repeated committing (κατεργαζόμενοι) of behavior that is disgraceful (τὴν ἀσχημοσύνην). Their willingness to embrace the error this deceptive lifestyle promotes (τῆς πλάνης αὐτῶν) carries with it a necessary penalty (τὴν ἀντιμισθίαν ἣν ἔδει) that affects them personally (ἐν ἑαυτοῖς).

3. God hands over to perverted conduct (1:28–32).

Paul alters his argument slightly by introducing the third statement about God's handing over with the reason behind God's action. In so doing, he repeats the theme of humankind's rejecting the truth about God (cf. 1:18, 21, 23, 25): they did not see fit to have God in their knowledge. The verb "did not see fit" (οὐκ ἐδοκίμασαν) describes the action of drawing a conclusion about something on the basis of testing.[28] They tested the available evidence and drew the wrong conclusion. Accordingly, the punishment to which God handed them over is "an unfitting mind" (εἰς ἀδόκιμον νοῦν). Elsewhere, Paul uses "mind" (ὁ νοῦς, νοός) to refer to moral reasoning and volition (7:23, 25; 11:34; 12:2; 14:5), and the outworking of their unfitting minds is apparent in their repeated doing of "things that are not fitting" (ποεῖν τὰ μὴ καθήκοντα). The extent of humankind's unfitting reasoning and behavior becomes clear as Paul introduces an extended list of twenty-one vices (1:29–31). The absence of a connecting conjunction (asyndeton) draws attention to the list, which paints "a picture of comprehensive wickedness."[29]

The first four vices embrace general categories, a fact highlighted by the introductory adjective "all" (πάσῃ). "Unrighteousness" (ἀδικία) describes a lack of respect for God and his righteous order (cf. 1:18); "wickedness" (πονηρίᾳ) describes a lack of moral values; "covetousness" (πλεονεξίᾳ) describes a desire to have more; "evil" (κακίᾳ) describes malice or ill will.

---

27. See Romans 2:27; 1 Corinthians 11:14; Galatians 2:15; 4:8; Ephesians 2:3 for other occurrences of "natural" and Romans 11:24 for another argument where Paul uses the ideas of "in accordance with" and "contrary to" nature. Philo (Spec Leg 3.39) and Josephus (Ag Ap 2.27) use the same language in discussions of homosexuality.
28. BDAG 255d.
29. Schreiner, *Romans*, 98.

The next five terms are dependent on the adjective "full" (μεστούς), which describes the state of being thoroughly characterized by something.[30] "Envy" (φθόνου) points to jealousy that aggressively seeks to do harm; "murder" (φόνου) points to the intentional taking of life (cf. Exod. 20:13; Deut. 5:17);[31] "strife" (ἔριδος) points to engaging in contention; "deceit" (δόλου) points to taking advantage through craft or underhandedness; "meanness" (κακοηθείας) points to character that results in hurting others.

The next eight vices are more loosely grouped. Some commentators see them as four pairs. "Gossips" (ψιθυριστάς) and "slanderers" (καταλάλους) destroy the reputations of others. The first do so through rumor and secret slander; the second do so by openly speaking evil of others. The active sense, "haters of God" (θεοστυγεῖς), is better than the passive sense, "hated by God"; someone who is "insolent" (ὑβριστάς) treats others with contempt. The two words might be paired because both groups express contempt for their object. One group directs the contempt vertically; the other directs it horizontally. "Arrogant" (ὑπερηφάνους) and "boastful" (ἀλαζόνας) are naturally related because someone who is haughty or proud tends to seek to impress others by bragging. Jewett suggests that "inventors of evil" (ἐφευρετὰς κακῶν) and "disobedient to parents" (γονεῦσιν ἀπειθεῖς) both contribute to the destruction of community. The first group does so in political affairs by specializing in stirring up trouble; the second group does so in domestic affairs by weakening the honor and respect due to parents.[32]

The final four terms are linked by common vowel sounds (assonance), and all denote the absence of positive qualities. "Without understanding" (ἀσυνέτος) describes someone who lacks intellectual and moral capacity (cf. 1:21); "without faithfulness" (ἀσυνθέτους) describes someone who does not keep his or her word; "without affection" (ἀστόργους) describes someone who lacks positive feelings for others; "without mercy" (ἀνελεήμονας) describes someone who lacks concern for those who are in need.

Paul concludes the paragraph by returning to the idea of humankind's rejecting the truth they know (cf. 1:18, 21, 23, 25, 28). Here, truth goes beyond general revelation to God's righteous requirement (τὸ δικαίωμα τοῦ θεοῦ). That requirement makes it clear that people who practice vices such as those included in the preceding list (οἱ τὰ

---

30. BDAG 636a.
31. Cranfield notes that envy can ultimately lead to murder and cites the example of Cain and Abel in Genesis 4 (*Romans*, 130).
32. Jewett, *Romans*, 188.

τοιαῦτα πράσσοντες) deserve death (ἄξιοι θανάτου εἰσίν). Although they know (ἐπιγνόντες) this requirement, they repeatedly do (ποιοῦσιν) the same acts (αὐτά) that requirement condemns. Further, they regularly join in approval (συνευδοκοῦσιν) of others who practice those vices (τοῖς πράσσουσιν). As Jewett notes, this closing statement "is the last plank in the rhetorical bridge called 'suppression of the truth'."[33] It also underlines the fact that those who suppress God's truth suppress both the general revelation of creation (cf. 1:20) and the special revelation of God's law (cf. 2:26; 8:4), are totally without excuse (cf. 1:20), and deserve the wrath he visits on them (cf. 1:18).

Theology and Appropriation

God's wrath is a topic Christians often prefer to avoid, although it is a divine attribute and relates directly to God's righteousness. If the topic is discussed at all, the common focus tends to be on end-time judgment rather than on God expressing his wrath in the contemporary world. Yet Paul's focus in these verses is precisely on the latter aspect. God's wrath is his reaction to sin with righteous anger and righteous action. That reaction is neither irrational nor temperamental; it is rational and judicial. Yet, it is not without an emotional component, since God's righteousness means that he hates sin and is repulsed by it. He will punish sin fully and finally at the last judgment, and he has chosen to defer that judgment to demonstrate his righteousness in the gospel (Rom. 3:25–26), but he cannot ignore sin. It is in keeping with his character, therefore, that God reveals his wrath against human ungodliness and unrighteousness and does so in the present as well as in the future.

God reveals his wrath by "handing over" humankind to their own sinful desires (1:24), passions (1:26), and thought processes (1:28). The basic meaning of the verb (παραδίδωμι) is "hand over, give over, deliver." In the Old Testament, the verb describes what God did to Israel's enemies (e.g., Exod. 23:31; Deut. 7:23) as well as what God did to Israel for their own punishment (e.g., Josh. 7:7; Judg. 2:14; 6:1). In the New Testament, the verb describes Judas's act of handing over Jesus (Matt. 26:15–16, 20–25), God's own act of handing over Jesus (Rom. 8:32), Paul's act of handing over unrepentant believers (1 Cor. 5:5; 1 Tim. 1:20), and the Gentiles' act of handing over themselves to sin (Eph. 4:19). The idea, then, is more than a passive withholding or release of restraint. It describes an active, purposeful transfer of someone to the control of another. The act reflects the natural consequences ("the penalty that is

---

33. Jewett, *Romans*, 191.

fitting") of sin (1:27), but it is not the origin of sinful acts, because it is in response to "the lusts of their hearts" that God hands over humankind (1:24). God's purpose in the handing over is retributive (1:27, 32), but it may also be seen as merciful (cf. 2:4; Isa. 19:22).[34]

Paul's primary purpose in writing this paragraph is to explain how suppressing God's truth results in God visiting wrath upon those who do the suppressing. It is the natural sequel to 1:18–23. Together, these paragraphs develop Paul's opening declaration that God reveals his wrath from heaven against human ungodliness and unrighteousness. The previous paragraph describes *why* God reveals his wrath (1:18b); this paragraph describes *how* God reveals his wrath (1:18a). The need we share with Paul's Roman readers is a realization of the way in which the decision to reject God's truth shows itself in increasingly perverted thought and behavior. Such a realization will help us understand the actions of those around us and will challenge us to respond appropriately to God's revealed truth.

The idea of fitting/unfitting could provide a point of connection, because everyone holds to some explicit or implicit standard of what is or is not appropriate regardless of the context(s) in which they might apply that standard. The passage corrects the ideas that idolatrous practices and homosexual acts are acceptable in the sight of the one true God. Paul condemns both and makes it clear that both are the result of foolish minds and darkened hearts that, in turn, have their origin in the fundamental sin of rejecting God. The passage commends the rejection of attitudes and actions that characterize those who have been "handed over" by God. Those actions carry an intrinsic penalty in this life as well as being worthy of death in the life to come. The primary objective in communicating this passage should be to help others understand that rejecting God's truth has serious consequences so that they will commit themselves to aligning their lives with God's righteous requirement.

---

34. See Cranfield, *Romans*, 121.

ROMANS 2:1–16

Text and Translation

1 Therefore, you are without excuse, oh man, every one *of you who is* judging;[1] for in *that* which you are judging the other *person*, you are condemning yourself, for *you who are* judging are practicing the same things. **2** Now we know that God's judgment[2] is according to truth upon *those who are* practicing[3] such things. **3** But are you imagining this— oh man *who is* judging[4] those *who are* practicing such things and is doing them—that you will escape God's judgment? **4** Or are you despising the riches of his goodness and forbearance and longsuffering, because you are ignorant[5] that the kindness of God is trying to lead[6] you to repentance? **5** But according to your hardened and unrepentant heart you are treasuring up wrath for yourself in the day of wrath and the revelation of God's righteous judgment,

    6   who will repay to each one according to his works;

    7   on the one hand, eternal life to the ones who, according to perseverance that produces a good work,[7] are seeking glory, and honor and incorruptibility,

    8   on the other hand, wrath and fury to the *ones who are motivated by* selfishness[8] and are disobeying[9] truth but obeying unrighteousness.

    9   Tribulation and distress upon every soul of the person *who is* working evil, both Jew first and Greek;

    10   but glory and honor and peace to everyone who is working good, both to Jew first and to Greek;

    11   for there is no partiality before God.

---

1. Ὁ κρίνων is a substantival participle (twice).
2. The phrase τὸ κρίμα τοῦ θεοῦ denotes a judicial verdict that comes directly from God. Τοῦ θεοῦ is a subjective genitive. So also in the next verse.
3. Τοὺς πράσσοντας is a substantival participle. So also in the next verse.
4. Ὁ κρίνων . . . καὶ ποιῶν are compound substantival participles. The article-participle-καί-participle construction is an example of the Granville Sharp rule (cf. Wallace, *Grammar*, 274–75).
5. Ἀγνοῶν is an adverbial participle of cause.
6. Ἄγει is a conative present.
7. Ἔργου ἀγαθοῦ is an objective genitive.
8. Τοῖς . . . ἐξ ἐριθείας is substantival and describes motivation.
9. Ἀπειθοῦσι and πειθομένοις are both substantival participles; both present tenses are iterative.

12 For as many as sin apart from law, will also[10] perish apart from law, and as many as sin in law, through law will be judged; **13** for not the hearers of law[11] are righteous before God, but the doers of law will be justified. **14** For whenever Gentiles, *who* are not having the law, are by nature, doing the things of the law, these, *although they are* not having the law,[12] are a law to themselves; **15** who are showing the work the law requires[13] written in their hearts, while their conscience is bearing witness[14] and their reasonings are alternately[15] accusing or even[16] defending *them,* **16** on the day[17] when God will judge the things humans hide[18] according to the gospel I preach[19] through[20] Christ Jesus.[21]

Context and Structure

    II. Letter Body (1:18–15:13)
        A. The Gospel as the Revelation of God's Righteousness (1:18–4:25)
            1. The gospel reveals God's righteousness through wrath (1:18–3:20)
                a. Because humankind suppresses God's truth (1:18–23)
                b. Because the Gentiles practice unrighteousness (1:24–32)
                c. **Because the moral person judges others (2:1–16)**
                d. Because the Jews transgress the law (2:17–29)
                e. Because God always acts righteously (3:1–8)
                f. Because all are under sin (3:9–20)

---

10. Καί is adjunctive.
11. Νόμου is an objective genitive (in the next clause also).
12. Ἔχοντα is an adverbial participle of concession.
13. Τοῦ νόμου is a subjective genitive.
14. Συμμαρτυρούσης αὐτῶν τῆς συνειδήεως is a genitive absolute of time (as are κατηγορούντων and ἀπολογουμένων).
15. A literal translation of μεταξύ ἀλλήλων is "between one another."
16. Καί is ascensive.
17. Ἐν + dative is temporal.
18. Τῶν ἀνθρῶπων is a subjective genitive.
19. Μου is a subjective genitive; compare GNB and NLT.
20. Διά + genitive denotes agency.
21. Although Metzger decides for Χριστοῦ Ἰησοῦ because it is supported by "the oldest extant witnesses" (*Textual Commentary*, 448), Paul tends to use Ἰησοῦ Χριστοῦ with διά (cf. 1:8; 5:1, 21; 7:25; 15:30; 16:27).

A shift from third person to second person marks a new movement of Paul's argument in which he uses a diatribe style for the first time (cf. 2:17–24; 3:1–8). The paragraph divides into three sections. The first is a diatribe section that introduces the topic of God's judgment (2:1–5). The second section is carefully structured and describes the basis for God's impartiality in judging (2:6–11).[22] The third section uses Hebrew parallelism as well as Greek syntactic construction to explain how God applies his impartial judgment to both those with and those without the law (2:12–16).

Basic Message and Exegetical Outline

God's judgment of every human being is deserved, based on works, and applied impartially.

God's Judgment (2:1–16)
1. God's judgment is deserved (2:1–5)
   a. By those who practice what they judge (2:1–3)
   b. By those who despise God's goodness (2:4–5)
2. God's judgment is based on works (2:6–11)
   a. Rewarding those who do good (2:7, 10)
   b. Punishing those who do evil (2:8–9)
3. God's judgment is applied impartially (2:12–16)
   a. To those who have the law (2:12–13)
   b. To those who do not have the law (2:14–16)

Explanation of the Text

1. God's judgment is deserved (2:1–5).

As Paul looks back to 1:18–32, he draws a conclusion (διό) about every person who passes unfavorable judgment on the life or actions of another (πᾶς ὁ κρίνων).[23] He addresses directly the person who responds in that way (ὦ ἄνθρωπε) and asserts that such a person shares the same verdict as the person who suppresses God's self-revelation in creation: both are without excuse (ἀναπολόγητος; cf. 1:20). The explanation (γάρ) for Paul's assertion resides in the nature of passing judgment. In the act

---

22. Most commentators view the structure as inverted (e.g., Harvey, *Romans*, 52); Longenecker proposes an alternate understanding based on antithetical parallelism (*Romans*, 253–54). He also views the section as "a traditional portion of confessional material" that Paul incorporated into his letter.
23. BDAG 567d.

of passing unfavorable judgment on another (ἐν ᾧ κρίνεις τὸν ἕτερον), that person pronounces a sentence on him/herself (σεαυτὸν κατακρίνεις), because (γάρ) he/she practices the same sort of actions (τὰ αὐτά).[24] Paul takes it as an accepted fact (οἴδαμεν δὲ ὅτι)[25] that his audience will agree that God's judgment (τὸ κρίμα τοῦ θεοῦ) meets a true standard (κατὰ ἀλήθειαν) when he judges those who practice such things (ἐπὶ τοὺς τὰ τοιαῦτα πράσσοντας). For that reason, they should not imagine (λογίζῃ) that they will escape the peril of God's judgment (ἐκφεύξῃ τὸ κρίμα τοῦ θεοῦ) when they do the same things they are judging in others (ὁ κρίνων τοὺς τὰ τοιαῦτα πράσσοντας καὶ ποιῶν αὐτά).

The other side (ἤ) of God's judgment is his goodness, and the moral person must be careful not to view that goodness with contempt (καταφρονεῖς).[26] The riches of God's goodness (τοῦ πλούτου τῆς χρηστότητος αὐτοῦ) include his forbearance (τῆς ἀνοχῆς) and his patience (τῆς μακροθυμίας). Extrabiblical use suggests that God expresses his goodness by patiently withholding his judgment.[27] Not only does God's goodness lead him to withhold judgment, it is intended to lead his people to repentance (εἰς μετάνοιάν σε ἄγει).[28] Because people are ignorant of that goodness (ἀγνοῶν τὸ χρηστὸν τοῦ θεοῦ), though, their natural human condition is a heart that is hardened (σκληρότητα) and unrepentant (ἀμετανόητον). The result is a storing up of wrath (θησαυρίζεις σεαυτῷ ὀργὴν) for the day of wrath (ἐν ἡμέρᾳ ὀργῆς) when God will reveal his righteous judgment (ἀποκαλύψεως δικαιοκρισίας τοῦ θεοῦ). Both hypocritical condemnation of others' actions (2:1–3) and uninformed contempt for God's goodness (2:4–5) result in God's judgment expressed in his wrath.

2. God's judgment is based on works (2:6–11).

Paul uses a relative clause to introduce an extended discussion of God (ὅς) and his righteous judgment. The opening clause (2:6) highlights three aspects of that judgment: (1) it is a repayment; (2) it is individual; and (3) it is based on the standard of works. The verb "repay"

---

24. Paul's understanding of the double-edged nature of "judging" echoes Jesus's own in the Sermon on the Mount (Matt. 7:1–2).
25. The disclosure formula introduces an accepted fact that establishes common ground between the writer and his audience (cf. 3:19; 7:14; 8:22, 28).
26. BDAG 529d.
27. E.g., Wisdom of Solomon 15:1–2 (cf. Rom. 3:25–26). See Moo's discussion (*Romans*, 132–33).
28. Wallace notes that the four other times Paul uses "repentance" (2 Cor. 7:9, 10; 12:21; 2 Tim. 2:25), it refers to believers (*Grammar*, 289 n.92)

(ἀποδώσει) affirms that the payment is equitable (cf. "due penalty" in 1:27). The substantized adjective "each one" (ἑκάστῳ) makes it clear that no one is exempt. In the next two verses (2:7–8), Paul discusses the "works" (κατὰ τὰ ἔργα αὐτοῦ) two groups of individuals perform and the repayment each group receives.

God rewards[29] the first group (μὲν) with eternal life (ζωὴν αἰώνιον) because they are seeking (ζητοῦσιν) qualities that reflect him and his character (cf, 1:23): glory (δόξαν), honor (τιμὴν), and incorruptibility (ἀφθαρσίαν). The standard against which the first group is measured is perseverance that produces a good work (καθ' ὑπομονὴν ἔργου ἀγαθοῦ)— in other words, they persistently pursue godliness. God repays the second group (δέ) in accordance with what they have earned: wrath (ὀργή) and fury (θυμός). This group is motivated by selfishness (ἐξ ἐριθείας), rejects God's truth (ἀπειθοῦσι τῇ ἀληθείᾳ), and embraces the unrighteousness (πειθομένοις τῇ ἀδικίᾳ) against which God reveals his wrath (1:18)—in other words, they constantly pursue godlessness.

Paul then retraces his argument (2:9–10), beginning with the second group he has just described. The absence of a connecting conjunction (asyndeton) creates an abruptness that calls attention to the shift. The second group is now characterized more directly as those who are producing that which is morally and socially reprehensible (τοῦ κατεργαζομένου τὸ κακὸν).[30] Every member of this group (ἐπὶ πᾶσαν ψυχήν ἀνθρώπου) will receive outward affliction (θλῖψις) and inward anguish (στενοχωρία), whether that person is Jew or Greek (cf. 1:16). In contrast (δέ), the first group is characterized as those who are producing that which is socially beneficial and acceptable (τῷ ἐργαζομένου τὸ ἀγαθόν).[31] Every member of that group (παντί) will receive the godliness he or she is seeking (δόξα καὶ τιμὴ καὶ εἰρήνη), whether that person is Jew or Greek (cf. 1:16; 2:9).

The repetition of "both to Jew first and to Greek" (Ἰουδαίῳ το πρῶτον καὶ Ἕλληνι) in verses 9 and 10 leads naturally to the final explanation (γάρ) of God's judgment based on works: there is no partiality before God (παρὰ τῷ θεῷ). "Partiality" (προσωπολημψία) occurs only three other times in the New Testament (Eph. 6:9; Col. 3:25; James 2:1), all with negative connotations.[32] The same idea occurs in Galatians 2:6: "God

---

29. Although verses 7–10 lack finite verbs, "he will repay" (ἀποδώσει) in verse 6 should be understood as governing the entire construction.
30. See BDAG 501c on κακός, -ή, -όν.
31. See BDAG 4b on ἀγαθός, -ή, -όν.
32. The cognate noun occurs in Acts 10:34, the cognate verb in James 2:9, and the cognate adverb in 1 Peter 1:17.

does not receive the face of a man" (πρόσωπον ἀνθρώπου οὐ λαμβάνει), which probably reflects the word's Old Testament background (e.g., Lev. 19:15; Deut. 1:17; 16:19). KJV translates the cognate noun in Acts 10:34 with "God is no respecter of persons." As a conclusion to the section, this statement reinforces Paul's opening assertion that God evaluates each person against the same standard (2:6). The intervening discussion makes it clear that there are two options: to pursue godliness or to pursue godlessness. Each choice leads to a distinct outcome: eternal life or wrath and fury. None of the readers, therefore, can conclude that it is possible to avoid God's impartial evaluation of their lives (cf. 2:3).

3. God's judgment is applied impartially (2:12–16).
   Paul provides a further explanation (γάρ) of God's impartial judgment by applying the principle to two groups: those who have the law and those who do not. He establishes the composition of those groups with a carefully balanced couplet in synonymous parallelism (2:12):

| As many as apart from law | sin, | also apart from law | will be ruined. |
| As many as in law | sin, | through law | will be judged. |

The first group consists of those who sin without the advantage of access to the Mosaic law (ἀνόμως).[33] All the members of that group will perish (ἀπολοῦνται). The second group consists of those who have regular access to the Mosaic law (ἐν νόμῳ). All the members of that group will be judged (κριθήσονται). Both groups face the same destiny for failing to meet God's standard: his righteous judgment and wrath (cf. 2:5, 8). Paul sets out the reason (γάρ) those with access to the law cannot avoid judgment in a second couplet, this time using antithetical parallelism (2:13):

| Not | the hearers of law | {are} righteous | before God. |
| But | the doers of law | will be declared righteous. | |

Those who possess the law are expected to obey the law.[34] For that reason, the Jews cannot claim an advantage simply because they know the law; they must also do it.
   What about those who do not possess the law? They, too, will be judged on the basis of their works, because whenever they "do the law," they demonstrate a knowledge of God's standard of right and wrong

---

33. BDAG 86b.
34. James explains the same requirement in his letter (1:22–25).

(οὗτοι . . . ἑαυτοῖς εἰσιν νόμος).[35] Gentiles (ἔθνη) might not have the same access to the Mosaic law the Jews do (τὰ μὴ νόμον ἔχοντα), but there are occasions when some of them do (ὅταν . . . ποιῶσιν) "some of the law's commands" (τὰ τοῦ νόμου).[36] When they do, it is "by nature" (φύσει) rather than because they possess the law. Although they do not possess any special revelation (νόμον μὴ ἔχοντες), they demonstrate that the kind of work the law requires (ἐνδείκνυνται τὸ ἔργον τοῦ νόμου) is written in their hearts (γραπτὸν ἐν ταῖς καρδίαις αὐτων). That is, they understand the sort of works the law expects without the ability to do those works as the law demands. For that reason, their conscience (αὐτῶν τῆς συνειδήσεως) and their reasonings (τῶν λογισμῶν) alternately (μεταξὺ ἀλλήλων) accuse and defend them (κατηγορούντων ἢ καὶ ἀπολογουμένων). Those internal human debates (τὰ κρυπτὰ τῶν ἀνθρώπων) will finally be settled on the day of divine judgment (ἐν ἡμέρᾳ ὅτε κρίνει ὁ θεός). That judgment will be executed by Christ Jesus (διὰ Χριστοῦ Ἰησοῦ) according to the standard of the gospel that has been entrusted to Paul (cf. 1:1) and that he faithfully preaches (κατὰ τὸ εὐαγγέλιόν μου). Ultimately, both Jew and Gentile will be judged impartially on the basis of the extent to which they have done the law rather than whether or not they have heard it.

Theology and Appropriation

Paul's teaching in this paragraph on God's judgment is clear. God judges all impartially (2:11), that is, both Jew and Gentile (2:9, 10), and he judges on the basis of works (2:16), that is, on doing rather than simply hearing the law (2:13). The details of his argument, however, raise questions. In particular, three questions have been the focus of considerable scholarly discussion: (1) Who earns eternal life by works (2:7, 10)? (2) Who are the Gentiles who do the law (2:14–15)? (3) Is it possible to be justified by works (2:12–13)?

Suggested answers to the first question include unbelievers, Old Testament believers, and Christians.[37] Longenecker resorts to the explanation that Paul is using traditional Jewish and/or Jewish Christian materials.[38] It seems more likely, however, that Paul is stating a general principle that describes two lifestyles and the results of each. Such an understanding would be in line with the Old Testament "two

---

35. See Moo, *Romans*, 151.
36. Longenecker, *Romans*, 275. He also suggests "instinctively" as a translation for φύσει.
37. Various combinations have also been proposed. See Cranfield for ten options (*Romans*, 152–53).
38. Longenecker, *Romans*, 266–69.

ways" teaching that is clearly present in the Old Testament (e.g., Ps. 1:1–6) and in Jesus's teaching (e.g., Matt. 7:13–27) and that finds expression in Paul's own "antithetical" teaching (e.g., Gal. 5:16–26).[39] In this context, his point is that God will judge men and women—Jew or Gentile—on the basis of whether they consistently pursue lives of godliness or lives of godlessness.

Suggested identities of the Gentiles in 2:14–15 include pagan Gentiles, pre-Christian Gentiles, and Gentile Christians. Paul has already made it clear, however, that the Gentiles know and reject God's righteous requirement (1:32). The best understanding of these verses is that *some* of the Gentiles on occasion keep some of the requirements of the Mosaic law.[40] Paul's point is that Gentiles possess at least an instinctive understanding of the moral norms included in the Mosaic law. Their knowledge of right and wrong is adequate to render them without excuse (2:1), but it is inadequate to save them.

Elsewhere in Romans and his other letters, Paul argues that God declares a person righteous solely through faith (3:21–30; 4:1–25; 9:1–11:36; cf. Gal. 3:1–29; Eph. 2:8–9). The background of Paul's statement that those who do the law will be declared righteous (2:13) is Leviticus 18:5. Paul also alludes to that verse in 10:5, although he rejects its premise in Galatians 3:11–12. His statement in 2:13, however, is parallel to James 1:22–25, and suggests that "Paul is not as far from James as some suggest."[41] Elsewhere, Paul highlights the importance of good works for the believer (e.g., Rom. 14:10–12; 2 Cor. 5:10; Eph. 2:10; 6:7–9; Col. 3:25) and the fact that works affect an individual's entry into the kingdom (e.g., 1 Cor. 6:9–11; Gal. 5:21; Eph. 5:5). Paul teaches that works are important *in response to* being declared righteous not *in order to be* declared righteous. In this context, Paul's point is that knowing the law—either by precept or by instinct—does not result in God justifying a person; doing the law does. Both Jew and Gentile stand on the same footing before God: they will be evaluated on the basis of their works. Neither does the law perfectly (1:32; 2:21–24) and, therefore, both are without excuse (1:20; 2:1).

Paul's primary purpose in including this paragraph was to help his readers understand that the moral person who condemns sin in others also falls short of the divine standard of absolute holiness. We share with his Roman readers the need to realize that we have no right to

---

39. See the Introduction and Harvey, *Pauline Letters*, 79–85.
40. See Longenecker (*Romans*, 275), Moo (*Romans*, 149), and Schreiner (*Romans*, 124) who hold similar positions.
41. Schreiner, *Romans*, 115.

expect special treatment from God simply because we claim that we hold to a higher moral standard than others. Possible points of connection include judgment and good works. The judicial system provides regular examples of rulings issued and judgments rendered, while public recognition bestowed on individuals for their good works is a common news story. The passage corrects the idea that God plays favorites, the suggestion that the same eternal destiny awaits everyone, and a judgmental attitude that looks down on others because we view their conduct as sub-Christian. It commends the persistent pursuit of righteousness that aligns with God's standard as well as the active doing of what Scripture teaches (cf. James 1:22–25). The primary objective in communicating this passage should be to help others understand that God judges individuals impartially on the basis of the works they do so that they will acknowledge their own moral bankruptcy before God and look to him for his grace.

ROMANS 2:17–29

Text and Translation

17 Now if *it is true that*[1] you are calling yourself[2] a Jew and are resting in the law and are boasting in God **18** and are knowing his[3] will and are approving the *things that are* excellent[4] *because you are* being instructed[5] out of the law, **19** and have persuaded[6] yourself that you are a guide to the blind,[7] a light to *those who are* in darkness, **20** an instructor to those who lack judgment, an instructor of the childlike,[8] *because you are* having[9] the embodiment of knowledge and truth[10] in the law— **21** Therefore, you who are teaching the other *person*, are you not teaching yourself? You who are preaching not to steal, are you stealing? **22** You who are saying not to commit adultery, are you committing adultery? You who are detesting idols, are you robbing temples? **23** *You* who are boasting in the law, are you dishonoring God through your transgression of the law?[11] **24** For **"God's name is being blasphemed among the Gentiles because of you,"** just as it has been written. **25** For on the one hand circumcision is of value, if you are practicing the law;[12] on the other hand if you are a transgressor of the law,[13] your circumcision has become uncircumcision. **26** Therefore, if the uncircumcised *person* is keeping the law's righteous requirement, *that person's* uncircumcision will be counted for circumcision, will it not? **27** And the *person who is* uncircumcised by nature—*if that person* is keeping[14] the law—will judge you who through letter and circumcision are a transgressor of the law. **28** For

---

1. Εἰ + indicative introduces a first-class condition.
2. Ἐπονομάζῃ is a direct middle.
3. The definite article functions as a possessive pronoun.
4. Τά διαφέροντα is substantival; compare Philippians 1:10 for the combination δοκιμάζειν . . . τά διαφέροντα.
5. Κατηχούμενος is an adverbial participle of cause.
6. Πέποιθάς is a second adverbial participle of cause.
7. Τυφλῶν is an objective genitive.
8. Ἀφρόνων and νηπίων are both objective genitives.
9. Ἔχοντα is an adverbial participle of cause.
10. Γνώσεως and ἀληθείας are descriptive genitives.
11. Τοῦ νόμου is an objective genitive.
12. The third class condition (ἐὰν . . . πράσσῃς) says nothing about the likelihood of fulfillment. So also in the next clause and in verse 26.
13. Νόμου is an objective genitive (also in verse 27).
14. Τελοῦσα is an adverbial participle of condition.

not the *one who is* evident is a Jew, and not that *which is* evident in the flesh *is* circumcision, **29** but the one who is hidden *is* a Jew, and circumcision of the heart[15] by the Spirit[16] not by letter *is circumcision*, whose praise is not from humans but from God.

Context and Structure

II. Letter Body (1:18–15:13)
   A. The Gospel as the Revelation of God's Righteousness (1:18–4:25)
      1. The gospel reveals God's righteousness through wrath (1:18–3:20)
         a. Because humankind suppresses God's truth (1:18–23)
         b. Because the Gentiles practice unrighteousness (1:24–32)
         c. Because the moral person judges others (2:1–16)
         d. **Because the Jews transgress the law (2:17–29)**
         e. Because God always acts righteously (3:1–8)
         f. Because all are under sin (3:9–20)

In the first section of the paragraph, Paul returns to the diatribe style to address the topics of Jewish advantage, obligation, and transgression, particularly as they relate to the law (2:17–24). In the second section, he uses a series of antitheses to explore the topics of true circumcision and uncircumcision (2:25–29).

Basic Message and Exegetical Outline

Although they possess the law and the sign of circumcision, the Jews' transgressions negate both and bring dishonor to God.

   The Case against the Jews (2:17–29)
      1. Possessing the law does not exempt from judgment (2:17–24)
         a. Four advantages of being instructed from the Mosaic law (2:17–18)
         b. Four obligations that result from possessing the Mosaic law (2:19–20)

---

15. Καρδίας is an objective genitive.
16. Ἐν + dative is instrumental (twice).

    c. Four transgressions of the Mosaic law (2:21–23)
    d. Proof of guilt from the Mosaic law (2:24)
  2. Being circumcised does not exempt from judgment
     (2:25–29)
    a. The relation of circumcision to the law (2:25)
    b. The relation of uncircumcision to the law (2:26–27)
    c. The nature of true Jewishness and true circumci-
       sion (2:28–29)

Explanation of the Text

1. Possessing the law does not exempt from judgment (2:17–24).
Having made it clear that both Jew and Gentile are accountable before God on the basis of what they do, Paul transitions (δέ) to
an indictment of his Jewish readers based on their failure to do the
Mosaic law. Working on the premise (εἰ + indicative) that they identify with the religious heritage of Judaism (σὺ Ἰουδαῖος ἐπονομάζῃ),
he lists four advantages of being a Jew: they find inner security in
the Mosaic law (ἐπαναπαύῃ νόμῳ);[17] they take pride in their special
relationship with the one true God (καυζᾶσαι ἐν θεῷ); they possess
insight into God's will (γινώσκεις τὸ θέλημα); and they are able to approve those attitudes and actions God considers excellent (δοκιμάζεις
τὰ διαφέροντα). The reason they are able to claim these advantages
resides in the fact that they possess access to and instruction from
the Mosaic law (κατηχούμενος ἐκ τοῦ νόμου).
    Further (τε), they have convinced themselves (πέποιθας σεαυτόν)
that they have four obligations to others:[18] they are to help those
who are spiritually blind find their way (ὁδηγὸν τυφλῶν); they are to
shine the light of God's truth in the darkness around them (φῶς τῶν
ἐν σκότει); they are to provide instruction to those who lack good judgment (παιδευτὴν ἀφρόνων); and they are to teach those who are spiritually immature (διδάσκαλον νηπίων). This sense of obligation has its
roots in the Old Testament (cf. Isa. 42:6–7; 49:6), and Jesus condemns
the Jewish religious leaders for failing to carry out those obligations
(Matt. 15:14; 23:16–22). The reason the Jews are able to pursue their
obligations, again, resides in the fact that they possess the law, which
is the embodiment par excellence of knowledge and truth (ἔχοντα τὴν
μόρφωσιν τῆσ γνώσεως καὶ τῆς αληθείας).

---

17. Moo suggests that the Jews believed their reliance on the law would ex-
    empt them from final judgment (*Romans*, 160).
18. Jewett relates the obligations specifically to the Gentiles (*Romans*, 225).

The conclusion Paul asks his readers to draw from considering their advantages and obligations consists of a series of rhetorical questions. The questions call the Jews among his readers to consider whether they are actually fulfilling the requirements and obligations set out in the Mosaic law. That law gives them their sense of identity, their sense of well-being, their source of pride, their ability to know God's will, and their calling to serve others. Paul's question is whether they simply hear the law or actually do it (cf. 2:12–13). Are they teaching themselves (σεαυτὸν οὐ διδάσκεις)? Are they keeping the commandments (κλέπτεις; . . . μοιχεύσεις)? Are they robbing temples (ἱεροσυλεῖς)?[19] Although they boast in the Mosaic law (ὅς ἐν νόμῳ καυχᾶσαι), are they dishonoring God by breaking that very law (διὰ τῆς παραβάσεως τοῦ νόμου τὸν θεὸν ἀτιμάζεις)? In fact (γάρ), as Isaiah 52:5 (LXX) affirms (καθὼς γέγραπται), the Jews and their actions (δι' ὑμᾶς) are causing God's name to be blasphemed (τὸ ὄνομα τοῦ θεοῦ . . . βλασφημεῖται) among the very Gentiles to whom they were called to be a light (ἐν τοῖς ἔθνεσιν). For that reason, the Jews should not consider themselves to be any better than the Gentiles whom they condemn.

2. Being circumcised does not exempt from judgment (2:25–29).

In addition to possessing the law, the Jews also possess the sign of circumcision as a mark of their special relationship with God. If the law does not protect them from God's judgment, perhaps circumcision would. Paul now provides a further explanation (γάρ) in response to that possible argument. His explanation is parallel to the principle he has set out in relation to the law: circumcision is of value (περιτομὴ . . . ὀφελεῖ) only if the person who is circumcised obeys the Mosaic law (ἐὰν νόμον πράσσῃς). Conversely (δέ), if a circumcised person transgresses the law (ἐὰν παραβάτης νόμου ᾖς), that person finds him/herself in the same state as an uncircumcised Gentile (ἡ περιτομὴ σου ἀκροβυστία γέγονεν).

Paul's point continues to be that God judges impartially on the basis of what individuals do rather than on the basis of what they know or, in this case, what supposed religious advantage they might possess. Not surprisingly, then, his argument echoes what he wrote in 2:14–15 when he turns to the example of uncircumcised Gentiles who keep the law.[20] If some Gentiles (ἡ ἀκροβυστία) keep the righteous requirements

---

19. See Moo for a helpful discussion of why Paul chose these particular transgressions. He concludes, "It is not, then, that all Jews commit these sins, but that these sins are representative of the contradiction between claim and conduct that *does* pervade Judaism" (*Romans*, 165, italics in original).
20. See "Theology and Appropriation" under 2:1–16.

of the law (τὰ δικαιώματα τοῦ νόμου φυλάσση), they will be counted as possessing circumcision (εἰς περιτομὴν λογισθήσεται). That is, they will be considered to have the same relationship with God that obedient Jews have. Further, if those physically uncircumcised individuals (ἡ ἐκ φύσεως ἀκροβυστία) keep the law (τὸν νόμον τελοῦσα), they will judge (κρινεῖ) those Jews who possess both the law and circumcision (διὰ γράμματος καὶ περιτομῆς) but break the law (τὸν παραβάτην νόμου).

Paul's summary explanation (γάρ) is structured using antithetical parallelism, but it is also extremely succinct and requires additional words.

For	not the one who is evident	is a Jew,
and	not that which is evident in the flesh	is circumcision,
but	the one who is hidden	is a Jew,
and	circumcision of the heart by the Spirit not by letter	is circumcision.

The final line unlocks the preceding three lines. It is not external appearance—whether in regard to letter of law or rite of circumcision—that makes the difference in God's sight; it is the Spirit's inner work in the heart.[21] The former receives praise from men (ἐξ ἀνθρώπων); the latter receives praise from God (ἐκ τοῦ θεοῦ).

Theology and Appropriation

Paul has already raised the issue of Jewish priority (1:16; 2:2, 10). In this paragraph he introduces the issue of Jewish privilege and obligation (2:17–20), a topic on which he touches in 3:1–2 and to which he returns in 9:4–5. In this context, Paul's focus is on the law and circumcision. Knowing and being instructed in the law is the starting point for the other advantages he mentions, and Dunn notes that "circumcision was not something other than law-keeping; on the contrary, it was the most fundamental act of the covenant and its law."[22] In other words, as an observant Jew, having a son circumcised or being circumcised as a proselyte was the most important law to keep. Paul returns to the benefit of circumcision in 3:1–2 and notes that circumcision brings

---

21. For the idea of a circumcised heart see Leviticus 26:41; Deuteronomy 10:16; 30:6; Jeremiah 4:4; 9:26.
22. Dunn, *Romans*, 126.

with it being entrusted with the oracles of God. So, in a sense, law and circumcision formed a symbiotic relationship. In 9:4–5, Paul expands the list of advantages considerably to include the adoption as sons, the glory of God's presence, the covenants, the temple service, the promises, the patriarchs, and the Messiah.

There can be no doubt that Paul himself took pride in being a Jew (Phil. 3:5–6), and his pre-conversion perspective aligns well with the perspective of Second Temple Judaism (e.g., 4 Ezra 6:55–59; 2 Bar. 48:22–24; Pss. Sol. 17:1). The advantages he lists are intended to be read positively as an acknowledgment of the blessings God has bestowed on Israel. He also recognizes the obligation those blessings placed on Israel. It might well be that this sense of Jewish obligation informs his own sense of obligation as an apostle (1:14–15; cf. 15:27; 1 Cor. 9:16). The problem lies neither with the advantages, which are good, nor with the obligations, which are also good. The problem lies with the Jews' failure to keep the law and to fulfill their observations. They had correct knowledge of their heritage (cf. Deut. 7:6–9), but they presumed on that heritage (cf. Mic. 3:11).[23] By doing what they knew they should not do, and by leaving undone what they knew they should do, the advantages and obligations of their heritage condemned them rather than securing their salvation.

Paul's primary purpose in including this paragraph at this point in his letter was to correct Jewish reliance on the law and circumcision as means of finding a sense of spiritual security and well-being. In 1:18–32, he had demonstrated the guilt of the Gentiles, and in 2:1–16, he had demonstrated the guilt of those individuals, both Jew and Gentile, who claim to have high moral standards. He now demonstrates the guilt of the Jews, who rely on their religious heritage. The paragraph leads naturally to his conclusion in 3:1–20 that the whole world is accountable to God (3:19). The need we share with Paul's original readers is to realize that religious heritage, privilege, and practice is inadequate for finding right standing before God. Possible points of connection are the notion of hypocrisy and the common admonition to "practice what you preach." Essentially, Paul leveled those charges against the Jews of his day in the same way that people often level them today against followers of Jesus Christ. The passage corrects the idea that religious heritage or privilege is adequate to secure an individual's spiritual well-being. It is not enough to be a "charter member" of a congregation, to be a deacon/elder, or to be a "third-generation Presbyterian/Baptist/

---

23. Dunn notes that "the same presumption of God's favor . . . had resulted in the exile" (ibid.).

Anglican." God looks at the heart rather than at church membership (cf. 1 Sam. 16:7). The passage commends an honest self-evaluation of inner spiritual motivation and orientation, as well as a similar evaluation of the degree to which our religious practices align with our religious beliefs. The primary objective in communicating this passage should be to help others understand that God looks beyond "religiosity" to evaluate the heart, so that they will honestly evaluate how well what they say they believe corresponds (or does not correspond) to the way they live.

ROMANS 3:1–8

Text and Translation

1 Therefore, what special advantage does the Jew[1] have? Or what special benefit does circumcision offer? **2** Much in every respect! For of chief importance,[2] they were entrusted[3] with the oracles from God.[4] **3** What difference does it make?[5] If *it is true that* [6] some were unfaithful, their faithlessness will not make God's faithfulness[7] ineffective, will it? **4** May it never be! But God must be true, although every person *is* a liar, just as it has been written,

> **"In order that you might be proved to be righteous by your words**[8] **and might overcome when you yourself judge."**[9]

5 But if *we adopt the premise that* [10] our unrighteousness provides evidence of[11] God's righteousness, what shall we say? God *who* inflicts[12] wrath is not unrighteous, is he?—I am speaking from a human perspective. **6** May it never be! Otherwise how will God judge the world? **7** Now[13] if *we believe that* [14] God's truth abounds to his glory by my lie,[15] why am I *of all people* still being judged as a sinner? **8** And *why are we* not *saying*—just as we are being maligned and just

---

1. Ἰουδαίου is a subjective genitive, as is τῆς περιτομῆς.
2. See Schreiner *Romans*, 148.
3. Ἐπιστεύθησαν is a divine passive.
4. Τοῦ θεοῦ is a subjective genitive; the article is monadic.
5. See BDF §299.3.
6. Εἰ ἠπίστησάν is a first-class condition.
7. Τοῦ θεοῦ is a subjective genitive.
8. Ἐν τοῖς λόγοις σου denotes means.
9. Ἐν τῷ κρίνεσθαι is adverbial of time.
10. Εἰ ... συνίστησιν is a first-class condition.
11. Συνίστησιν carries the nuance of providing evidence in support of a claim (BDAG 973a). Although the verb does not fit within the semantic range of "revelation," the idea of the protasis is not far from 1:18.
12. Ὁ ἐπιφέρων is an adjectival participle.
13. The parallel with verse 5 suggests that δέ should be preferred over γάρ. See Metzger, *Textual Commentary*, 448.
14. Εἰ ... ἐπερίσσευσεν is a first-class condition.
15. Ἐν τῷ ἐμῷ ψεύσματι denotes means.

as some are saying that we are saying—"Let us do evil in order that good might come"? Their[16] judgment is just![17]

Context and Structure

    II. Letter Body (1:18–15:13)
        A. The Gospel as the Revelation of God's Righteousness (1:18–4:25)
            1. The gospel reveals God's righteousness through wrath (1:18–3:20)
                a. Because humankind suppresses God's truth (1:18–23)
                b. Because the Gentiles practice unrighteousness (1:24–32)
                c. Because the moral person judges others (2:1–16)
                d. Because the Jews transgress the law (2:17–29)
                e. **Because God always acts righteously (3:1–8)**
                f. Because all are under sin (3:9–20)

Paul returns to the diatribe style, using four double questions (3:1, 3, 5, 7) to raise and refute possible accusations against his teaching.

Basic Message and Exegetical Outline

By answering possible objections, Paul demonstrates that the gospel he preaches upholds God's promise, faithfulness, justice, and truth.

    Four Questions about Paul's Teaching (3:1–8)
        1. Paul's teaching upholds God's promise to Israel (3:1–2)
            a. Question: What is the benefit of being Jewish? (3:1)
            b. Answer: Israel was entrusted with God's revelation. (3:2)
        2. Paul's teaching upholds God's faithfulness (3:3–4)
            a. Question: Is God's faithfulness negated? (3:3)
            b. Answer: God must be faithful. (3:4)

---

16. The phrase ὧν τὸ κρίμα ("whose judgment") refers back to τινες and is best understood as a variation on the more common construction τὸ κρίμα αὐτῶν ("their judgment").
17. Ἔνδικος, -ον describes something that is just or deserved (BDAG 332c).

3. Paul's teaching upholds God's justice (3:5–6)
   a. Question: Is God unjust when he inflicts wrath? (3:5)
   b. Answer: God will judge righteously. (3:6)
4. Paul's teaching upholds God's truth (3:7–8)
   a. Question: Does Paul's teaching promote doing evil? (3:7–8a)
   b. Answer: Those who suggest such things deserve condemnation. (3:8b)

Explanation of the Text

1. Paul's teaching upholds God's promise to Israel (3:1–2).

Having argued that possessing the law and circumcision does not protect the Jews from God's impartial judgment, Paul uses a pair of questions to raise the logical conclusion (οὖν): there would appear to be no special advantage to being a Jew (τί τὸ περσσὸν τοῦ Ἰουδαίου) and no special benefit to being circumcised (τίς ἡ ὠφέλεια τῆς περτομῆς). Paul emphatically rejects such a conclusion (πολὺ κατὰ πάντα τρόπον) with an answer the NEB translates as "Great in every way!" and highlights the great privilege of being a Jew. From a long list of possible privileges (cf. 9:4–5) Paul chooses the fact that God entrusted the Jews (ἐπιστεύθησαν) with his self-revelation in the Old Testament as the item of chief importance (πρῶτον μέν). Schreiner notes that the phrase "oracles of God" (τὰ λόγια τοῦ θεοῦ) extends beyond both the possession of the Scriptures and the stewardship that accompanies their possession to include "promises from God ensuring them of future salvation."[18] Paul's gospel, therefore, does not call into question God's promise to Israel; it upholds that promise.

2. Paul's teaching upholds God's faithfulness (3:3–4).

Two more questions raise a second potential objection—this one related to God's faithfulness.[19] Paul begins with the premise (εἰ) that at least some Jews have been unfaithful (ἠπίστησάν τινες). Their faithlessness (ἡ ἀπιστία αὐτῶν), however, does not nullify (μή . . . καταργήσει) God's faithfulness (τὴν πίστιν τοῦ θεοῦ). Paul responds to that suggestion with an emphatic rejection that becomes characteristic for the letter: May it never be (μὴ γένοιτο)![20] God's character, in fact, demands that he remain

---

18. Schreiner, *Romans*, 149.
19. Τί γάρ is best taken as a separate question: "What difference does it make?"
20. Other occurrences are 3:6, 31; 6:2, 15; 7:7, 13; 9:14; 11:1, 11.

true to his promises (γινέσθω ὁ θεὸς ἀληθής) even if every human being is untrustworthy (πᾶς ἄνθρωπος ψεύστης).[21] The Old Testament supports (καθὼς γέγραπται) Paul's assertion when David affirms (Ps. 51:4 LXX) that both God's pronouncements (ἐν τοῖς λόγοις σου) and his verdicts (ἐν τῷ κρίνεσθαί σε) are proved to be right (δικαιωθῇς). Paul's gospel, therefore, does not call into question God's faithfulness; it upholds that faithfulness.

3. Paul's teaching upholds God's justice (3:5–6).

What conclusion should Paul's readers draw (τί ἐροῦμεν) from his premise (εἰ) that human unrighteousness (ἡ ἀδικία ἡμῶν) allows God to provide evidence of his righteousness (θεοῦ δικαιοσύνην συνίστησιν)? Does that teaching somehow suggest that God is unrighteous (μὴ ἄδικος ὁ θεός) when he inflicts wrath on human beings (ὁ ἐπιφέρων τὴν ὀργήν) who do not meet the righteous requirement he has set?[22] Such a perspective is purely human (κατὰ ἄνθρωπον λέγω) and should be emphatically rejected (μὴ γένοιτο). The reason to reject such an idea (ἐπεί) is that God's righteousness is necessary for him to judge the world justly (κρινεῖ ὁ θεὸς τὸν κόσμον). Since Paul only alludes to final judgment rather than addressing it directly, it appears he believes it is a doctrine both he and his readers hold in common (2:5–6, 16; 13:11). Logically, therefore, they should agree that Paul's gospel does not call into question God's justice; it upholds that justice as seen in the final judgment.

4. Paul's teaching upholds God's truth (3:7–8).[23]

It is possible to draw a further false conclusion (δέ) from the idea that human faithlessness and unrighteousness (ἐν τῷ ἐμῷ ψεύσματι) magnify (ἐπερίσσευσεν) God's truth (ἡ ἀλήθεια τοῦ θεοῦ) and bring him glory (εἰς τὴν δόξαν αὐτοῦ). Following that premise (εἰ) to its logical

---

21. The idea of "liar" (ψεύστης) echoes "they exchanged the truth of God for a lie" (ἐν τῷ θεύδει) in 1:25.

22. Note the similar question in 9:14, where Paul's specific focus is Israel.

23. The primary exegetical difficulty in these verses is whether the first person ("my/I" and "we/us") refers to Paul himself (e.g., Longenecker, *Romans*, 350) or represents Paul's Jewish objector (e.g., Jewett, *Romans*, 249). In other words, is Paul saying others accuse him of propagating a lie and blasphemy, or is the objecting Jew adopting Paul's reference to a "lie" (3:4) and using it ironically? The former understanding seems to fit at least the parenthetical statement of verse 8 most naturally. The latter understanding would connect verse 7 with the first person question in verse 5 ("What shall we say?"). Cranfield's compromise solution is to view the two questions as raised by the objector and the parenthesis as Paul speaking about himself *(Romans*, 187).

conclusion could lead individuals to conclude that they should not be judged as "sinners" (τί ἔτι κἀγὼ ὡς ἁμαρτωλός κρίνομαι) and should, therefore, actually do evil (ποιήσωμεν τὰ κακά) in order that good might result (ἵνα ἔλθῃ τὰ ἀγαθά). Paul's parenthetical interjection suggests that such accusations have been leveled against him, and he dismisses both the false conclusion and those accusations brusquely: "Their judgment is just!" (ὧν τὸ κρίμα ἔνδικόν ἐστιν). Longenecker elaborates, "These are, Paul implies, simply libelous charges based on sophistic reasoning, which show that those who mount them know nothing regarding the nature of God, the message of the Christian gospel, or the character of those who are Christ's people."[24] Paul's gospel, therefore, does not call into question God's truth; it upholds that truth.

Theology and Appropriation

Paul's argument in this paragraph brings together three divine attributes: God's faithfulness (τὴν πίστιν τοῦ θεοῦ) in verse 3, God's righteousness (θεοῦ δικαιοσύνην) in verse 5, and God's truth (ἡ ἀλήθεια τοῦ θεοῦ) in verse 7. Faith (ἡ πίστις, -εως) occurs in Paul's thesis statement (1:16–17), and cognate words of that stem (πιστ-) are prominent.[25] Righteousness (ἡ δικαιοσύνη, -ης) also occurs in Paul's thesis statement, and cognate words of that stem (δικαι-) are the predominant word group in Romans (61 times).[26] Truth (ἡ ἀλήθεια, -ας) has been a key concept in chapters 1–2 (1:18, 25; 2:2, 8, 20), and elsewhere in Paul's letters it describes the content of the gospel (cf. Gal. 2:5; 5:7; 1 Tim. 2:4; 2 Tim. 3:7).

Each of these words describes both God's character and his conduct. Faithfulness describes God's dependability; because he is faithful, he acts reliably. Righteousness describes God's justness; because he is righteous, he acts equitably. Truth describes God's integrity; because he is true, he acts consistently. Paul's argument in 3:1–8 also suggests an interesting set of relationships involving these three attributes: God's faithfulness validates his truth (3:3–4); his righteousness undergirds his judgment (3:5–6); and his truth promotes his glory (3:7–8). By highlighting these attributes in answering questions about his teaching, Paul makes it clear that the gospel he preaches aligns perfectly with both God's character and his redemptive activity.

---

24. Longenecker, *Romans*, 351.
25. In other letters, the adjective (πιστός, -ή, -όν) carries the sense of "faithful" (cf. 1 Cor. 1:9; 10:13; 2 Cor. 1:18; 1 Thess. 5:24; 2 Thess. 3:3; 2 Tim. 2:13), and the translation "God's faithfulness" fits the context of 3:3.
26. For an analysis of the distribution, see Harvey, *Listening*, 125.

Paul's primary purpose in including this paragraph in his letter is to address possible charges that God has acted unjustly in visiting judgment on humankind for their sin. In fact, Paul argues, God always acts faithfully, justly, and truthfully in his dealings with sinful humankind, and the realization of that truth is the need we share with Paul's original readers. Possible points of connection include the contrasting values of truth and lie, the idea of raising objections to a given idea or argument, and the possibility of individuals or social systems acting unjustly. The passage corrects any suggestion that God is unjust or unfaithful. It also refutes the philosophies of antinomianism[27] and libertinism[28] as worthy of condemnation by rejecting the suggestion that we should do evil in order to promote good. It commends a stance of confidence in God's faithfulness, justice, and truth. The primary objective in communicating this passage should be to help others understand that God always acts faithfully and justly so that they will affirm an attitude of confidence and trust in God and his working.

---

27. Antinomianism is the teaching that God's grace frees us from any relationship to his law.
28. Libertinism is the teaching that we are free from any moral restraints.

ROMANS 3:9–20

Text and Translation

9 What then? Are we *Jews* having an advantage?[1] Not at all! For we ourselves charged[2] both Jews and Greeks all to be under the rule of sin.[3] **10** Just as it has been written that

> **There is not *one who is* righteous,**
>> **not even one.**
> **11 There is not one who is understanding;** [4]
>> **there is not one who is seeking God.**
>
> **12 All have turned aside;**
>> **together they have been made worthless.** [5]
> **There is not one who is doing good;[6]**
>> **there is not[7] even one.**
>
> **13 Their throat is an open[8] tomb;**
>> **they deceive with their tongues.[9]**
> **The poison of asps is under their lips;**
> **14   their[10] mouth is full of curses and bitterness.**
>
> **15 Their feet are swift to pour out[11] blood;**
> **16   destruction and misery are in their paths;**
> **17   and they have not known[12] the way of peace.**

---

1. Προεχόμεθα is a middle form with active meaning (Robertson, *Grammar*, 816).
2. Προῃτιασάμεθα is an indirect middle.
3. Ὑπό + accusative denotes subordination.
4. Ὁ συνίων and ὁ ἐκζητῶν are substantival participles.
5. Both ἐξέκλιναν and ἠχρειώθησαν are consummative aorists.
6. Ὁ ποιῶν is a substantival participle.
7. Although it is the longer reading, οὐκ ἔστιν is supported by most manuscripts (ℵ, A, D, 33) and could have been deleted (B) as superfluous.
8. Ἠγνεῳγμένος is an adjectival participle; the perfect tense is intensive.
9. Ταῖς γλώσσαις is an instrumental dative.
10. The ὧν τὸ στόμα ("whose mouth") is a stylistic variant on the more common τὸ στόμα αὐτῶν ("their mouth").
11. Ἐκχέαι is an infinitive of purpose.
12. Ἔγνωσαν is a consummative aorist.

18   There is no fear of God[13] before their eyes.

19 Now we know that as many things as the law is saying, it is speaking to those in the law, in order that every mouth might be shut and the entire world might be accountable to God; **20** because no flesh[14] will be declared righteous in his sight by[15] works of the law,[16] for through the law *is* the knowledge of sin.[17]

Context and Structure

  II. Letter Body (1:18–15:13)
   A. The Gospel as the Revelation of God's Righteousness (1:18–4:25)
      1. The gospel reveals God's righteousness through wrath (1:18–3:20)
        a. Because humankind suppresses God's truth (1:18–23)
        b. Because the Gentiles practice unrighteousness (1:24–32)
        c. Because the moral person judges others (2:1–16)
        d. Because the Jews transgress the law (2:17–29)
        e. Because God always acts righteously (3:1–8)
        f. **Because all are under sin (3:9–20)**

Paul uses a fifth pair of questions (3:9) to introduce the conclusion to the first major portion of his argument (1:18–3:20). A string of Old Testament proofs demonstrates the universality of sin (3:10–12), the extent of that sin as expressed in speech (3:13–14), and the extent of that sin as expressed in action (3:15–18). A disclosure formula introduces a summary of the law's role in God revealing his righteousness (3:19–20).

---

13. Θεοῦ is an objective genitive.
14. Οὐ . . . πᾶσα σάρξ is a Hebraism equivalent to οὐδείς (Robertson, *Grammar*, 752).
15. Ἐκ + genitive denotes means.
16. Νόμου is a subjective genitive; Schreiner suggests "works commanded by the law" (*Romans*, 177).
17. Ἁμαρτίας is an objective genitive.

Basic Message and Exegetical Outline

The Old Testament provides proof that both Jew and Greek are under sin, makes all people accountable before God, and brings the knowledge of sin.

    The Case against Humankind (3:9–20)
    1. Jews and Greeks are both under sin (3:9)
        a. Jews have no advantage (3:9a)
        b. Jews and Greeks are both under sin (3:9b)
    2. The Old Testament provides proof of guilt (3:10–18)
        a. No one is righteous (3:10–11)
        b. Everyone turns away from God (3:12)
        c. Everyone speaks corruptly (3:13–14)
        d. Everyone acts corruptly (3:15–17)
        e. No one fears God (3:18)
    3. The law makes accountable and brings the knowledge of sin (3:19–20)
        a. It makes all accountable before God (3:19)
        b. It brings the knowledge of sin (3:20)

Explanation of the Text

1. Jews and Greeks are both under sin (3:9).
    What conclusion (τί οὖν) should Paul's readers draw from his discussion of humankind's guilt? In particular, should the Jews think they are having an advantage (προεχόμεθα)?[18] Paul rejects that idea emphatically (οὐ πάντως) and explains (γάρ) that the proper conclusion to draw is that both Jews and Greeks ('Ιουδαίους τε καὶ ''Ελληνας) are all under the rule of sin (πάντας ὑφ' ἁμαρίαν εἶναι). The verb Paul uses (προητιασάμεθα) carries the idea of arriving at a guilty verdict; the prefix (προ-) suggests that Paul's readers should have reached that verdict for themselves by this point in the letter.

2. The Old Testament provides proof of guilt (3:10–18).
    To support his conclusion, Paul turns to the Old Testament (καθὼς γέγραπται). The primary source for his catena of quotations is the LXX

---

18. An alternate understanding of the verb's voice (i.e., as passive) changes the sense of the question to "Are we at a disadvantage?" (cf. Jewett, *Romans*, 257).

version of Psalm 13:2–3.[19] The quotations demonstrate five facts: (1) no one is righteous (3:10–11); (2) everyone turns away from God (3:12); (3) everyone speaks corruptly (3:13–14); (4) everyone acts corruptly (3:15–17); and (5) no one fears God (3:18). Humankind's total lack of righteousness (οὐκ ἔστιν δίκαιος) is demonstrated by their lack of spiritual understanding (οὐκ ἔστιν ὁ συνίων) and their failure to exert any effort to seek that understanding (οὐκ ἔστιν ὁ ἐκζητῶν τὸν θεόν). Their act of turning away from God (πάντες ἐξέκλιναν) has made them worthless (ἅμα ἠχρεώθησαν) and unable to deal uprightly with those around them (οὐκ ἔστιν ὁ ποιῶν χρηστότητα). Their speech is characterized by rottenness (τάφος ἀνεῳγμένος), deceit (ἐδολιοῦσαν), poison (ἰός), curses (ἀρᾶς), and bitterness (πικρίας). Their conduct is characterized by an eagerness to shed blood (ὀξεῖς οἱ πόδες αὐτῶν ἐκχέαι αἷμα), destruction (σύντριμμα), misery (ταλαιπωρία), and an utter ignorance of what it means to live peacefully with others (ὁδὸν εἰρηνης οὐκ ἔγνων). The root of this universal sinfulness in thought, word, and deed is humankind's total lack of reverence for God (οὐκ ἔστιν φόβος θεοῦ ἀπέναντι τῶν ὀφθαλμῶν αὐτῶν), which is precisely where Paul began his argument in 1:18–32.

3. The law makes accountable and brings the knowledge of sin (3:19–20).

Because both Jews and Gentiles are guilty before God, and because the Mosaic law expresses God's righteous requirements against which they are judged, Paul concludes this paragraph and the entire section (1:18–3:20) with a summary of the law's role in revealing God's righteousness. It should be a point of common agreement between Paul and his readers (οἴδαμεν ὅτι) that whatever the law says (ὅσα ὁ νόμος λέγει), it speaks specifically to those who possess and are instructed by it (τοῖς ἐν τῷ νόμῳ λαλεῖ). The law speaks with the purpose (ἵνα) of silencing objections (πᾶν στόμα φραγῇ) and placing the entire world under God's divine indictment (ὑπόδικος γένηται πᾶς ὁ κόσμος τῷ θεῷ). So, the role of the law is not to enable anyone to be declared righteous by keeping it (ἐξ ἔργων νόμου οὐ δικαιωθήσεται πᾶσα σάρξ); rather, the law is the means by which men and women come to recognize sin (διὰ νόμου ἐπίγνωσις ἁμαρτίας). Having established that everyone lives under God's righteous judgment and that no one can escape his judgment by keeping the law (1:18–3:20), Paul is ready to move to his explanation of how the gospel reveals God's righteousness apart from the law (3:21–4:25).

---

19. The first line is drawn from Sirach 7:20; the second and third lines are drawn from Psalm 13:2 (cf. Ps. 52:3–4); the remainder of the catena is from Psalm 13:3 (cf. Pss. 5:9; 10:7; 35:2; 139:4; Isa. 59:7–8.

Theology and Appropriation

Paul began his indictment of humankind in Romans 1 by writing that men and women refuse to give God the glory and thanksgiving he deserves (1:21), suppress his truth (1:18), exchange what they know about him for a lie (1:23, 25), and engage in corrupt worship (1:24–25), corrupt sex (1:26–27), and corrupt conduct (1:28–32). They are totally without excuse (1:20; 2:1). Along the way, he has demonstrated that Gentiles (1:18–32), individuals with high moral standards (2:1–16), and Jews (2:17–29) are all guilty, because they know God's righteous requirements as set out in the law (1:32; 2:26), but they fail to do those requirements (2:12–13). In Romans 3, Paul's argument comes full circle. Humankind's root sin is their refusal to give God the respect he deserves (3:18). They refuse to seek him (3:11), and they turn away from him (3:12). As a result, their speech is corrupt (3:13–14), and their conduct is corrupt (3:15–17). They are totally without excuse (3:19) and have no defense when facing judgment (3:19; cf. 1:18; 2:3, 5, 16). All humankind, therefore, is "under sin" (3:9). Not only do they deserve the penalty for their sin; they are also under sin's power. Every part of their being has been corrupted, and they exist in a state that theologians term "total depravity." It is this state of guilt and corruption that the gospel addresses.

Paul's primary purpose for including this paragraph was to provide Old Testament proof in support of his argument that all are guilty before God. If his readers have not been convinced by his argument to this point, the clear testimony of Scripture provides the deciding reason in support of his claim. The need we share with his original readers is the realization that all of us are without excuse or defense before God and are totally corrupt in every aspect of our being. One possible point of connection is the notion of corrupt speech and conduct, because many recognize that there are certain ways of speaking and acting that are not appropriate in certain situations. Another possible point of connection is the idea of seeking God, since many churches attempt to design their services to be "seeker friendly." The passage corrects any suggestion that human beings are somehow inherently good. Paul removes any doubt about humankind's total depravity when he writes, "There is none who does good; there is not even one." The passage commends the recognition of our own sinfulness and our need for God's deliverance. The primary objective in communicating this passage should be to help others understand that they are all guilty before God so that they will look to him for his help.

ROMANS 3:21–26

Text and Translation

21 But now apart from the law God's righteousness, *which is* being witnessed by the law and the prophets,[1] has been made evident, **22** that is,[2] God's righteousness *which is* by faith[3] in Jesus Christ[4] to all[5] the *ones who* are believing;[6] for there is no difference, **23** for all sin[7] and fall short of God's glory, **24** *and* are being declared righteous[8] freely[9] by his grace through the redemption *that is* in Christ Jesus; **25** whom God himself displayed[10] *as* a propitiation through faith[11] by his blood[12] for a demonstration of his righteousness[13] because of the passing over of previously committed[14] sins **26** because of[15] God's forbearance, for the demonstration[16] of his righteousness in the present time, in order for

---

1. The participial phrase μαρτυρουμένη ὑπὸ τοῦ νόμου καὶ τῶν προφητῶν is adjectival, modifying δικαιοσύνη θεοῦ, and has been brought forward accordingly. The present tense is progressive.
2. Δέ is explanatory.
3. Διά + genitive denotes means.
4. Ἰησοῦ Χριστοῦ is an objective genitive.
5. The variant εἰς πάντας ("to all") has stronger manuscript (𝔓40· ℵ*, A, B, C) support than ἐπί πάντας ("upon all"). See Metzger, *Textual Commentary*, 444. Εἰς + accusative denotes advantage.
6. Τοὺς πιστεύοντας is a substantival participle; the present tense is progressive. Wallace notes that the New Testament authors prefer the present tense with the participle of πιστεύω to denote continual belief (*Grammar*, 621, n.22).
7. Ἥμαρτον is a gnomic aorist and states a timeless truth.
8. The participle δικαιούμενοι is adjectival, further explaining πάντες in verse 23.
9. Δωρεάν (feminine accusative singular) functions as an adverb denoting manner.
10. Προέθετο is an indirect middle.
11. The manuscript evidence is divided between including (𝔓40, B, C3, D2, 33) or omitting (ℵ, C*, D*) the definite article with πίστεως. See Metzger for a discussion (*Textual Commentary*, 449).
12. The prepositional phrase ἐν τῷ αὐτοῦ αἵματι is instrumental.
13. Τῆς δικαιοσύνης is an objective genitive.
14. Τῶν προγεγονότων is an adjectival participle.
15. Ἐν + dative denotes cause.
16. Πρός + accusative denotes purpose.

him to be righteous in that[17] he is the *one who* declares righteous[18] the one *who is* of faith in Jesus.[19]

Context and Structure

  II. Letter Body (1:18–15:13)
      A. The Gospel as the Revelation of God's Righteousness (1:18–4:25)
          1. The gospel reveals God's righteousness through wrath (1:18–3:20)
          2. The gospel reveals God's righteousness apart from law (3:21–31)
             a. **Through faith in Christ (3:21–26)**
             b. Apart from works of law (3:27–31)

In Romans 3:21, Paul moves from a discussion of the negative aspects of God's revealed righteousness to an explanation of the positive aspect. He opens his argument with an extended three-part sentence in periodic style.[20] Although some scholars find a pre-Pauline formula in 3:24–26, it is just as likely that Paul composed the entire paragraph.[21]

Basic Message and Exegetical Outline

God's righteousness through faith is manifested apart from the law, is available without distinction to all who believe, and is displayed in Christ's propitiatory sacrifice that vindicates that righteousness.

    God's Righteousness through Faith (3:21–26)
      1. God's righteousness is manifested apart from the law (3:21–22b)
         a. By the law and the prophets (3:21b)
         b. Through faith in Christ (3:22a)
         c. To all who believe (3:22b)

---

17. The conjunction καὶ is explicative ("in that") rather than connective ("and").
18. Δικαιοῦντα is a substantival participle.
19. Ἐκ πίστεως denotes source; Ἰησοῦ is an objective genitive.
20. D. A. Campbell, *The Rhetoric of Righteousness in Romans 3:21–26* (Sheffield: Sheffield Academic Press, 1992), 81.
21. Jewett argues in favor of a pre-Pauline formula (*Romans*, 270–71); Schreiner is not persuaded by such arguments (*Romans*, 187–88).

2. God's righteousness is available to all without distinction (3:22c–24)
   a. Because all sin and lack God's glory (3:23)
   b. Because all must be declared righteous (3:24)
3. God's righteousness is displayed in Christ's propitiatory sacrifice (3:25–26)
   a. Through faith (3:25a)
   b. By Christ's blood (3:25b)
   c. To demonstrate God's righteousness (3:25c; 3:26b)
   d. For God to be just and justifier (3:26d)

Explanation of the Text

1. God's righteousness is manifested apart from the law (3:21–22b).

"But now" (νυνὶ δέ) establishes both an explicit contrast with what precedes and a contrast implicit in Paul's thought. The explicit contrast is that the law reveals sin (3:20), but God has made his righteousness evident apart from the Mosaic law (χωρὶς νόμου).[22] The implicit contrast is between "what was" in Adam and "what is" in Christ (cf. 6:22; 7:6). With Christ's death, resurrection, and ascension a new era has begun that introduces a new element into the equation. The manifestation of God's righteousness, however, is not new, because the perfect tense (πεφανέρωται) highlights completed action with continuing results. In fact, the law and prophets—the entire Old Testament—continue testifying to it. Paul repeats "God's righteousness" (δικαιοσύνη δὲ θεοῦ) to refocus his topic and develops it with two prepositional phrases. The means God uses to communicate his righteousness is through faith (διὰ πίστεως) that has Jesus Christ as its object.[23] That faith-based righteousness is credited to the advantage of all (εἰς πάντας) those who are believing (τοὺς πιστεύοντας).

---

22. Although νόμου is anarthrous, it is definite and refers to the Mosaic law (Robertson, *Grammar*, 796).
23. There is considerable scholarly discussion on whether πίστις Ἰησοῦ Χριστοῦ should be understood as a subjective genitive ("faithfulness of Jesus Christ") or an objective genitive ("faith in Jesus Christ"). Schreiner has a good discussion that includes the pertinent bibliography and decides in favor of the objective genitive (*Romans*, 181–86).

2. God's righteousness is available to all without distinction (3:22c–24).

The final clause of verse 22 is best taken with verses 23 and 24 as introducing the second part of the passage. The reason (γάρ) God's righteousness is credited to all who believe resides in divine impartiality: there is no distinction (οὐ . . . ἐστιν διαστολή).[24] This impartiality is explained (γάρ) by two factors. First, there is no distinction because all human beings stand under God's condemnation as Paul has pointed out in 1:18–3:20. Specifically, all people sin (πάντες ἥμαρτον). As a result, they all lack God's glory (ὑστεροῦνται τῆς δόξης τοῦ θεοῦ).[25] That glory was lost at Adam's fall and cannot be regained apart from final redemption at Christ's return.[26] Second, there is no distinction because all who are declared righteous (δικαιούμενοι) receive that status in the same way. It comes as a free gift (δωρεάν); it comes by means of God's grace (τῇ αὐτοῦ χάριτι); and it comes through redemption in Christ Jesus (διὰ τῆς ἀπολυτρώσεως τῆς ἐν Χριστῷ Ἰησοῦ).[27]

3. God's righteousness is displayed in Christ's propitiatory sacrifice (3:25–26).

An extended relative clause with Christ Jesus as its antecedent forms the third part of the passage. In it Paul describes how God can declare sinful human beings righteous without violating his own righteousness. "Display" (προέθετο) means to set forth publicly (cf. Gal. 3:1) and takes a double accusative.[28] The remainder of the clause consists of seven prepositional phrases and an infinitival phrase; the relationship among those elements is complex and must be understood accurately.

The first two prepositional phrases describe Christ's propitiatory sacrifice rather than the act of displaying it. Faith (διὰ τῆς πίστεως) describes the means by which his sacrifice is appropriated, and his blood (ἐν τῷ αὐτοῦ αἵματι) is the instrument by which God's wrath is satisfied. The third phrase modifies the main verb and explains that the purpose of displaying Christ as a sacrifice was to demonstrate

---

24. See 10:12–13 for a fuller statement of God's impartiality (cf. 2:11).
25. The conjunction καί adds the consequences of sin; the present tense of ὑστεροῦνται is gnomic; the middle voice calls attention to πάντες.
26. See Dunn, *Romans*, 168.
27. See below for a discussion of redemption.
28. The relative pronoun ὅν is the object, and the noun ἱλαστήριον is the complement. See below for a discussion of propitiation.

God's righteousness (εἰς ἔνδειξιν τῆς δικαιοσύνης αὐτοῦ).[29] The fourth phrase explains why God needed to demonstrate his righteousness: he had passed over sins committed prior to Christ's sacrifice (διὰ τὴν πάρεσιν τῶν προγεγονότων ἁμαρτημάτων). He did not forgive those sins, but he postponed imposing the full penalty for them. The fifth phrase establishes God's forbearance (ἐν τῇ ἀνοχῇ τοῦ θεοῦ) as his motivation for passing over those sins.

The sixth prepositional phrase parallels the third and reinforces God's purpose of demonstrating his righteousness (πρὸς τὴν ἔνδειξιν τῆς δικαιοσύνης αὐτοῦ).[30] The seventh phrase designates the time of that demonstration as the present age (ἐν τῷ νῦν καιρῷ) and echoes the opening words of the passage. The concluding infinitival phrase (εἰς τὸ εἶναι . . .) is adverbial to the main verb and establishes the ultimate purpose of God's actions. By displaying Christ as a propitiatory sacrifice, he upholds his righteous character (δίκαιον) in that he both punishes sin and declares righteous (δικαιοῦντα) the individual who places faith in Jesus (τὸν ἐκ πίστεως Ἰησοῦ).

Theology and Appropriation

At its core, Paul's theology emphasizes the transfer by grace through faith from what followers of Christ once were in Adam to what they now are in Christ.[31] Three important soteriological terms in this passage highlight that transfer: justification (3:24), redemption (3:24), and propitiation (3:25). *Justification* (δικαίωσις) occurs only twice in Paul's letters (Rom. 4:25; 5:18), although the cognate verb (δικαιόω) occurs twenty-seven times including Romans 3:24. Taken from a law court context, the noun carries the idea of being declared righteous by a judge. Justification, therefore, highlights the transfer to righteous status that results from Jesus taking on the guilt of our sin. *Redemption* (ἀπολύτρωσις) and its cognates occur nine times in Paul's letters (Rom. 3:24; 8:23; 1 Cor. 1:30; Gal. 4:5; Eph. 1:7, 14; 4:30; Col. 1:14; Titus 2:14). The noun carries the idea of release from a captive condition, and uses outside Paul's letters support the view that it involves the payment of

---

29. Ἔνδειξις denotes something that compels acceptance and can be translated as "demonstration" or "proof." In this context, δικαιοσύνη most naturally points to God's righteous character rather than to right standing before him (cf. Moo, *Romans*, 240).
30. Moo argues that the εἰς phrase points to God's past act of passing over sins and the πρός phrase points to his present act of declaring sinners righteous (*Romans*, 241).
31. Harvey, *Interpreting the Pauline Letters*, 79–88.

a ransom (Mark 10:45; 1 Peter 1:18; cf. Acts 20:28; 1 Peter 1:19; Rev. 5:9). Redemption, therefore, highlights the transfer to freedom that results from Jesus purchasing our release from the bondage of sin and death. *Propitiation* (ἱλαστήριον) and its cognates occur only five times in the New Testament (Rom. 3:25; Heb. 2:17; 9:15; 1 John 2:2; 4:10). Twenty-one of the twenty-seven LXX occurrences refer to the mercy seat as the place of sacrifice, set the word in a cultic context, and point to the idea of turning away wrath. Propitiation, therefore, highlights our transfer to being objects of God's favor that results from Jesus satisfying divine wrath by his sacrifice. Together these soteriological terms reinforce the totality of the change that occurs when individuals place their faith in Christ and, so, experience the revelation of God's righteousness available in the new era inaugurated by his life, death, resurrection, and ascension.

These terms also relate directly to Paul's primary purpose in the paragraph: to highlight the centrality of Jesus Christ in the revelation of God's righteousness. He reinforces that purpose by mentioning faith in Christ (twice), redemption in Christ, and Christ's propitiatory work. Christ is, therefore, both the source of our deliverance and the object of our faith. Our shared need with the original audience is to respond in faith to this revelation of God's righteousness in Christ. Faith (mentioned three times) is a natural point of connection because everyone exercises faith to some degree, although not always in the same object. The passage corrects several potential misconceptions, including the idea that law-keeping is somehow central to gaining God's favor ("apart from the law"), the idea that God's plan somehow changed between the Old and New Testaments ("witnessed by the law and the prophets"), and the idea that certain individuals are somehow better than others ("all sin and lack God's glory"). Positively, the passage commends the benefits that accrue to all those who place their faith in Christ: righteous status before God (justification), freedom from the bondage of sin and death (redemption), and favor in God's sight (propitiation). The objective in communicating this passage should be to help others understand how Jesus Christ reveals God's righteousness so that they respond in faith to him and experience the benefits he offers.

ROMANS 3:27–31

Text and Translation

27 Therefore, where *is* boasting? It is excluded.[1] Through what kind of law? *A law* of works? No, but through a law of faith. **28** For[2] we are considering a person to be declared righteous by faith apart from works of law. **29** Or *is* God *the God* of the Jews only? Not also of the Gentiles? Certainly also of the Gentiles. **30** After all,[3] God *is* one, who will declare righteous the circumcised person out of faith[4] and the uncircumcised person through the same[5] faith. **31** Therefore, are we *trying to* render[6] the law ineffective through faith? May it never be! Rather,[7] we are establishing the law.

Context and Structure

II. Letter Body (1:18–15:13)
   A. The Gospel as the Revelation of God's Righteousness (1:18–4:25)
      1. The gospel reveals God's righteousness through wrath (1:18–3:20)
      2. The gospel reveals God's righteousness apart from law (3:21–31)
         a. Through faith in Christ (3:21–26)
         b. **Apart from works of law (3:27–31)**

Paul returns to a question-and-answer (diatribe) style that allows him to raise and refute possible objections to his teaching (cf. 3:1–8). The resulting dialogical interchange allows Paul to draw three important

---

1. Ἐξεκλείσθη is a consummative aorist and a divine passive.
2. The variant γάρ has stronger manuscript support (ℵ, A, D*) than οὖν (B, C, D²); grammatical context also favors the reading (Metzger, *Textual Commentary*, 450).
3. Εἴπερ ("if after all") introduces the reason God is the God of both Jew and Gentile.
4. Both ἐκ πίστεως and διὰ τῆς πίστεως denote means; the difference in prepositions carries no fine distinction.
5. The definite article in διὰ τῆς πίστεως is anaphoric.
6. The present tense of καταργοῦμεν is conative.
7. The combination μή . . . ἀλλά establishes a strong contrast.

implications from his previous discussion of righteousness through faith apart from law (3:21–26).

Basic Message and Exegetical Outline

The fact that God bestows righteousness through faith apart from law shuts the door on human boasting, establishes him as the God of both Jew and Gentile, and validates the role of the Old Testament law.

The Implications of Righteousness through Faith (3:27–31)
1. Righteousness by faith shuts the door on human boasting (3:27–28)
   a. Through the principle of faith (3:27)
   b. Because it rests on faith apart from works of law (3:28)
2. Righteousness by faith establishes God as the God of both Jew and Gentile (3:29–30)
   a. He is also the God of the Gentiles (3:29)
   b. Because he justifies both by faith (3:30)
3. Righteousness by faith validates the role of the Old Testament law (3:31)

Explanation of the Text

1. Righteousness by faith shuts the door on human boasting (3:27–28).
The first implication (οὖν) Paul draws from the truth that righteousness is revealed apart from the law relates to "boasting" (ἡ καύχησις).[8] Paul declares emphatically (οὐχί) that God shuts the door (ἐξεκλείσθη)[9] on any boasting that has its basis anywhere other than in him.[10] The means (διά) through which boasting is excluded is faith, not works, because (γάρ) a proper understanding of the gospel leads to the settled

---

8. In his letters, Paul uses the verb (καυχάομαι) and its cognates thirty times, the noun that describes the cause of boasting (καύχημα) ten times, and the noun that describes the act of boasting (καύχησις) ten times. In Romans the idea most commonly has a negative connotation (1:30; 2:17, 23; 3:27; 4:2; 11:8), although it can also have a positive connotation (5:2, 11; 15:17; cf. 2 Cor. 1:14; Phil. 1:26; 1 Thess. 2:19).
9. The passive voice is a divine passive; Jewett suggests "to shut the door in one's face" (*Romans*, 296).
10. Elsewhere, Paul states clearly that the proper basis for boasting is God and what he has done (1 Cor. 1:31; 2 Cor. 10:17; both times quoting Jer. 9:24).

conclusion (λογιζόμεθα) that a person (ἄνθρωπον) is declared righteous (δικαιοῦσθαι) by faith (πίστει) and apart from works of law (χωρὶς ἔργθν νόμου). Paul's use of the phrases "a law of works" and "a law of faith" have generated considerable discussion. Although "principle" is a possible understanding, the more natural understanding in this context is that "law" refers to the Mosaic law.[11] Paul is suggesting, then, that it is possible to view the law from two perspectives.[12] The "law-of-works" perspective (νόμου τῶν ἔργων) focuses on accomplishments that humans pursue (2:17–20; cf. Phil. 3:5–6). The "law-of-faith" perspective (νόμου πίστεως) focuses on a requirement that God fulfills in Christ (3:21–26; cf. 8:3–4). The former perspective enhances boasting; the latter perspective excludes it.

2. Righteousness by faith establishes God as the God of both Jew and Gentile (3:29–30).

A second implication (ἤ) relates to the scope of God's justifying work. Paul follows his double rhetorical question about whether God is the God of both Jews and Gentiles with an answer that leaves no room for doubt: "Certainly also of the Gentiles" (ναὶ καὶ ἐθνῶν). In stating the reason God is the God of both Jew and Gentile (εἷς ὁ θεός), Paul echoes the Shema of Deuteronomy 6:4: "Hear, O Israel, the Lord is our God, the Lord is one" (Ἄκουε, Ἰσραηλ· κύριος ὁ θεὸς ὑμῶν κύριος εἷς ἐστιν). Since he is the one God of both Jew and Gentile, he has a single plan to declare both righteous (δικαιώσει); he will declare the circumcised Jew (περιτομήν) righteous out of faith (ἐκ πίστεως), and he will declare the uncircumcised Gentile (ἀκορβυστίαν) righteous through the same faith (διὰ τῆς πίστεως). The same God uses the same means to declare everyone righteous: faith.

3. Righteousness by faith validates the role of the Old Testament law (3:31).

The third implication (οὖν) Paul raises relates to the role of the Mosaic law. Should Paul's readers conclude that his teaching about faith as the means God uses (διὰ τῆς πίστεως) somehow abolishes the law or renders the law ineffective (νόμον καταργοῦμεν)? Paul's response to that suggestion is emphatic: "May it never be!" (μὴ γένοιτο). In fact, his teaching validates the law and its role in God's plan (νόμον

---

11. Longenecker (*Romans*, 445) and Moo (*Romans*, 249) argue for "principle." Cranfield (*Romans*, 220), Dunn (*Romans*, 186), and Schreiner (*Romans*, 202) argue for the Mosaic law.
12. See Jewett, *Romans*, 297.

ἱστάνομεν). Scholars disagree, however, on the way in which Paul's gospel, "establishes" the Mosaic law. Moo summarizes the three main suggestions as testifying (i.e., the gospel validates the law's role in testifying to the centrality of faith in God's plan), convicting (i.e., the gospel validates the law's role in condemning sinners and preparing the way for Christ), and commanding (i.e., the gospel validates the law's role in commanding righteousness that Christ provides).[13] Advocates of each understanding tend to argue from an either/or standpoint. It seems more natural to consider all of what Paul has written since at least 3:19. Using that approach, Paul's teaching validates the role of the law in at least three ways: (1) as God's revelation that brings the knowledge of sin (3:19–20), (2) as God's requirement that he fulfills in Christ (3:21–26), and (3) as part of God's plan to exclude boasting and justify both Jew and Gentile by faith (3:27–30).

Theology and Appropriation

Paul first mentioned the combination "Jew and Greek" in his thesis statement (1:16–17). He then used the same combination in discussing divine impartiality (2:9–10). In this paragraph he varies his wording to "circumcision and uncircumcision" (3:30), but the referents are the same. Longenecker correctly adds this passage to those that highlight Paul's "universalistic emphasis" (1:16–17; 3:21–23, 29–30).[14] Paul's statement in verse 30, however, goes further in saying that the one true God has one plan. There are not, and never have been, two ways of salvation, because God "will declare righteous the circumcised person out of faith and the uncircumcised person through the same faith."

It is possible to trace that one plan through the first three chapters of the letter. All human beings have a knowledge of God's existence (1:18–23) and his moral standard (2:12–16). All will be judged according to their works (2:6–11). All are responsible to live up to the light they have (2:17–24) and will be evaluated on their inner reality rather than on their outer appearance (2:25–29). All are under the rule of sin (3:9), have a knowledge of sin (3:20), and have committed actual sins (3:23). As a result, all are accountable before God (3:19) and fall short of his glory (3:23). For that reason, all are declared righteous freely on the basis of God's grace (3:24) by means of faith apart from works of law (3:28, 30). Israel's "one God," therefore, is also the God of the Gentiles (3:29), who extends mercy to Jew and Gentile alike (9:23–29; 11:32) and incorporates the Gentiles into his people (15:8–12). So, the one plan of the one

---

13. Moo, *Romans*, 253.
14. Longenecker, *Romans*, 465.

God creates one people in which ethnicity, social status, and gender are not factors (Gal. 3:23–29; cf. 1 Cor. 12:13; Eph. 2:13–18; Col. 3:11).

Paul's purpose in including this paragraph at this point in his letter was to draw out further implications of his gospel in which a person is declared righteous by faith and apart from the law. We share with his original audience the need to understand how the gospel affects the way we think about our supposed accomplishments, God's plan, and the law's role in that plan. Possible points of connection include the concepts of boasting and the law. The idea of one God might also connect with some who like to think that "all roads lead to the same God," although that idea is theologically incorrect. The passage corrects the idea that our works and/or our accomplishments somehow give us special status before God. It also corrects the idea that there are two ways of salvation, whether Old Testament versus New Testament, law versus grace, or Israel versus the church. Finally, the passage corrects the idea that the Old Testament law no longer has a role to play in God's plan for his people. The passage commends faith as the means God has established for relating to him. The phrase "through faith" occurs three times (3:22, 25, 31) as do "by faith" (3:28) and "out of faith" (3:30). This fivefold repetition of faith makes it the central idea in the passage. The primary objective in communicating this passage should be to help others understand that God has always had one plan for all people across all time, so that they will respond to his working in humble faith, realizing that they have no ground for pride or boasting.

ROMANS 4:1–12

Text and Translation

1 Therefore, what shall we say Abraham, our forefather according to the flesh, has found?[1] **2** For if *it is true that*[2] Abraham was declared righteous by works,[3] he has grounds for boasting, but not toward God. **3** For what does the Scripture say? **"And Abraham believed God,[4] and it was counted[5] to him for righteousness."** **4** Now to *the one who* is working,[6] the reward is not counted according to grace but according to debt, **5** but to *the one who* is not working but is believing upon the one who is declaring righteous the ungodly, that person's[7] faith is counted for righteousness; **6** just as David also speaks of the blessedness of the person[8] to whom God is counting righteousness apart from works,

> **7** **Blessed is that person whose[9] lawless deeds are pardoned[10]**
> **and whose sins are covered;**
> **8** **blessed is the person whose sins the Lord never counts.[11]**

9 Therefore, *is* this blessing *bestowed* upon the circumcised person or also[12] upon the uncircumcised person? For we are saying, **"Faith was counted to Abraham for righteousness."** **10** Therefore, how was it counted? While he was[13] in *the state of* circumcision,[14] or *in the state of* uncircumcision? Not in *the state of* circumcision, but in *the state of*

---

1. Προπάτορα is preferred as more difficult and has stronger manuscript support. The omission of εὑρηκέναι in B appears to be an isolated variant.
2. Εἰ . . . ἐδικαιώθη is a first-class condition.
3. Ἐξ ἔργων denotes impersonal means.
4. Τῷ θεῷ is a dative of indirect object.
5. Ἐλογίσθη is a divine passive.
6. In verses 4–5, ἐργαζομέμῳ (twice), πιστεύοντι, and δικαιοῦντα are substantival participles.
7. The antecedent of αὐτοῦ is the person described in the first half of the verse.
8. Τοῦ ἀνθρώπου is an objective genitive.
9. The relative pronoun ὧν includes an embedded demonstrative pronoun (οὗτοι).
10. Ἀφέθησαν and ἐπεκαλύφθησαν are both divine passives.
11. Οὐ μὴ λογίσηται is emphatic negation.
12. Καί is adjunctive.
13. Ὄντι is an adverbial participle of time.
14. Ἐν + dative denotes state (four times); also in verse 12.

uncircumcision; **11** for[15] he received *the* sign that is circumcision,[16] a seal that confirmed his righteousness[17] that came from the faith[18] that[19] *was his while he was* in uncircumcision, in order for him to be the father of all *those who are* believing[20] through uncircumcision—so that[21] the same[22] righteousness is counted to them[23]—**12** and the father of circumcision not only *with reference* to those who are out of circumcision[24] but also with reference to those who are walking in the footsteps of the faith[25] our father Abraham had *while he was* in *the state of* uncircumcision.

Context and Structure

    II. Letter Body (1:18–15:13)
        A. The Gospel as the Revelation of God's Righteousness (1:18–4:25)
            1. The gospel reveals God's righteousness through wrath (1:18–3:20)
            2. The gospel reveals God's righteousness apart from law (3:21–31)
            3. The gospel reveals God's righteousness in response to faith (4:1–25)
                a. **Apart from works or circumcision (4:1–12)**
                b. Apart from law (4:13–25)

Paul uses a rhetorical question to introduce the experience of Abraham, who serves to support Paul's claim that God declares a

---

15. Καί is explanatory.
16. Περιτομῆς is a genitive of apposition.
17. Τῆς δικαιοσύνης is an objective genitive; the definite article functions as a possessive pronoun.
18. Πίστεως is a subjective genitive.
19. The definite article functions as a relative pronoun.
20. Τῶν πιστευόντων is a substantival participle; the present tense denotes continuing belief (cf. Wallace, *Grammar*, 621n22).
21. Εἰς τὸ εἶναι is adverbial of result (cf. Cranfield, *Romans*, 237).
22. The definite article is anaphoric.
23. Although the inclusion in some manuscripts (א², C, D) of an ascensive καί after λογισθῆναι highlights the inclusion of the Gentiles, it is omitted in א*, A, B, and is probably a later addition. (See Schreiner, *Romans*, 232.)
24. The dative constructions τοῖς ἐκ περιτομῆς and τοῖς στοιχοῦσιν denote reference; στοιχοῦσιν is a substantival participle.
25. Πίστεως is a descriptive genitive.

person righteous solely on the basis of faith (4:1–3). To that claim he adds evidence that neither works (4:4–8) nor circumcision (4:9–12) play a role in God's action.

Basic Message and Exegetical Outline

Abraham was declared righteous because he believed God, apart from works or circumcision.

Lessons from Abraham's Experience, Part 1 (4:1–12)
1. Abraham was declared righteous because he believed God (4:1–3)
2. Abraham was declared righteous apart from works (4:4–8)
   a. The one who works is owed a reward (4:4)
   b. The one who believes is credited with righteousness (4:5)
   c. The one whom God declares righteous apart from works is blessed (4:6–8)
3. Abraham was declared righteous apart from circumcision (4:9–12)
   a. He was declared righteous when he was circumcised (4:9–10)
   b. He received circumcision as a seal of his righteousness by faith (4:11–12)

Explanation of the Text

1. Abraham was declared righteous because he believed God (4:1–3).

Paul uses a rhetorical question to introduce Abraham as a case study and draw his readers into his argument (τί οὖν ἐροῦμεν). It is natural to explore what Abraham discovered (εὑρηκέναι Ἀβραάμ) in connection with the topic under discussion, since Jews considered him the founder of their ethnic and national line (τὸν προπάτορα ἡμῶν κατὰ σάρκα). In particular, Abraham's experience helps explain (γάρ) the issues of works and boasting Paul has raised earlier (cf. 3:27–28). If the suggestion that Abraham was declared righteous on the basis of his works is true (εἰ Ἀβραὰμ ἐξ ἔργων ἐδικαιώθη), he has a reason to boast (ἔχει καύχημα). The problem, however, is that his boasting would be worthless before God (ἀλλ᾽ οὐ πρὸς θεόν), because (γάρ) his reasoning would run counter to the witness of Genesis 15:6 (τί ἡ γραφὴ λέγει). That verse clearly records God's act of crediting righteousness to

Abraham's account (ἐλογίσθη αὐτῷ εἰς δικαιοσύνην), because he believed God (ἐπίστευσεν Ἀβραὰμ τῷ θεῷ). Abraham's belief was the reason God declared him righteous.

2. Abraham was declared righteous apart from works (4:4–8).

Paul uses antithetical parallelism to structure the implications he draws from Genesis 15:6. His basic point may be summarized as:

| To the one who is working | reward | is counted | according to debt |
| To the one who is believing | faith | is counted | for righteousness |

The person who works (τῷ ἐργαζομένῳ) is credited (λογίζεται) with a reward (ὁ μισθός). That reward, however, is given according to the wrong standard—obligation (κατὰ ὀφείλυμα). The correct standard is God's grace (κατὰ χάριν). In contrast (δέ), the person who chooses to believe (πιστεύοντι) rather than work (τῷ μὴ ἐργαζομέμῳ) is credited (λογίζεται) with righteousness (εἰς δικαιοσύνην). That person's faith (ἡ πίστις αὐτοῦ) has as its object the one who declares righteous those who have violated the norms of a proper relationship with God (ἐπὶ τὸν δικαιοῦντα τὸν ἀσεβῆ).[26] Believing, therefore, is the antithesis of working, and a person is declared righteous on the basis of faith, not works. Paul supports this conclusion with a second Old Testament quotation (καθάπερ Δαυὶδ λέγει).

Paul connects Psalm 32:1–2 with Genesis 15:6 because both use the key word "count/credit" (λογίζομαι). He equates God's "counting" righteousness to an individual (Gen. 15:6) with his "not counting" sin against an individual (Ps. 32:2). The person David describes is—like Abraham—the person to whom (ᾧ) God counts righteousness (ὁ θεὸς λογίζεται διακιοσύνην) apart from works (χωρὶς ἔργων). That person experiences God's blessing (τὸν μακαρισμὸν τοῦ ἀνθρώπου), because God graciously pardons his/her lawless deeds (ὧν ἀφέθησαν αἱ ἀνομίαι) and covers his/her sins (ὧν ἐπεκαλύφθησαν αἱ ἁμαρτίαι). That person is blessed (μακάριος ἀνήρ) because the Lord never counts sin against him/her (οὐ μὴ λογίσηται κύριος ἁμαρτίαν). God's declaration of righteousness, therefore, is the result of his forgiving sins, not of a person's performing certain works. The righteousness so given meets the correct standard—the standard of grace (4:4).

---

26. Although Christ is more frequently the object of faith in Paul's letters (Harris, *Prepositions*, 237), here Paul notes that God is the object of Abraham's faith in line with Genesis 15:6. He uses the adjective "ungodly" (ἀσεβής, -ές) again in 5:6 to describe those for whom Christ died.

3. Abraham was declared righteous apart from circumcision (4:9–12).

Having explained the nature of the blessing that comes from being declared righteous apart from works (4:6), Paul uses another rhetorical question to draw the further implication (οὖν) of how this blessing (ὁ μακαρισμὸς οὗτος) relates to circumcision (cf. 3:29–30). Does it apply only to those who are circumcised (ἐπὶ τὴν περιτομήν), or also to those who are uncircumcised (ἢ καὶ ἐπὶ τὴν ἀκροβυστίαν)? Genesis 15:6 is, again, the reason (γάρ) behind Paul's question. That verse states clearly that Abraham's faith was counted for righteousness. The next logical question to ask is when that faith was so counted (πῶς οὖν ἐλογίσθη)—before or after Abraham was circumcised (ἐν περιτομῇ ὄντι ἢ ἐν ἀκροβυστίᾳ)? The Genesis record is unambiguous: his faith was counted as righteousness while he was uncircumcised (οὐκ ἐν περιτομῇ ἀλλ᾽ ἐν ἀκροβυστίᾳ). It is clear, therefore, that circumcision was not the basis for God declaring Abraham righteous.

Circumcision was, in fact, a sign Abraham received (σημεῖον ἔλαβεν περιτομῆς) that confirmed his righteousness (σφραγῖδα τῆς δικαιοσύνης). That righteousness, however, came from the faith (τῆς πίστεως) Abraham demonstrated while he was uncircumcised (τῆς ἐν τῇ ἀκροβυστίᾳ). God's purpose in circumcising Abraham was that he would be (εἰς τὸ εἶναι αὐτον) "the point of union between all who believe, whether circumcised or uncircumcised,"[27] with the result that the same righteousness could be counted to them (εἰς τὸ λογισθῆναι αὐτοις τὴν δικαιοσύνην). Verse 11 applies Paul's teaching to the Gentiles (πάντων τῶν πιστευόντων δι᾽ ἀκροβυστίᾳ); then, verse 12 applies it to the Jews.[28] It is not enough simply to be circumcised (τοῖς οὐκ ἐκ περιτομῆς μόνον); there must also be an inward response of faith (cf. 2:28–29). Those who are circumcised must also walk in conformance with the footsteps (τοῖς στοιχοῦσιν τοῖς ἴχνεσιν) of the faith that characterized Abraham while he was uncircumcised (τῆς ἐν ἀκροβυστίᾳ πίστεως). It is faith in action—not circumcision—that makes Abraham the father of both believing Jew and believing Gentile (τοῦ πατρὸς ἡμῶν Ἀβραάμ).

Theology and Appropriation

Abraham's prominence in Jewish history leads three New Testament writers to include him in their letters as an example: Paul,

---

27. Cranfield, *Romans,* 236.
28. See Schreiner for a nuanced discussion of the grammatical issues in verse 12 (*Romans*, 226).

James, and the author of Hebrews.[29] Traditional Jewish thinking regarding Abraham included at least six elements: (1) he was their father (Isa. 51:2); (2) his descendants would inherit the earth (Sir. 44:21); (3) he was perfect in his works (Jub. 23:10); (4) he performed the entire law before it was given to Moses (Jub. 24:11; 2 Bar. 57.2; Sir. 44:20); (5) his faithfulness in temptation was imputed to him for righteousness (1 Macc. 2:52); (6) his faith was connected with his circumcision. The New Testament authors affirm the first two elements, but Paul in particular takes issue with the other four.

Paul uses Abraham as an example four times in his letters, twice in Romans and twice in Galatians. In Romans 4:1–22, Paul's focus is on righteousness by faith: God declared Abraham righteous apart from works (4:1–8), Abraham received the blessing of forgiveness apart from circumcision (4:9–12), and he received the promise that he would be the heir of the world apart from law (4:13–22). Each of these arguments serves to highlight the fact that God declares a person righteous solely on the basis of faith. In Romans 9:6–9, Paul uses Abraham's sons, Ishmael and Isaac, to reinforce a point he has made earlier in the letter: simply being a descendant of Abraham does not guarantee a person status among the children of promise (cf. 2:25–29; 3:29–30). In Galatians 3:6–29, Paul's focus is again on righteousness by faith: God declared Abraham righteous on the basis of his own promise and Abraham's faith (3:6–10), Abraham's righteousness by faith preceded the Mosaic law by 430 years (3:15–18), and his offspring include Jew, Greek, slave, free, male, and female (3:26–29). In Galatians 4:21–31, Paul's allegory provides the basis for rejecting any teaching that would add anything to faith as the basis for God declaring a person righteous.

James uses Abraham's offering of Isaac as proof that his faith was "perfected" by his works (James 2:21–24). The author of Hebrews highlights Abraham's faithful obedience in connection with four promises from God: that God would give Abraham many descendants (6:13–15), that God would give him a land as an inheritance (11:8–10), that God would give Sarah the ability to conceive Isaac (11:11–12), and that Abraham would receive Isaac back from the dead if he followed God's instruction to offer Isaac (11:17–19). These latter two writers focus on the expression of Abraham's faith, while Paul focuses on Abraham's faith as a basis for being declared righteous. The two emphases are complementary, not contradictory. Both Abraham's initial response of

---

29. For an extended treatment, see R. N. Longenecker, "The 'Faith of Abraham' Theme in Paul, James and Hebrews: A Study in the Circumstantial Nature of New Testament Teaching," *JETS* 20 (1977): 203–12.

faith and his continuing obedience of faith are essential to living the Christian life.

Paul's primary purpose for including this paragraph, as well as the following paragraph, in his letter was to present Abraham as a case study illustrating that a person is declared righteous on the basis of faith, not of works, circumcision, or law. In this paragraph, he addresses the first two issues and seeks to correct the traditional Jewish understanding of Abraham by demonstrating that he was an example of faith rather than of works. With Paul's Roman readers we need to understand the single criterion God uses for declaring a person righteous so that we can discard reliance on any additional criteria others might suggest. Possible points of connection include tracing a family tree to identify important ancestors; the ideas of obligation, debt, and reward; and the practice of something being credited to a person's account. The passage highlights the futility of trying to work ourselves into God's favor and, so, corrects any teaching that suggests a person must meet any prerequisites other than faith in order to have a relationship with God. The passage commends Abraham's example as one we should follow. The primary objective in communicating this passage should be to help others understand that faith, not works (including any specific religious "work"), is the means of being declared righteous before God, so that they will follow Abraham's example of faith.

ROMANS 4:13–25

Text and Translation

13 For the promise to Abraham or to his seed that he was to be the heir of the world[1] *was* not through law[2] but through righteousness that comes from faith.[3] **14** For if *it is true that* those *who are* out of law *are* heirs,[4] his[5] faith has been caused to be without effect, and the promise has been rendered ineffective; **15** for the law brings about wrath; but[6] where there is no law, neither *is there* transgression. **16** For this reason, *the promise* is because of[7] faith, in order that *it might be* according to grace, in order for the promise to be[8] guaranteed to all his[9] seed, not only to *the one who is* out[10] of the law but also to *the one who is* out of the faith of Abraham,[11] who is the father of us all, **17** just as it has been written that **"I have made you the father of many nations,"** in the face of which *promise* he believed the God who gives life[12] to the dead and calls the *things that* are not as *things that* are;[13] **18** who[14] against hope in hope[15] believed in order so that he became[16] the father of many nations according to that which has been written,[17] **"So will your**

---

1. Κόσμου is an objective genitive. An alternate translation is, "He would inherit the world."
2. "Through law" (διὰ νόμου) stands first in the Greek text for emphasis. It is moved later in this translation to conform to more natural English syntax.
3. Πίστεως is a subjective genitive.
4. Εἰ introduces a first-class condition.
5. The article with πίστις functions as a possessive pronoun and refers to Abraham.
6. The manuscript support for δέ (ℵ*, A, B, C) rather than γάρ is strong.
7. Ἐκ + genitive denotes cause.
8. Εἰς τό + infinitive denotes purpose.
9. The definite article functions as a possessive pronoun.
10. Ἐκ + genitive denotes source (twice).
11. Although Ἀβραάμ is indeclinable, it is a subjective genitive ("the faith Abram demonstrated").
12. Τοῦ ζῳοποιοῦντος . . . καὶ καλοῦντος are both substantival participles; the construction is an example of the Granville Sharp rule.
13. Both occurrences of the participle ὄντα are substantival.
14. The antecedent of ὅς is Abraham.
15. A literal translation would be "beside hope upon hope." NASB translates as "in hope against hope."
16. Εἰς τό + infinitive denotes result.
17. Εἰρομένον is a substantival participle.

seed be," **19** and because he was not weak with reference to faith,[18] he considered[19] his own body as already[20] having been put to death,[21] because it was[22] about one hundred *years old*, and Sarah's dead womb;[23] **20** and did not doubt with reference to the promise God made because of unbelief[24] but was strengthened[25] in his[26] faith, giving[27] glory to God **21** and being fully persuaded that *the one* who[28] promised is able also[29] to do *it*. **22** Therefore, indeed,[30] **"It was counted to him for righteousness."**

23 Now it was not written because of[31] him only that it was counted to him, **24** but also because of us to whom it is being counted,[32] to *those who* are believing[33] in the *one who* raised[34] Jesus our Lord from the dead.

---

18. Ἀσθενήσας is an adverbial participle of cause; τῇ πίστει is a dative of reference.
19. Western and Byzantine manuscripts (D, G, K, P, Ψ) include the negative particle οὐ before κατενόησεν; Alexandrian manuscripts (ℵ, A, B, C) omit it. Omitting the particle is the more difficult reading, and Paul's intent seems to be to highlight Abraham's active consideration of the situation.
20. Although omitting ἤδη is the shorter reading, the manuscript evidence (ℵ, A, C, 33) supports its inclusion.
21. Τὸ ἑαυτοῦ σῶμα (object) . . . νενεκρωμένον (complement) is a double accusative construction.
22. Ὑπάρχων is an adverbial participle of cause.
23. Τῆς μήτρας is an attributed genitive.
24. Εἰς + accusative denotes reference; Θεοῦ is a subjective genitive; ἀπιστία is a dative of cause.
25. Ἐνδυναμώθη is a divine passive.
26. The definite article functions as a possessive pronoun.
27. The participles δούς and πληροφορηθείς are adverbial of manner.
28. The relative pronoun includes an embedded demonstrative.
29. Καί is adjunctive.
30. Καί is emphatic. The manuscript evidence for its inclusion (ℵ, A, C, D¹) or omission (B, D*) is evenly balanced.
31. Διά + accusative denotes cause, also in the second half of the statement.
32. Although the combination μέλλει λογίζεσθαι points to the future lexically ("is about to be counted"), the action refers to those who exercise faith subsequent to Abraham (cf. Jewett, *Romans*, 341).
33. Τοῖς πιστεύουσιν is a substantival participle standing in apposition to the relative pronoun οἷς.
34. Ἐπί + accusative denotes the one to whom faith is directed; ἐγείραντα is a substantival participle.

25 Who was handed over because of[35] our wrongdoings,
and was raised because of our justification.[36]

Context and Structure

II. Letter Body (1:18–15:13)
  A. The Gospel as the Revelation of God's Righteousness
    (1:18–4:25)
    1. The gospel reveals God's righteousness through wrath
      (1:18–3:20)
    2. The gospel reveals God's righteousness apart from law
      (3:21–31)
    3. The gospel reveals God's righteousness in response to
      faith (4:1–25)
      a. Apart from works or circumcision (4:1–12)
      b. **Apart from law (4:13–25)**

The theme of "promise" unites a brief rejection of the law (4:13–15) and a longer affirmation of faith (4:16–22). A short concluding paragraph highlights the importance of Abraham's experience for the readers (4:23–25).

Basic Message and Exegetical Outline

Abraham's response of faith to God's promise serves as an example for his spiritual descendants, who believe in the God who is able to do what he promises.

Lessons from Abraham's Experience, Part 2 (4:13–25)
  1. The promise was not given to Abraham on the basis of
    the law (4:13–15)
    a. The law would nullify the promise (4:14)
    b. The law provokes wrath and reveals sin (4:15)
  2. The promise was given to Abraham on the basis of
    faith (4:16–22)
    a. To guarantee the promise to his spiritual descendants (4:16)
    b. Because of his response to God's promise (4:17–21)

---

35. Διά + accusative in both lines denotes cause (cf. Harris, *Prepositions*, 81–82).
36. A paraphrase is, "Who was handed over because we sinned against God and was raised because God declared us righteous" (Harvey, *Romans*, 122).

      i. He believed the God who does the impossible (4:17)

      ii. He believed God's promise (4:18)

      iii. He considered the obstacles (4:19)

      iv. He rejected unbelief and doubt (4:20–21)

    c. So that his faith was counted for righteousness (4:22)

  3. The promise was given to Abraham for our sake (4:23–25)

Explanation of the Text

1. The promise was not given to Abraham on the basis of the law (4:13–15).

So far, Paul has not mentioned the Mosaic law.[37] That omission makes sense, because Abraham lived 430 years before the law was given to Israel (cf. Gal. 3:15–18). Nevertheless, in explaining (γάρ) how Abraham came to be the father of both those who are circumcised and those who are uncircumcised (4:9–12), Paul begins with the emphatic qualifier "not through law" (οὐ διὰ νόμου) and continues with the strong contrast "but through righteousness that comes from faith" (ἀλλὰ διὰ δικαιοσύνης πίστεως). In so doing, he corrects the traditional Jewish thinking that Abraham received the promise because he kept the entire law before it was given to Moses (e.g., Jub. 24:11; 2 Bar. 57.2; Sir. 44:20). Neither Abraham nor his descendants (τῷ Ἀβραὰμ ἢ τῷ σπέρματι αὐτοῦ) received the promise by doing the law.

The specific promise (ἡ ἐπαγγελία) to which Paul points (cf. Gen. 17:1–8) was that Abraham would inherit the world (τὸ κληρονόμον αὐτὸν εἶναι κόσμου). That promise must be realized through faith for two reasons (γάρ). First, involving the law would nullify the promise (v. 14). Any arrangement in which individuals who "base their lives on the Mosaic law"[38] are heirs (εἰ οἱ ἐκ νόμου κληρονόμοι) has two results: it causes faith to have no impact (κεκένωται ἡ πίστις), and it renders the promise ineffective (κατήργηται ἡ ἐπαγγελία). Second, the law's role is to reveal and judge transgressions (v. 15; cf. 2:12–13; 3:19–20), not to validate promises. The law exists to point out acts that deviate from God's established norm (οὗ δὲ οὐκ ἔστιν νόμος, οὐδὲ παράβασις) and, so, brings about the wrath of judgment (ὁ νόμος ὀργὴν κατεργάζεται).

---

37. "Law" (ὁ νόμος, -ου) occurs five times in verses 13–16 and refers to the Mosaic law.

38. Longenecker, *Romans,* 512.

2. The promise was given to Abraham on the basis of faith (4:16–22).

Logically (διὰ τοῦτο), the promise must be based on faith (ἐκ πίστεως) in order for it to meet the standard of grace (ἵνα κατὰ χάριν).[39] Basing the promise on faith also guarantees it (εἰς τὸ εἶναι βεβαίαν τὴν ἐπαγγελίαν) for all of Abraham's descendants (παντὶ τῷ σπέρματι)— not only the Jewish Christian (οὐ τῷ ἐκ τοῦ νόμου μόνον)[40] but also the Gentile Christian (ἀλλὰ καὶ τῷ ἐκ πίστεως Ἀβραάμ)—and makes him the father of all (ὅς ἐστιν πατὴρ πάντων ἡμῶν) who exercise faith. Genesis 17:5 provides the Old Testament proof (καθὼς γέγραπται) that God would make Abraham the father of many nations (πατέρα πολλῶν ἐθνῶν τέθεικά σε), not just the Jews.

Paul now includes an extended description of Abraham's response to God's promise (κατέναντι οὗ).[41] First, Abraham believed God (ἐπίστευσεν θεοῦ). Specifically, he believed the God who does the impossible—the God who gives life to the dead (τοῦ ζῳοποιοῦντος τοὺς νεκρούς) and who calls into existence things that are not yet in existence (καὶ καλοῦντος τὰ μὴ ὄντα ὡς ὄντα). Second, Abraham believed God's promise (Gen. 15:5). His faith was characterized by the confident expectation in God's word the New Testament describes as "hope" (παρ' ἐλπιδα ἐπ' ἐλπιδι ἐπίστευσεν). As a result of that confident expectation, God fulfilled his promise (εἰς τὸ γενέσθαι αὐτὸν πατέρα πολλῶν ἐθνῶν). Third, Abraham considered the obstacles. Because he was not weak with reference to faith (μὴ ἀσθενήσας τῇ πίστει), he was able to reflect objectively (κατενόησεν) on the difficulties involved. Specifically, his body was as good as dead (τὸ ἑαυτοῦ σῶμα ἤδη νενεκρωμένον), he was almost 100 years old (ἑκατονταετής που ὑπάρχων), and Sarah's womb was barren (καὶ τὴν νέκρωσιν τῆς μήτρας Σάρρας). Fourth, Abraham did not succumb to unbelief (τῇ ἀπιστίᾳ) that might cause him to doubt God's promise (εἰς τὴν ἐπαγγελίαν τοῦ θεου οὐ διεκρίθη). Instead (ἀλλ'), God strengthened him in his faith (ἐνεδυναμώθη τῇ πίστει) so that he was able to glorify God (δοὺς δόξαν τῷ θεῷ) and be fully persuaded (καὶ πληροφορηθείς)[42] that God was able to do what he had promised to do (ὅ ἐπήγγελται δυνατός ἐστιν καὶ ποιῆσαι). For these reasons (διό) Abraham's faith was counted to him for righteousness (ἐλογίσθη αὐτῷ εἰς δικαιοσύνην) as Genesis 15:6 records (cf. 4:3).

---

39. Paul has previously highlighted the importance of grace in 3:24 and 4:4.

40. See Moo for an explanation of this understanding of the phrase "to the one who is out of the law" (*Romans*, 278–79).

41. See Harvey for a discussion of the phrase "in the face of which promise" (*Romans*, 117).

42. Πληροφορέω describes the attitude of being fully persuaded without any limitation created by doubt (BDAG 827d).

3. The promise was given to Abraham for our sake (4:23–25).

Paul's summary application continues his stress on the truth that Abraham's experience also applies to those who follow his example. The statement in Genesis 15:6 that God credited righteousness to Abraham's account (ἐλογίσθη αὐτῷ) was not written only for Abraham's sake (οὐκ ἐγράφη δι' αὐτον μονον), but also for our sake (ἀλλὰ καὶ δι' ἡμᾶς). Echoing verse 17, Paul declares that righteousness is also being credited to the account (μέλλει λογίζεσθαι) of those who are believing (τοῖς πιστεύουσιν) in the God who raised Jesus from the dead (ἐπι τὸν ἐγείραντα Ἰησοῦν τὸν κύριον ἡμῶν ἐκ νεκρῶν).

Paul concludes 1:18–4:25 with a carefully constructed statement in synonymous parallelism that some consider a traditional Christian confession:[43]

who	was handed over	because of our wrongdoings,
and	was raised	because of our justification.

In these two lines, Paul captures the doctrines of Jesus's passive obedience and his active obedience. His death on the cross (passive obedience) paid the penalty for our sins (παρεδόθη διὰ τὰ παραπτώματα ἡμῶν), and his righteous life (active obedience) made it possible for his righteousness to be credited to our account (ἠγέρθη διὰ τὴν δικαίωσιν ἡμῶν). Together, these lines encompass the entirety of Christ's work on our behalf and remind us that in him we are more than simply "not guilty"—we are, in fact, positively righteous before God.

Theology and Appropriation

Paul most frequently writes of God's promise to Abraham (singular). That promise is first recorded in Genesis 12:1–3:

> Go from your country, and from your relatives, and from your father's house, to the land I will show you.
> And I will make you a great nation, and will bless you, and make your name great, so that you shall be a blessing.
> And I will bless those who bless you, and the one who curses you I will curse; and in you all the families of the earth shall be blessed.

This unitary promise is often understood to include three components: a land, a people, and a blessing. It is worth noting that both the second

---

43. See, for example, Longenecker, *Romans*, 535.

and the third lines conclude with Abraham being a blessing, and the third line extends that blessing to all the families of the earth.

God repeats his promise to Abraham three times. In Genesis 15, the Lord promises that Abraham's descendants will be as numerous as the stars of the heavens (1–5) and that those descendants will possess the land of Canaan (18–21). In Genesis 17, the Lord promises to multiply Abraham exceedingly so that he will be the father of many nations (1–6) and to make the land of Canaan an everlasting possession (7–8). In Genesis 22, the angel of the Lord promises to bless Abraham greatly, to multiply his seed greatly, and to bless all the nations through his seed (15–18). God further specifies three times that Isaac will be the son through whom he will fulfill his promise (Gen. 17:15–19; 18:9–15; 21:12).

Paul uses Isaac in his argument in Romans 9:6–9, but his primary focus—after Abraham's initial response of faith (Rom. 4:3, 9, 22; Gal. 3:6)—is the universal scope of God's promise. In Romans 4:13, Paul refers to Abraham as "the heir of the world." In 4:17–18, he refers to Abraham as the "father of many nations." In Galatians 3:8, he notes that "all the nations" would be blessed in Abraham. Paul understood, therefore, that the Old Testament promise to Abraham extended beyond the Jews to the Gentiles. Indeed, Christ had commissioned Paul "to bear [his] name before the Gentiles" (Acts 9:15; 22:21), and he identified himself as "an apostle of Gentiles" (Rom. 11:13). That understanding informed both his ministry practice and his gospel preaching. In Romans 4, the latter is clearly at the fore in that those who are Abraham's descendants ("seed") share in the blessing of God's promise solely on the basis of faith, apart from any acts of Jewish piety, including works, circumcision, and keeping the law. The response God desires is faith that believes him and his promises, objectively considers the obstacles, does not waver in unbelief, and is fully persuaded that he is able to do what he promises. In such a person, God fulfills his promise to Abraham.

Paul's primary purpose for including this paragraph was to help his readers understand that they share in God's promises to Abraham, if they follow his example of faith. As was true for those original readers, we, too, share the need to realize that by faith we inherit the blessings that flow from those promises. Possible points of connection include promise, heir, and inheritance. Everyone can identify with the idea of promises, either kept or broken, and most individuals have a concept of what is involved in receiving an inheritance from a family member who has passed on. This passage corrects the idea that faith is "blind" in having no objective basis, or that faith is idealistic and ignores potential obstacles. From a human perspective, Abraham faced insurmountable obstacles. Yet he focused on God's promise, faced those obstacles squarely, rejected unbelief and doubt, and as a result, grew stronger in his faith. The passage commends confidence in God and his ability to keep his promises. The primary objective in communicating this passage should be to help others understand that we have the opportunity to share in the blessings of God's promises so that they will believe God and his promises in the face of obstacles and opportunities for unbelief and doubt.

ROMANS 5:1–8:39

The Gospel as the Demonstration of God's Power

The body of Romans consists of four major parts, each of which unpacks one of the four topics Paul includes in his thematic statement of 1:16–17. The central topic of Romans 5:1–8:39 is **the demonstration of God's power** in the gospel. Paul's argument makes it clear that God demonstrates his power to save from wrath (5:1–11), to save from condemnation (5:12–21), to save from sin (6:1–23), to save from the law (7:1–25), to save from the flesh (8:1–30), and to save from all opposition (8:31–39).

II. Letter Body (1:18–15:13)
    B. The Gospel as the Demonstration of God's Power
        (5:1–8:39)
        1. The gospel demonstrates God's power to save from
            wrath (5:1–11)
        2. The gospel demonstrates God's power to save from
            condemnation (5:12–21)
        3. The gospel demonstrates God's power to save from sin
            (6:1–23)
           a. Because we died with Christ (6:1–14)
           b. Because we serve a new master (6:15–23)
        4. The gospel demonstrates God's power to save from the
            law (7:1–25)
           a. Because dying with Christ brings release from the
              law (7:1–6)
           b. Because the law brings knowledge of sin (7:7–12)
           c. Because sin uses the law to produce death
               (7:13–25)

5. The gospel demonstrates God's power to save from the flesh (8:1–30)
    a. Because the Spirit gives us life and assurance (8:1–17)
    b. Because the Spirit gives us hope of glory (8:18–30)
6. The gospel demonstrates God's power to save from all opposition (8:31–39)

ROMANS 5:1–11

Text and Translation

1 Therefore, because we have been justified by faith[1] we are having[2] peace with God[3] through our Lord Jesus Christ, **2** through whom also[4] we have[5] our entrance by faith[6] into this grace in which we are standing, and we are boasting[7] on the basis of hope in God's glory.[8] **3** And not only *this*, but also we are boasting in our[9] tribulations, because we know[10] that tribulation produces perseverance, **4** and perseverance *produces* proven character, and proven character *produces* hope. **5** And hope does not put to shame, because God's love *for us*[11] has been poured out[12] in our hearts through the Holy Spirit *who has been* given[13] to us. **6** For while we were still weak,[14] still at the appointed time Christ died on behalf of[15] the ungodly. **7** For scarcely on behalf of a righteous person will anyone die; for on behalf of a good person someone might even[16] dare to die; **8** but God commends his own love toward us, in that[17] while we were still sinful Christ died on our behalf. **9** Therefore,

---

1. Δικαιωθέντες is an adverbial participle of cause; the aorist tense is consummative; ἐκ + genitive denotes means.
2. The indicative reading ἔχομεν is to be preferred over the subjunctive. Elsewhere in Paul's letters, peace is something God gives (2 Cor. 13:11; Phil. 4:7, 9; 2 Thess. 3:16) rather than something believers are exhorted to pursue.
3. Πρός + accusative denotes relationship.
4. Καί is adjunctive.
5. Ἐσχήκαμεν and ἐστήκαμεν are both intensive perfects.
6. Of the three variant readings, τῇ πίστει is the most likely original (cf. Metzger, *Textual Commentary*, 452).
7. Καυχώμεθα is indicative; καί joins it to ἔχομεν in verse 1.
8. Ἐπί + dative denotes basis; τῆς δόξης is an objective genitive; τοῦ θεοῦ is a possessive genitive.
9. The definite article functions as a possessive pronoun.
10. Εἰδότες is an adverbial participle of cause.
11. Τοῦ θεοῦ is a subjective genitive.
12. Ἐκκέχυται is an extensive perfect.
13. Δοθέντες is an adjectival participle; the aorist tense is consummative.
14. Of the six textual variants, ἔτι γάρ . . . ἔτι has the strongest manuscript support (ℵ, A, C, D); ὄντων ἡμῶν ἀσθενῶν is a genitive absolute and adverbial of time.
15. Ὑπέρ + genitive denotes substitution; the preposition occurs with this sense four times in verses 6–8.
16. Καί is ascensive.
17. Ὅτι is short for ἐν τούτῳ ὅτι (cf. BDF §394).

all the more certainly,[18] now, because we have been justified by *means of* his blood, we will be saved from wrath through him. **10** For if[19] *it is true that* while we were[20] enemies we were reconciled[21] to God through his death, all the more certainly, because we have been reconciled,[22] we will be saved by his life; **11** and not only *this*, but also *we are* boasting[23] in God through our Lord Jesus Christ, through whom now we have received[24] the reconciliation.

Context and Structure

II. Letter Body (1:18–15:13)
   A. The Gospel as the Revelation of God's Righteousness (1:18–4:25)
   B. The Gospel as the Demonstration of God's Power (5:1–8:39)
      1. **The gospel demonstrates God's power to save from wrath (5:1–11)**
      2. The gospel demonstrates God's power to save from condemnation (5:12–21)
      3. The gospel demonstrates God's power to save from sin (6:1–23)
      4. The gospel demonstrates God's power to save from the law (7:1–25)
      5. The gospel demonstrates God's power to save from the flesh (8:1–30)
      6. The gospel demonstrates God's power to save from all opposition (8:31–39)

The first paragraph of the second major portion of Paul's argument divides into three sections. The first offers a summary of the present results of being declared righteous by faith (5:1–5; cf. 3:21–4:25). The

---

18. NEB; πολλῷ μᾶλλον combines a dative of degree with the adverb "more" to form an emphatic comparison.
19. Εἰ introduces a first-class condition.
20. Ὄντες is an adverbial participle of time.
21. Κατηλλάγημεν is a divine passive.
22. Καταλλαγέντες is an adverbial participle of cause; the aorist tense is consummative.
23. The participle καυχώμενοι functions as the main verb in the clause (cf. Wallace, *Grammar*, 653).
24. The aorist tense of ἐλάβομεν is consummative.

second establishes Christ's death as the reason for those benefits (5:6–8). The third adds the promise of future salvation from wrath (5:9–11).

Basic Message and Exegetical Outline

Because Christ's death reconciled those who are weak, ungodly, and sinful, we have peace, grace, hope, and salvation from wrath.

Three Dimensions of Being Declared Righteous by Faith (5:1–11)
1. The present results of being declared righteous are peace, grace, and hope (5:1–5)
   a. We have peace with God (5:1)
   b. We have access into grace (5:2a)
   c. We have hope in God's glory (5:2b–5)
2. The past basis of being declared righteous is Christ's death for us (5:6–8)
   a. We were not righteous or good (5:7)
   b. We were weak, ungodly, and sinful (5:6, 8)
3. The future promise of being declared righteous is salvation from wrath (5:9–11)
   a. Because we are declared righteous by Christ's blood (5:9)
   b. Because we are reconciled through Christ's death (5:10–11)

Explanation of the Text

1. The present results of being declared righteous are peace, grace, and hope (5:1–5).

Paul now introduces the implications (οὖν) of being declared righteous by faith (δικαιωθέντες ἐκ πίστεως) apart from works, circumcision, or law (3:21–4:25). Longenecker suggests that beginning with 5:1 Paul moves to "more personal, relational, and participatory language,"[25] and the occurrences of peace (εἰρήνη), grace (χάρις), and hope (ἐλπίς) in these verses support his suggestion.[26] Of those three benefits, hope receives the greatest emphasis (five times), but Paul begins with the

---

25. Longenecker, *Romans*, 539.
26. A comparison of repeated words in chapters 1–4 and chapters 5–8 is instructive. Faith/believe appears thirty-three times in 1–4 but only three times in 5–8. Grace (15 times), hope (7 times), and life (24 times) become more prominent in 5–8.

peace we have (εἰρήνην ἔχομεν) in relation to God (πρὸς τὸν θεόν) that comes through Christ (διὰ τοῦ κυρίου ἡμῶν Ἰησοῦ Χριστοῦ). Peace includes both the Greek concept of divinely bestowed favor and the Hebrew concept of divinely bestowed well-being (cf. 1:7), and it refers to an objective state rather than a subjective emotion. We were at war with God, but now we are at peace with him.[27] Not only is Christ the agent through whom we have peace with God, he is also (καί) the agent (δι' οὗ) who provides access into God's grace. We have that way of approach (τὴν προσαγωγὴν ἐσχήκαμεν) into grace (εἰς τὴν χάριν ταύτην) by means of faith (τῇ πίστει). As a result, we exist in a continuing state of grace (ἐν ᾗ ἑστήκαμεν).[28]

The third benefit we receive because we have been declared righteous by faith is hope. Previously, Paul has portrayed boasting as a negative behavior, but now he underlines a positive side to boasting (καυχώμεθα) because of the basis on which we boast: hope in God's glory (ἐπ' ἐλπίδι τῆς δόξης τοῦ θεοῦ). Later in the letter Paul will make it clear that hope is eager and confident expectation of what we do not yet see (8:18–24; cf. 4:18). In this context, hope gains its impetus from what we know: God's love for us leads him to develop our character. For that reason, Paul can say that we boast in the trouble and distress outward circumstances inflict on us[29] (καυχώμεθα ἐν ταῖς θλίψεσιν), because we know that (εἰδότες ὅτι) God will use those troubles. Difficult circumstances produce the capacity to bear up in the face of those difficulties[30] (ἡ θλῖψις ὑπομονὴν κατεργάζεται); that capacity produces character that has withstood the test[31] (ἡ ὑπομονὴ δοκιμήν), which in turn produces hope (ἡ δοκιμὴ ἐλπίδα) that brings neither shame nor disappointment (ἡ ἐλπὸς οὐ καταισχύνει). The reason (ὅτι) hope does not disappoint is the love for us that God has poured out in our hearts (ἡ ἀγάπη τοῦ θεοῦ ἐκκέχυται ἐν ταῖς καρδίαις ἡμῶν) by giving us his Holy Spirit (διὰ πνεύματος ἁγίου τοῦ δοθέντος ἡμῖν). The next sections set out the way in which God has demonstrated his love for us and why that demonstration confirms our hope.

2. The past basis of being declared righteous is Christ's death for us (5:6–8).

---

27. Paul resumes this idea later in the paragraph under the theme of reconciliation (5:10–11).
28. The idea of grace becomes prominent in 5:12–21.
29. BDAG 457c.
30. BDAG 1039a.
31. BDAG 256a.

The reason (γάρ) we have peace, grace, and hope (5:1–5) is the demonstration of God's love in Christ.[32] Paul begins by highlighting our condition at the time when Christ died: we were still weak (ἔτι ὄντων ἡμῶν ἀσθενῶν). Nevertheless (ἔτι) at the appointed time (κατὰ καιρόν), Christ died on behalf of those who were ungodly (ὑπὲρ ἀσεβῶν). Paul then explains (γάρ) the significance of what Christ has done. It would be rare (μόλις) for someone to die (τις ἀποθανεῖται) on behalf of a person who is morally upright (ὑπὲρ δικαίου). Similarly (γάρ), it is within the realm of possibility (τάχα) that someone might be bold enough to die (τις τολμᾷ ἀποθανειν) on behalf of a person who is kind and generous[33] (ὑπερ τοῦ ἀγαθοῦ). In contrast to unlikely human action (δέ), though, God provides tangible evidence (συνίστησιν . . . ὁ θεός) of his own love (τὴν ἑαυτοῦ ἀγάπην) by his concrete action toward us (εἰς ἡμᾶς). After the hypothetical aside of verse 7, Paul returns to the actual situation— not only were we weak (ἀσθενῶν) and godless (ἀσεβῶν), we were also "sinful" (ἔτι ἁμαρτωλῶν ὄντων ἡμῶν). In those circumstances, Christ died (Χριστὸς . . . ἀπέθανεν) not on behalf of the righteous (ὑπὲρ δικαίου) or on behalf of the good (ὑπερ τοῦ ἀγαθοῦ) but on our behalf (ὑπὲρ ἡμῶν). The Spirit's witness to Christ's death on behalf of individuals who were anything but deserving is proof positive of the Father's love that gives us hope.

3. The future promise of being declared righteous is salvation from wrath (5:9–11).

Paul sets out the conclusion that logically follows from Christ's death on our behalf (οὖν) in a "from lesser to greater" argument. Because it is a reality in the present time (νῦν) that we have been declared righteous by means of Christ's blood (δικαιωθέντες ἐν τῷ αἵματι αὐτοῦ),[34] we can expect even greater (πολλῷ μᾶλλον) results in the future. The future promise is that we will also be saved from wrath (σωθησόμεθα . . . ἀπὸ

---

32. Paul's emphasis on Christ is clear from the way in which he places the noun Χριστός at the beginning of verse 6 in the Greek text, delays the finite verb ἀπέθανεν until the end of the first clause, and places his full statement on Christ's death at the end of verse 8. The threefold repetition of ἔτι reinforces the circumstances that existed when Christ died, and the fourfold repetition of ὑπέρ + genitive reinforces our weak, godless, sinful condition.

33. BDAG 4a. Schreiner (*Romans*, 261) and Cranfield (*Romans*, 265) argue for someone who functions as a "benefactor."

34. "By means of his blood" denotes impersonal means. Another understanding is instrumental of price ("at the price of his blood").

τῆς ὀργῆς) through Christ (δι᾽ αὐτοῦ). Paul then explains (γάρ) why we can count on that promise. While we were enemies (ἐχθροὶ ὄντες), God reconciled us to himself (κατηλλάγημεν τῷ θεῷ) through Christ's death (διὰ τοῦ θανάτου τοῦ υἱοῦ αὐτοῦ). With our reconciliation through his death an established fact (καταλλαγέντες), we can expect that his life (ἐν τῇ ζωῇ) will bring the even greater (πολλῷ μᾶλλον) result of future salvation (σωθησόμεθα). Further (οὐ μόνον ἀλλὰ καί), because we have received reconciliation through Christ (δι᾽ οὗ νῦν τὴν καταλλαγὴν ἐλάβομεν), we have every reason to boast in God (καυχώμενοι ἐν τῷ θεῷ) through Christ (διὰ τοῦ κυρίου ἡμῶν Ἰησοῦ Χριστοῦ). Rather than having any reason to be ashamed of Christ or the gospel (cf. 5:5; 1:16), we have every reason to take pride in both. In this way, Paul brings the discussion full circle by echoing the idea of boasting in God (5:2) and repeating the refrain "through our Lord Jesus Christ."[35]

Theology and Appropriation

Romans 3:21–26 introduces three key soteriological terms: justification, redemption, and propitiation. This passage introduces a fourth: reconciliation (noun, καταλλαγή; verb, καταλλάσσω). Taken from the context of interpersonal relations, the term describes the process of bringing into agreement two parties who have been at odds with one another. Reconciliation, therefore, highlights our change in status before God from that of being his enemies to that of being his friends. Outside Paul, the idea occurs only in Matthew 5:24, where it refers to the reconciliation of human beings with one another.[36] In Paul's letters the emphasis falls heavily on the reconciliation of human beings with God (Rom. 5:9–11; 11:15; 2 Cor. 5:18–21; Eph. 2:13–18; Col. 1:19–22). The theological context of reconciliation is the enmity that exists between us and God apart from Christ (Rom. 5:10), and the need is to overcome that alienation and hostility (Col. 1:21). Reconciliation is God's work, not ours (2 Cor. 5:18), and the result is that we are reconciled to him (Rom. 5:10; 2 Cor. 5:18–19; Col. 1:20). Reconciliation is effected through Christ's work (Rom. 5:6–8, 10; 2 Cor. 5:18–19, 21; Col. 1:20), includes the forgiveness of sins (2 Cor. 5:19), and promises salvation from wrath (Rom. 5:9–10). The scope of reconciliation is universal in that it extends to both Jew and Gentile (Rom. 11:15; 2 Cor. 5:19; Col. 1:20) and brings Jew and Gentile together into one new race (Eph. 2:16). Reconciliation has an impact on the way we live (Col. 1:22–23),

---

35. The phrase also gives unity to all of 5:1–8:39, marking the ends of divisions within the section (5:11, 21; 6:23; 7:25; 8:39).
36. Paul mentions reconciliation on the human level in 1 Corinthians 7:11.

and it establishes us as ambassadors of Christ who are entrusted with both the message and the ministry of reconciliation (2 Cor. 5:19–20).

Paul's primary purpose for including this passage at this point in his letter was to help his readers understand the relational benefits that result from being declared righteous by faith. With the original readers we share the need to realize both the change in relationship that has taken place between God and us and the hope it brings. Because of what Christ has done, we now have peace, grace, hope, reconciliation, and deliverance from wrath. Possible points of connection include peace, hope, and the idea of former enemies becoming allies. The passage corrects the idea that trials are bad; in fact, Paul teaches that God uses difficulties to build our character and to give us hope. It also reminds us that we are estranged from God—we are weak, ungodly, and sinful—and can do nothing to overcome that hostility and alienation. The passage commends confident expectation in our ultimate salvation from wrath and highlights that expectation using the "from lesser to greater" argument form. The objective in communicating this passage should be to help others understand the benefits that they receive because of what Christ has done for them so that they will live with their focus on the hope of God's glory.

ROMANS 5:12–21

Text and Translation

12 Because of this,[1] as through one person[2] sin has entered[3] into the world and through sin death, and so death has passed to all persons, for[4] all sinned—**13** For until the law, sin was in the world, but sin is not being charged to an account when there is no law,[5] **14** but death reigned from Adam until Moses, even[6] over *those who* did not sin[7] after the likeness of Adam's transgression,[8] who is a type of *the one who* is to come.[9] **15** But not as the trespass, so also *is* the grace gift; for if *it is true that* [10] by the trespass of the one the many died, all the more certainly[11] the grace of God and the gift by[12] grace by the one man, Jesus Christ, abounded to *the benefit of* [13] the many. **16** And not as through *the one who* sinned[14] *is* the free gift; for on the one hand the judgment *was* out of one *sin* resulting in condemnation; on the other hand the grace gift *was* out of many trespasses resulting in acquittal. **17** For if *it is true that* [15] by the trespass of the one, death reigned through the one *man*, all the more certainly *those who* are receiving[16] the abundant grace[17] and the free gift that is righteousness[18] will reign in life through

1. The conceptual antecedent of τοῦτο is what Paul has written in 5:1–11.
2. Ἑνός ἀνθρώπου refers to Adam.
3. The aorist tense of εἰσῆλθεν is consummative; the same is true of διῆλθεν later in the verse.
4. Ἑφ' ᾧ is short for ἐπί τούτο ὅτι and denotes cause (cf. 2 Cor. 5:4; Phil. 3:12; 4:10). It is best to understand the antecedent of the relative pronoun as the first part of the verse: "Because sin entered the world through Adam" (cf. Schreiner, *Romans,* 274).
5. Μὴ ὄντος νόμου is a genitive absolute of time.
6. Καί is ascensive.
7. Τοὺς μὴ ἁμαρτήσαντες is a substantival participle.
8. Although indeclinable, Ἀδάμ is a subjective genitive.
9. Τοῦ μέλλοντος is a substantival participle.
10. Εἰ introduces a first-class condition.
11. Πολλῷ μᾶλλον; also in verse 17.
12. Ἑν χάριτι is instrumental.
13. Εἰς + accusative denotes advantage.
14. Ἑνὸς ἁμαρτήσαντός is a substantival participle.
15. Εἰ introduces a first-class condition.
16. Οἱ ... λαμβάνοντες is a substantival participle.
17. Χάριτος is an attributed genitive; δικαιοσύνης is an epexegetical genitive.
18. Τῆς δικαιοσύνης is an epexegetical genitive.

the one *man*, Jesus Christ. **18** Consequently,[19] as because of one *man's* trespass[20] to all people resulting in condemnation, in this way also[21] because of one *man's* righteous act to all people resulting in acquittal of life; **19** for as because of one man's[22] *act* of disobedience many were appointed sinners, in this way also because of one man's *act* of obedience many will be appointed righteous. **20** And the law entered alongside, in order that the trespass might increase; but where sin increased, grace abounded much more, **21** in order that, as sin reigned in death, in this way also[23] grace might reign through righteousness resulting in eternal life through Jesus Christ our Lord.

Context and Structure

   II. Letter Body (1:18–15:13)
     A. The Gospel as the Revelation of God's Righteousness (1:18–4:25)
     B. The Gospel as the Demonstration of God's Power (5:1–8:39)
       1. The gospel demonstrates God's power to save from wrath (5:1–11)
       2. **The gospel demonstrates God's power to save from condemnation (5:12–21)**
       3. The gospel demonstrates God's power to save from sin (6:1–23)
       4. The gospel demonstrates God's power to save from the law (7:1–25)
       5. The gospel demonstrates God's power to save from the flesh (8:1–30)
       6. The gospel demonstrates God's power to save from all opposition (8:31–39)

Paul twice interrupts his argument in order to clarify what he has written. He begins a discussion of the impact of Adam's sin (5:12) but breaks it off to explain the situation that existed between Adam and the coming of the Mosaic law (5:13–14). After stating that Adam is a

---

19. Ἄρα οὖν is a strong inferential conjunction that draws the discussion to a conclusion.
20. In both clauses of the sentence, διά + genitive denotes cause (BDF §481). So also in verse 19.
21. Καί is adjunctive.
22. In both clauses of the sentence, τοῦ ἑνός is a subjective genitive.
23. Καί is adjunctive.

type of Christ (5:14b), he breaks off again to identify the ways in which Adam and Christ differ (5:15–17). He then returns to his original comparison of Adam and Christ (5:18–19). He concludes the paragraph with a note on the subordinate role of the law (5:20–21).

Basic Message and Exegetical Outline

Although Adam's act of disobedience resulted in the reign of sin and death, Christ's act of obedience results in the reign of righteousness and life.

> Salvation History in a Nutshell (5:12–21)
> 1. Adam's sin had widespread impact (5:12–14)
>   a. Sin entered the world (5:12a)
>   b. Death passed to all (5:12b)
>   c. Death reigned from Adam until Moses (5:13–14)
> 2. Adam and Christ differ in four respects (5:15–17)
>   a. Adam's act was a violation of law; Christ's act was a gift of grace (5:15a)
>   b. In Adam, many died; in Christ, grace abounds to many (5:15b)
>   c. In Adam, judgment brought condemnation; in Christ, grace brings acquittal (5:16)
>   d. In Adam, death reigned; in Christ, life reigns (5:17)
> 3. Christ's obedience also had widespread impact (5:18–19)
>   a. His righteous act leads to life (5:18)
>   b. His obedience leads to righteous status (5:19)
> 4. The law's role is subordinate (5:20–21)
>   a. The law causes sin to increase (5:20a)
>   b. Sin causes grace to increase even more (5:20b–21)

Explanation of the Text

1. Adam's sin had widespread impact (5:12–14).
Paul gathers up 5:1–11 (διὰ τοῦτο) and begins a comparison (ὥσπερ) he leaves incomplete until verse 18. The reason Paul ultimately wants to offer in support of what he has just written is that Christ's obedience has countered Adam's disobedience and results in justification of life (5:18–19). First, however, he must develop the impact of Adam's sin. Through the one man (δι' ἑνὸς ἀνθρώπου), Adam, sin entered the world (ἡ ἁμαρτία εἰς τὸν κόσμον εἰσῆλθεν), and through sin (καὶ διὰ

τῆς ἁμαρτίας) death (ὁ θάνατος) also entered.[24] As a consequence (καὶ οὕτως) death spread throughout the entire human race (εἰς πάντας ἀνθρώπους ὁ θάνατος διῆλθεν). Because sin entered the world through Adam (ἐφ᾽ ᾧ), all sinned (πάντες ἥμαρτον).[25]

In order to reinforce the universal reign of sin, Paul breaks off his initial comparison to explain (γάρ) that sin and death reigned even during the time between Adam's sin and the giving of the Mosaic law. Sin was in the world (ἁμαρτία ἦν ἐν κόσμῳ) prior to the giving of the law (ἄχρι νόμου), even though sin is not charged to a person's account (ἁμαρτία δὲ οὐκ ἐλλογεῖται) when there is no law (μὴ ὄντος νόμου).[26] Nevertheless (ἀλλά), sin exercised royal authority (ἐβασίλευσεν ὁ θάνατος) during the time period that extended from Adam to Moses (ἀπὸ Ἀδὰμ μέχρι Μωϋσέως), even over those who did not sin (καὶ ἐπὶ τοὺς μὴ ἁμαρτήσαντας) in the same way as Adam, who violated a clear divine command (ἐπὶ τῷ ὁμοιώματι τῆς παραβάσεως Ἀδάμ). There is, however, a larger topic Paul wants to address in connection with Adam: he is a "type" of Christ, who is "the one who was to come" (ὅς ἐστιν τύπος τοῦ μέλλοντος).[27]

2. Adam and Christ differ in four respects (5:15–17).

Because typology focuses on one specific way in which a type prefigures its antitype, Paul makes it a point to clarify the ways in which Adam (type) and Christ (antitype) are different before he completes his original comparison. The first contrast (οὐχ ὡς ... οὕτως καί) is the nature of the work each performed. Adam's work was a wrongdoing that violated God's moral standard (τὸ παράπτωμα), while Christ's work was a gift that is freely and graciously given (τὸ χάρισμα). Appropriately, Paul uses a "from lesser to greater" argument (πολλῷ μᾶλλον) to explain (γάρ) the second difference—the difference in magnitude between Adam's act and Christ's act. It is by the trespass of the one (τῷ τοῦ ἑνὸς παραπτώματι), Adam, that many died (οἱ πολλοὶ ἀπέθανον). In contrast, by the one man, Jesus Christ (τῇ τοῦ ἑνὸς ἀνθρώπου Ἰησοῦ Χριστοῦ),

---

24. Schreiner describes sin and death as "twin powers that entered the world when Adam transgressed" (*Romans*, 272).
25. As might be expected, the way in which "all sinned" has generated considerable discussion. See "Theology and Appropriation" below for a summary.
26. Paul's point is not that sin somehow fails to make a person guilty when there is no law, but that sin cannot be viewed as equivalent to a violation of law when there is no law to violate.
27. A "type" is a person or event that prefigures another person or event related to future redemption. The person or event prefigured is the "antitype."

God's grace (ἡ χάρις τοῦ θεοῦ) and his gift in grace (ἡ δωρεὰ ἐν χάριτι) overflow to the many (εἰς τοὺς πολλούς) to an extent that is not ordinarily encountered (ἐπερίσσευσεν).

The third difference relates to the consequences of the two acts. While Adam's sin (δι' ἑνὸς ἁμαρτήσαντος) brings judgment (τὸ κρίμα) and the judicial verdict of condemnation (εἰς κατάκριμα), Christ's gift (τὸ δώρημα) brings the judicial verdict of acquittal (εἰς δικαιώμα). Further, it took a single trespass (ἐξ ἑνός) to bring condemnation, while the gift covers many trespasses (ἐκ πολλῶν παραπτωμάτων). The final difference highlights the contrasting results of Adam's act and Christ's act, particularly the abundance resulting from the latter. By the trespass of the one (τῷ τοῦ ἑνὸς παραπτώματι), Adam, death reigned through that one man (ὁ θάνατος ἐβασίλευσεν διὰ τοῦ ἑνός). In contrast, through the one man, Jesus Christ (διὰ τοῦ ἑνὸς Ἰησοῦ Χιρστοῦ), those who are receiving (οἱ . . . λαμβάνοντες) God's abundant grace (τὴν περισσείαν τῆς χάριτος) and the gift that is righteousness (τῆς δωρεᾶς τῆς δικαιοσύνης) will reign in life (ἐν ζωῇ ἐβασιλεύσουσιν).[28]

3. Christ's obedience also had widespread impact (15:18–19).

Having completed the explanations in verses 13–17, Paul is now ready to summarize his argument (ἄρα οὖν) by resuming the comparison (ὡς) he began in verse 12. He makes his point twice, although with different points of emphasis, using two carefully constructed parallel statements. The first statement focuses on the contrast in the verdicts (5:18):

Because of one man's trespass	to all people	resulting in condemnation;
because of one man's righteous act	to all people	resulting in acquittal.

In the same way that Adam's trespass (δι' ἑνὸς παραπτώματος) resulted in a verdict of condemnation (εἰς κατάκριμα), Christ's righteous act (δι' ἑνὸς δικαιώματος) results in a verdict of acquittal that is accompanied by life (εἰς δικαίωσιν ζωῆς). Both acts had widespread impact (εἰς πάντας ἀνθρώπους).[29] The second statement focuses on the contrast in the results (5:19):

---

28. Dunn notes that the "piling up of [Paul's] language . . . is . . . an attempt to mirror the superabundant quality of grace given and received" (*Romans*, 281).

29. Seeking to draw fine distinctions between the synonymous uses of "all" (5:18) and "many" (5:15, 19) does more than Paul's language intends. The contrast he is seeking to highlight is between one person and a large number of people. In other words, Adam's and Christ's actions both

| Because of one man's act of disobedience | many | were appointed sinners; |
| because of one man's act of obedience | many | will be appointed righteous. |

In the same way that Adam's act of disobedience (διὰ τῆς παρακοῆς τοῦ ἑνὸς ἀνθρώπου) resulted in a status of "sinner" (ἁμαρτωλοὶ κατεστάθησαν οἱ πολλοί), Christ's act of obedience (διὰ τῆς ὑπακοῆς τοῦ ἑνός) results in a status of "righteous" (δίκαιοι κατεστάθήσονται οἱ πολλοί). Although commentators are divided on whether Christ's act of obedience refers to the active obedience of his entire life or the passive obedience of his death, it is probably best not to make a sharp distinction between the two, since his active obedience made his passive obedience possible. The verb translated "appoint" (καθίστημι) may be understood in a number of ways. Moo suggests "'inaugurated into' the state of sin/righteousness."[30]

4. The law's role is subordinate (5:20–21).

Having concluded his comparison of Adam and Christ, Paul returns to his previous mention of the Mosaic law (5:13). The law "entered alongside" (νόμος παρεισῆλθεν) in the sense that it had a subordinate role when compared to the roles Adam and Christ played in salvation history.[31] That role was to cause sin to increase (ἵνα πλεονάσῃ παράπτωμα). Cranfield suggests that the law caused sin to increase in three ways: (1) by making it known, (2) by making it more sinful, (3) by increasing its quantity.[32] Moo adds a fourth way: by intensifying its seriousness.[33] The increased abundance of sin (οὗ ἐπλεόνασεν ἡ ἁμαρτία), however, resulted in a superabundance of grace (ὑπερεπερίσσευσεν ἡ χάρις), with the express purpose (ἵνα) of the reign of grace and life replacing the reign of sin and death. In Adam, sin exercised royal authority in the death that followed it (ἐβασίλευσεν ἡ ἁμαρτία ἐν τῷ θανάτῳ). In Christ, grace exercises royal authority through righteousness resulting in eternal life (ἡ χάρις βασιλεύσῃ διὰ δικαιοσύνης εἰς ζωὴν αἰώνιον).

---

produced results that reached far beyond their own lives. Moo writes, "Christ affects those who are his as certainly as Adam does those who are his" (*Romans*, 343). Even more significantly, Christ's obedience delivers us from the results of Adam's disobedience (5:19).

30. Moo, *Romans*, 345, including n. 144.
31. Compare Morris, *Romans*, 241.
32. Cranfield, *Romans*, 293.
33. Moo, *Romans*, 348.

Theology and Appropriation

Paul's statement in 5:12 that "all sinned" has generated multiple interpretations;[34] of those, five are most common. The Divine Decree view holds that all humans sinned in line with God's decision that if Adam sinned, all would be judged guilty of sin. This view asserts no causal relation between Adam's sin and the sin of the human race. The Moral Example view holds that all humans sin in their own person, independently of Adam but after his example.[35] The Natural Headship view holds that, because all humanity existed biologically and genealogically in Adam, each person comes into the world as an individualization of sinful Adam. The Mediate Imputation view holds that all humans inherit a corrupt nature from Adam and, as a result, commit sin that makes them guilty before God.[36] The Immediate Imputation view holds that all humans are accounted guilty because of Adam's sin and, as a consequence, are born with a corrupt nature that infallibly leads them to commit sin that confirms their guilt before God.[37]

Several arguments have been offered in support of the Immediate Imputation view. First, Scripture describes human history in terms of two individuals: Adam and Christ (1 Cor. 15:21–22, 45–49). Second, Scripture draws a parallel between Adam's relation to humanity and Christ's relation to humanity (Rom. 5:12–19). Third, Adam's sin has a direct relationship to the sin, condemnation, and death of all (Rom. 5:12–19). Fourth, Scripture conceives of righteousness being imputed directly to humans (Rom. 4:1–25; Gal. 3:6–7). Fifth, the results of Jesus's work are imputed directly to those who respond to the gospel in faith; they are not transmitted naturally (Rom. 6:1–11).

If Paul teaches that "all sinned" in Adam (5:12), does he also teach that all are saved through Christ (5:18)? Several pieces of evidence argue against that conclusion. In the immediate context, Paul's emphasis is on the parallel operation rather than on numerical extent. In the larger context of the letter, Paul's consistent stress is on faith

---

34. For a helpful summary, see S. L. Johnson, "Romans 5:12—An Exercise in Exegesis and Theology." Pages 298–316 in *New Dimensions in New Testament Study*, edited by R. N. Longenecker and M. C. Tenney (Grand Rapids: Zondervan, 1974).

35. This position is commonly labeled the Pelagian view after the monk to whom it is attributed.

36. This position is attributed to Placaeus. Cranfield (*Romans*, 279), Longenecker (*Romans,* 591), and Schreiner (*Romans*, 276) adopt this position.

37. This position is attributed to Turrettin. Murray (*Romans,* 186), Stott (*Romans*, 154), and Moo (*Romans*, 326) adopt this position.

as the means by which a person is declared righteous (e.g., 4:1–25). In parallel passages, Paul uses "all" in a way that is limited to followers of Christ (e.g., Rom. 8:32; 1 Cor. 15:21–22). Elsewhere in his letters, Paul teaches that there are two distinct destinies for individuals based on their responses to the gospel (e.g., 2 Thess. 1:5–10). Paul's point throughout the passage, therefore, is that it is certain beyond a doubt that the benefits of Christ's work will be credited to all who respond in faith to the gospel, because the same dynamic that was at work in Adam's sin and death is at work in Christ's righteousness and life.[38]

Demonstrating that certainty was Paul's primary purpose in including this paragraph at this point in Romans. He wanted his readers to know that righteousness, acquittal, and life now apply to them because of what Christ has done as certainly as sin, condemnation, and death previously applied to them because of what Adam did. With his Roman readers we share the need to realize that, in Christ, we experience in far greater abundance blessings that deliver us from the effects of Adam's sin. Possible points of connection to the passage include concepts drawn from the legal system (e.g., judgment, condemnation, acquittal), conduct that is characterized by obedience and/or disobedience, and the idea of someone reigning over others (e.g., a monarchial system of governing). The passage corrects the idea that Adam was simply a myth or legend as well as the idea that some people might somehow be exempt from sin and judgment. The passage commends confidence in what Christ has done for us, an attitude of praise in response to his work, and commitment to live out the blessings we have in him. The objective in communicating this passage should be to help others understand the all-encompassing impact of Christ's work in reversing what they were in Adam so that they will embrace who they are in Christ and will share with others the possibility of experiencing that transfer from being in Adam to being in Christ.

---

38. Moo writes, "The point is that there can be assurance of justification and life on one side that is just a strong and certain as the assurance of condemnation on the other. Paul wants to show . . . how Christ has secured the benefits of that righteousness for all who belong to him" (*Romans*, 343).

ROMANS 6:1–14

Text and Translation

1 Therefore, what shall we say? Shall we continue in sin, in order that grace might increase? **2** May it never be! *We who died with refer*-ence to sin,[1] how shall we still live according to its standard?[2] **3** Or are you ignorant that as many *of us* as were baptized into *relation-ship with* Christ Jesus[3] were baptized into his death? **4** Therefore,[4] we were buried with him through baptism into his[5] death, in order that as Christ was raised from the dead because of the glory it would bring to the Father,[6] so also we might walk in new life.[7] **5** For if *it is true that* we have been[8] united *with him* in the likeness of his death, indeed also[9] we will be in the likeness of his[10] resurrection; **6** because we know[11] this: that our old man was crucified with *him*, in order that our sinful body[12] might be rendered ineffective, so that we might no longer keep on serving sin; **7** for the *one who* died[13] has been declared righteous from sin. **8** Now[14] if *it is true that* we died[15] with Christ, we are believing that we will live with him, **9** because we know[16] that after Christ was raised[17] from the dead, he no longer dies; death no longer

---

1. Τῇ ἁμαρτίᾳ is a dative of reference; see also verse 10.
2. Ἐν αὐτῇ denotes standard (cf. Wallace, *Grammar*, 372).
3. Harris argues that εἰς Χριστὸν Ἰησοῦν denotes relationship with and be-longing to Christ (*Prepositions*, 229).
4. The reading οὖν has considerably stronger manuscript support (א, A, B, C, D, 33) than either of the other two variants (γάρ; omit).
5. The definite article functions as a possessive pronoun.
6. Διά + genitive denotes the efficient cause; τοῦ πατρός is an objective genitive.
7. Ζωῆς is an attributed genitive.
8. Εἰ ... γεγόναμεν is a first-class condition.
9. Ἀλλά is emphatic; καί is adjunctive.
10. The definite article functions as a possessive pronoun.
11. Γινώσκοντες is an adverbial participle of cause.
12. The definite article functions as a possessive pronoun; ἁμαρτίας is an at-tributed genitive.
13. Ἀποθανών is a substantival participle.
14. Although 𝔓46 supports γάρ over δέ, the latter reading has considerably stronger support (א, A, B, C, D).
15. Εἰ ... ἀπεθάνομεν is a first-class condition.
16. Εἰδότες is an adverbial participle of cause.
17. Ἐγερθείς is an adverbial participle of time.

rules over him. **10** For what he died, he died *with reference* to sin once for all, and what he lives, he lives *with reference* to God. **11** So also[18] you must keep on considering[19] yourselves to be, on the one hand dead *with reference* to sin, on the other hand alive[20] *with reference* to God *because you are* in Christ Jesus.[21] **12** Therefore, sin must not continue ruling[22] in your mortal body so that *you* keep on obeying[23] its lusts,[24] **13** and stop presenting[25] your members to sin *as* instruments *for the purpose* of unrighteousness,[26] but present yourselves to God as alive from the dead and your members to God as instruments *for the purpose* of righteousness. **14** For sin will not rule over you; for you are not under law[27] but under grace.

Context and Structure

    II. Letter Body (1:18–15:13)
        A. The Gospel as the Revelation of God's Righteousness (1:18–4:25)
        B. The Gospel as the Demonstration of God's Power (5:1–8:39)
           1. The gospel demonstrates God's power to save from wrath (5:1–11)

---

18. Καί is adjunctive.
19. Λογίζεσθε is best understood as a progressive present in the imperative.
20. Ζῶντας is an adjectival participle functioning as a predicate accusative following εἶναι; see also verse 13.
21. Harris suggests that ἐν Χριστῷ Ἰησοῦ is causal (*Prepositions*, 124). The longer variant that includes τῷ κυρίῳ ἡμῶν is most likely an assimilation to 5:1, 21; 6:33 (cf. Moo, *Romans*, 353n10).
22. The third person singular prohibition μή ... βασιλευέτω is best translated using "must not"; the present tense highlights continuing action.
23. Εἰς τὸ ὑπακούειν is best understood as result; the present tense highlights continuing action.
24. The UBS[5] reading (ταῖς ἐπιθυμίαις αὐτοῦ) is the more difficult and has good Alexandrian manuscript support (𝔓[94], ℵ A, B, C*). The Western reading (αὐτῇ) is probably an attempt to clarify the original by understanding ἡ ἁμαρτία as the antecedent. The Byzantine reading (αὐτῇ ἐν ταῖς ἐπιθυμίαις αὐτοῦ) is a conflation of the other two.
25. Μηδέ παριστάνετε is a present tense prohibition and stands in strong contrast to the aorist tense command (ἀλλά παραστήσατε) that follows.
26. Both ἀδικίας and δικαιοσύνης are objective genitives describing purpose.
27. Ὑπό + accusative denotes subordination in both phrases; Harris suggests "under the rule of" (*Prepositions*, 221).

2. The gospel demonstrates God's power to save from condemnation (5:12–21)
3. The gospel demonstrates God's power to save from sin (6:1–23)
   a. **Because we died with Christ (6:1–14)**
   b. Because we serve a new master (6:15–23)
4. The gospel demonstrates God's power to save from the law (7:1–25)
5. The gospel demonstrates God's power to save from the flesh (8:1–30)
6. The gospel demonstrates God's power to save from all opposition (8:31–39)

Paul uses a series of rhetorical questions to raise a possible false conclusion that might be drawn from the previous discussion (6:1–2). In response, he uses the analogy of baptism to introduce the truth of identification with Christ's death, burial, and resurrection (6:3–4) and draw out the implications of that truth (6:5–11). He concludes with practical injunctions on how to live in light of those implications (6:12–14).

Basic Message and Exegetical Outline

Because we are united with Christ in his death, resurrection, and life, we must reject sin's rule in our lives by presenting ourselves to God.

Dead to Sin; Alive to God (6:1–14)
1. Baptism into Christ incorporates us into his death and resurrection (6:1–4)
   a. We should not continue living in sin (6:1–2)
   b. We should walk in new life (6:3–4)
2. We are incorporated into his death (6:5–7)
   a. Our "old man" was crucified with Christ (6:6)
   b. We have been declared righteous regarding sin (6:7)
3. We are incorporated into his resurrection (6:8–11)
   a. Death no longer rules Christ (6:9)
   b. Christ died to sin and lives to God (6:10–11)
4. Dying and rising (as one entity) with Christ calls us to reject sin's reign in our lives (6:12–14)
   a. We must not present our members to sin and unrighteousness (6:13a)
   b. We must present our members to God and righteousness (6:13b)

Explanation of the Text

1. Baptism into Christ incorporates us into his death and resurrection (6:1–4).

What conclusion should Paul's readers draw from what he has just written (τί οὖν ἐροῦμεν)? If one of the roles of the law is to cause sin to increase, and if the increase of sin causes grace to overflow (5:19), should they continue in sin (ἐπιμένομεν τῇ ἁμαρτίᾳ) in order to cause that overflow of grace to increase even more (ἵνα ἡ χάρις πλεονάσῃ)?[28] Paul emphatically rejects such a suggestion (μὴ γένοιτο), because it is illogical to think that someone who has died with reference to sin (οἵτινες ἀπεθάνομεν τῇ ἁμαρτίᾳ) would somehow choose to continue living according to the standard dictated by sin (πῶς ἔτι ζήσομεν ἐν αὐτῷ).[29]

In fact, they should realize (ἢ ἀγνοεῖτε) that their incorporation into Christ (ὅτι ὅσοι ἐβαπτίσθημεν εἰς Χριστὸν Ἰησοῦν) also incorporates them into the fact of his death (εἰς τὸν θάνατον αὐτοῦ ἐβαπτίσθημεν).[30] There is a logical implication (οὖν) to draw from the pattern of Christ's death: he died because his resurrection from the dead would bring glory to God (ἠγέρθη Χριστὸς ἐκ νεκρῶν διὰ τῆς δόξης τοῦ θεοῦ). In the same way (οὕτως καί), those who have been incorporated into Christ through baptism (διὰ τοῦ βαπτίσματος) have been incorporated into his death and burial (συνετάφημεν . . . εἰς τὸν θάνατον)[31] for the purpose (ἵνα) of walking in new life (ἡμεῖς ἐν καινότητι ζωῆς περιπατήσωμεν),[32] which will in turn, bring glory to God. Continuing to live in sin (6:1), therefore, would nullify the entire purpose of Christ's death.

---

28. Compare the similar false conclusion in 3:7–8.
29. It is as illogical to think that someone who has had a guilty verdict reversed and a death sentence commuted would choose to continue living on death row as it is to think that someone who has died with reference to sin would choose to continue living in sin. The possibility exists, but it makes little sense. Stott offers two other illustrations (*Romans*, 178–79).
30. In this passage, baptism is a sign of incorporation, not a picture of death and resurrection.
31. Paul's repeated use of words with the prefix συν- (συνετάφημεν, σύμφυτοι, συνεσταυρώθη, συζήσομεν) highlights our close association with Christ.
32. Paul states only parts of each side of the parallel, but the full sequence is clear when both sides are taken into account.

Christ:	death	{burial}	resurrection	{new life}	God's glory
Believer:	death	burial	{resurrection}	new life	{God's glory}

2. *We are incorporated into his death (6:5–7).*

Paul's first explanation (γάρ) of our incorporation into Christ focuses on our incorporation into his death. It follows logically that being united with Christ in the likeness of his death (εἰ σύμφυτοι γεγόναμεν τῷ ὁμοιώματι τοῦ θανάτου αὐτοῦ) will result in being united with him in his resurrection (ἀλλὰ καὶ τῆς ἀναστάσεως ἐσόμεθα). The reason we know we will be in the likeness of Christ's resurrection (τοῦτο γινώσκοντες) is that we have been crucified with him (cf. 2 Cor. 5:14). All that we were in Adam prior to our conversion (ὁ παλαιὸς ἡμῶν ἄνθρωπος) [33] was put to death when we were crucified with Christ (συνεσταυρώθη).[34] The purpose of being crucified with Christ (ἵνα) is that the whole person controlled by sin (τὸ σῶμα τῆς ἁμαρτίας)[35] might be deprived of power (καταργηθῇ). The result is that we no longer need to continue conducting ourselves in total service to sin (τοῦ μηκέτι δουλεύειν ἡμᾶς τῇ ἁμαρτίᾳ). The sequence, therefore, is: in-Adam existence crucified—sin deprived of power—delivered from sin's slavery. Paul's summary statement (6:7) explains (γάρ) the primary focus of his argument in this section: being crucified with Christ pays the penalty of sin: the person who has died (ὁ ἀποθανών) has been declared righteous (δεδκιαώται)[36] in regard to sin (ἀπὸ τῆς ἁμαρτίας).

3. *We are incorporated into his resurrection (6:8–11).*

Paul's second explanation (γάρ) of our incorporation into Christ focuses on our incorporation into his resurrection. It follows logically that having died with Christ (εἰ ἀπεθάνομεν σὺν Χριστῷ) we should believe that we will live with him (πιστεύομεν ὅτι καὶ συζήσομεν αὐτῷ).

---

33. Paul refers to the two spheres of human existence interchangeably as being "in Adam" and "in Christ" (e.g., 1 Cor. 15:21–22) or as "the old man" and "the new man" (e.g., Eph. 4:23–24; Col. 3:10–11).
34. The idea of being crucified with Christ here (Rom. 6:6) is distinct from the idea of crucifying the flesh (Gal. 5:24; cf. Rom. 8:13). The latter is something we do continually in order to subdue the lusts of sin (cf. 6:12). The former is something that was done to us once in order to pay the penalty of sin; it is closer to Galatians 2:20.
35. The translation "sinful body" should not be understood to suggest that the body is inherently sinful or evil. Romans 7 makes it clear that indwelling sin is the culprit. "Body" is best understood as referring to "the whole person controlled by sin" (Cranfield, *Romans*, 309).
36. Although most English versions translate δεδικαίωται as "has been set free," Paul uses ἐλευθερόω for the idea of being set free (6:15–23). It is more natural to retain the "righteousness" nuance of the verb. See Stott, *Romans*, 177.

Christ himself provides the basis for this expectation. After he was raised from the dead (ἐγερθεὶς ἐκ νεκρῶν), he no longer dies (οὐκέτι ἀποθνῄσκει), and death no longer exercises authority over him (θάνατος αὐτοῦ οὐκέτι κυριεύει). Paul's summary statement (6:10) explains (γάρ) that the primary focus of his argument in this section is the once-for-all (ἐφάπαξ) change Christ's death and resurrection accomplish.

| For what he died, | he died | with reference to sin | once for all, |
| and what he lives, | he lives | with reference to God | |

The once-for-all death involved was specifically "with reference to sin" (τῇ ἁμαρτίᾳ). Since Christ did not possess a sinful nature (Heb. 7:26) or commit actual sins (1 Peter 2:21–22), the death he died to sin was to its penalty (2 Cor. 5:21). His resurrection was the demonstration that sin no longer has any legal claim on him. The life he is now living (ζῇ), he lives "with reference to God" (τῷ θεῷ)—that is, he lives continually under God's total claim on him.[37] In the same way (οὕτως), those who are in Christ (ὑμεῖς) must also (καί) view themselves from the same perspective (λογίζεσθε ἑαυτούς). On the one hand (μέν), they are dead to sin (νεκροὺς τῇ ἁμαρτίᾳ), and sin has no claim on them. On the other hand (δέ), they are alive to God (ζῶντας τῷ θεῷ), and he has total claim on them.

4. Dying and rising (as one entity) with Christ calls us to reject sin's reign in our lives (6:12–14).
The truth of our dying and rising with Christ leads logically (οὖν) to action. Since it no longer has any legal claim on us (6:7, 10), sin must not exercise any authority over us (μὴ βασιλευέτω ἡ ἁμαρτία).[38] As was true in verse 6, the battleground is the whole person (ἐν τῷ θνητῷ ὑμῶν σώματι); the result of submitting to sin's reign is that we obey its lusts (εἰς τὸ ὑπακούειν ταῖς ἐπιθυμίαις αὐτοῦ). The essential decision involves the authority at whose disposal we are. We can choose repeatedly to place ourselves at sin's disposal (παριστάνετε τὰ μέλη ὑμῶν . . . τῇ ἁμαρτίᾳ) for the purpose of unrighteousness (ὅπλα ἀδικίας), or we can choose promptly to place ourselves at God's disposal (παραστήσατε ἑαυτοὺς . . . καὶ τὰ μέλη ὑμῶν . . . τῷ θεῷ) for the purpose of righteousness

---

37. The present tense of ζῇ is customary and denotes an ongoing state (cf. Wallace, *Grammar*, 521–22).
38. Cranfield's vivid comment is, ". . . now they must fight—they must not let sin go on reigning unopposed over their daily life, but must revolt in the name of their rightful ruler, God, against sin's usurping rule" (*Romans*, 316).

(ὅπλα δικαιοσύνης).[39] The basis on which the second choice rests and which, therefore, should drive our decision is our new life in Christ (ὡσεὶ ἐκ νεκρῶν ζῶντας). Further, sin is not our ruler (ἁμαρτία ὑμῶν οὐ κυριεύσει), because (γάρ) we have been transferred from being under law (οὐ . . . ὑπὸ νόμον) to being under grace (ἀλλὰ ὑπὸ χάριν)—that is, we have moved from the old state ("in Adam") that was administered according to law and was characterized by sin and death to the new state ("in Christ") that is administered according to grace and is characterized by righteousness and life.

Theology and Appropriation

Although it is not as prominent as the "in Christ" theme, the "with Christ" motif that occurs in Romans 6:1–14 occurs thirty-six times in Paul's letters.[40] It touches on multiple areas and highlights the extent of our identification with Christ. In the past, we were crucified with Christ (Rom. 6:6; Gal. 2:20), died with him (Rom. 6:5, 8; 2 Tim. 2:11), were buried with him (Rom. 6:4; Col. 2:12), were made alive with him (Eph. 2:5; Col. 2:13), were raised with him (Eph. 2:6; Col. 2:12; 3:1), and were seated with him in the heavenlies (Eph. 2:6). In the present, we are hidden in Christ in the heavenlies (Col. 3:3), live with him (Rom. 6:8; 2 Cor. 13:4; 2 Tim. 2:11), are empowered by him (Rom. 8:32; 2 Cor. 13:4), suffer with him (Rom. 8:17), and are being conformed to him (Rom. 8:29; Phil. 3:10). In the future, we will be heirs with Christ (Rom. 8:17), will be raised with him (2 Cor. 4:14), will be transformed to be like him (Phil. 3:21; Col. 3:4), will return with him (1 Thess. 4:14, 17), will live with him (Phil. 1:23; 1 Thess. 5:10), and will reign with him (2 Tim. 2:12). In fact, in every aspect of our Christian lives—past, present, and future—we are identified with Christ. Past participation in Christ's work gives us a new status that challenges us to live in a new way. Present life with Christ gives us the resources we need to be conformed to his example. Anticipation of future transformation to become like Christ gives us hope as we face the challenges of this life.

Paul's primary purpose for including this passage in his letter was to help his readers understand the significance of Christ's death and resurrection for the way they live. With those original readers,

---

39. The difference in verb tenses is significant. The present tense of μηδὲ παριστάνετε prohibits an action Paul views as happening regularly ("do not keep on presenting"); the aorist tense of παραστήσατε, although describing summary action, issues a more urgent command ("present—right now!").

40. For a full treatment, see Harvey, "The 'With Christ' Motif in Paul's Thought," *JETS* 35 (1992): 329–40.

we need to realize that our sinful patterns of thought and behavior should no longer control or characterize us. We live in a new era in which new paradigms apply. The natural points of connection for this passage are the ideas of life and death, which dominate the passage and to which every human being can relate. The passage corrects the idea that the way in which we live makes no difference. In fact, a correct understanding of our identification with Christ in his death and resurrection should lead to a total makeover of the way in which we live. The passage commends a wholehearted commitment to living under the rule of God and his grace. The objective in communicating this passage should be to help others understand that we have been incorporated into Christ's death and resurrection so that others will choose to submit to his authority and live righteously in a way that will bring glory to God.

ROMANS 6:15–23

Text and Translation

15 What then? Shall we continue sinning, because we are not under law but under grace? May it never be! **16** Do you not know that *to the one* to whom you are presenting yourselves as slaves resulting in obedience,[1] you are slaves *to that one* whom you are obeying, whether sin resulting in death or obedience resulting in righteousness? **17** But thanks *be* to God, because[2] you were enslaved by sin[3] but obeyed from the heart the form of teaching to which you were handed over, **18** and when you were set free[4] from sin, you were enslaved to righteousness. **19** I am speaking in human terms because of the weakness[5] of your flesh. For as you presented your members *as* slaves to uncleanness and lawlessness resulting in lawlessness,[6] so now present your members *as* slaves to righteousness resulting in sanctification. **20** For when you were enslaved to sin, you were free with reference to righteousness.[7] **21** Therefore, what fruit were you having at that time from those things about which[8] you are now ashamed? For the end brought about by those *things* [9] *is* death. **22** But now because you have been set free[10] from sin and have been enslaved with reference to God, you are having your fruit resulting in sanctification,[11] and the end *is* eternal life. **23** For the wages sin pays[12] *are* death, but the grace gift God gives is eternal life in Christ Jesus our Lord.

Context and Structure

    II. Letter Body (1:18–15:13)
        A. The Gospel as the Revelation of God's Righteousness
           (1:18–4:25)

---

1. Εἰς + accusative denotes result (three times in verse 16).
2. Ὅτι is best understood as causal.
3. Ἁμαρτίας is a subjective genitive; see also verse 20.
4. Ἐλευθερωθέντες is an adverbial participle of time.
5. Διά + accusative denotes cause.
6. Εἰς + accusative denotes result in both phrases.
7. Τῇ δικαιοσύνῃ is a dative of reference.
8. Ἐφ' οἷς is short for ἐπί τούτοις ἐφ' οἷς and supplies the basis for the shame.
9. Ἐκείνων is a genitive of production.
10. Both ἐλευθερωθέντες and δουλωθέντες are adverbial participles of cause.
11. Εἰς + accusative denotes result.
12. Both τῆς ἁμαρτίας and τοῦ θεοῦ are subjective genitives.

B. The Gospel as the Demonstration of God's Power
(5:1–8:39)
1. The gospel demonstrates God's power to save from wrath (5:1–11)
2. The gospel demonstrates God's power to save from condemnation (5:12–21)
3. The gospel demonstrates God's power to save from sin (6:1–23)
a. Because we died with Christ (6:1–14)
b. **Because we serve a new master (6:15–23)**
4. The gospel demonstrates God's power to save from the law (7:1–25)
5. The gospel demonstrates God's power to save from the flesh (8:1–30)
6. The gospel demonstrates God's power to save from all opposition (8:31–39)

Paul uses another rhetorical question to raise a false conclusion from what he has just written (6:15) and responds by introducing a basic principle about obedience and slavery (6:16). He then explains the change of masters that takes place at conversion (6:17–19). He concludes by contrasting the results of the two slaveries and, so, provides implicit motivation to embrace being enslaved to God (6:20–23).

Basic Message and Exegetical Outline

Obedience to the teaching of the gospel sets free from sin and death, enslaves to God and righteousness, and results in eternal life.

Freed from Sin; Enslaved to God (6:15–23)
1. You are slaves to the one you obey (6:15–16)
2. You once were slaves to sin but now are slaves to righteousness (6:17–19)
a. Your master has changed (6:17–18)
b. Your conduct should also change (6:19)
3. The two slaveries have contrasting results (6:20–23)
a. Slavery to sin results in death (6:20–21, 23a)
b. Slavery to God results in eternal life (6:22, 23b)

Explanation of the Text

1. You are slaves to the one you obey (6:15–16).

Lest his readers draw the wrong conclusion (τί οὖν) from what he has just written (6:14), Paul uses another rhetorical question that allows him to refute the possible objection. He rejects emphatically (μὴ γένοιτο) the idea that being under grace rather than law might lead to continued sinful conduct (ἁμαρτήσωμεν ὅτι οὐκ ἐσμὲν ὑπὸ νόμον ἀλλὰ ὑπὸ χάριν). Paul changes metaphors from death to slavery to show that such a conclusion runs counter to common knowledge (οὐκ οἴδατε). Since slaves present themselves to the master to whom they are bound for obedience (ᾧ παριστάνετε ἑαυτοὺς δούλους εἰς ὑπακοήν), obedience demonstrates whom a slave serves (δοῦλοι ἐστε ᾧ ὑπακούετε)—whether sin resulting in death (ἤτοι ἁμαρτίας εἰς θάνατον) or obedience resulting in righteousness (ἢ ὑπακοῆς εἰς δικαιοσύνην). As Paul will show, continuing in sin would demonstrate that his readers were obeying the wrong master.

2. You were once slaves to sin but now are slaves to righteousness (6:17–19).

Paul is confident (χάρις τῷ θεῷ) that his readers have experienced the transfer from being slaves of their old master, sin (ἦτε δοῦλοι τῆς ἁμαρτίας), to being slaves of a new master. The evidence of that transfer is their heartfelt obedience (ὑπηκούσατε ἐκ καρδίας) to the form of teaching (τύπον διδαχῆς) to which they have been handed over (εἰς ὃν παρεδόθητε).[13] Being released from sin (ἐλευθερωθέντες ἀπὸ τῆς ἁμαρτίας), their old master, does not leave them without a master. They are now enslaved to a new master: righteousness (ἐδουλώθητε τῇ δικαιοσύνῃ). That change of masters has practical implications, and Paul states them in another parallel construction.

As you presented your members	to uncleanness and lawlessness	resulting in lawlessness,
so now present your members	to righteousness	resulting in sanctification.

Previously, their slavery was to uncleanness and lawlessness (τῇ ἀκαθαρσίᾳ καὶ τῇ ἀνομίᾳ) and resulted in the process of becoming even more lawless (εἰς τὴν ἀνομίαν). Now (νῦν) their slavery is to righteousness (τῇ δικαιοσύνῃ) and results in the process of becoming holy (εἰς

---

13. It would seem more natural to speak of the teaching being handed over to them rather than of them being handed over to the teaching, but the awkward syntax emphasizes God's role in the process (cf. Schreiner, *Romans*, 336).

ἁγιασμόν). Their responsibility is to present themselves (παραστήσατε τὰ μέλη ὑμῶν) to their new master.

3. The two slaveries have contrasting results (6:20–23).
The reason (γάρ) to present ourselves to our new master resides in the far better consequences that ensue. Although a slave of sin (ὅτε δοῦλοι ἦτε τῆς ἁμαρτίας) is free with respect to righteousness (ἐλεύθεροι ἦτε τῇ δικαιοσύνῃ), he/she produces fruit leading to shame (καρπὸν εἴχετε . . . ἐφ᾿ οἷς . . . ἐπαισχύνεσθε), and the end result is death (τὸ τέλος ἐκείνων θάνατος). In contrast, a slave of God (δουλωθέντες τῷ θεῷ) is free with respect to sin (ἐλευθερωθέντες ἀπὸ τῆς ἁμαρτίας), produces fruit leading to sanctification (ἔχετε τὸν καρπὸν ὑμῶν εἰς ἁγιασμόν), and the end result is eternal life (τὸ τέλος ζωὴν αἰώνιον). Paul summarizes the contrast in a concise, parallel statement.

The wages	sin pays	are death;
the gift	God gives	is eternal life.

Our old master, sin, pays us the wages we have earned (τὰ ὀψώνια τῆς ἁμαρτίας): death (θάνατος). Our new master, God, freely and graciously gives us a gift we have not earned (τὸ χάρισμα τοῦ θεοῦ): eternal life (ζωὴ αἰώνιος). Why would we choose to serve any master other than God?

Theology and Appropriation
Paul's letters make it clear that being in Christ eliminates differences of gender, ethnicity, and socioeconomic status (1 Cor. 12:13; Gal. 3:28; Col. 3:11). His letter to Philemon directly addresses the impact the gospel has on the relationship between slaves and their masters. Yet, as is clear from Romans 6:15–23, the metaphor of slavery is one that appears repeatedly in his letters. Paul identifies himself as a "slave of Jesus Christ" in three salutations (Rom. 1:1; Phil. 1:1; Titus 1:1), and he applies the same label to Epaphras (Col. 4:12). There are at least three suggestions for why Paul would label himself a slave. Longenecker, for example, connects it to the "Servant of Yahweh" (e.g., Isa. 49:1–6) as an Old Testament prophetic designation.[14] Jewett relates it to the title "slave of Caesar" as indicating influential representatives in the imperial service.[15] More likely, however, are connotations of "humility, devotion, and service,"[16] since, for

---

14. Longenecker, *Romans*, 51.
15. Jewett, *Romans*, 100.
16. Moo, *Romans*, 41.

example, Paul writes to Timothy that "the Lord's bondservant must not be quarrelsomel, but be kind to all . . . patient when wronged, with gentleness correcting those who are in opposition" (2 Tim. 2:24–25; cf. Rom. 14:18; 16:18). Such an understanding would also be in keeping with the example of Jesus, who "emptied himself, taking the form of a bondservant . . . humbled himself by becoming obedient to the point of death, even death on a cross," and as a result was highly exalted, received "the name that is above every name," and is confessed as Lord by every tongue (Phil. 2:5–11).

In Romans 6:15–23, Paul's emphasis is on our new slavery to God that replaces our old slavery to sin. That former slavery involved total ownership, total obedience, and total accountability. His challenge is that we should present ourselves to God with the same single-minded devotion we had when we served sin. Passages in which Paul writes about the way in which human slaves should relate to their human masters help us catch a glimpse of what he has in mind in Romans 6. There are three such passages. Ephesians 6:5–8 highlights obedience, sincerity, willingness, a heartfelt pursuit of God's will, and the expectancy of receiving back from his master. The parallel passage in Colossians 3:22–24 highlights obedience, sincerity of heart, and the expectation of the reward of an inheritance. Titus 2:9 highlights submission, lack of an argumentative attitude, good faith, and a life that adorns the doctrine of God in every respect. These passages provide a good look at what it means to obey "from the heart the form of teaching to which you were handed over" as a slave of Jesus Christ (Rom. 6:17).

Paul's primary reason for including this passage in Romans was to help his readers understand that Christ's work on their behalf has fully and finally severed any obligation they have to obey sin and its lusts. They might still choose to obey sin, but they are no longer obligated to do so. With his original readers we share the need to realize fully our freedom to say "No" to sin and "Yes" to righteousness. Points of connection to this passage include obedience, the servant/master relationship, and the contrast between wages that are earned and a gift that is not earned. This passage corrects the idea that it is possible to claim to follow Jesus and not obey him. Since obedience demonstrates ownership, followers of Jesus who consistently obey sin and its lusts must examine their claim to be his. The passage commends embracing the new ownership arrangement by wholeheartedly obeying our new master: Jesus. The objective in communicating this passage should be to help others understand that their obligation to sin has ended so that they will say "No" to sin and "Yes" to righteous living.

ROMANS 7:1–6

Text and Translation

1 Or are you ignorant, brothers—for I am speaking to those who are knowing[1] the law—that the law rules over a person[2] for as much time as that person is living? **2** For the married woman has been bound by law to the living[3] husband; but if the husband dies[4] she has been released from the law of her husband.[5] **3** Consequently, while her[6] husband is living[7] she is being called an adulteress, if she becomes[8] another man's *wife*;[9] but if her husband dies, she is free from the law, so that she is not[10] an adulteress if she becomes another man's *wife*. **4** So then, my brothers, you also[11] were put to death *with reference* to the law[12] through the body of Christ in order for you to become[13] another's,[14] the *one who* was raised[15] from the dead, in order that you might bear fruit to God. **5** For when you were in the flesh, the sinful[16] passions that are through the law were working[17] in your members, in order to bear fruit[18] to death; **6** but now you were released from the law, because you died[19] *with reference to that* by which[20] you were being held

1. Γινώσκουσιν is a substantival participle and functions as an indirect object.
2. Τοῦ ἀνθρώπου is a genitive of direct object; definite article identifies a category.
3. Ζῶντι is an adjectival participle modifying ἀνδρί.
4. Ἐάν ... ἀποθάνῃ is a third class condition.
5. The definite article functions as a possessive pronoun; τοῦ ἀνδρός is an objective genitive; Cranfield suggests "the law that binds the wife to the husband" (*Romans*, 333–34).
6. The definite article functions as a possessive pronoun.
7. Ζῶντος τοῦ ἀνδρός is a genitive absolute of time.
8. Ἐάν ... ἀποθάνῃ is a third class condition (twice in verse 3).
9. Ἀνδρί ἑτέρῳ is a possessive dative (twice in verse 3).
10. Τοῦ μὴ εἶναι denotes result.
11. Καί is adjunctive.
12. Τῷ νόμῳ is a dative of reference.
13. Εἰς τὸ γενέσθαι denotes purpose.
14. Ἑτέρῳ is possessive dative.
15. Τῷ ... ἐγερθέντι is a substantival participle in apposition to ἑτέρῳ.
16. Τῶν ἁμαρτιῶν is a genitive of quality.
17. Ἐνηργεῖτο is a progressive imperfect that highlights constant activity.
18. Εἰς τὸ καρποφορῆσαι denotes result.
19. Ἀποθανόντες is an adverbial participle of cause.
20. Ἐν ᾧ is short for τούτῳ ἐν ᾧ and denotes means.

fast, so that you might serve[21] in newness that comes from the Spirit[22] and not in oldness that comes from the letter.

Context and Structure

II. Letter Body (1:18–15:13)
- A. The Gospel as the Revelation of God's Righteousness (1:18–4:25)
- B. The Gospel as the Demonstration of God's Power (5:1–8:39)
  1. The gospel demonstrates God's power to save from wrath (5:1–11)
  2. The gospel demonstrates God's power to save from condemnation (5:12–21)
  3. The gospel demonstrates God's power to save from sin (6:1–23)
  4. The gospel demonstrates God's power to save from the law (7:1–25)
     - a. **Because dying with Christ brings release from the law (7:1–6)**
     - b. Because the law brings knowledge of sin (7:7–12)
     - c. Because sin uses the law to produce death (7:13–25)
  5. The gospel demonstrates God's power to save from the flesh (8:1–30)
  6. The gospel demonstrates God's power to save from all opposition (8:31–39)

Paul phrases a disclosure formula as another question that allows him to explain how his readers are no longer under law (7:1). He uses an analogy from marital law to establish the basic principle that the death of one of the parties in a relationship ends the obligation of the other party (7:2–3). He then applies that principle to his readers in light of their death with Christ (7:4–6).

Basic Message and Exegetical Outline

Because Christ's death releases us from the law's obligation and stigma, we are free to bear fruit for and serve God.

---

21. Ὥστε δουλεύειν denotes result.
22. Πνεύματος and γράμματος are both genitives of source.

Released from the Law; joined to Christ (7:1–6)
1. The law rules a person as long as he/she lives (7:1–3)
   a. Death releases from the law's obligation (7:2)
   b. Death sets free from the law's stigma (7:3)
2. Christ's death severs our obligation to the law (7:4–6)
   a. So that we might bear fruit to God (7:4)
   b. So that we might serve in newness of the Spirit (7:5–6)

Explanation of the Text

1. The law rules a person as long as he/she lives (7:1–3).

Because he is writing to readers who know the Mosaic law (γινώσκουσιν νόμον λαλῶ), Paul expects them to understand (ἢ ἀγνοεῖτε, ἀδελφοί) a further implication of their incorporation into Christ: their death with Christ ends their relationship to the law, just as it ends their ownership by sin (6:15–23). The basic principle is that the law exercises authority over a person as long as that person lives (ὁ νόμος κυριεύει τοῦ ἀνθρώπου ἐφ᾽ ὅσον χρόνον ζῇ).

An example from Jewish marital law illustrates (γάρ) the principle. As long as her husband lives (τῷ ζῶντι ἀνδρί), a married woman (ἡ ὕπανδρος γυνή) is bound to him by law (δέδεται νόμῳ). If her husband were to die (ἐὰν ἀποθάνῃ ὁ ἀνήρ), however, she would be released from the law that bound her to her husband (κατήργηται ἀπὸ τοῦ νόμου τοῦ ἀνδρός). It follows logically (ἄρα οὖν), therefore, that the widow would be free to marry another man. As long as her husband lives (ζῶντος τοῦ ἀνδρός), she would be called an adulteress (μοιχαλὶς χρηματίσει) if she were to marry another man (ἐὰν γένηται ἀνδρὶ ἑτέρῳ). The death of her husband (ἐὰν ἀποθάνῃ ὁ ἀνήρ), though, would have two results. First, she would be free from her obligation to the law (ἐλευθέρα ἐστὶν ἀπὸ τοῦ νόμου), and second, she would no longer need to fear the stigma of being labeled an adulteress (τοῦ μὴ εἶναι μοιχαλίδα) if she were to remarry (γενομένην ἀνδρὶ ἑτέρῳ).

2. Christ's death severs our obligation to the law (7:4–6).

The application Paul draws for his readers (ὥστε, ἀδελφοί μου, καὶ ὑμεῖς) speaks directly to their relationship to the Mosaic law. By means of Christ's crucifixion (διὰ τοῦ σώματος τοῦ Χριστοῦ), God ended their obligation to the law and its authority over them (ἐθανατώθητε τῷ νόμῳ).[23] The purpose of dying with Christ is that they might be joined

---

23. "The body of Christ" is best understood as "his person put to death on the cross" (Cranfield, *Romans*, 336). The idea of being "put to death with

to another (εἰς τὸ γενέσθαι ὑμᾶς ἑτέρῳ) who was raised from the dead (τῷ ἐκ νεκρῶν ἐγερθέντι), and the purpose of being joined to Christ is to bear fruit for God (ἵνα καρποφορήσωμεν τῷ θεῷ).

Paul explains (γάρ) the resulting difference in two verses that preview his discussion of life lived in the flesh (7:5; cf. 7:7–25) and life lived in the Spirit (7:6; cf. 8:1–39). Prior to their conversion, believers were "in the flesh" (ὅτε ἦμεν ἐν τῇ σαρκὶ).[24] That existence was dominated by sinful passions (τὰ παθήματα τῶν ἁμαρτιῶν) that constantly used the law (τὰ διὰ τοῦ νόμου ἐνηργεῖτο) to produce fruit resulting in death (εἰς τὸ καρποφορῆσαι τῷ θανάτῳ).[25] Now, however, they have been released from the law (νυνὶ δὲ κατηργήθημεν ἀπὸ τοῦ νόμου) because they have died to its imprisonment (ἀποθανόντες ἐν ᾧ κατειχόμεθα).[26] The result of dying to the law and its imprisonment is that we serve in "the new state determined by the Spirit" (ὥστε δουλεύειν ἡμᾶς ἐν καινότητι πνεύματος) rather than "the old state determined by the letter" (οὐ παλαιότητι γράμματος) of the law.[27]

Theology and Appropriation

Perhaps the most prominent motif that runs throughout Romans 5–8 is the change that takes place when God transfers a person from being in Adam to being in Christ. The most extensive treatment, of course, is in 5:12–21, where Paul contrasts the immediate effect, the resulting status, and the ultimate effect.[28] Chapter 6 continues the contrast when Paul describes believers as dead to sin but alive to God (6:1–14) as well as freed from sin but enslaved to God (6:15–23). At the beginning of the latter section, Paul also declares that believers are "not under law but under grace" (6:15). He elaborates on that change in 7:1–6. Specifically, Christ's death on our behalf brings an end to that aspect of being in Adam related to the law as the administrative

---

reference to the law" is best understood in terms similar to 6:14. Our old existence ("in Adam")—administered according to law and characterized by sin and death—has ended.

24. In 8:8–9, Paul explicitly contrasts existence "in the flesh" (ἐν σαρκί) and existence "in the Spirit" (ἐν πνεύματι).

25. The phrase "in our members" (ἐν τοῖς μέλεσιν ἡμῶν) denotes the location in which sin used the law and includes our physical, cognitive, and emotional faculties. Paul reiterates the idea when he talks about "the sin that is dwelling in us" (7:17, 21).

26. Κατέχω describes the act of confining someone or something within certain limits. In extrabiblical literature it can describe being imprisoned.

27. The suggested translations are Moo's (*Romans*, 421n64).

28. See also Harvey, *Pauline Letters*, 82–83.

system under which we must relate to God. As a result, we are no longer obligated to try to keep the letter of the law as a means of pursuing the life it promises (cf. Lev. 18:5). We are now free to pursue life under the new administrative system superintended by the Holy Spirit (cf. 2 Cor. 3:1–18). This paragraph in Romans adds one more stone to the foundation upon which Paul builds his call to the life in the Spirit in Romans 8.

Paul's primary purpose for including this paragraph at this point in his letter was to help his readers understand that they were released from the law as a governing system and were free to live under the new system into which they were transferred by Christ's death. With his original readers we need to realize that we are free from any sense of obligation or guilt arising from our previous attempts to keep the law. Given the example Paul uses in verses 2–3, the natural point of connection to this passage is the institution of marriage, including the experiences of widowhood and remarriage. This passage corrects any teaching that suggests we are under an arrangement that depends on the Old Testament law as its governing authority. Rather, the passage commends living in newness of life by the power of the Holy Spirit. The objective in communicating this passage should be to help others understand that they are now free from any sense of obligation to the law as a governing authority so that they will live under the Holy Spirit as the new governing authority.

ROMANS 7:7–12

Text and Translation

7 Therefore, what shall we say? *Is* the law[1] sin? May it never be! Indeed[2] I did not know sin except through the law;[3] for indeed[4] I did not know coveting except the law was saying, **"You shall not covet."** **8** And sin opportunistically took advantage[5] *and* through the commandment produced in me all *kinds* of coveting;[6] for apart from the law, sin *was* dead. **9** Now once I was alive apart from the law, but when the commandment came,[7] sin came alive,[8] **10** but I died, and the commandment—which was *intended* to result in life—this *commandment* was found to result in death for me. **11** For sin opportunistically took advantage through the law *and* deceived me, and through it I died. **12** So then, indeed,[9] the law *is* holy, and the commandment *is* holy and just and good.

Context and Structure

II. Letter Body (1:18–15:13)
   A. The Gospel as the Revelation of God's Righteousness (1:18–4:25)
   B. The Gospel as the Demonstration of God's Power (5:1–8:39)
      1. The gospel demonstrates God's power to save from wrath (5:1–11)
      2. The gospel demonstrates God's power to save from condemnation (5:12–21)
      3. The gospel demonstrates God's power to save from sin (6:1–23)
      4. The gospel demonstrates God's power to save from the law (7:1–25)

---

1. Throughout the paragraph, νόμος refers to the Mosaic law (cf. Schreiner, *Romans*, 358).
2. Ἀλλά is emphatic.
3. Νόμου is definite although anarthrous.
4. Τε is emphatic.
5. Λαβοῦσα is an adverbial participle of manner; see also verse 11.
6. Πᾶσαν is qualitative and designates a class.
7. Ἐλθούσης is an adverbial participle of time.
8. Ἀνέζησεν is an ingressive aorist.
9. Μέν is emphatic.

    a. Because dying with Christ brings release from the law (7:1–6)
    b. **Because the law brings knowledge of sin (7:7–12)**
    c. Because sin uses the law to produce death (7:13–25)
  5. The gospel demonstrates God's power to save from the flesh (8:1–30)
  6. The gospel demonstrates God's power to save from all opposition (8:31–39)

Paul continues his question-and-answer style to clarify the nature of the law: it brings the knowledge of sin (7:7) and is divine in its origin, character, and purpose (7:12). A central panel, framed by ring-composition, explains that the problem is sin's opportunistic use of the law to deceive and kill (7:8–11).

Basic Message and Exegetical Outline

Although the law is good and makes sin known, sin uses the law to deceive and kill.

    Law Good; Sin Bad (7:7–12)
  1. The law is not sin; it makes sin known (7:7)
  2. Sin uses the law to deceive and kill (7:8–11)
    a. Apart from the law, sin cannot achieve its purpose (7:8)
    b. When the law comes, sin springs to life and brings death (7:9–10)
    c. Sin takes opportunity through the law to deceive and kill (7:11)
  3. The law is holy, just, and good (7:12)

Explanation of the Text

1. The law is not sin; it makes sin known (7:7).

    If sin constantly uses the law to bear fruit that results in death (7:5), should the Romans conclude (τί οὖν ἐροῦμεν) that the law is sin (ὁ νόμος ἁμαρτία)? Paul emphatically rejects that idea (μὴ γένοιτο). In fact, (ἀλλά), we would not arrive at a knowledge of what sin truly is (τὴν ἁμαρτίαν οὐκ ἔγνων) apart from the Mosaic law (εἰ μὴ διὰ νόμου).[10] Paul uses coveting as a representative example: we would not know what it means to covet (τήν ἐπιθυμίαν οὐκ ᾔδειν) apart from the specific commandment that says "You shall not covet" (εἰ μὴ ὁ νόμος ἔλεγεν οὐκ ἐπιθυμήσεις). The law is not sin; it makes sin known.

2. Sin uses the law to deceive and kill (7:8–11).

Further, the law is not the problem; sin is the problem. Sin uses the commandment as an opportunity (ἀφορμὴν λαβοῦσα ἡ ἁμαρτία διὰ τῆς ἐντολῆς) to produce all kinds of coveting in a person (κατειργάσατο ἐν ἐμοὶ πᾶσαν ἐπιθυμίαν), because sin is "incapable of achieving its purpose"[11] of inducing violations of God's will (ἁμαρτία νεκρά) apart from the law (χωρὶς νόμου). Human experience testifies to the interaction of sin and the law.[12] Prior to knowing the law (χωρὶς νόμου ποτέ), we were ignorant of the fact that we were living contrary to God's will (ἐγώ ἔζων).[13] The arrival of the commandment (ἐλθούσης τῆς ἐντολῆς) had a double-edged effect: sin "sprang to life again" (ἡ ἁμαρτία ἀνέζησεν), but we died (ἐγὼ ἀπέθανον). To our disadvantage (μοι), the commandment—which promises life for the one who obeys it (ἡ εἰς ζωήν)[14]—proved to be a source of death (εὑρέθη . . . ἡ ἐντολὴ . . . εἰς θάνατον), because (γάρ) sin takes advantage of the opportunity provided by the commandment (ἡ ἁμαρτία ἀφορμὴν λαβοῦσα διὰ τῆς ἐντολῆς), deceives us (ἐξηπάτησέν με), and kills us (καὶ δι' αὐτῆς ἀπέκτεινεν). Now, rather than sinning in ignorance, we are guilty of violating known expressions of God's will. Such violations confirm our sinfulness and guilt before God and will ultimately result in both physical and eternal death.

---

10. Cranfield observes that we would not understand that sin is a deliberate disobedience of God's revealed will apart from the law (*Romans*, 349).
11. Jewett, *Romans*, 450. The adjective νεκρός, -ά, -όν can mean "dead" (cf. James 2:26), "useless" (cf. Heb. 9:14), or "powerless" (cf. Eph. 2:5). The third nuance applies here.
12. The identity of "I" in Romans 7 has consumed considerable scholarly energy. The three most common interpretations are Adam (Dunn, *Romans*, 381–84), Israel (Moo, *Romans*, 437–39), or Paul himself (Schreiner, *Romans*, 363–65). The best option might well be Paul in solidarity with the human experience we all share.
13. Paul has already made it clear that ignorance of God's specific commandments does not exempt anyone from the ultimate penalty of sin (cf. Rom. 5:12–14).
14. Leviticus 18:5; Psalm 19:7–10; Ezekiel 20:11; Luke 20:38.

3. The law is holy, just, and good (7:12).

Paul's conclusion from verses 7–11 (ὥστε) relates to the Mosaic law as a whole (ὁ νόμος) and to specific commandments that constitute the law (ἡ ἐντολή). "Holy" (ἅγιος) points to the law's divine origin; "just" (δίκαιος) points to its divine character; "good" (ἀγαθός) points to its divine purpose. Although sin takes advantage of the law to deceive and kill, the law is not sin (7:7). It is "a gift of God, given to serve his purposes."[15]

Theology and Appropriation

Seventy-five of the 122 occurrences of "law" (νόμος) in Paul's letters are concentrated in Romans.[16] At this point in his letter, Paul has raised the issue of law in every chapter except the first. Most commonly, "law" describes the divine requirements given to Israel through Moses. From Paul's perspective, the Mosaic law is holy, just, good, and spiritual (7:12, 14). The law was intended to result in life (7:10) and promises life for perfect obedience (10:5; cf. Lev. 18:5). Because sin is not counted as a violation of God's will apart from the law (5:13), the law brings a knowledge of sin (3:20; 7:7) and, with that knowledge, wrath (4:15). The law makes all the world accountable before God (3:19), and everyone will be judged according to the standard of whether or not they do the law (2:12–15).

Although it causes sin to increase (5:20), the law is not sin (7:7), and being released from the law does not provide an occasion to continue sinning (6:15). The problem is indwelling sin, which uses the law as an occasion to provoke sinful acts (7:5, 8–11, 17, 20). Under these circumstances, the law can never be a means by which any individual is declared righteous (3:20, 28). Instead, Christ brings an end to the law with regard to righteousness to everyone who believes (10:4). Our incorporation into Christ's death and resurrection means that we are now under grace rather than law (6:14) because he has fulfilled the righteous requirement of the law (8:3–4). We are, therefore, free from the law as an administrative system for relating to God (7:4; cf. 2 Cor. 3:5–11). Nevertheless, as we walk according to the Spirit (8:4) and love our neighbor, we fulfill the intent of the law (13:8–10). Paul can say, therefore, that his gospel establishes the law (3:31) as God's revelation that brings the knowledge of sin, as God's requirement that he fulfills in Christ, and as God's expression of his moral norms for living.

---

15. Dunn, *Romans*, 402.
16. The second largest concentration is in Galatians (32). The remaining fifteen occurrences are in 1 Corinthians (9), Ephesians (1), Philippians (3), and 1 Timothy (2).

Paul's primary purpose for including this paragraph at this point in his letter was to help his readers understand the relationship between law and sin. Because he wanted the Romans to live in newness of life (7:6), they needed to know that the law makes sin known, but sin uses the law for its own purposes. He will explain the latter aspect at greater length in the following paragraph. With those original readers we need to realize that the interplay between the law and sin is complex and, so, need to be alert to the way in which sin uses the law to deceive and kill. A natural point of connection to the passage is the concept of law. The idea of commandments might be an additional point of connection, including the more specific example of the Ten Commandments. The passage corrects any notion that the law is inherently evil or sinful or that it promotes sin. In contrast, it commends a proper perspective on the law as holy, just, and good because it comes from God. The objective in communicating this passage should be to help others understand that, although the law is inherently good, sin uses it for evil so that they will be alert to the way in which sin uses the law to deceive and kill.

ROMANS 7:13–25

Text and Translation

13 Therefore, has that which is good become¹ death to me? May it never be! But sin—in order that sin might become apparent—*was* producing² death in me³ through that which is good, in order that sin might become exceedingly⁴ sinful through the commandment. **14** For we know⁵ that the law is spiritual, but I am fleshly, having been sold⁶ under *the authority of* sin.⁷ **15** For I am not knowing what I am doing; for what I am wishing, this I am not practicing, but what I am hating, this I am doing. **16** Now if what I am not wishing, this I am doing, I am agreeing with the law that it *is* good. **17** But now I am no longer doing it but the sin *that is* dwelling⁸ in me. **18** For I know that *the capacity to do* good is not dwelling in me—that is, in my flesh; for the willing⁹ is present with me,¹⁰ but the working of the good *is* not;¹¹ **19** for I am not doing the good that I am wishing, but the evil that I am not wishing, this I am practicing. **20** Now if *it is true that* what I am not wishing,¹² this I¹³ am doing, I am no longer doing it, but the sin *that is* dwelling in me. **21** Therefore, I am finding the principle—in

---

1. Ἐγένετο is a consummative aorist.
2. The sentence lacks a verb. The simplest solution is to supply ἦν and understand κατεργαζομένη as a periphrastic participle that is part of the main verb. (See Moo, *Romans*, 452n29.)
3. Μοι is locative.
4. The prepositional phrase καθ᾽ ὑπερβολήν functions adverbially to modify the adjective ἁμαρτωλός.
5. Οἴδαμεν has good manuscript support (א, A, B*, C, D). The variant reading (οἶδα μεν) is most likely influenced by the use of the first person singular elsewhere in 7:7–25.
6. Εἰμι πεπραμένος is a periphrastic participle; the intensive perfect emphasizes the existing state.
7. Ὑπό + accusative denotes subordination.
8. Οἰκοῦσα is an adjectival participle; see also verse 20.
9. Θέλειν and κατεργάζεσθαι are substantival infinitives.
10. Μοι is a dative of association.
11. The reading οὔ is shorter, more difficult, and has better manuscript support (א, A, B, C) than either of the two longer variants.
12. Εἰ . . . ποιῶ is a first-class condition.
13. The manuscript evidence to include (א, A, 33) or omit (B, C, D) the pronoun ἐγώ is evenly balanced, and the meaning of Paul's statement is not affected either way.

me, the *one who* is wishing[14] to be doing the good—that evil is present in me;[15] **22** for I am delighting in[16] God's law[17] according to the inner man, **23** but I am seeing another law in my members that is warring against[18] the law of my mind and is taking me captive[19] to the law of sin[20] that is[21] in my members. **24** Wretched man *that* I *am*; who will rescue me from this dead body?[22] **25** Thanks *be* to God[23] through Christ Jesus our Lord. Consequently, on the one hand I myself am serving God's law with my[24] mind, on the other hand *I am serving* sin's law with my flesh.

Context and Structure

II. Letter Body (1:18–15:13)
   A. The Gospel as the Revelation of God's Righteousness (1:18–4:25)
   B. The Gospel as the Demonstration of God's Power (5:1–8:39)
      1. The gospel demonstrates God's power to save from wrath (5:1–11)
      2. The gospel demonstrates God's power to save from condemnation (5:12–21)
      3. The gospel demonstrates God's power to save from sin (6:1–23)

---

14. Τῷ θέλοντι is a substantival participle in apposition to ἐμοί; the participial phrase is parenthetical.
15. Ἐμοί is locative.
16. BDAG highlights the association explicit in the prefix of συνήδομαι by translating the verb as "experience joy in connection" (971c).
17. The reading θεοῦ is strongly supported (ℵ, A, C, D, 33); the variant reading νοός is most likely an assimilation to verse 23.
18. Ἀντιστρατυόμενον is an adjectival participle modifying ἕτερον νόμον; τῷ νόμῳ is a dative of disadvantage.
19. Αἰχμαλωντίζοντα is an adjectival participle modifying ἕτερον νόμον.
20. Ἐν τῷ νόμῳ is equivalent to εἰς + accusative; τῆς ἁμαρτίας is a subjective genitive.
21. Τῷ ὄντι is a substantival participle in apposition to τῷ νόμῳ.
22. Τοῦ θανάτου is an attributive genitive.
23. Metzger concludes that the UBS[5] reading best explains the other three variants (*Textual Commentary*, 455). Schreiner has a helpful summary (*Romans*, 394).
24. The definite article functions as a possessive pronoun.

    4. The gospel demonstrates God's power to save from the law (7:1–25)
       a. Because dying with Christ brings release from the law (7:1–6)
       b. Because the law brings knowledge of sin (7:7–12)
       c. **Because sin uses the law to produce death (7:13–25)**
    5. The gospel demonstrates God's power to save from the flesh (8:1–30)
    6. The gospel demonstrates God's power to save from all opposition (8:31–39)

Paul begins his third and longest paragraph in his discussion of the law with another question that allows him to address another possible false conclusion (7:13). Two parallel sections (7:14–17 and 7:18–20) explain how indwelling sin (not the law) produces death and end with identical wording. The final section summarizes the resulting "spiritual schizophrenia" and makes it clear that only Christ can deliver from that wretched condition (7:21–25).

Basic Message and Exegetical Outline

Only Christ can deliver us from a life of futility and death caused by indwelling sin.

    The Role of Indwelling Sin (7:13–25)
    1. The law does not cause death; sin uses the law to produce death (7:13)
    2. We are sold under sin (7:14–17)
       a. We agree that the law is good, but we do what we hate (7:15–16)
       b. Indwelling sin is the problem (7:17)
    3. Good does not dwell in us (7:18–20)
       a. We want to do good, but we do evil instead (7:18b–19)
       b. Indwelling sin is the problem (7:20)
    4. The result is "spiritual schizophrenia" (7:21–25)
       a. Our mind serves the law of God (7:22, 25b)
       b. Our flesh serves the law of sin (7:23, 25c)
       c. The solution is Jesus Christ (7:24–25a)

Explanation of the Text

1. The law does not cause death; sin uses the law to produce death (7:13).

It would be wrong to conclude (οὖν), based on what Paul has just written, that the law causes death (τὸ ἀγαθὸν ἐμοὶ ἐγένετο θάνατος).[25] Paul emphatically rejects such a suggestion (μὴ γένοιτο). Instead (ἀλλά), as Paul has already written in verses 8–11, the culprit is sin. It is sin that produces death (ἡ ἁμαρτία . . . κατεργαζομένη θάνατον). In so doing, sin shows its true character (ἵνα φανῇ ἁμαρτία) and becomes "exceedingly sinful" (ἵνα γένηται καθ᾽ ὑπερβολὴν ἁμαρτωλὸς ἡ ἁμαρτία). In both instances, the law is the instrument sin uses (διὰ τοῦ ἀγαθοῦ . . . διὰ τῆς ἐντολῆς). Paul will explain how sin uses the law for its own purposes in the two parallel sections that follow (7:14–17, 18–20).

2. We are sold under sin (7:14–17).

Paul draws his readers into his first explanation (γάρ) of how sin becomes exceedingly sinful by suggesting that the concept he is going to describe is common knowledge (οἴδαμεν). Not only is the law holy, just, and good (7:12), it is also spiritual (ὁ νόμος πνευματικός ἐστιν)— that is, the law belongs "to the sphere of the Spirit of God"[26] rather than to the sphere of the flesh. In contrast (δέ), our human nature[27] is fleshly (ἐγὼ σάρκινός εἰμι)[28] and has been sold into the captivity of slavery under the authority and power of sin (πεπραμένος ὑπὸ τὴν ἁμαρτίαν). When we live as slaves under the authority and power of sin, we experience cognitive and behavioral dysfunction. We do not understand our own behavior (ὃ κατεργάζομαι οὐ γινώσκω). We do what we hate (ὃ μισῶ τοῦτο ποιῶ) rather than practicing what we wish (οὐ ὃ θέλω τοῦτο πράσσω). The very fact, however, that we do what we do not wish (εἰ δὲ ὃ οὐ θέλω τοῦτο ποιῶ) means we agree that the law is good (σύμφημι τῷ νόμῳ ὅτι καλός). Logically then (νυνὶ δέ), indwelling sin is the culprit (ἡ οἰκοῦσα ἐν ἐμοι ἁμαρτία); we are not (οὐκέτι ἐγὼ κατεργάζομαι αὐτὸ).

---

25. "That which is good" is a reference to the law that reflects Paul's statement in 7:12 that the law is "holy, just, and good."
26. Longenecker, *Romans*, 662. Cranfield suggests that "spiritual" affirms the divine origin, majesty, and authority of the law, as well as its source, character, and mode of operation (*Romans*, 355–56).
27. See "Theology and Appropriation" for a discussion of the identity of "I."
28. See 1 Corinthians 3:1–3 for the contrast between "fleshly" (i.e., ungodly) and "spiritual" (i.e., godly).

3. Good does not dwell in us (7:18–20).

Paul's second explanation (γάρ) reflects personal experience (οἶδα) and parallels the negative premise of verse 14b: in ourselves (τοῦτ' ἐν τῇ σαρκί μου), we lack the capacity to do good (οὐκ οἰκεῖ ἐν ἐμοί . . . ἀγαθόν). Cognitively, we want to do good (τὸ θέλειν παράκειταί μοι), but behaviorally we do not follow through (τὸ δὲ κατεργάζεσθαι τὸ καλὸν οὔ). Instead of doing the good we wish (οὐ ὃ θέλω ποιῶ ἀγαθόν) we practice the evil we do not wish (ὃ οὐ θέλω κακὸν τοῦτο πράσσω). The conclusion is the same as that of verse 17: if we do what we do not wish (εἰ ὃ οὐ θέλω ἐγὼ τοῦτο ποιῶ), indwelling sin is the culprit (ἡ οἰκοῦσα ἐν ἐμοὶ ἁμαρτία); we are not (οὐκέτι ἐγὼ κατεργάζομαι αὐτό).

4. The result is "spiritual schizophrenia" (7:21–25).

Paul states his conclusion (ἄρα) as a principle[29] (εὑρίσκω τὸν νόμον): although we are wishing to do what is good (τῷ θέλοντι ἐμοὶ ποεῖν τὸ καλόν), evil is present in us (ἐμοὶ τὸ κακὸν παράκειται). The explanation (γάρ) describes two sides engaged in an internal struggle. Our "inner man" (κατὰ τὸν ἔσω ἄνθρωπον) denotes the inward, spiritual self that is oriented toward God (cf. 2 Cor. 4:16; Eph. 3:16). Our "members" (τοῖς μέλεσίν μου) denote the physical, cognitive and emotional faculties that are oriented toward sin (cf. 7:5).[30] Our God-oriented self experiences joy in connection with God's law (συνήδομαι τῷ νόμῳ τοῦ θεοῦ). Our sin-oriented self, however, wages war against God's law (ἀντιστρατευόμενον τῷ νόμῳ τοῦ νοός μου) and takes us captive to the power of sin (αἰχμαλωτίζοντά με ἐν τῷ νόμῳ τῆς ἁμαρτίας).

This internal struggle evokes the emotional outburst: "Wretched man that I am!" (ταλαίπωρος ἐγὼ ἄνθρωπος) and a cry for help: "Who will rescue me from this dead body?" (τίς με ῥύσεται ἐκ τοῦ σώματος τοῦ θανάτου τούτου). The confident answer is found in Jesus Christ (χάρις τῷ θεῷ διὰ Ἰησοῦ Χριστοῦ τοῦ κυρίου ἡμῶν). In summary (ἄρα οὖν), with our minds we serve God's law (αὐτὸς ἐγὼ τῷ νοΐ δουλεύω νόμῳ θεῷ), but in our flesh we serve the power of sin (τῇ δὲ σαρκὶ νόμῳ ἁμαρτίας). Having explained the struggle that ensues when we live

---

29. Τὸν νόμον is best understood as "the principle." The different uses of "law" in these verses are best understood as follows: (a) τὸν νόμον in verse 21 refers to a general principle; (b) τῷ νόμῳ τοῦ θεοῦ in verse 22, τῷ νόμῳ τοῦ νοός in verse 23, and νόμῳ θεοῦ in verse 25 all refer to the Mosaic law; (c) ἕτερον νόμον in verse 23, τῷ νόμῳ τῆς ἁμαρτίας in verse 23, and νόμῳ ἁμαρτίας in verse 25 all refer to the authority or power of sin.

30. In this context, "our members" is equivalent to "flesh" (cf. 6:19; 7:18, 25).

in the flesh (cf. 7:5), Paul turns to the solution in chapter 8: life in the Spirit (cf. 7:6).

Theology and Appropriation

As might be expected, there is considerable discussion over the identity of "I" in Romans 7:7–25. Is it Paul? If so, is the struggle he describes normal for Christians? Is there any hope for us? If it is not Paul, who is "I"? Moo identifies four basic directions in interpretation.[31] The autobiographical direction understands the "I" as Paul describing his own experience. The Adamic direction understands the "I" as Paul describing the experience of prototypical Adam. The Israelite direction understands the "I" as Paul describing the experience of Israel. The existential direction understands the "I" as Paul describing the experience of humankind in general. Beyond these four basic directions, proponents of the autobiographical approach disagree on whether Paul is describing his life before or after his encounter with Christ on the Damascus Road.[32] There is also a tendency to differentiate between the "I" in verses 7–12 and the "I" in verses 13–25. The following table seeks to summarize the positions found in six major commentaries.

Commentator	Romans 7:7–12	Romans 7:13–25
Cranfield *Romans*, 342–47	No specific individual or group	Christians in general, "including the very best and most mature"
Dunn *Romans*, 399–405	Adam, as every human being at the fall	Paul, as every human being after the fall
Jewett *Romans*, 441–45	"Paul the Zealot" (i.e., pre-conversion)	"Paul the Zealot" (i.e., pre-conversion)
Longenecker *Romans*, 642, 651–60	Pre-conversion Paul	All humankind
Moo *Romans*, 430–31, 442–48	Paul in solidarity with Israel when confronted with the Mosaic law	Pre-conversion Paul as representative of Israel under the Mosaic law
Schreiner *Romans*, 359–65, 379–90	Paradigmatic of all humankind	Neither pre-conversion nor post-conversion Paul

---

31. Moo, *Romans*, 424–31.
32. Schreiner has the most detailed summary of the arguments for unregenerate (pre-conversion) and regenerate (post-conversion) Paul (*Romans*, 379–90).

The combinations are bewildering. There is, however, a tendency to see the "I" as describing an experience that extends beyond Paul, whether to Adam, Israel, Christians, or humankind. For that reason, it is best not to expend time and energy trying to decide, for example, whether "I" describes Paul before or after his conversion. It is more profitable to understand the experiences described as those that characterize any human being—whether Christian or non-Christian—who tries to live for God by obeying the Mosaic law apart from the resources of Christ and the Holy Spirit.[33] As Schreiner notes, the passage "centers on the inability of the law to transform."[34] Although the law is spiritual (7:14), indwelling sin uses the law to take us captive to its power (7:23). The result is futility and frustration, from which only Christ can deliver.

Paul's primary purpose for including this passage was to help his readers understand the futility and frustration of trying to live life in the flesh, that is, in their own power. With his readers we share the need to realize that we cannot live the Christian life in our own power. Points of connection to the passage include internal conflict over a course of action, a person doing something he or she does not want to do, and the mental disorder in which two or more personality states show in a person's behavior.[35] The passage corrects the belief that we are able to serve God using our own resources. It commends total dependence on Christ in order to serve God. The objective in communicating this passage should be to help others understand that sin takes advantage of the law to frustrate our attempt to serve God apart from his help so that they will commit to depending on God to deliver them from a lifestyle of futility and frustration.

---

33. Longenecker's suggestion is "the tragic plight of people who attempt to live their lives apart from God, that is, by means of their own resources and abilities" (*Romans*, 659).
34. Schreiner, *Romans*, 379.
35. The disorder is technically diagnosed as dissociative identity disorder and sometimes popularly known as a "split personality."

ROMANS 8:1–17

Text and Translation

1 Therefore, now *there is* no condemnation for those *who are* in Christ Jesus.[1] **2** For the law that is the Spirit who gives life[2] in Christ Jesus set you[3] free from the law that is sin and produces death.[4] **3** For *that* which was impossible for the law[5]—because[6] it was weak through the flesh—God, by sending[7] his own Son in the likeness of sinful flesh and with reference to sin,[8] condemned sin in his[9] flesh, **4** in order that the law's[10] righteous requirement might be fulfilled[11] in us, the *ones who* are not walking[12] according to the flesh but according to the Spirit. **5** For the *ones who* are[13] according to the flesh are setting their minds on the things of the flesh, but the *ones who* are according to the Spirit *are setting their minds on* the things of the Spirit. **6** For the mind-set that comes from the flesh[14] *is* death, but the mind-set that comes from the Spirit *is* life and peace; **7** because the mind-set that comes from the flesh *is* hostile toward God,[15] for it is not subjecting itself[16] to God's law,

---

1. Τοῖς ἐν Χριστῷ Ἰησοῦ is the shorter reading and has good manuscript support (ℵ*, B, C², D*). The two longer readings are most likely assimilations to verse 4.
2. Τοῦ πνεύματος is a genitive of apposition; ζωῆς is a genitive of product.
3. Of the four variant readings, two (ἡμᾶς; omit) have minimal manuscript support. Both με (ℵ, B) and σε (A, D) are well supported, but the latter reading is viewed as the more difficult because the first person singular occurs so frequently in the preceding chapter (e.g., Moo, *Romans*, 470n11).
4. Τῆς ἁμαρτίας is a genitive of apposition; τοῦ θανάτου is a genitive of product.
5. Τοῦ νόμου is a subjective genitive.
6. Ἐν ᾧ is causal.
7. Πέμψας is an adverbial participle of means.
8. Περί + genitive denotes reference.
9. The definite article functions as a possessive pronoun referring to Christ.
10. Τοῦ νόμου is a genitive of source/origin.
11. Πληρωθῇ is a divine passive.
12. Τοῖς περιπατοῦσιν is a substantival participle in apposition to ἡμῖν.
13. Οἱ ὄντες is a substantival participle (twice).
14. Τῆς σαρκός and τοῦ πνεύματος are subjective genitives; see also τῆς σαρκός in verse 7.
15. Εἰς + accusative denotes disadvantage.
16. Ὑποτάσσεται is a direct middle.

for it is not even[17] able *to do so*; **8** and the *ones who* are[18] in the flesh are not able to please God.[19] **9** But you are not in the flesh but in the Spirit, if indeed God's Spirit is dwelling in you. And if *it is true that* someone is not having Christ's Spirit, [20] this one is not his. **10** But if *it is true that* Christ *is* in you,[21] on the one hand the body *is* dead because of sin,[22] on the other hand the Spirit *is* life because of righteousness. **11** And if[23] *it is true that* the Spirit of the *one who* raised[24] Jesus from the dead is dwelling in you, the *one who* raised[25] Christ from the dead will also[26] make alive our mortal bodies through the Spirit *who is* dwelling[27] in you. **12** Consequently, brothers, we are debtors, not to the flesh so as to live[28] according to the flesh—**13** For if *it is true that* you are living[29] according to the flesh, you are about to die, but if *it is true that* by the Spirit you are putting to death the *fleshly* practices that come to expression through the body,[30] you will live. **14** For as many as are being led by God's Spirit, these are God's sons. **15** For you did not receive a Spirit who makes you slaves[31] for the purpose of fear[32] again, but you received a Spirit who makes you adopted sons, by whom we are crying out "Abba, Father." **16** The Spirit himself is bearing witness with our spirit[33] that we are God's children. **17** And if *we are* children, *we are* also heirs; on the one hand we receive an inheritance from God, on the

---

17. Οὐδέ is ascensive.
18. Οἱ ὄντες is a substantival participle.
19. Τῷ θεῷ is the object of the infinitive.
20. Εἰ ... ἔχει is a first-class condition.
21. Εἰ introduces a first-class condition; ἐστίν is understood.
22. Διά + accusative denotes cause (twice).
23. Δέ is resumptive ("and"); εἰ ... οἰκεῖ is a first-class condition that Paul uses to draw his readers into the argument.
24. Τοῦ ἐγείραντος is a substantival participle; the genitive is possessive.
25. Ὁ ἐγείρας is a substantival participle.
26. Καί is adjunctive.
27. Ἐνοικοῦντος is an adjectival participle. The manuscript evidence is divided between the genitive (א, A, C) and the accusative (B, D, 33). Cranfield provides four reasons to prefer the genitive reading (*Romans*, 391–92).
28. Τοῦ ... ζῆν is an epexegetical infinitive.
29. Εἰ ... ζῆτε is a first-class condition, as is εἰ ... θανατοῦτε.
30. Τοῦ σώματος is a subjective genitive. Moo suggests "deeds worked out through the body under the influence of the flesh" (*Romans*, 495).
31. Δουλείας and υἱοθεσίας are objective genitives.
32. Εἰς + accusative denotes purpose.
33. Τῷ πνεύματι ἡμῶν is a dative of association.

other hand we receive the inheritance with Christ,[34] if indeed we are suffering together *with him*, in order that we might also[35] be glorified together *with him.*

Context and Structure

II. Letter Body (1:18–15:13)
- A. The Gospel as the Revelation of God's Righteousness (1:18–4:25)
- B. The Gospel as the Demonstration of God's Power (5:1–8:39)
    1. The gospel demonstrates God's power to save from wrath (5:1–11)
    2. The gospel demonstrates God's power to save from condemnation (5:12–21)
    3. The gospel demonstrates God's power to save from sin (6:1–23)
    4. The gospel demonstrates God's power to save from the law (7:1–25)
    5. The gospel demonstrates God's power to save from the flesh (8:1–30)
        a. **Because the Spirit gives us life and assurance (8:1–17)**
        b. Because the Spirit gives us hope of glory (8:18–30)
    6. The gospel demonstrates God's power to save from all opposition (8:31–39)

After opening the next paragraph of his argument with what Longenecker calls "a theological pronouncement" in 8:1,[36] Paul introduces five changes the Holy Spirit effects as part of life in the new era brought about in Christ. The Spirit sets free from the law of sin and death (8:2–4). The Spirit produces a mind-set of life and peace (8:5–8). The Spirit gives life now and in the future (8:9–11). The Spirit puts to death the deeds of the body (8:12–13). The Spirit bears witness to adoption as God's children (8:14–17).

---

34. Κληρονόμοι θεοῦ is a subjective genitive; συγκληρονόμοι Χριστοῦ is a genitive of association.
35. Καί is adjunctive.
36. Longenecker, *Romans,* 684.

Basic Message and Exegetical Outline

The indwelling Spirit sets free from condemnation, sin, and death, produces a mind-set of life and peace, gives life now and in the future, puts to death the deeds of the body, and bears witness to adoption as God's children.

The Role of the Indwelling Spirit (8:1–17)
1. The Spirit sets free from condemnation, sin, and death (8:1–4)
   a. There is no condemnation for those in Christ (8:1)
   b. The Spirit sets free from sin and death, because God condemned sin and fulfilled the law's righteous requirement in Christ (8:2–4)
2. The Spirit produces a mind-set of life and peace (8:5–8)
   a. Focusing on the Spirit results in a mind-set of life and peace (8:5–6)
   b. Focusing on the flesh results in a mind-set of hostility and rebellion (8:7–8)
3. The Spirit gives life now and in the future (8:9–11)
   a. If the Spirit dwells in us, we are Christ's (8:9)
   b. If the Spirit dwells in us, our spirit is alive (8:10)
   c. If the Spirit dwells in us, God will give life to our bodies (8:11)
4. The Spirit puts to death the deeds of the body (8:12–13)
   a. We are no longer debtors to the flesh (8:12)
   b. If we live according to the flesh, we will die (8:13a)
   c. If, by the Spirit, we put to death the deeds of the body, we will live (8:13b)
5. The Spirit bears witness to adoption as God's children (8:14–17)
   a. The Spirit leads those who are God's (8:14)
   b. The Spirit confirms our adoption by the Father (8:15)
   c. The Spirit bears witness to our status as children and heirs (8:16–17)

Explanation of the Text

1. The Spirit sets free from condemnation, sin, and death (8:1–4).
By using the combination "Therefore, now . . ." Paul not only ties

his argument back to 7:6 (ἄρα) but also highlights the contrast of the new era (νῦν) with the immediately preceding description of life lived under the old era that was governed by the law and sin (7:13–25). The elliptical way in which Paul states his thesis gives special emphasis to the negative adjective and highlights the absolute absence of condemnation (οὐδὲν κατάκριμα) for those who are incorporated into Christ Jesus (τοῖς ἐν Χριστῷ Ἰησοῦ).[37]

The reason (γάρ) there is now no condemnation is that we have been transferred into a new domain. That domain (ἐν Χριστῷ Ἰησοῦ) is under the governing authority (ὁ νόμος) of the Holy Spirit who produces life (τοῦ πνεύματος τῆς ζωῆς). The Spirit has set us free (ἠλευθέρωσεν σε) from the old domain[38] that was governed by sin and death (ἀπὸ τοῦ νόμου τῆς ἁμαρτίας καὶ τοῦ θανάτου). Paul then explains (γάρ) that the means by which we have been transferred is God's action of sending Christ. First, he highlights briefly the inability of the Mosaic law to deliver (τὸ ἀδύνατος τοῦ νόμου) because the flesh weakens its effectiveness (ἐν ᾧ ἠσθένει διὰ τῆς σαρκός).[39] By sending his own Son (ὁ θεὸς τὸν ἑαυτοῦ υἱὸν πέμψας), however, God accomplished what the law could not: he broke sin's power by sentencing and judging it in Christ's death on the cross (κατέκρινεν τὴν ἁμαρτάν ἐν τῇ σαρκι).[40] God's purpose (ἵνα) for condemning sin in Christ was that he might fulfill in us the righteous requirement the law establishes (τὸ δικαίωμα τοῦ νόμου πληρωθῇ ἐν ἡμῖν) as we consistently walk under the control of the Spirit (τοῖς ... περιπατοῦσιν ... κατὰ πνεῦμα) rather than under the control of the flesh (μὴ κατὰ σάρκα).[41]

---

37. The Greek text is οὐδὲν ἄρα νῦν κατάκριμα τοῖς ἐν Χριστῷ Ἰησοῦ, which, woodenly translated, would be, "No therefore now condemnation to those in Christ Jesus." Placing οὐδὲν ("no") first gives it special emphasis and is equivalent to using capital letters, bold font, italics, and an exclamation point ("[There is], therefore, now *NO!* condemnation. . .").

38. That old domain is captured by the phrase "in Adam."

39. He has already described that weakness at some length in 7:13–25.

40. "In his flesh" (ἐν τῇ σαρκί) captures in shorter form "in the likeness of sinful flesh" (ἐν ὁμοιώματι σαρκὸς ἁμαρτίας), which describes Christ's identity and involvement with humanity. The prepositional phrase "with reference to sin" (περὶ ἁμαρτίας) should be understood as referring to sacrifice (Moo, *Romans,* 480n48), most likely as a reference to sacrifice for sin (Dunn, *Romans,* 422).

41. There is some discussion over what Paul means when he says the law is fulfilled in us. Moo argues for our incorporation into Christ (*Romans,* 484), while Schreiner argues for our active obedience (*Romans,* 405). The immediate context of Romans 8 as well as the parallel in 13:8–10 suggests

2. The Spirit produces a mind-set of life and peace (8:5–8).

The reason (γάρ) those who are in Christ can fulfill the righteous requirement of the law (8:4) resides in the fact that they possess the Spirit while those who are in Adam do not. Those whose existence is according to the flesh (οἱ κατὰ σάρκα ὄντες) have two problems. First, they set their minds on (φρονοῦσιν) the affairs of the flesh (τὰ τῆς σαρκὸς), and the mind-set that comes from the flesh produces death (τὰ φρόνημα τῆς σαρκὸς θάνατος). In contrast (δέ) those whose existence is according to the Spirit (οἱ κατὰ πνεῦμα) set their minds on the affairs of the Spirit (τὰ τοῦ πνεῦμα),[42] and the mind-set that comes from the Spirit produces life and peace (τὸ φρόνημα τοῦ πνεύματος ζωὴ καὶ εἰρήνη). Second, the mind-set that comes from the flesh (τὸ φρόνημα τῆς σαρκός) is hostile toward God (ἔχθρα εἰς θεόν) and is totally unable (οὐδὲ δύναται) to submit itself to God's law (τῷ νόμῳ τοῦ θεοῦ οὐχ ὑποτάσσεται). As a consequence, those who are in the flesh (οἱ ἐν σαρκὶ ὄντες) are not able to please God (θεῷ ἀρέσαι οὐ δύνανται). As Schreiner writes, "[These verses] do not constitute an exhortation to live according to the Spirit or to fulfill the law. Rather, they describe what is necessarily the case for the one who has the Spirit or is still in the flesh."[43]

3. The Spirit gives life now and in the future (8:9–11).

Paul's readers, however, are unambiguously in the sphere of the Spirit (ὑμεῖς δὲ οὐκ ἐστὲ ἐν σαρκὶ ἀλλὰ ἐν πνεύματι),[44] "if indeed" it is true (εἴπερ) that God's Spirit dwells in them (πνεῦμα θεοῦ οἰκεῖ ἐν ὑμῖν).[45] The readers' situation differs drastically from those who are outside the sphere of the Spirit. Those who do not have the Spirit (τις πνεῦμα Χριστοῦ οὐκ ἔχει) are not Christ's (οὗτος οὐκ ἔστιν αὐτοῦ) and—by implication—face the insurmountable problems described in verses 5–8. In contrast (δέ), the Spirit of Christ dwells in Paul's readers (Χριστὸς ἐν ὑμῖν).[46] Their bodies might face death because of sin (τὸ σῶμα νεκρὸν διὰ ἁμαρτίαν), but the indwelling Spirit guarantees

---

    that Paul is thinking of Spirit-empowered obedience to God's moral norms expressed in the law.

42. The verb φρονοῦσιν is understood from the antithetical parallelism.

43. Schreiner, *Romans*, 409.

44. Δέ is adversative, ὑμεῖς is emphatic, and οὐκ . . . ἀλλά creates a strong contrast between the two spheres.

45. Paul's implication is that, indeed, the Spirit does dwell in them. See also Wallace, *Grammar*, 694.

46. Χριστός in verse 10 is equivalent to πνεῦμα θεοῦ and πνεῦμα Χριστοῦ in verse 9 (cf. Dunn, *Romans*, 430); ἐστίν is understood.

life because of God's gift of righteousness in Christ (τὸ πνεῦμα ζωὴ διὰ δικαιοσύνην).⁴⁷

To reinforce his point, Paul adds (δέ) a summary statement that expounds on the way in which the indwelling Spirit is "life." He begins with the premise (εἰ) that his readers know the Spirit of the one who raised Jesus from the dead (τὸ πνεῦμα τοῦ ἐγείραντος τὸν Ἰησοῦν ἐκ νεκρῶν) dwells in them (οἰκεῖ ἐν ὑμῖς). They can, therefore, also be confident that the same God who raised Jesus from the dead (ὁ ἐγείρας τὸν Χριστὸν ἐκ νεωρῶν) will also give life to their mortal bodies (ζῳοποιήσει καὶ τὰ σώματα ὑμῶν) through his indwelling Spirit (διὰ τοῦ ἐνοικοῦντος αὐτοῦ πνεύματος ἐν ὑμῖν) at the resurrection.⁴⁸

4. The Spirit puts to death the deeds of the body (8:12–13).

Having demonstrated that the indwelling Spirit sets us free from condemnation, sin, and death (8:1–4), produces a mind-set of life and peace (8:5–8), and gives us life now and in the future (8:9–11), Paul moves to the practical implications (ἄρα οὖν) for daily living. The first implication is that, instead of living according to the flesh, we are now free to live according to the Spirit. Because we are in the sphere of the Spirit, we are no longer under obligation to the flesh (ὀφειλέται ἐσμέν οὐ τῇ σαρκί) to continue living according to the standard the flesh demands (τοῦ κατὰ σάρκα ζῆν). The pragmatic reason (γάρ) for living according to the Spirit rather than according to the flesh resides in the contrasting consequences. When someone lives according to the flesh (εἰ κατὰ σάρκα ζῆτε), that person faces the certainty of death (μέλλετε ἀποθνήσκειν), both in this life and in the future. In contrast (δέ), when someone lives according to the Spirit (εἰ πνεύματι), that person faces the certainty of life (ζήσεσθε), both in this life and in the future. Specifically, the Spirit is the agent through whom believers regularly root out and put to death (θανατοῦτε) the disgraceful deeds the flesh brings to expression through their bodies (τὰς πράξεις τοῦ σώματος). Just as death to sin allows us to present our bodies to God (6:1–14), so

---

47. Τὸ πνεῦμα ζωή refers to the Holy Spirit who gives life—both spiritual life now and physical life in the future—rather than to the human spirit (cf. 8:2, 6, 11). Δικαιοσύνην is Christ's righteousness imputed to the believer by God (cf. Moo, *Romans*, 492).

48. Although most commentators conclude that Paul is referring to the Spirit's future work at the final resurrection (e.g., Cranfield, *Romans*, 391), a minority position holds that he is referring to the Spirit's present work in the lives of believers (e.g., Jewett, *Romans*, 492–93). The latter idea seems to be more clearly in view in verses 2 and 6.

being indwelt by the Spirit allows us to break free of sin's power in our lives.[49]

5. The Spirit bears witness to adoption as God's children (8:14–17).

The second implication is that, instead of living as slaves, we are to live as children.[50] The regular practice of putting to death the deeds of the body (8:13), provides evidence that a person is led by the Spirit. In turn, all who are regularly being led by God's Spirit (ὅσοι πνεύματι θεοῦ ἄγνοται) are God's children (οὗτοι υἱοὶ θεοῦ εἰσιν).[51] Again, Paul highlights the drastic difference that results from receiving the Spirit. That difference involves both our state and our response. In contrast to our previous existence, we did not receive a Spirit who makes us slaves (οὐ ἐλάβετε πνεῦμα δουλείας) but a Spirit who makes us adopted children (ἀλλὰ ἐλάβετε πνεῦμα υἱοθεσίας). As a result, our response is no longer one of fear (εἰς φόβον) but one of confidence that expresses itself in the fervent Spirit-enabled exclamation, "Abba, Father!" (ἐν ᾧ κράζομεν Αββα ὁ πατήρ). That heartfelt cry is the product of the Holy Spirit himself (αὐτὸ τὸ πνεῦμα) joining our human spirits in testifying (συμμαρτυρεῖ τῷ πνεύματι ἡμῶν) that we are God's children (ὅτι ἐσμὲν τέκνα θεοῦ). Along with our new status as God's children (εἰ δὲ τέκνα) comes the added status of being heirs (καὶ κληρονόμοι). We inherit what God promises (κληρονόμοι θεοῦ) because of our identity with Christ (συγκληρονόμοι Χριστοῦ). The caveat (εἴπερ) of which Paul reminds his readers (and us) is that the future promise of sharing in inherited glory with Christ (συνδοξασθῶμεν) also comes with the present reality of sharing in suffering with him (συμπάσχομεν).

Theology and Appropriation

Adoption (υἱοθεσία) is the fifth key soteriological term in Romans.[52] Taken from the context of family relations, the term describes the process of bestowing the rights and privileges of family membership on a person. Adoption, therefore, highlights our change in status before God from that of being slaves to that of being sons. Longenecker

---

49. Schreiner also notes the similarity between 6:1–11 and 8:12–13 (*Romans*, 419).
50. Longenecker argues that γάρ is connective rather than causal or explanatory (*Romans*, 702).
51. As is true in Galatians 5:16–18, being "led by the Spirit" describes the practice of holy living rather than the promise of divine guidance.
52. The other four are justification, redemption, propitiation (all in 3:21–26), and reconciliation (in 5:1–12).

notes four important features of the Greco-Roman practice of adoption: "1. An adopted son was taken out of his previous situation and placed in an entirely new relationship to his new adopting father, who became his new *paterfamilias*. 2. An adopted son started a new life as part of his new family, with all his old debts canceled. 3. An adopted son was considered no less important than any other biologically born son in his adopting father's family. 4. An adopted son experienced a changed status, with his old name set aside and a new name given him by his adopting father."[53]

The term does not appear in the MT or LXX, although the idea of being "sons of God" does (Ps. 29:1; Hos. 2:1), as does the concept of Israel as God's son (Exod. 4:22). The word occurs five times in Paul's letters (Rom. 8:15, 23; 9:4; Gal. 4:5; Eph. 1:5). Those verses describe adoption as a past act (Eph. 1:5), a present reality (Rom. 8:15; Gal. 4:6), and a future hope (Rom. 8:23). The same verses highlight the work of all three persons of the Trinity: "The Father predestines us to adoption (Eph. 1:15) . . . our adoption rests on the basis of Christ's completed work (Gal. 4:4–5). The Spirit . . . confirms our adoption and makes us aware of it" (Rom. 8:15–17).[54] By adopting us, God gives us assurance, delivers us from fear, delivers us from the bondage of the flesh and the law, and promises us an inheritance.[55]

In Romans 8:14–17, Paul's point of emphasis is on the change in status from being slaves to being sons. As Dunn writes, "Though many slaves could and did rise to positions of considerable importance and influence within households . . . the idea of slavery . . . focuses on the slave's lack of freedom, as one who orders his life at another's behest, who must live within the terms of a code that restricts him firmly in servitude, and who . . . is divided in status from members of the family by an unbridgeable gulf. Whereas sonship . . . including adoptive sonship . . . speaks of freedom and intimate mutual trust, where filial concerns can be assumed to provide the motivation and direction for living, and conduct be guided by spontaneous love rather than by law."[56]

Paul's primary purpose in including this paragraph was to help his readers understand their new status, response, and behavior that results from being indwelt by the Holy Spirit. They no longer exist in the realm of the flesh, but in the realm of the Spirit; they should live accordingly. Along with Paul's original readers we need to realize the

---

53. Longenecker, *Romans*, 704.
54. Harvey, *Anointed with the Spirit and Power*, 148.
55. Cranfield has a helpful discussion of inheritance (*Romans*, 407–9).
56. Dunn, *Romans*, 460.

new status that is ours and that our new status has implications for our daily living—we are to live according to the Spirit rather than according to the flesh. Possible points of connection include adoption and inheritance. Adoption is a common practice in the West, with families sometimes traveling to another country and culture to adopt a child. Stories of individuals inheriting large sums from their "dead uncle/aunt" are common, if sometimes apocryphal. The passage corrects any idea that it is possible to serve God apart from the Holy Spirit's enabling and that the law is somehow able to set us free from slavery to the flesh. It commends a commitment to and dependence on the Holy Spirit and challenges us to root out and put to death the attitudes and actions of the flesh. The objective in communicating this passage should be to help others understand the difference that results from being indwelt by the Holy Spirit so that they will reject the old mind-set and patterns of the flesh and, instead, adopt the new mind-set and patterns of the Spirit.

ROMANS 8:18–30

Text and Translation

18 For I am considering that the sufferings the present time produces[1] *are* not comparable to the glory *that is* about to be revealed[2] to us. **19** For the eager longing of the creation[3] waits expectantly for the revelation of the sons of God. **20** For the creation was subjected in futility,[4] not willingly[5] but because of the *one who* subjected[6] it, in hope **21** that[7] also[8] creation itself will be set free[9] from the slavery *that is* corruption[10] *and will come* to the freedom[11] resulting from the glory bestowed on God's children.[12] **22** For we know that all creation is groaning together and suffering pain together until now; **23** and not only *this*, but also we ourselves,[13] because we are having[14] the firstfruits of the Spirit, we ourselves also[15] are groaning in ourselves while we are waiting expectantly[16] for adoption,[17] the redemption of our body.[18] **24** For we

---

1. The adverb νῦν functions as an adjective; τοῦ καιροῦ is a subjective genitive.
2. Μέλλουσιν is an adjectival participle; ἀποκαλυφθῆναι is a complementary infinitive.
3. Τῆς κτίσεως is a subjective genitive; τῶν υἱῶν is an objective genitive.
4. Τῇ ματαιότητι is a dative of manner; ὑπετάγη is a divine passive.
5. Ἑκοῦσα is an adjective used adverbially to indicate manner.
6. Τὸν ὑποτάξαντα is a substantival participle.
7. Although διότι is the more difficult reading and has significant manuscript support (ℵ, D*), ὅτι is the more likely original reading. It has stronger manuscript support (𝔓⁴⁶, A, B, C, D², 33) and makes better sense contextually by introducing the content of the hope Paul as just mentioned.
8. Καί is adjunctive.
9. Ἐλευθερωθήσεται is a divine passive.
10. Τῆς φθορᾶς is a genitive of apposition.
11. Εἰς + accusative denotes the anticipated goal.
12. See Harvey, *Romans,* 205. The translation takes τῆς δόξης as a subjective genitive and τῶν τέκνων as an objective genitive.
13. Αὐτοί functions as an intensive pronoun.
14. Ἔχοντες is an adverbial participle of cause.
15. The combination of ἡμεῖς (personal pronoun), καί (adjunctive use), and αὐτοί (intensive pronoun) is strongly emphatic.
16. Ἀπεκδεχόμενοι is an adverbial participle of time.
17. The reading that omits υἱοθεσίαν (𝔓⁴⁶, D) simplifies the syntax and resolves any perceived contradiction with Paul's previous statement that we have already received adoption (8:12–14). Including υἱοθεσίαν, however, is the more difficult reading and has stronger manuscript support (ℵ, A, B, C).
18. Τοῦ σώματος is an objective genitive.

were saved in hope;[19] but hope that is being seen[20] is not hope. For who is hoping[21] for what[22] he is seeing? **25** But if *it is true that* we are hoping[23] for what we are not seeing, we are waiting expectantly with perseverance.[24] **26** And in the same way also[25] the Spirit is helping our weakness;[26] for we are not knowing what we should pray[27] as it is necessary, but the Spirit himself is interceding[28] *for us* with wordless groanings;[29] **27** and the *one who is* searching[30] our[31] hearts is knowing how the Spirit thinks,[32] because he is interceding according to God on behalf of the saints.[33] **28** And we know that all things[34] are working together in the interest of[35] the *ones who are* loving God *and are* being[36] called according to *his* purpose. **29** Because *those* whom[37] he foreknew he also[38] predestined *to be* conformed to the image[39] of his Son, in order

---

19. Τῇ ἐλπίδι is dative of manner.
20. Βλεπομένη is an adjectival participle.
21. Ἐλπίζει (𝔓⁴⁶, ℵ², B, C, D, 33) has stronger manuscript support than ὑπομένει (ℵ*, A) and makes better sense contextually.
22. The textual tradition is divided among four variants. The unaccompanied interrogative pronoun τίς is the shortest reading.
23. Εἰ . . . ἐλπίζομεν is a first-class condition.
24. Διά + genitive denotes manner.
25. Καί is adjunctive.
26. Τῇ ἀσθενείᾳ is a dative of direct object.
27. Τί προσευχώμεθα refers to the object of prayer rather than manner (cf. Harvey, *Romans,* 207).
28. The reading ὑπερεντυγχάνει is the shortest of three readings and has good manuscript support (ℵ*, A, B, D). Nevertheless, the ὑπέρ- prefix carries the sense of "in behalf of" (Robertson, *Grammar,* 629). See the clear statement of representation (ὑπὲρ ἁγίων) at the end of verse 27.
29. Στεναγμοῖς ἀλαλήτοις is a dative of manner.
30. Ὁ ἐραυνῶν is a substantival participle.
31. The definite article functions as a possessive pronoun.
32. Τοῦ πνεύματος is a subjective genitive (cf. CEB).
33. Ὑπέρ + genitive denotes representation.
34. Πάντα is best understood as the subject. The textual variant that adds ὁ θεός after συνεργεῖ is probably an explanatory addition (cf. Metzger, *Textual Commentary,* 458).
35. Εἰς + accusative denotes advantage, as does the dative of the substantival participle τοῖς ἀγαπῶσιν.
36. Τοῖς οὖσιν is a substantival participle in apposition to τοῖς ἀγαπῶσιν.
37. The relative pronoun οὕς includes an embedded demonstrative.
38. Καί is adjunctive.
39. Τῆς εἰκόνος is a genitive of association.

for him to be[40] the firstborn among many brothers; **30** and *those* whom he predestined, these he also called, and *those* whom he called, these he also declared righteous, and *those* whom he declared righteous, these he also glorified.

Context and Structure

II. Letter Body (1:18–15:13)
   A. The Gospel as the Revelation of God's Righteousness (1:18–4:25)
   B. The Gospel as the Demonstration of God's Power (5:1–8:39)
      1. The gospel demonstrates God's power to save from wrath (5:1–11)
      2. The gospel demonstrates God's power to save from condemnation (5:12–21)
      3. The gospel demonstrates God's power to save from sin (6:1–23)
      4. The gospel demonstrates God's power to save from the law (7:1–25)
      5. The gospel demonstrates God's power to save from the flesh (8:1–30)
         a. Because the Spirit gives us life and assurance (8:1–17)
         b. **Because the Spirit gives us hope of glory (8:18–30)**
      6. The gospel demonstrates God's power to save from all opposition (8:31–39)

After stating his firm conviction about the sufferings we encounter in this life (8:18), Paul sets out four reasons we can view the future with hope. Creation will be set free from corruption (8:19–21). We possess the firstfruits of the Spirit (8:22–25). The Spirit helps our weakness (8:26–27). God's calling is purposeful, beneficial, and effectual (8:28–30). References to "glory" in verses 18 and 30 frame the paragraph.

Basic Message and Exegetical Outline

We can view the future with hope, because creation will be set free from futility, slavery, and corruption; because we have the firstfruits of

---

40. Εἰς τό + infinitive denotes purpose.

the Spirit; because the Spirit helps our weakness; and because God's calling is purposeful, beneficial, and effectual.

The Hope of Glory (8:18–30)
1. Creation will be set free from futility, slavery, and corruption (8:18–21)
   a. Creation waits for deliverance (8:19)
   b. Creation was subjected in hope (8:20–21)
2. We have the firstfruits of the Spirit (8:22–25)
   a. We wait for the redemption of the body (8:23c)
   b. We wait with hopeful endurance (8:24–25)
3. The Spirit helps us in our weakness (8:26–27)
   a. The Spirit intercedes with wordless groanings (8:26)
   b. God knows the Spirit's mind (8:27)
4. God's calling is purposeful, beneficial, and effectual (8:28–30)
   a. He predestines those he foreknows (8:29)
   b. He calls those he predestines (8:30a)
   c. He declares righteous those he calls (8:30b)
   d. He glorifies those he declares righteous (8:30c)

Explanation of the Text

1. Creation will be set free from futility, slavery, and corruption (8:18–21).

Paul's connection of suffering with glory (8:17) leads him to provide a more extended explanation (γάρ) of that connection. Much as he did in 8:1, he begins with a thesis statement (8:18) that he develops at greater length in the remainder of the paragraph. Cranfield describes Paul's thesis (λογίζομαι ὅτι) as a "firm conviction reached by rational thought."[41] His conviction is that there is no comparison (οὐκ ἄξια . . . πρός) between the sufferings we experience as the result of living in the present age (τὰ παθήματα τοῦ νῦν καιροῦ) and the glory we will inherit in the future age (τὴν μέλλουσαν δόξαν ἀποκαλυφθῆναι εἰς ἡμᾶς).[42]

---

41. Cranfield, *Romans*, 408.
42. The Greek word order is unusual, but it emphasizes the future nature of the event to which Paul refers (cf. Harvey, *Romans*, 203). Schreiner notes that "'glory' refers to the eschatological inheritance of believers" (*Romans*, 434) and provides support from elsewhere in Paul's letters (Rom. 2:7, 10; 5:2; 2 Cor. 4:17; Phil. 3:21; Col. 3:4; 1 Thess. 2:12; 2 Tim. 2:10).

The first reason (γάρ) Paul offers in support of his thesis is creation's confident expectation (ἡ ἀποκαραδοκία τῆς κτίσεως) as it eagerly waits for (ἀπεκδέχεται) God to reveal his children in all their glory (τὴν ἀποκάλυψιν τῶν υἱῶν τοῦ θεοῦ).[43] Creation is "on tiptoe" (Phillips) because, when God glorifies his children, he will also set creation free from the futility, slavery, and corruption resulting from the curse he imposed after Adam's fall (cf. Gen. 3:17–19). When God put the earth in subjection (ἡ κτίσις ὑπετάγη), it became futile and lost its ability to fulfill its intended purpose (τῇ ματαιότητι).[44] Although God subjected creation (τὸν ὑποτάξαντα) against its will (οὐχ ἑκοῦσα), he did so in hope (ἐφ' ἐλπίδι). The content of creation's hope (ὅτι) is that God will set it free (αὐτὴ ἡ κτίσις ἐλευθερωθήσεται) from slavery and corruption (ἀπὸ τῆς δουλείας τῆς φθορᾶς) with the goal that it will have the same "freedom resulting from the glory bestowed on God's children" (εἰς τὴν ἐλευθερίαν τῆς δόξης τῶν τέκνων τοῦ θεοῦ).[45] The promise of glory God gives to his children is a promise that extends to his creation as well.

2. We have the firstfruits of the Spirit (8:22–25).

The second reason (γάρ) Paul offers in support of his thesis is the hope that results because we have the firstfruits of the Holy Spirit. As followers of Christ, we share a common conviction (οἴδαμεν ὅτι) that things are not as they should be. Not only (οὐ μόνον) is the whole creation groaning and suffering pain together until the present time (πᾶσα ἡ κτίσις συστενάζει καὶ συνωδίνει ἄχρι τοῦ νῦν),[46] we also are sighing inwardly (ἡμεῖς καὶ αὐτοὶ ἐν ἑαυτοῖς στενάζομεν). We are sighing because we have the firstfruits of the Spirit (τὴν ἀπαρχὴν τοῦ πνεύματος ἔχοντες) while we are waiting expectantly for the final step in our adoption (υἱοθεσίαν ἀπεκδεχόμενοι): the redemption of our body (τὴν ἀπολύτρωσιν τοῦ σώματος ἡμῶν). Our expectant waiting is explained (γάρ) by the hope in which we were saved (τῇ ἐλπίδι ἐσώθημεν). Hope is not based on what is seen (ἐλπὶς βλεπομένη οὐκ ἔστιν ἐλπίς), and no one

---

43. See BDAG 112c for ἀποκαραδοκία. "Creation" is best understood as "the sum-total of sub-human nature both animate and inanimate" (Cranfield, *Romans*, 411) and, therefore, begins an extended figure of personification (Harvey, *Romans*, 203). Paul also uses ἀπεκδέχομαι to describe Christian hope in Romans 8:19, 23, 25; 1 Corinthians 1:7; Philippians 3:20.

44. See BDAG 621c.

45. See Harvey, *Romans*, 205.

46. Paul uses the verb συνωδίνω to emphasize common experience. Elsewhere, the cognate noun (ἡ ὠδίν, -ῖνος) and verb (ὠδίνω) describe the pains associated with childbirth (cf. Gal. 4:19; 1 Thess. 5:3; Rev. 12:2).

hopes for what can be seen (ὅ βλέπει τίς ἐλπίζει). Instead (δέ) we wait persistently and expectantly (δι' ὑπομονῆς ἀπεκδεχόμεθα) and hope for what we do not see (ὅ οὐ βλέπομεν ἐλπίζομεν). The promise of glory, of which the indwelling Holy Spirit is the firstfruits, gives us hope as we face the sufferings of the present age.

3. The Spirit helps us in our weakness (8:26–27).

The third reason the sufferings of the present age are not comparable to the glory of the future age is the help the Holy Spirit provides. In the same way (ὡσαύτως) that he gives us hope (8:22–25), the Spirit also gives us help (καὶ τὸ πνεῦμα συναντιλαμβάνεται τῇ ἀσθενείᾳ ἡμῶν).[47] The specific weakness the Spirit helps is our lack of understanding (οὐκ οἴδαμεν) of what we should pray (τὸ τί προσευξώμεθα καθὸ δεῖ). The Spirit's help stands in contrast (ἀλλά) to our weakness and lack of understanding. Because we do not know what to pray, the Spirit himself intercedes for us (αὐτὸ τὸ πνεῦμα ὑπερεντυγχάνει). Paul highlights three aspects of the Spirit's intercession. First, the manner in which the Spirit intercedes is "with wordless groanings" (στεναγμοῖς ἀλαλήτοις). Although this phrase has been explained in multiple ways, it seems best to understand it to refer to unspoken longings in our hearts, which "the Holy Spirit takes . . . and presents . . . before God in an articulate form."[48] Second, the reason the Spirit is able to intercede for us is his intimate relationship with the Father. The Father who searches our hearts (ὁ ἐραυνῶν τὰς καρδίας) knows what the Spirit—who indwells us—is thinking (οἶδεν τί τὸ φρόνημα τοῦ πνεύματος) and, so, is able to answer his prayers on our behalf. Third, the standard by which the Spirit intercedes for us is set by God (κατὰ θεὸν ἐντυγχάνει ὑπὲρ ἁγίων).[49] The NEB captures the idea by translating the clause as "he pleads for God's people in God's own way." The promise of glory for which we yearn is sustained and nurtured by the Spirit's intercession on our behalf.

4. God's calling is purposeful, beneficial, and effectual (8:28–30).

The fourth reason the sufferings of the present age are not comparable to the glory of the future age is that God uses all things—including suffering (cf. 5:3–5)—for good in our lives. As followers of

---

47. Τῇ ἀσθενείᾳ ἡμῶν is best understood as the direct object, resulting in the translation "the Spirit helps our weakness" (cf. Harvey, *Romans*, 207).

48. Schreiner, *Romans*, 446. See his excellent discussion of suggested interpretations (444–46).

49. "According to God" (κατὰ θεόν) is most likely shorthand for "according to God's will" (cf. Cranfield, *Romans*, 424).

Christ, we share a common conviction (οἴδαμεν ὅτι) that God has our best interests at heart. Because God calls us according to his divine purpose (τοῖς κατὰ πρόθεσιν κλητοῖς οὖσιν),[50] we love him (τοῖς ἀγαπῶσιν τὸν θεόν) and can be confident that every circumstance we encounter assists in achieving a beneficial purpose (πάντα συνεργεῖ εἰς ἀγαθόν). The certainty of God's calling, plan, and purpose is the reason (ὅτι) for our confidence as Paul makes clear in the well-known rhetorical climax of verses 29–30.

The verbal chain begins with "*those* whom he foreknew" (οὓς προέγνω), which describes "God's special knowledge of a person . . . rather than a prior knowledge of how a person will respond to God."[51] Murray suggests that the verb (προγινώσκω) connotes "distinguishing affection and delight,"[52] and Schreiner concludes that it highlights God's "covenantal love and affection for those whom he has chosen."[53] The starting point is not our response to God but his love for us (cf. Eph. 2:4–5). God's love for those who are his leads him to "predestine" them (προώρισεν). Here as elsewhere, Paul writes that God predestines his people to one of the blessings of salvation rather than to salvation itself.[54] The particular blessing Paul has in mind is conformity to Christ's image (συμμόρφους τῆς εἰκόνος τοῦ υἱοῦ αὐτοῦ). He further describes that image as "firstborn among many brothers" (πρωτότοκον ἐν πολλοῖς ἀδελφοῖς). In addition to highlighting the status and privileges associated with being the "firstborn,"[55] the adjective (πρωτότοκος, -ον) points to the glory and preeminence Jesus possesses as a result of his resurrection (Col. 1:15, 18; cf. Heb. 1:6). It is the expectation of Jesus's post-resurrection glory that far outweighs the sufferings of the present age.

Paul deals more concisely with the remaining three links in his verbal chain. Having predestined to glory those upon whom he has set his love, God calls them to himself (οὓς προώρισεν τούτους καὶ ἐκάλεσεν). His calling is an act that accomplishes his divine purpose

50. Elsewhere in Paul's letters πρόθεσις always refers to God's divine purpose (cf. Rom. 9:11; Eph. 1:1; 3:11; 2 Tim. 1:9).
51. Harvey, *Romans*, 210. In particular, see 1 Peter 1:20 where the apostle describes Christ as "foreknown before the foundation of the world but made manifest at the end of the times."
52. Murray, *Romans*, 317.
53. Schreiner, *Romans*, 453.
54. In 1 Corinthians 2:7 and Ephesians 1:11, the blessing is glory; in Ephesians 1:5, it is adoption.
55. BDAG 894a.

(cf. 8:28); it is not "an invitation that [is] up to [us] to accept or reject."[56] Having summoned his people to himself, God declares them righteous (οὓς ἐκάλεσεν τούτους ἐδικαίωσεν)—solely on the basis of grace, by means of faith in Christ, apart from works, circumcision, or law-keeping. Having declared his people righteous, God decrees that they will ultimately experience the post-resurrection glory of Christ (οὓς ἐδικαίωσεν τούτους καὶ ἐδόξασεν).[57] With this final verb, the paragraph comes full circle: first, considering the glory God will reveal to us (8:18), next, waiting eagerly for the glory God has promised to us (8:21), then, conformed to the glory to which God has predestined us (8:29), and finally, certain of the glory God has waiting for us (8:30).

Theology and Appropriation

Romans 8:18–30 is Paul's concluding paragraph on what it means to live life in the Spirit (cf. 7:6).[58] His primary focus in this paragraph is on the hope of future glory the Spirit provides (8:18–25) and the help the Spirit provides for our prayer weakness (8:26–27). Those aspects of the Spirit's work are the sixth and seventh Paul includes in chapter 8. The seven aspects may be summarized under the following headings: liberation (8:1–4), aspiration (8:5–8), regeneration (8:9–11), mortification (8:12–13), attestation (8:14–17), glorification (8:18–25), and supplication (8:26–30).[59] Since God's provisions enable us to fulfill our obligations, those provisions always bring with them implicit obligations. The following chart seeks to set out the provisions and obligations that constitute Paul's discussion of living life in the Spirit.

---

56. Moo, *Romans*, 530.
57. The aorist tense of ἐδόξασεν is most likely proleptic (Wallace, *Grammar*, 562), describing a future event as already completed—and from God's perspective, it is.
58. For a fuller discussion of the Spirit in Romans 8, see J. D. Harvey, "Life in the Spirit according to McQuilkin and Paul." Pages 117–35 in *Transformed from Glory to Glory: Celebrating the Legacy of J. Robertson McQuilkin*, edited by C. R. Little (Fort Washington, PA: CLC Publications, 2015). The table below is a revised form of the one that appears on page 134 of that chapter.
59. The starting point for this list is Stott's classic work, *Men Made New: An Exposition of Romans 5-8* (Downers Grove, IL: InterVarsity, 1970). See pages 91–92 for his discussion of "mortification" and "aspiration," which inspired the other five headings.

Romans 8	The Spirit's Provision	Our Obligation
Liberation (8:1–4)	The Spirit sets us free from condemnation, sin, and death.	We must live under the control of and according to the values of the Spirit.
Aspiration (8:5–8)	The Spirit produces in us a mind-set of life and peace.	We must adopt the orientation and attitudes of the Spirit.
Regeneration (8:9–11)	The Spirit gives us spiritual life now and physical life in the future.	We must live out Christ's righteousness that is imputed to us.
Mortification (8:12–13)	The Spirit puts to death the deeds worked out through our bodies.	We must allow the Spirit to establish in us new patterns of thought and behavior.
Attestation (8:14–17)	The Spirit bears witness to our adoption as God's children.	We must follow the Spirit's leading and endure the sufferings that lead to glory.
Glorification (8:18–25)	The Spirit guarantees the final redemption of our bodies.	We must hope and wait expectantly for what we do not yet see.
Supplication (8:26–30)	The Spirit intercedes for us with wordless groanings.	We must trust that God's sovereign working always accomplishes his purposes.

As we live life by the Spirit, therefore, "it might be said that whether we struggle with the flesh, groan under present suffering, grow impatient with the delay of promised glory, or sense our weakness in prayer, we can be confident that the Spirit will provide the strength (8:12–13), the assurance (8:14–17), the hope (8:23–25), and the help (8:26–27) we need."[60]

Paul's primary purpose for including this paragraph in his letter was to help his readers understand the glorious future that awaited them and to motivate them to live expectantly in light of that future. We share with the Romans the need to realize the way in which the truth about our future should affect the way we view present circumstances, especially suffering. There are multiple possible points of connection in this passage, including weakness, suffering, hope, and eager

---

60. Harvey, *Anointed with the Spirit and Power*, 150.

expectation. The words Paul uses for eager waiting and expectation (ἀποκαραδοκία, ἀπεκδέχομαι), for instance, paint a picture of someone leaning forward out of intense interest, craning the neck, and standing on tiptoe. The passage corrects the idea that our present existence is "all there is" or "as good as it gets." It also corrects philosophies that conclude life is futile, purposeless, and/or without hope. It commends hope, expectation, and confidence in our future destiny that promises freedom, redemption, and glory. The objective in communicating this passage should be to help others understand the truth about their future hope so that they will have confidence that God uses the tribulations and reverses of life for their present benefit and ultimate good.

ROMANS 8:31–39

Text and Translation

31 Therefore, what shall we say to these things? If *it is true that* God *is* for us,[1] who *can be* against us?[2] **32** *The one* who indeed[3] did not spare his own son[4] but handed him over on our behalf,[5] how will he not also[6] with him graciously give to us all things? **33** Who will bring a charge against *the ones* God has chosen?[7] God *is the one who* is declaring righteous.[8] **34** Who *is the one who* is condemning?[9] Christ Jesus[10] *is the one who* died, indeed[11] rather was raised,[12] who also[13] is at the right *hand* of God, who also is interceding for us. **35** What will separate us from the love Christ[14] has for us?[15] Tribulation, or distress, or persecution, or famine, or nakedness, or danger, or sword? **36** Just as it is written that

Because of you we are being put to death all day long,
we were counted as sheep destined for slaughter.[16]

37 But in all these things we hyper-conquer through the *one who* loved[17] us. **38** For I am persuaded[18] that neither death, nor life, nor angels, nor

---

1. Εἰ introduces a first-class condition; ὑπέρ + genitive denotes advantage.
2. Κατά + accusative denotes opposition; see also verse 33.
3. The relative pronoun included an embedded demonstrative; the antecedent is Θεός in the preceding question; γε is emphatic.
4. Τοῦ ἰδίου υἱοῦ is a genitive of direct object.
5. Ὑπέρ + genitive denotes representation; see also verse 34.
6. Καί is adjunctive.
7. Θεοῦ is a subjective genitive.
8. Ὁ δικαιῶν is a substantival participle.
9. Ὁ κατακρινῶν is a substantival participle.
10. The manuscript evidence is divided among three variants; UBS[5] includes Ἰησοῦς in brackets; and Schreiner notes the scribal tendency to add names (*Romans*, 467). Nevertheless, the poetic style of the context suggests that the full name should be preferred.
11. Δέ is emphatic.
12. Both ἀποθανῶν and ἐγερθείς are substantival participles.
13. Καί is adjunctive (twice).
14. Of the three variant readings, θεοῦ (ℵ) and θεοῦ τῆς ἐν Χριστῷ Ἰησοῦ (B) are most likely assimilations to 8:39. UBS[5] gives Χριστοῦ (C, D, 33) an [A] rating.
15. Τοῦ Χριστοῦ is a subjective genitive.
16. Σφραγῆς is an objective genitive.
17. Τοῦ ἀγαπήσαντος is a substantival participle.
18. Πέπεισμαι is an intensive perfect.

rulers, nor things *that are* present,[19] nor things *that are* about to be, nor powers,[20] **39** nor height, nor depth, nor any other created thing will be able to separate us from the love God has for us[21] *which is* in Christ Jesus our Lord.

Context and Structure

II. Letter Body (1:18–15:13)
  A. The Gospel as the Revelation of God's Righteousness (1:18–4:25)
  B. The Gospel as the Demonstration of God's Power (5:1–8:39)
    1. The gospel demonstrates God's power to save from wrath (5:1–11)
    2. The gospel demonstrates God's power to save from condemnation (5:12–21)
    3. The gospel demonstrates God's power to save from sin (6:1–23)
    4. The gospel demonstrates God's power to save from the law (7:1–25)
    5. The gospel demonstrates God's power to save from the flesh (8:1–30)
    6. **The gospel demonstrates God's power to save from all opposition (8:31–39)**

Paul concludes both chapter 8 and the second major section of the letter body (5:1–8:39) with a rhetorical flourish consisting of a question section (8:31–36) and an answer section (8:37–39). The final occurrence of the refrain "through/in our lord Jesus Christ" closes the paragraph (cf. 5:1, 11, 21; 6:23; 7:24).

Basic Message and Exegetical Outline

God's love for us in Christ assures us of victory over every opponent and circumstance.

---

19. Both ἐνεστῶτα and μέλλοντα are anarthrous substantival participles.
20. The reading ἐνεστῶτα . . . μέλλοντα . . . δυνάμεις has the strongest manuscript support ($\mathfrak{P}^{27}$, $\mathfrak{P}^{46}$, ℵ, A, B).
21. Θεοῦ is a subjective genitive.

Total Victory! (8:31–39)
1. Paul asks four rhetorical questions (8:31–36)
   a. Who will oppose us? (8:31–32)
   b. Who will accuse us? (8:33)
   c. Who will condemn us? (8:34)
   d. What will separate us? (8:35–36)
2. Paul gives two resounding answers (8:37–39)
   a. We are more than conquerors through God's love (8:37)
   b. Nothing can separate us from God's love in Christ (8:38–39)

Explanation of the Text

1. Paul asks four rhetorical questions (8:31–36).

What conclusion should we draw from what Paul has written in 5:1–8:30 (τί οὖν ἐροῦμεν πρὸς ταῦτα:)? The apostle follows his opening question with four more specific questions. The first question is, "Who will oppose us?" (τίς καθ' ἡμῶν). In support of the premise that God is on our side (εἰ ὁ θεὸς ὑπὲρ ἡμῶν), Paul points to what God has done for us in Christ using a strong contrast (οὐκ . . . ἀλλά) that highlights the significance of his act. He chose not to spare his very own Son (τοῦ ἰδίου υἱοῦ οὐκ ἐφείσατο) but, instead, handed over that Son on our behalf (ὑπὲρ ἡμῶν πάντων παρέδωκεν αὐτόν). Since God has handed over his Son, he will most certainly (πῶς οὐχὶ καί) graciously and freely give us whatever we might need in the face of opposition (σὺν αὐτῷ τὰ πάντα ἡμῖν χαρίσεται).

The second question is, "Who will accuse us?" The verb Paul uses (ἐγκαλέσει) describes the act of bringing charges against (κατά) someone in a judicial context. The futility of such an action in our case is clear for two reasons: God has chosen us (ἐκλεκτῶν θεοῦ), and God has declared us righteous (θεὸς ὁ δικαιῶν). The latter verb occurred twelve times prior to chapter 8.[22] Most recently, Paul used it twice in the "golden chain" of 8:29–30 that assures us of our future glory. As noted above, God's choice is the basis for his foreknowledge and all the subsequent links in that chain.[23] Given the certainty that God has chosen us and has declared us righteous, any accusations against us are doomed to fail.

---

22. Romans 2:13; 3:4, 20, 24, 26, 28, 30; 4:2, 5; 5:1, 9; 6:7.
23. Paul uses the noun ἐκλογή five times (Rom. 9:11; 11:5, 7, 28; 1 Thess. 1:4), the adjective ἐκλεκτός six times (Rom. 8:33; 16:13; Col. 3:12; 1 Tim. 5:20; 2 Tim. 2:10; Titus 1:1), and the verb ἐκλέγομαι four times (1 Cor. 1:27 [twice], 28; Eph. 1:4).

The third question is "Who will condemn us?" (τίς ὁ κατακρινῶν). In response to this question (that echoes his initial declaration in 8:1) Paul offers four reminders, all of which describe Christ's work. He died (ὁ ἀποθανών) to pay the penalty for our sins. He was raised (ἐγερθείς) to secure our righteousness. He ascended to God's right hand (ἐστιν ἐν δεξιᾷ τοῦ θεοῦ) to take the ultimate position of prestige and power. He intercedes for us (ἐντυγχάνει ὑπὲρ ἡμῶν) to insure that our righteous status prevails in any verdict. With Christ as our risen, heavenly advocate, what chance of success does any attempt to condemn us have?

The final question is, "What will separate us?" (τίς ἡμᾶς χωρίσει). What Paul has written in response to the immediately preceding question highlights the love Christ has for us (τῆς ἀγαπῆς τοῦ Χριστοῦ), which becomes the key concept in the remainder of the paragraph (8:37, 39). By enumerating seven different forms of suffering Paul effectively eliminates every possible source of separation.[24] His quotation of Psalm 44:22 (LXX), however, makes it clear that suffering and, possibly, death should come as no surprise to followers of Christ (cf. 8:17). Nevertheless, those experiences—however extreme—cannot affect the way in which God relates to us because that relationship rests on what Christ has done for us.

2. Paul gives two resounding answers (8:37–39).

In contrast (ἀλλ') to the short-lived sufferings we might possibly encounter is the ultimate victory we will certainly enjoy (cf. 2 Cor. 4:17). Christ's love for us (διὰ τοῦ ἀγαπήσαντος ὑμᾶς) insures that we will be totally victorious (ὑπερνικῶμεν) in the face of every obstacle we might face (ἐν τούτοις πᾶσιν). In fact, Paul is absolutely convinced (πέπεισμαι ὅτι) that nothing can separate us from that love, and he lists four categories of hostile forces in order to make his point. Death (θάνατος) and life (ζωή) encompass the full range of human existence.[25] Angels (ἄγγελοι), rulers (ἀρχαί), and powers (δυνάμεις) encompass the full range of cosmic spiritual powers.[26] Things present (ἐνεστῶτα) and

---

24. Tribulation (θλῖψις) describes affliction (BDAG 457b); distress (στενοχωρία) describes stressful circumstances (BDAG 943a); persecution (διωγμός) describes a process of oppression (BDAG 253d); famine (λιμός) describes the danger of dying from lack of food (BDAG 596c); nakedness (γυμνότης) describes the state of being so destitute as to lack adequate clothing (BDAG 208d); danger (κίνδυνος) describes risk/peril in general (BDAG 544d); sword (μάχαιρα) is a metonymy for violent death (BDAG 622b).
25. Cf. Jewett, *Romans*, 550–51.
26. Cf. Dunn, *Romans*, 507.

things about to be (μέλλοντα) encompass the full extent of temporal events. Height (ὕψωμα) and depth (βάθος) encompass the full extent of the created order.[27] To be clear that he is excluding every possibility, Paul adds "nor any other created thing" (οὔτε τις κτίσις ἑτέρα). Because of God's love for us (τῆς ἀγάπης τοῦ θεοῦ) as focused and expressed in Christ Jesus (τὴν ἐν Χριστῷ 'Ιησοῦ τῷ κυρίῳ ἡμῶν), we can know that nothing is able to separate us from him (δυνήσεται ἡμᾶς χωρίσαι).

Theology and Appropriation

Although the noun "love" (ἀγάπη) and its cognates appear 169 times in Paul's letters, only twenty occurrences refer to the love God has for us (e.g., 2 Cor. 13:14).[28] The fact that the idea occurs three times in the nine verses of Romans 8:31–39, therefore, suggests that it might well be the key concept in the paragraph. The facets of love that appear in that paragraph are congruent with what Paul writes on the topic elsewhere in his letters. God's love for us as his children is great (Eph. 2:4; 3:19), and he views us as "beloved" (Rom. 1:7). Objectively, his love is linked with his act of choosing us (1 Thess. 1:4; 2 Thess. 2:13) and his act of declaring us righteousness (Rom. 8:33). Subjectively, his love is poured out in our hearts through the Holy Spirit (Rom. 5:5). His love gives us encouragement (2 Thess. 2:16), hope (2 Thess. 2:16), and peace (2 Cor. 13:11). His love also gives us confidence because nothing can separate us from it (Rom. 8:35, 39). God's love for us is focused and expressed in Jesus Christ (Rom. 8:37, 39; 2 Tim. 1:13). God demonstrated his love for us by giving Christ to die for us (Rom. 5:8). He chose not to spare his Son but, instead, delivered him up for us (Rom. 8:32) because of our wrongdoing (Rom. 4:25). Christ himself not only loved us, but he also gave himself for us (Gal. 2:20; Eph. 5:2, 25). As a result, he continues to mediate God's love for us as he intercedes for us from his place at God's right hand (Rom. 8:34).

Paul's purpose for including this paragraph in his letter was to reinforce the hope his readers should have because of what Christ has done for them. Along with his Roman readers, we need to realize the infinite scope of God's love for us as focused in and demonstrated by Christ and his work on our behalf. There are multiple possible points of connection between this paragraph and contemporary audiences. They

---

27. Cf. Schreiner, *Romans*, 465.
28. The noun (ἀγάπη) occurs eleven times (Rom. 5:5, 8; 8:35, 39; 2 Cor. 13:11, 14; Eph. 2:4; 3:19; 5:2; 2 Thess. 3:5; 2 Tim. 1:13); the verb (ἀγαπάω) occurs eight times (Rom. 8:37; Gal. 2:20; Eph. 2:4; 5:2, 25; 1 Thess. 1:4; 2 Thess. 2:13, 16); the adjective (ἀγαπητός) occurs once (Rom. 1:7).

include opposition, accusation, condemnation, separation, tribulation, suffering, and victory. The compound verb Paul uses for being "totally victorious" (ὑπερνικάω), for example, adds the preposition from which we get "hyper-" (ὑπέρ) to the verb for victory (νικάω) from which Nike, Inc., the athletic apparel and equipment corporation, derives its name. The passage corrects any idea that the Christian life is free from troubles or difficulties. It also argues strongly against the suggestion that it is possible for a follower of Christ somehow to "separate him/herself" from a relationship that God himself has established. It commends an attitude of confidence and ultimate victory in the face of short-term opposition. The objective in communicating this passage should be to help others understand the extent of God's love for them so that they will persevere in following Christ, because they can be confident that the gospel is God's power to save them not only from wrath (5:1–11), condemnation (5:12–21), sin (6:1–23), the law (7:1–25), and the flesh (8:1–30), but also from all opposition (8:31–39).

ROMANS 9:1–11:36

The Gospel as the Fulfillment of God's Plan

The body of Romans consists of four major parts, each of which unpacks one of the four topics Paul includes in his thematic statement of 1:16–17. The central topic of Romans 9:1–11:36 is **the fulfillment of God's plan** in the gospel. Paul's argument makes it clear that God fulfills his plan to keep his word (9:6–29), to use Israel's unresponsiveness (9:30–10:21), and to show mercy to all 11:1–32). He emphasizes his personal interest in God's plan by expressing his concern for Israel (9:1–5), and he confirms his absolute confidence in that plan by closing with a doxology to God's wisdom (11:33–36).

        c.   By demonstrating his kindness and severity (11:17–24)

        d.   By restoring Israel (11:25–32)

    5.   Paul's doxology of praise to God for his working (11:33–36)

ROMANS 9:1-5

Text and Translation

1 I am speaking *the* truth in Christ; I am not lying; while my conscience is bearing witness[1] with me[2] by the Holy Spirit,[3] **2** that my[4] grief is great and *there is* unceasing sorrow in my heart. **3** For I could almost be praying[5] that I myself were anathema from the Messiah on behalf of my brothers,[6] my kinsmen according to the flesh,[7] **4** who are *the* Israelites, who possess[8] the adoption as sons and the glory and the covenants[9] and the giving of the law and the temple service and the promises, **5** who are descended from the fathers and from whom[10] *is* the Messiah according to the flesh, the *one who* is[11] God over all, blessed to the ages.[12] Amen.

Context and Structure

---

1. Συμμαρτυρούσης ... τῆς συνειδήσεώς μου is a genitive absolute of time.
2. Μοι is a dative of association.
3. Ἐν + dative is instrumental.
4. Μοι is a dative of possession.
5. Wallace, following Fanning, classifies ηὐχόμην as a potential indicative (*Grammar*, 451n22) and a tendential imperfect (ibid., 552n27), indicating that Paul repeatedly considered the action but did not bring himself to the point of actually making the request.
6. Ὑπέρ + genitive denotes substitution.
7. Κατά + accusative denotes natural lineage. So also in verse 5.
8. The genitive of the relative pronoun ὧν denotes possession; in verse 5 it denotes relationship.
9. The plural reading αἱ διαθῆκαι (ℵ, C, 33) is the more difficult, and there would be no compelling reason to change a singular to the plural.
10. Ἐκ + genitive denotes natural lineage.
11. Ὁ ὤν is a substantival participle.
12. Of the several punctuation variants, Jewett's suggestion of commas after σάρκα and θεός is probably the best choice (Jewett, *Romans*, 567–69).

4. The gospel fulfills God's plan to show mercy to all (11:1–32)
5. Paul's doxology of praise to God for his working (11:33–36)

The absence of a connecting conjunction (asyndeton) marks the beginning of a new major section in the letter. This brief opening paragraph consists of two sentences, in which Paul expresses the depth of his concern for Israel (9:1–2) and provides the reason for that concern (9:3–5).

Basic Message and Exegetical Outline

Israel's unresponsiveness affects Paul deeply and personally, because they ignore the blessings God has bestowed on them.

Paul's Grief over Israel (9:1–5)
1. He feels their lack of responsiveness deeply (9:1–2)
   a. Christ, the Spirit, and his own conscience bear witness to his grief (9:1)
   b. His grief is profound, constant, and heartfelt (9:2)
2. He takes their lack of responsiveness personally (9:3–5)
   a. They are his kinsmen (9:3)
   b. They ignore God's blessings (9:4–5)

Explanation of the Text

1. He feels their lack of responsiveness deeply (9:1–2).
Paul calls attention to the next major section of his letter by omitting a connecting conjunction and using an "attestation statement" [13] (ἀλήθειαν λέγω ἐν Χριστῷ) that highlights Christ as "the absolute guarantor of the truth." [14] He underlines his own truthfulness by adding two parenthetical statements. The first assures the Romans that he does not lie (οὐ ψεύδομαι); the second adds the witness of his own conscience (συμμαρτυρούσης μοι τῆς συνειδήσεώς μου) and the witness of the Holy Spirit (ἐν πνεύματι ἁγίῳ) in support of his truthfulness. [15] The truth he has taken such pains to reinforce is the depth of his own sorrow at the

---

13. Longenecker, *Romans*, 781.
14. Cranfield, *Romans*, 452.
15. By citing three witnesses, Paul meets the Old Testament requirement for veracity (Deut. 17:6; 19:15).

Jews' lack of responsiveness to the gospel. He describes his grief as profound (λύπη μοί ἐστιν μεγάλη) and his anguish as both unceasing (ἀδιάλειπτος ὀδύνη) and heartfelt (τῇ καρδίᾳ μου).

2. He takes their lack of responsiveness personally (9:3–5).

The depth of his concern for his kinsmen leads Paul to consider an extreme option. If it were possible, he would pray (ηὐχόμην) that he could be handed over to "the divine wrath of eschatological judgment"[16] (ἀνάθεμα εἶναι αὐτὸς ἐγώ) of being separated from Christ (ἀπὸ τοῦ Χριστοῦ) as a substitute for his fellow Jews (ὑπὲρ τῶν ἀδελφῶν μου τῶν συγγενῶν μου κατὰ σάρκα). As a people, the Jews enjoy nine divinely bestowed benefits that should increase their responsiveness to the gospel but, instead, increase their accountability before God. As Israelites (οἵτινές εἰσιν Ἰσραηλῖται), they possess special status as God's people. God graciously adopted them as his own (ἡ υἱοθεσία), gave them the visible sign of his glorious presence (ἡ δόξα), and granted them all the rights and privileges associated with the Old Testament biblical covenants (αἱ διαθῆκαι). He also gave them the Mosaic law (ἡ νομοθεσία), the temple service (ἡ λατρεία), the Old Testament promises (αἱ ἐπαγγελίαι)—including those related to Messiah—and their connection to the patriarchs (ὧν οἱ πατέρες). Finally, the Messiah himself derives his natural lineage from Israel (ἐξ ὧν ὁ Χριστὸς τὸ κατὰ σάρκα). Paul concludes with three truths about Messiah: he is God (ὁ ὢν . . . θεός); he is sovereign (ἐπὶ πάντων); and he is eternal (εὐλογητὸς εἰς τοὺς αἰῶνας). Yet despite these benefits and the knowledge they possess, the Jews remain unresponsive to the gospel.

Theology and Appropriation

The nine benefits Paul enumerates in Romans 9:4–5 have Old Testament roots. "Israel" was the name God gave to Jacob on his return from Paddan-aram (Gen. 32:24–32) and was subsequently applied to his offspring as "the sons of Israel" (Gen. 32:32; 46:8). Moo notes that it designated the Israelites as "a people chosen by God to belong to him in a special way and to be the vessels of his plan of salvation for the world."[17] The term "adoption" does not occur in the Old Testament with relation to Israel, but it summarizes the Old Testament idea of Israel as "God's sons" (e.g., Exod. 4:22–23; Deut. 14:1–2; Isa. 43:6; 63:16; 64:8; Jer. 31:9; Hos. 1:10; 11:1; Mal. 1:6; 2:10). God's "glory" was the visible sign of his presence with his people in the wilderness

---

16. Harvey, *Romans*, 224.
17. Moo, *Romans,* 561n30.

(Exod. 16:7, 10), at Sinai (Exod. 24:16–17), in the tabernacle (Exod. 40:34–35) and the temple (1 Kings 8:11). Israel's wickedness resulted in his glory departing from the temple (Ezek. 10:15–19; 11:22–23), but Messiah would bring that glory to the nations (Luke 2:32; cf. Isa. 60:1–3). The Old Testament records God establishing four "covenants" with Israel.[18] The Abrahamic covenant (Gen. 12:1–3; 17:1–8) promised God's blessing; the Mosaic covenant (Exod. 19:1–24:18) promised God's presence; the Davidic covenant (2 Sam. 7:8–17) promised Israel a king; the new covenant (Jer. 31:31–34) promised forgiveness of sins. The repeated element common to all four covenants is the promise that God would be their god and would make them his people (Gen. 17:7; Exod. 19:5; 20:2; 2 Sam. 7:14; Jer. 31:33).

Paul has addressed the Mosaic law throughout the letter, noting that it was holy, just, and good (7:12), a special source of pride for the Jews (2:17–23), and a special responsibility God had entrusted to them (3:2). The "temple service" is described in Exodus (chapters 25–30) and Leviticus (chapters 1–7, 16–17, 21–25). The "promises" are best understood as the promises given to Abraham (Gen. 12:1–3; 13:14–15; 15:4–5; 17:4–8; 21:12–13; 22:16–18), Isaac (Gen. 26:3–5), Jacob (Gen. 28:13–15; 35:11–12), Moses (Deut. 18:18–19), and David (2 Sam. 7:8–16). The "patriarchs," Abraham, Isaac, Jacob, and perhaps Jacob's twelve sons, are the leading characters in Genesis 12–50 and the founding fathers of Israel. The Old Testament origin of "Christ" (Messiah) is found in the practice of anointing Israel's high priests (Exod. 29:21; 30:30) and kings (1 Sam. 16:1–13). The anointed king became closely connected to God's "Son" (Ps. 2:7), and Israel's king—David in particular—is called God's servant (2 Sam. 7:1–17; Pss. 78:70; 89:20). "Servant" also carried messianic overtones, perhaps as an anointed prophet (Isa. 43:1–13; 49:1–7; 50:1–11; 52:13–53:12). Each of these ideas informed Jewish expectations during the intertestamental period, with the kingly aspect being most prominent.

Paul's primary purpose for including this passage at this point in his letter was to introduce his extended treatment of Jewish unresponsiveness and help his readers understand his own concern for Israel. With the original readers we share the need to realize that religious, ethic, and cultural heritage do not guarantee that anyone will respond positively to God's grace. One possible point of connection is grief over a situation involving friends, immediate family, or relatives. Another

---

18. The biblical covenants also include the Adamic covenant (Gen. 3:14–21) and the Noahic covenant (Gen. 9:8–17). They promise a redeemer and preservation, respectively, although they preceded God's call of Abraham.

is the concept of religious heritage or privilege. The passage corrects any sense that religious heritage is all an individual or a people group needs in order to have a right relationship with God. It commends a godly concern for the lost. The objective in communicating this passage should be to help others understand the responsibility that accompanies a godly heritage (cf. 2 Tim. 3:14–15) so that they will take seriously the eternal significance—for themselves and others—of the gospel message.

ROMANS 9:6–13

Text and Translation

6 But *it is* by no means as though[1] God's word has failed.[2] For not all the *ones who are* from Israel[3] *are* Israel; **7** and *it is* not that all children are Abraham's seed, but **"Through Isaac your[4] seed will be called."** **8** That is, not the children who belong to the flesh[5] are God's children, but the children who belong to the promise will be counted as a seed. **9** For the word of promise[6] *is* this, **"According to this time I will come and Sarah[7] will have a son." 10** And not only this, but also when Rebekah was having a sperm[8] from[9] one *man*, Isaac our father—**11** for when they had not yet been born[10] and had not practiced any good or bad thing, in order that God's purpose according to election might remain, **12** not on the basis of[11] works but on the basis of the *one who* calls[12]—it was said to her, **"The greater will serve the lesser."**[13] **13** Just as it is written, **"Isaac I loved, but Esau I hated."**

Context and Structure

    II. Letter Body (1:18–15:13)
        C. The Gospel as the Fulfillment of God's Plan (9:1–11:36)
            1. Paul's concern for Israel (9:1–5)
            2. The gospel fulfills God's plan to keep his word (9:6–29)
                a. **According to his calling (9:6–13)**

---

1. According to BDAG (701d), οὐχ οἷον ὅτι is a combination of οὐχ οἷον ("by no means") and οὐχ ὅτι ("not as if").
2. Ἐκπέπτωκεν is an extensive perfect.
3. Ἐκ + genitive denotes natural lineage.
4. Σοι is a dative of possession.
5. Τῆς σαρκός is a possessive genitive, as is τῆς ἐπαγγελίας.
6. Ἐπαγγελίας is a descriptive genitive.
7. Τῇ Σάρρᾳ is a possessive dative.
8. Ἔχουσα is an adverbial participle of time; κοίτην ἔχειν is best understood as a seminal emission (BDAG 554b).
9. Ἐκ + genitive denotes source.
10. Γεννηθέντων and πραξάντων are genitive absolutes of time; the implied subjects of both participles are Jacob and Isaac.
11. Ἐκ + genitive (twice) denotes the basis on which the action rests; see BDAG 297c; cf. Harris, *Prepositions*, 104.
12. Τοῦ καλοῦντος is a substantival participle.
13. Τῷ ἐλάσσονι is a dative of direct object.

        b.   Out of his mercy (9:14–18)
        c.   Under his authority (9:19–29)
     3.   The gospel fulfills God's plan to use Israel's unrespon-
        siveness (9:30–10:21)
     4.   The gospel fulfills God's plan to show mercy to all
        (11:1–32)
     5.   Paul's doxology of praise to God for his working
        (11:33–36)

Paul opens the next section of his argument (9:6–29) with the claim that God's word has not failed (9:6). In this first paragraph, he supports that claim by using the examples of Isaac (9:7–9) and Jacob (9:10–13) to demonstrate that God's sovereign calling determines to whom the word of promise applies. Four Old Testament quotations (Gen. 21:12; 18:10; 25:23; Mal. 1:2–3) begin the collection of thirty-two such quotations that occur in chapters 9–11.

Basic Message and Exegetical Outline

The examples of Isaac and Jacob demonstrate that God's promise applies to those he sovereignly calls.

    God's Sovereign Calling (9:6–13)
     1.   God word is trustworthy (9:6)
     2.   The promise is applied to Isaac, but not to Ishmael
        (9:7–9)
        a.   Not on the basis of flesh (9:7a, 8a)
        b.   But on the basis of promise (9:7b, 8b–9)
     3.   The promise is applied to Jacob, but not to Esau
        (9:10–13)
        a.   Not on the basis of works (9:10–11)
        b.   But on the basis of calling (9:12–13)

Explanation of the Text

1. God's word is trustworthy (9:6).
    Paul begins by stating his thesis for the next section of his argument (9:6–29): Israel's lack of responsiveness does not mean that God's declared purpose for his people has somehow failed (οὐχ οἷον δὲ ὅτι ἐκπέπτωκεν ὁ λόγος τοῦ θεοῦ). The first step in understanding Israel's current situation is to realize that God's promise is selective—it does not apply to every individual who traces his or her ancestry to Abraham

(οὐ πάντες οἱ ἐξ Ἰσραήλ οὗτοι Ἰσραήλ). In fact, as Paul will demonstrate with two examples from Israel's history, the determining factor is God's sovereign calling.[14]

2. The promise is applied to Isaac, but not to Ishmael (9:7–9).

Paul's first example involves Abraham's two sons and uses the messianic term "seed" (σπέρμα), which first appears in Genesis 3:15, is repeated in Genesis 4:25, and is a key to Paul's argument in Galatians 3:15–20 (cf. Gen. 9:9; 12:7). That term does not apply equally to all of Abraham's children (οὐδ' ὅτι εἰσὶν σπέρμα Ἀβραάμ πάντες τέκνα). Instead, in Abraham's case, it applied only to Isaac, as God's promise in Genesis 21:12 makes clear: "But through Isaac your seed will be called" (ἀλλ' ἐν Ἰσαὰκ κληθήσεταί σοι σπέρμα). As the product of Abraham's and Sarah's attempt to "help" God, Ishmael exemplifies the "children of the flesh" (τὰ τέκνα τῆς σαρκός) and is clearly not counted among the "children of God" (τέκνα τοῦ θεοῦ). In contrast, Isaac exemplifies the "children of the promise" (τὰ τέκνα τῆς ἐπαγγελίας) and, so, is counted as a seed (λογίζεται εἰς σπέρμα). The promise (ἐπαγγελίας ὁ λόγος οὗτος) specifically applied to Sarah's son (καὶ ἔσται τῇ Σάρρα υἱός),[15] not to Hagar's son. God's promise, therefore, is selective.

3. The is promise applied to Jacob, but not to Esau (9:10–13).

Paul's second example is even more conclusive (οὐ μόνον δέ ἀλλὰ καί). Although Ishmael and Isaac had the same father, they had different mothers. Jacob and Esau, however, both had the same parents. In fact, Rebekah conceived both sons from the same sperm she received from Isaac (Ῥεβέκκα ἐξ ἑνὸς κοίτην ἔχουσα Ἰσαὰκ τοῦ παρτὸς ἡμῶν). In order to make it clear that God's promise is selective, Paul highlights the timing of that promise. God spoke it before either son was born (μήπω γεννηθέντων) and before either had the opportunity to do anything good or bad (μηδὲ πραξάντων τι ἀγαθὸν ἢ φαῦλον). God's promise is selective (ἡ κατ' ἐκλογὴν πρόθεσις τοῦ θεοῦ), has its source in divine calling (ἐκ τοῦ καλοῦντος) rather than in human works (οὐκ ἐξ ἔργων), and is specific. In this particular instance, God declared that Rebekah's older son would serve the younger son (ὁ μείζων δουλεύσει τῷ ἐλάσσοντι)—that is, the promise applied to Jacob rather than to Esau. The prophet Malachi subsequently confirmed the principle of

---

14. Note the repetition of καλέω in verses 9 and 12.
15. Cf. Genesis 18:10.

selectivity when he wrote, "Jacob I loved, but Esau I hated" (τὸν Ἰακὼβ ἠγάπησα τὸν δὲ Ἡσαῦ ἐμίσησα).[16]

Theology and Appropriation

Walter Kaiser notes that the term "seed" carries two nuances in the Old Testament: one corporate, the other representative.[17] The initial mention is singular, clearly carries the latter nuance, and promises one who will counteract the effects of Adam's fall (Gen. 3:15). The second mention (by Eve) continues that aspect (Gen. 4:25). With Noah, however, the term broadens into the corporate sense of "descendants" (Gen. 9:9), the aspect that assumes prominence throughout the remainder of Genesis (e.g., Gen. 13:15–16; 15:3; 17:7; 26:3–4; 28:13–14; 35:12). God promises those descendants that they will possess a land (Gen. 15:18; 17:8; 26:3–4; 28:13–14; 35:12) and that they will be a blessing to the nations (Gen. 22:18; cf. Isa. 54:3). He also makes it clear that the promise is traced through specific individuals beginning with Isaac (Gen. 17:19; 21:12). The hint of a promised king (Num. 24:7) becomes explicit in God's covenant with David, where the term again narrows to the singular "seed" and refers to David's son whose throne God will establish forever (2 Sam. 7:12–13; cf. Ps. 89:4, 29, 36; Jer. 23:5–8).

The New Testament focuses on the representative aspect of the "seed," which reflects the expectation in Jesus's time that the Christ would be one of David's descendants (John 7:42). Although Luke and Paul identify David's seed as Savior (Acts 13:23) and God's Son (Rom. 1:3), the New Testament authors more frequently connect the promised seed to Abraham traced through Isaac (Rom 9:7; Heb. 11:18; cf. Gen. 21:12). Paul in particular makes clear the selectivity of the promise (Gal. 3:16, 19), connects the promise to Christ (2 Tim. 2:8; cf; Heb. 2:16), extends the promise to those in Christ who have faith like Abraham's (Rom. 4:13, 16; Gal. 3:29), and highlights the universal blessing of that promise (Rom. 4:8; cf. Gen. 22:18; Acts 3:25). It is the representative/ selective aspect of God's working that Paul highlights in this passage.

Paul's primary purpose for including this passage at this point in his letter, therefore, was to make it clear that God's promise is selective and does not apply to every individual who traces his or her ancestry to Abraham. With the original readers we share the need to realize that God calls to himself those to whom his sovereign promise applies.

---

16. Malachi 1:2. Cranfield concludes that "love" and "hate" are best understood in terms of election and rejection (*Romans*, 480).

17. W. C. Kaiser Jr., *The Promise-Plan of God* (Grand Rapids: Zondervan, 2008), 56–57.

There are at least two possible points of connection to the passage. Negatively, the idea of broken promises echoes the rhetorical question with which Paul opens the paragraph. Positively, the idea of "favorite child" status reflects the selectivity at work in God's choice of Isaac over Ishmael and Jacob over Esau. The passage corrects both the idea that God's word is somehow faulty or in error and the idea that God might possibly fail to follow through on what he has promised. It commends confidence in God's word and purposes and gratitude for God's gracious calling. The objective in communicating this passage should be to help others understand that God works selectively to fulfill his purposes so that they will trust his sovereignty in calling to himself those men and women he has chosen.

ROMANS 9:14–18

Text and Translation

14 Therefore, what shall we say? *There is* no unrighteousness with regard to God,[1] is there? May it never be! **15** For to Moses he says,

> **I will have mercy** *on anyone* **on whom**[2] **I am having mercy,**
>> **and I will have compassion** *on anyone* **on whom I am having compassion.**

16 Consequently, *it is* not dependent on the *one who* is willing,[3] and not on the *one who* is running, but on God, the *one who* is having mercy. **17** For the Scripture says to Pharaoh that,

> **For this very purpose**[4] **I brought you to power,**
>> **so that I might show my power through you**[5]
>> **and so that my name might be proclaimed in all the earth.**

18 Consequently, he is having mercy on *the one* whom[6] he wishes, and he is hardening *the one* whom he wishes.

Context and Structure

---

1. Παρά + dative denotes association.
2. Both relative pronouns (ὅς, ἄν) are indefinite and include embedded demonstratives.
3. The three substantival participles θέλοντες . . . τρέχοντες . . . ἐλεῶντες are all genitive of source.
4. Εἰς αὐτὸ τοῦτο is a classical idiom of purpose.
5. Ἐν + dative is instrumental.
6. Both accusative relative pronouns include embedded demonstratives.

Once again, Paul uses a rhetorical question to raise a possible false conclusion: Are God's actions in dealing with Israel unfair (9:14)? In support of his emphatic denial Paul uses God's statements to Moses (9:15–16) and to Pharaoh (9:17–18) to demonstrate that God's exercise of his mercy depends solely on him. Two Old Testament quotations (Exod. 33:19; 9:16) add scriptural proof to his argument.

Basic Message and Exegetical Outline

God's statements to Moses and Pharaoh demonstrate that God exercises his mercy justly, in accordance with his character, and in order to make himself known.

God's Sovereign Mercy (9:14–18)
1. God acts justly (9:14)
2. God acts in accordance with his character (9:15–16)
   a. Not contingent on human desire or action (9:16a–b)
   b. Out of his character (9:16c)
3. God acts in order to make himself known (9:17–18)
   a. To show his power (9:17b)
   b. To proclaim his name (9:17c)

Explanation of the Text

1. God's acts justly (9:14).

Does the selectivity of God's promise somehow imply that he is unrighteous (μὴ ἀδικία παρὰ τῷ θεῷ)? Paul rejects that suggestion emphatically (μὴ γένοιτο). In fact, rather than reflecting any sort of unrighteousness, God's actions are just and rooted in his sovereign mercy.[7] Two related statements from Israel's history demonstrate that truth.

2. God acts in accordance with his character (9:15–16).

God's statement to Moses in Exodus 33:19 (τῷ Μωϋσεῖ λέγει) highlights the divine origin of his actions. He has mercy upon whomever he wishes (ἐλεήσω ὃν ἂν ἐλεῶ), and he shows compassion to whomever he wishes (οἰκτιρήσω ὃν ἂν οἰκτίρω). He alone determines the identity of the individual who experiences both. His actions are not contingent on human will (οὐ τοῦ θέλοντος) or human effort (οὐδὲ τοῦ τρέχοντος).

---

7. Note the fourfold repetition of ἐλεέω in verses 15, 16, and 18.

Instead, they have their source solely in God, who shows mercy (ἀλλὰ τοῦ ἐλεῶντος θεοῦ).

3. God acts in order to make himself known (9:17–18).

The fact that God chooses to extend his mercy to some (ὃν θέλει ἐλεεῖ) means that he also chooses to withhold his mercy from others (ὃν θέλει σκληρύνει). In Pharaoh's case, God's act of withholding mercy is characterized as "hardening." Moo notes that the verb "is used consistently in Scripture to depict a spiritual condition that renders one unreceptive and disobedient to God and his word."[8] In the context of this divine hardening, God's statement to Pharaoh in Exodus 9:16 (λέγει ἡ γραφὴ τῷ Φαραώ) highlights the twofold purpose of his actions. He brought Pharaoh to power (εἰς αὐτὸ τοῦτο ἐξήγειρά σε) in order to show his power (ὅπως ἐνδείξωμαι ἐν σοὶ τὴν δύναμίν μου) and in order to proclaim his name in all the earth (ὅπως διαγγελῇ τὸ ὄνομά μου ἐν πάσῃ τῇ γῇ).

Theology and Appropriation

For the Greeks, mercy was primarily "the emotion aroused by contact with an affliction which comes undeservedly on someone else."[9] In the Old Testament, however, the idea relates most closely to "proper covenant behavior,"[10] that is, the exercise of kindness, mercy, and/or pity based on a commitment to a covenant partner. It is primarily God's gracious gift expressed in acts (Exod. 34:6–9; Pss. 25:10; 40:11), including deliverance (Ps. 6:4) and the forgiveness of sins (Ps. 32:1). God's exercise of his mercy makes him an object of hope (Pss. 13:5; 20:7; 33:18).

In the New Testament, human mercy is seldom in view (Matt. 5:7; 18:33; Luke 16:24; Rom. 12:8), but God's people are expected to exercise mercy (Matt. 9:13; 12:7) because of their own experience of divine mercy (Matt. 5:7; 2 Cor. 4:1; cf. 1 Cor. 7:25; 1 Tim. 1:13, 16). God's own mercy is characterized as great (Luke 1:58), rich (Eph. 2:4), and abundant (1 Peter 1:3). He is, therefore, the source of grace, mercy, and peace (1 Tim. 1:2; 2 Tim. 1:2; Titus 1:4; 2 John 3; cf. Jude 2). Because he is merciful, we can expect him to act in accordance with his character by expressing his mercy in acts. He extends his mercy to those who call on him (e.g., Matt. 17:15; Mark 10:47–48; Luke 17:13), to those who fear him (Luke 1:50), and to those who do not deserve his mercy (Rom. 11:30–31; 1 Peter 2:10). He does so sovereignly (Rom. 9:15, 18), in order to have mercy on all (Rom. 11:32), and because it brings him glory (Rom. 15:9).

---

8. Moo, *Romans*, 596.
9. *TDNT* 2.477.
10. *NIDNTT* 2.594.

Paul's primary purpose for including this passage at this point in his letter was to help his readers understand that God acts justly in extending his mercy to some but not to others. With the original readers we need to realize that God exercises his mercy sovereignly and justly. One possible point of connection to this passage is the idea of injustice, but a better approach would be to use the idea of mercy, for which any number of possible connections exist. The passage corrects any suggestion that God bases his actions on human will or effort. Instead, it highlights the fact that he works in accordance with his own character, and is within his rights to do so. It commends confidence and trust in God, who acts sovereignly and justly in line with his merciful character. The objective in communicating this passage should be to help others understand that God is merciful and expresses his mercy to those who call on him, to those who fear him, and to those who do not deserve his mercy so that they will trust him to extend his mercy as he knows best.

ROMANS 9:19–29

Text and Translation

19 Therefore, will you say to me, "Why, then, is he finding fault? For who has set himself against[1] his will?" **20** On the contrary,[2] O man, who are you, the *one who* is answering back[3] to God? That which is molded will not say to the *one who* molded[4] *it*, "Why did you make me like this," will it? **21** Or is the potter not having authority over the clay[5] out of his lump to make one[6] vessel for honor[7] *and* another vessel for dishonor? **22** Now *what* if[8] God—because he is willing[9] to show for himself[10] his wrath and to make known his power—bore with much patience[11] vessels destined for wrath[12] that are prepared[13] for destruction,[14] **23** and[15] in order that he might make known the riches that are his glory[16] upon vessels destined for mercy that he prepared beforehand for glory, **24** *that is, upon* us, *the ones* whom[17] he also[18] called, not only out of the Jews[19] but also out of the Gentiles? **25** As also it says in Hosea,

---

1. Ἀνθέστηκεν is a gnomic perfect with a middle sense.
2. Μενοῦνγε is adversative and corrects (cf. 10:18).
3. Ὁ ἀνταποκρινόμενος is a substantival participle that further explains the personal pronoun σύ.
4. Τῷ πλάσσοντι is a substantival participle.
5. Τοῦ πηλοῦ is a genitive of subordination.
6. The correlative combination ὅ μέν ... ὅ δέ ("one ... another") heightens the contrast.
7. Εἰς + accusative denotes purpose (twice).
8. Εἰ introduces the protasis of a first-class condition, but no apodosis follows (Moo, *Romans*, 604).
9. Θέλων is an adverbial participle of cause.
10. Ἐνδείξασθαι is an indirect middle.
11. Ἐν + dative denotes manner.
12. Ὀργῆς is a genitive of purpose; so also ἐλέους in verse 23.
13. Κατηρτισμένα is an adjectival participle modifying σκεύη.
14. Εἰς + accusative denotes purpose; also in verse 23.
15. The inclusion of καί has stronger manuscript support (𝔓⁴⁶, ℵ, A, D, 33) than does its omission (B).
16. Τῆς δόξης is a genitive of apposition.
17. The relative pronoun includes an embedded demonstrative.
18. Καί is adjunctive (twice).
19. Ἐκ + genitive denotes separation (twice).

> I will call the *one who is* not my people my people
> and the *one who* has not been loved[20] beloved;

26 and in the very [21]place where it was said to them, "You *are* not my people,"

> there they will be called sons of the living[22] God.

27 And Isaiah cries out concerning Israel,[23]

> If[24] the number of the sons of Israel were as the sand of the sea, the remnant[25] will be saved; **28** for the Lord will carry out his word quickly and finally[26] on the earth.

29 And just as Isaiah has said beforehand,

> Except[27] the Lord of hosts[28] had left behind a seed for us, we would have been caused to be[29] as Sodom and we would have been caused to resemble Gomorrah.

Context and Structure

  II. Letter Body (1:18–15:13)
    C. The Gospel as the Fulfillment of God's Plan (9:1–11:36)
      1. Paul's concern for Israel (9:1–5)
      2. The gospel fulfills God's plan to keep his word (9:6–29)
        a. According to his calling (9:6–13)
        b. Out of his mercy (9:14–18)
        c. **Under his authority (9:19–29)**
      3. The gospel fulfills God's plan to use Israel's unresponsiveness (9:30–10:21)
      4. The gospel fulfills God's plan to show mercy to all (11:1–32)

---

20. The first participle is substantival; the second is adjectival.
21. The definite article functions as a mild demonstrative pronoun.
22. Ζῶντος is an adjectival participle.
23. Ὑπέρ + genitive denotes reference.
24. Ἐάν introduces a third class condition.
25. Longenecker includes an extended excursus on the background of "remnant" (*Romans*, 803–13).
26. Συντελῶν and συντέμνων are both adverbial participles of manner. The two longer variant readings are most likely assimilations to the LXX.
27. Εἰ μή ("except") . . . ἄν introduces a second class condition.
28. English versions variously translate κύριος Σαβαώθ as "Lord of Sabaoth" (NASB), "Lord of hosts" (ESV), "Lord of armies" (NET), and "Lord Almighty" (NIV).
29. Both ἐγενήθημεν and ὡμοιώθημεν have causative nuances, reflecting the original Hebrew hiphil tense.

5. Paul's doxology of praise to God for his working (11:33–36)

Paul resumes his diatribe style by phrasing potential objections as two questions (9:19). He responds with three counterquestions (9:20–21). He then implies a fourth question by introducing the protasis of a conditional sentence but omitting the apodosis (9:22–24). A series of four Old Testament quotations (Hos. 2:23; 1:10; Isa. 10:22–23; 1:9) adds scriptural proof to his argument (9:25–29).

Basic Message and Exegetical Outline

God's absolute authority allows him to exercise his forbearance and extend his mercy as he sees fit.

God's Sovereign Authority (9:19–29)
1. God's authority is absolute (9:19–21)
   a. To create as he wishes (9:20)
   b. To make vessels for honor and for dishonor (9:21)
2. God's authority allows him to exercise his forbearance (9:22–24)
   a. To display his wrath and power (9:22)
   b. To reveal his glory (9:23–24)
3. God's authority allows him to extend his mercy (9:25–29)
   a. To the Gentiles (9:25–26)
   b. To the Jews (9:27–29)

Explanation of the Text

1. God's authority is absolute (9:19–21).

By demonstrating that God works selectively (9:6–13) and justly (9:14–18), Paul has highlighted God's absolute right to do what he knows is best. The doctrine of God's sovereignty, however, naturally leads to questions, and Paul introduces two possible objections others might have to that doctrine. First, is it fair for God to find fault with Israel for their lack of responsiveness (τί ἔτι μέμφεται)? Second, is it fair for God to expect anyone to act counter to his will (τῷ βουλήματι αὐτοῦ τίς ἀνθέστηκεν)? If God's authority is indisputable (and it is), how are we to understand the fact that he extends mercy to some and not to others? That is the issue Paul addresses in the rest of the paragraph.

To correct (μενοῦνγε) these objections, Paul responds with three questions of his own. The first question is emphatic and highlights the presumption of a human (ὦ ἄνθρωπε . . . σὺ τίς εἶ) talking back to the one true God (ὁ ἀνταποκρινόμεος τῷ θεῷ). The second question expects a "no" answer and compares the propriety of a human who questions God to the audacity of a created object (μὴ ἐρεῖ τὸ πλάσμα) that questions its creator (τῷ πλάσσοντι) by asking "Why did you make me this way?" (τί με ἐποίησας οὕτως). The third question expects a "yes" answer and makes the second more explicit by introducing the analogy of a potter, who has authority over his clay (ἢ οὐκ ἔξει ἐξουσίαν ὁ κεραμεὺς τοῦ πυλοῦ). The potter's authority is absolute. From exactly the same lump (ἐκ τοῦ αὐτοῦ φυράματος), he can make one vessel for an honorable purpose (ὅ μὲν εἰς τιμὴν σκεῦος) as well as a second vessel for a dishonorable purpose (ὅ δὲ εἰς ἀτιμίαν). The clay does not determine its use; the potter does. Paul has established his point by illustration: God's authority is absolute.

2. God's authority allows him to exercise his forbearance (9:22–24).

Paul continues his discussion of the two types of vessels (εἰς τιμὴν σκεῦος. . . εἰς ἀτιμίαν) but shifts the focus to God's ultimate purpose for each (σκεύη ὀργῆς . . . σκεύη ἐλέους).[30] The construction is incomplete grammatically; it begins with a condition (εἰ), but it lacks the expected conclusion. Nevertheless, what Paul writes highlights the forbearance that characterizes God's authority. The reason[31] God acts with forbearance is that doing so gives him the opportunity to put on display his wrath (ἐνδείξασθαι τὴν ὀργήν) and to make known his power (γνωρίσαι τὸ δυνατὸν αὐτοῦ). The great patience with which God exercises his forbearance (ἤνεγκεν ἐν πολλῇ μακρθυμίᾳ) "allow[s] the rebellion of his creation to gain force and intensity"[32] and confirms the identity of those who are "vessels of wrath prepared for destruction" (σκεύη ὀργῆς κατηρτισμένα εἰς ἀπώλειαν). His forbearance, however, has as its primary purpose the revelation of God's glory upon those to whom he extends his mercy (ἵνα γνωρίσῃ τὸν πλοῦτον τῆς δόξης αὐτοῦ ἐπὶ σκεύη ἐλέους). In fact, God "pre-prepared" (προητοίμασεν) those "vessels of mercy" for the purpose of displaying his glory (εἰς δόξαν). Paul personalizes his argument by identifying himself and his readers with the vessels of mercy he has been describing (οὓς καὶ ἐκαλεσεν ἡμᾶς). The mention of "calling" echoes

---

30. The genitives denote purpose and have been glossed as "destined for . . ." in the translation above. See 2 Timothy 2:20–21, where Paul also uses the concept of two types of vessels.
31. Θέλων is an adverbial participle of cause.
32. Cranfield, *Romans*, 606.

9:6–13, and Paul makes it clear that God's calling extends beyond the Jews (οὐ μόνον ἐξ Ἰουδαίων) to include the Gentiles (ἀλλὰ καὶ ἐξ ἐθνῶν).

3. God's authority allows him to extend his mercy (9:25–29).

Four Old Testament quotations—two from Hosea (Hos. 2:23; 1:10) and two from Isaiah (Isa. 10:22–23; 1:9)—support Paul's claim that the vessels destined for glory include both Gentiles and Jews. The idea of calling (καλέσω . . . κληθήσονται) frames a double quotation from the book of Hosea (ὡς καὶ ἐν τῷ Ὡσηὲ λέγει) that applies God's calling to the Gentiles. Previously, the Gentiles could claim neither the status of being God's people (τὸν οὐ λαόν μου . . . οὐ λαός μου ὑμεῖς) nor the experience of being loved (τὴν οὐκ ἠγαπημένην). Now, however, God describes them as "my people" (λαόν μου), "beloved" (ἠγαπημένην), and "sons of the living God" (υἱοὶ θεοῦ ζῶντος).

Two quotations from Isaiah explain that God also extends his mercy to Israel, and does so in the context of judgment. God will execute his work of judgment "quickly and with finality"[33] (λόγον συντελῶν καὶ συντέμνων ποιήσει κύριος ἐπὶ τῆς γῆς). For that reason, although the people of Israel might be as numberless as the grains of sand along the beach (ἐὰν ᾖ ὁ ἀριθμὸς τῶν υἱῶν Ἰσραὴλ ὡς ἡ ἄμμος τῆς θαλάσσης), only a relatively small surviving group will be saved (τὸ ὑπόλειμμα σωθήσεται). Only the sovereign work of the Lord of hosts makes it possible for some among Israel to be counted among Abraham's "seed" (εἰ μὴ κύριος Σαβαὼθ ἐγκατέλιπεν ἡμῖν σπέρμα). Otherwise, Israel would be as thoroughly destroyed as Sodom and Gomorrah were (ὡς Σόδομα ἂν ἐγενήθημεν καὶ ὡς Γόμορρα ἂν ὡμοιώθημεν).

The addition of "seed" (9:29) to "calling" (9:25, 26) returns Paul's argument to his opening premise, "not all those from Israel are Israel" (9:6). Instead, God's sovereign calling determines the identity of Abraham's seed (9:7, 12). Despite Israel's lack of responsiveness, God's word has not failed; he will extend mercy to Israel in his time and way.

Theology and Appropriation

In the midst of his discussion of God's authority, Paul writes that God called us "not only out of the Jews but also out of the Gentiles" (9:24). His mention of God's calling echoes 9:6–13, where the verb καλέω frames the paragraph. In the Old Testament the verb refers to the act of a superior toward a subordinate (e.g., Exod. 1:18; 12:21; 19:7). It describes a command rather than an invitation (e.g., Job 13:22), and it expects the individual who is called to hear and respond (e.g., Isa. 50:2; Jer.

---

33. NLT.

7:13). In a more limited sense, it describes God's creative call that brings into existence that which did not previously exist (e.g., Isa. 40:26; cf. Rom. 4:17). In the New Testament the verb sometimes describes the act of conferring a name (e.g., Matt. 1:21; John 1:42), and Paul uses καλέω with that sense in Romans 9:7 and 26. It can also describe the issuing of an invitation (e.g., John 2:2; Rev. 19:9). Paul adds a unique nuance of status or social position in 1 Corinthians (1:26; 7:18, 20, 21, 22, 24).

Paul, however, uses καλέω and its cognates primarily to describe God's divine calling.[34] In a narrow sense, it describes God's personal commission of Paul to be an apostle (Rom. 1:1; 1 Cor. 1:1; 15:9). More commonly, it describes God's act of calling individuals to be his. It is always God who issues the call (Rom. 9:24; 1 Cor. 1:9, 24; 7:15; Gal. 1:6, 15; 5:8; 1 Thess. 2:12; 4:7; 5:24; 2 Thess. 2:14).[35] He calls us in accordance with his purpose (Rom. 8:28, 30), by his grace (Gal. 1:6, 15), and using the means of the gospel (2 Thess. 2:14). Because he is faithful, God's calling is irrevocable (1 Thess. 5:24; Rom. 11:29). It is a high (Phil. 3:14) and holy (2 Tim. 1:9) calling that bestows on us the status of saints (Rom. 1:7; 1 Cor. 1:2). God's calling brings us into fellowship with Christ (1 Cor. 1:9) as part of one body (Col. 3:15). We also receive peace (1 Cor. 7:15), liberty (Gal. 5:13), and hope (Eph. 1:18; 4:4). God expects us to respond to his calling by walking worthy (Eph. 4:1; 2 Thess. 1:11) and to pursue sanctification (1 Thess. 4:7). The ultimate end of God's calling is his own glory (Rom. 9:24; cf. 8:29–30).

Paul's primary purpose for including this passage at this point in his letter was to address the attitude that lies behind possible objections to his teaching about God's sovereign working. With the original readers we need to realize that the way in which we respond to the teaching of Scripture reflects an underlying attitude toward God, his character, and the way in which he works. The logical point of connection to this passage is Paul's illustration of the potter and the clay, which lends itself well to an opening object lesson. The passage corrects an arrogant spirit that presumes humans have the right to question how a sovereign God works. Instead, it commends a humble spirit that accepts God's absolute authority to reveal his glory by exercising his wrath or extending his judgment. The objective in communicating this passage should be to help others understand that God deserves (and expects) respectful humility in response to revealed truth about the way in which he works so that they will accept his absolute authority to exercise his judgment and extend his wrath as he sees fit.

---

34. Paul uses καλέω 29 times, κλῆσις 8 times, and κλητός 7 times.
35. Cf. Longenecker, *Romans*, 68.

ROMANS 9:30–10:4

Text and Translation

30 Therefore, what shall we say? *We shall say* that the Gentiles, *who were* not trying to pursue[1] righteousness, attained righteousness, even[2] a righteousness that is based on faith,[3] **31** but Israel, *who were* trying to pursue[4] a law[5] that promises righteousness,[6] did not arrive at the law.[7] **32** Why? Because *they pursued* not based on faith but as based on works;[8] they stumbled with reference to the stone[9] that produces stumbling,[10] **33** just as it has been written,

Behold, I am placing[11] in Zion a stone
> **that produces stumbling and a rock that produces offense,**
and[12] the *one who* is believing[13] in him will not be put to shame.
1 Brothers, indeed[14] the desire of my heart[15] and my petition to God concerning them[16] *is* for *their* salvation.[17] **2** For I am bearing witness to them that they are having a zeal for God,[18] but not according to knowledge; **3**

---

1. Τά διώκοντα is an adjectival participle, modifying ἔθνη; the present tense is conative.
2. Δέ is ascensive.
3. Ἐκ + genitive denotes the basis on which righteousness rests; see also verse 32.
4. Διώκων is an adjectival participle modifying Ἰσραήλ; the present tense is conative.
5. Νόμον refers to the law of Moses (Moo, *Romans*, 624).
6. Δικαιοσύνης is an objective genitive and is best understood as a status (cf. Cranfield, *Romans*, 508n1).
7. Εἰς + accusative denotes destination; νόμον is definite although anarthrous.
8. Ἔργων is shorter, more difficult, and well-supported ($\mathfrak{P}^{46}$, ℵ*, A, and B). The omission of νόμου places emphasis on "works," not "law."
9. Τῷ λίθῳ is a dative of reference.
10. Τοῦ προσκόμματος is a genitive of product; see also verse 33.
11. Τίθημι is a perfective present that emphasizes continuing results.
12. The variant that adds πᾶς after καί is an assimilation to 10:11.
13. Ὁ πιστεύων is a substantival participle.
14. Μέν is emphatic.
15. Τῆς καρδίας is a genitive of source.
16. Ὑπέρ + genitive denotes reference. The reading αὐτῶν is well supported ($\mathfrak{P}^{46}$, ℵ, A, B, D); the longer readings most likely are later attempts to clarify the meaning.
17. Εἰς + accusative denotes goal.
18. Θεοῦ is an objective genitive.

for, because they are ignorant[19] of God's righteousness and are seeking to establish their own righteousness, they did not subject themselves[20] to God's righteousness; **4** for Christ *is* the termination of the law[21] with respect to righteousness[22] for everyone *who* is believing.[23]

Context and Structure

    II. Letter Body (1:18–15:13)
        C. The Gospel as the Fulfillment of God's Plan (9:1–11:36)
            1. Paul's concern for Israel (9:1–5)
            2. The gospel fulfills God's plan to keep his word (9:6–29)
            3. The gospel fulfills God's plan to use Israel's unresponsiveness (9:30–10:21)
                a. **In pursuing a law of righteousness (9:30–10:4)**
                b. In failing to embrace righteousness by faith (10:5–13)
                c. In failing to believe the gospel (10:14–21)
            4. The gospel fulfills God's plan to show mercy to all (11:1–32)
            5. Paul's doxology of praise to God for his working (11:33–36)

Paul uses the rhetorical question, "What shall we say?" to draw an implication from what he has just written (cf. 8:31; 11:7)—the problem does not lie with God's word, justness, or authority; it lies with Israel. In this paragraph, Paul highlights two key elements of Israel's failed pursuit of righteousness: they use the wrong means (9:30–33), and they have the wrong attitude (10:1–4).

Basic Message and Exegetical Outline

Israel has not arrived at the righteousness they pursue, because they use the wrong means and have the wrong attitude.

---

19. Ἀγνοοῦντες and ζητοῦντες are adverbial participles of cause.
20. Ὑπετάγησαν is passive form with a middle sense.
21. Νόμου is an objective genitive.
22. Εἰς + accusative denotes reference.
23. Παντὶ τῷ πιστεύοντι is a substantival participle; the dative denotes advantage.

Israel's Failed Pursuit (9:30–10:4)
1. They use the wrong means (9:30–33)
   a. They focus on the law (9:31)
   b. They focus on works (9:32–33)
2. They have the wrong attitude (10:1–4)
   a. They have zeal without knowledge (10:2)
   b. They do not subject themselves to God's righteousness (10:3–4)

Explanation of the Text

1. They use the wrong means (9:30–33).

Paul opens the next section of his argument with a rhetorical question (τί οὖν ἐροῦμεν). This time, rather than raising a possible objection (cf. 6:1; 7:7; 9:14), the question allows him to introduce the point he wants to make (cf. 4:1; 8:31). Even though the Gentiles did not pursue righteousness (ἔθνη τὰ μὴ διώκοντα δικαισύνην), they attained righteousness (κατέλαβεν δικαιοσύνην). The key factor, however, is that the righteousness they attained is based on faith (δικαιοσύνην τὴν ἐκ πίστεως). In contrast, the Jews' lack of responsiveness to the gospel is the result of pursuing the wrong kind of righteousness in the wrong way and with the wrong attitude.

The Jews engage in a "committed lifestyle"[24] of pursuing (διώκων) the Mosaic law, which promises righteousness (νόμον δικαιοσύνης) for perfect obedience.[25] That pursuit, however, cannot arrive at the desired destination (εἰς νόμον οὐκ ἔφθασεν), because it pursues righteousness in the wrong way. There are two ways of pursuing righteousness: on the basis of faith (ἐκ πίστεως) or on the basis of works (ἐξ ἔργων). The Jews choose the latter and, so, stumble (προσέκοψαν) with reference to the stone that causes people to stumble (τῷ λίθῳ τοῦ προσκόμματος)— Christ. As Isaiah makes clear (Isa. 28:16; cf. 8:14), God has divinely placed that stone in Zion (τίθημι ἐν Σιών). Although Christ can be a stone that causes stumbling (λίθον προσκόμματος) and a rock that causes offense (κέτραν σκανδάλου) for many, the proper response is continuing belief in him (ὁ πιστεύων ἐπ' αὐτῷ), which results in ultimate

---

24. Dunn, *Romans*, 581.
25. The idea of the Mosaic law promising life/righteousness for perfect obedience echoes Paul's previous comments in 7:10 and his subsequent comment in 10:5, both of which are based on Leviticus 18:5.

vindication (οὐ καταισχυνθέσεται).[26] Unfortunately, the Jews fail to respond with faith as God requires.

2. They have the wrong attitude (10:1–4).

Paul's heartfelt desire (ἡ εὐδοκία τῆς ἐμῆς καρδίας) and his urgent request to God (ἡ δέησις πρὸς τὸν θεόν) on behalf of his fellow Jews (ὑπὲρ αὐτῶν) is that they would be saved (εἰς σωτηρίαν). Their root problem is that they have a zeal for God (ζῆλον θεοῦ ἔχουσιν),[27] but they fail to comprehend the proper source of righteousness (ἀλλ' οὐ κατ' ἐπίγνωσιν). Because they are ignorant of God's righteousness (ἀγνοοῦντες τὴν τοῦ θεοῦ δικαιοσύνην), they seek to establish their own righteousness (τὴν ἰδίαν δικαιοσύνην ζητοῦντες στῆσαι). Because they pursue the wrong kind of righteousness (their own), they refuse to submit to the righteousness God requires (τῇ δικαιοσύνῃ τοῦ θεοῦ οὐκ ὑπετάγησαν)—the righteousness he bestows on the basis of faith.

Paul's bottom line is that faith in Christ eliminates any need to keep the law in an attempt to attain righteousness. His statement that "Christ is the end of the law" (τέλος νόμου Χριστός) raises an interpretive challenge. Does τέλος denote "goal" (e.g., 1 Tim. 1:5) as in "Jesus is the real meaning of the law" or "termination" as in "Jesus brings an end to the function of the law"? "Termination" is the more natural understanding, since the context focuses on the contrast between the law's righteousness by works and God's righteousness by faith.[28] Paul qualifies the way in which Christ brings an end to the law in two ways: (1) as a way of pursuing righteousness (εἰς δικαιοσύνην), and (2) for those who are in Christ (παντὶ τῷ πιστεύοντι). That is, those who place their faith in Christ receive the righteousness God bestows and must no longer seek to establish their own righteousness by keeping the Mosaic law.

Theology and Appropriation

Paul's reference to Jesus as the "stone that produces stumbling" (Rom. 9:32) and his supporting Old Testament quotation (Rom. 9:33) highlight two of three major threads in the New Testament christological use of Old Testament stone imagery. Neither David's confidence

---

26. Schreiner understands οὐ καταισχυνθήσεται as referring to vindication in eschatological judgment (*Romans*, 541).
27. Dunn describes ζῆλον θεοῦ as "a passionate consuming zeal focused on God, as evidenced by an overwhelming desire to do his will" (*Romans*, 586).
28. See Murray's discussion (*Romans*, 2:49–50; cf. Dunn, *Romans*, 597; Moo, *Romans*, 641; Schreiner, *Romans*, 545).

in God as his "rock" of safety and strength (2 Sam. 22:2–3; Pss. 31:2–3; 62:6–7; cf. Ps. 71:3) nor Daniel's record of the crushing "stone" in Nebuchadnezzar's first vision (Dan. 2:34; cf. 2:44–45) plays a role in the New Testament, although the latter acquired a messianic interpretation in Second Temple Judaism. The major Old Testament "stone" passages portray Messiah in three different ways.[29]

Psalm 118:22 portrays him as a rejected stone:
> **The stone which the builders rejected**
> **has become the chief cornerstone.**

Isaiah 8:14 portrays him as a stumbling stone:
> **Then he shall become a sanctuary;**
> **but to both the houses of Israel, a stone to strike**
> **and a rock to stumble over,**
> **and a snare and a trap for the inhabitants of**
> **Jerusalem.**

Isaiah 28:16 portrays him as a foundation stone:
> **Behold I am laying in Zion a stone, a tested stone,**
> **a costly cornerstone for the foundation, firmly**
> **placed.**
> **He who believes in it will not be disturbed.**

The rejected stone aspect is prominent in the Gospels and Acts, where Jesus applies Psalm 18:22 to himself (Matt. 21:42; Mark 12:10; Luke 20:17–18) and Peter applies the verse to Jesus (Acts 4:10–11). Paul uses the foundation stone imagery in Ephesians 2:19–22 and 1 Corinthians 3:10–15. Peter brings all three aspects together in 1 Peter 2:4–8. Longenecker suggests that the "stone" theme was "a significant feature" in early Christian thought and proclamation.[30]

Paul's quotation in Romans 9:33 combines the foundation stone and stumbling stone aspects in a way that is particularly appropriate to his argument. He brings together the first line of Isaiah 28:16 ("I am laying in Zion a stone"), the second line of Isaiah 8:14 ("a stone to strike and a rock to stumble over"), and the third line of Isaiah 28:16 ("he who believes in it will not be disturbed"). The declaration that God has placed the stone in Zion echoes Paul's argument in 9:6–29 that divine initiative is the starting point for Israel's current plight. God himself has made Christ central to his redemptive purpose. The

---

29. These three nuances are drawn from Longenecker's discussion (*Romans*, 842–44).

30. Longenecker's, *Romans*, 844.

very cornerstone of God's plan—who should have been a sanctuary for Israel—has become a barrier instead, and they have rejected Christ. The Gentiles, however, have responded with the faith God requires and, so, will not be put to shame when they stand before God at the final judgment. By including the third line of Isaiah 28:16 Paul has, in effect, demonstrated the truth of Psalm 118:22 without citing it. Although Israel has rejected Christ, the stone, he has become the chief cornerstone of the building God is constructing among the Gentiles (cf. Eph. 2:19–24). If Israel were to understand correctly the teaching of the Old Testament, they would pursue the righteousness God requires in the way he requires.

Paul defended God's role in Israel's plight, so Paul's primary purpose for including this passage at this point in his letter was to clarify the nature of Israel's role in their failed pursuit of righteousness. With the original readers we need to realize the importance of understanding correctly the nature of the righteousness God requires and how he expects us to pursue that righteousness. Possible points of connection to this passage include the ideas of pursuing something, being zealous about something, failing to understand something correctly, and failing to achieve a goal or reach an objective. The passage corrects three wrong concepts: (a) that it is possible for a person to establish his/her own righteousness, (b) that works are an effective means of attaining righteous status before God, and (c) that the way something is pursued is more important than what is actually pursued. The passage commends the importance of understanding correctly what God requires and expects. The objective in communicating this passage should be to help others understand that no amount of zeal in pursuing their own righteousness can compensate for pursuing the wrong goal in the wrong way, so that they will pursue what God offers in the way he requires.

ROMANS 10:5-13

Text and Translation

5 For Moses is writing with respect to the righteousness[1] *that is* based on the law[2] that

> **The person *who* does[3] them will live by them.**

6 But the righteousness that is based on faith speaks in this way,

> **Do not say in your heart, "Who will ascend into the heaven?"—**
>
> that is, to try to bring Christ down[4]—

7 or   **"Who will descend into the abyss?"—**

> that is, to try to bring Christ up from the dead.

8 But what does it say?

> **The word is near you, in your mouth and in your heart—**
>
> that is, the word that calls for faith[5] that we are preaching.

9 For if you confess[6] with your mouth that Jesus *is* Lord, and believe in your heart that God raised him from the dead, you will be saved;

10   for with the heart it is believed resulting in righteousness[7]

> and with the mouth it is confessed resulting in salvation.

11 For what does the Scripture say?

> **Everyone *who is* believing[8] in him will not be ashamed.**

12 For *there is* no distinction between a Jew and a Gentile,[9] for the same lord *is lord over* all,[10] who is rich[11] to all the *ones who* are calling upon[12] him; **13** for

---

1. Τήν δικαιοσύνην is an accusative of respect.
2. Ἐκ + genitive denotes the basis on which righteousness rests; see also verse 6.
3. Ὁ ποιήσας is a substantival participle.
4. Καταγαγεῖν is a conative present. See also ἀναγαγεῖν in verse 7.
5. Τῆς πίστεως is an objective genitive.
6. Ἐὰν ὁμολογήσῃς ... καὶ πιστεύσῃς forms the protasis of a third class conditional sentence.
7. Εἰς + accusative denotes result (twice).
8. Ὁ πιστεύων is a substantival participle.
9. The genitives following διαστολή and joined by τε καί carry the sense of "between" (Wallace, *Grammar*, 135; BDAG 237a).
10. Πάντων is an objective genitive.
11. Πλουτῶν is an adjectival participle modifying κύριος.
12. Τοὺς ἐπικαλουμένους is a substantival participle.

Everyone who might call upon[13] the name of the Lord
will be saved.

Context and Structure

II. Letter Body (1:18–15:13)
    C. The Gospel as the Fulfillment of God's Plan (9:1–11:36)
        1. Paul's concern for Israel (9:1–5)
        2. The gospel fulfills God's plan to keep his word (9:6–29)
        3. The gospel fulfills God's plan to use Israel's unresponsiveness (9:30–10:21)
           a. In pursuing a law of righteousness (9:30–10:4)
           b. **In failing to embrace righteousness by faith (10:5–13)**
           c. In failing to believe the gospel (10:14–21)
        4. The gospel fulfills God's plan to show mercy to all (11:1–32)
        5. Paul's doxology of praise to God for his working (11:33–36)

Paul clarifies the correct understanding of righteousness based on faith in three steps. First, he contrasts righteousness based on faith with righteousness based on law (10:5–8). Next, he explains the simplicity of righteousness based on faith (10:9–10). Finally, he provides Old Testament proof that righteousness based on faith has universal scope (10:11–13).

Basic Message and Exegetical Outline

Righteousness based on faith focuses on the simplicity of God's promise, which calls for a response of conviction and confession and applies to everyone who believes it.

    Israel's Flawed Understanding (10:5–13)
        1. Israel misunderstands the nature of righteousness based on faith (10:5–8)
           a. Righteousness based on law focuses on the complexity of doing God's commandments (10:5)
           b. Righteousness based on faith focuses on the simplicity of responding to God's promise (10:6–8)

---

13. Πᾶς ὅς ἄν ἐπικαλέσηται is the equivalent of a third class condition, with contingency of person.

2. Israel misunderstands the response of righteousness based on faith (10:9–10)
   a. It calls for inner conviction (10:9b, 10a)
   b. It calls for outward confession (10:9a, 10b)
3. Israel misunderstands the scope of righteousness based on faith (10:11–13)
   a. It applies to everyone who believes in Jesus (10:11)
   b. It extends impartially to both Jew and Gentile (10:12)
   c. It applies to everyone who calls on the name of the Lord (10:13)

Explanation of the Text

1. Israel misunderstands the nature of righteousness based on faith (10:5–8).

Paul begins his explanation (γάρ) of why Christ is the end of the law (cf. 10:4) by quoting what Moses writes (Μωϋσῆς γράφει) in Leviticus 18:5 regarding righteousness that is based on the law (τὴν δικαιοσύνην τὴν ἐκ τοῦ νόμου). The statement that "the person who does them will live by them" (ὁ ποιήσας αὐτὰ ἄνθρωπος ζήσεται ἐν αὐτοῖς) is best understood either as reflecting the exegesis of Paul's opponents (i.e., doing the Mosaic law results in life)[14] or as Paul's summary of the essence of the Mosaic law (i.e., blessing is contingent on obedience).[15] Under either understanding, the heart attitude that says (μὴ εἴπῃς ἐν τῇ καρδίᾳ σου) "doing" the law is a means of achieving righteousness stands in contrast to the righteousness that is based on faith (ἡ δὲ ἐκ πίστεως δικαιοσύνη) as Deuteronomy 30:12–14 makes clear. It is not necessary to do the work of ascending into heaven to bring Christ down (τίς ἀναβήσεται εἰς τὸν οὐρανόν . . . Χριστὸν καραγαγεῖν). Nor is it necessary to do the work of descending into the abyss to bring Christ up from the dead (τίς καταβήσεται εἰς τὴν ἄβυσσον . . . Χριστὸν ἐκ νεκρῶν ἀναγαγεῖν). Instead, the righteousness God requires is proclaimed in a word (τὸ ῥῆμα . . . ὃ κορύσσομεν) that is accessible (ἐγγύς σου τὸ ῥῆμά ἐστιν), is personal (ἐν τῷ στόματί σου καὶ ἐν τῇ καρδίᾳ σου), and calls for faith (τὸ ῥῆμα τῆς πίστεως).[16]

---

14. Schreiner, *Romans*, 555.
15. Moo, *Romans*, 648.
16. Τῆς πίστεως is an objective genitive.

2. Israel misunderstands the response of righteousness based on faith (10:9–10).

The word Paul proclaims is near. It is also personal, calling for a response of faith that embraces that word inwardly and verbalizes it outwardly. Initially, Paul adopts the word order of Deuteronomy 30:14 (στόματι . . . καρδίᾳ) but shifts the nuance of the prepositional phrases (ἐν + dative) from local ("in") to instrumental ("with"). The individual who outwardly professes allegiance to the Lord Jesus[17] (ὁμολογήσῃς ἐν τῷ στόματί σου κύριον Ἰησοῦν) and inwardly places trust in the truth that God raised Jesus from the dead (πιστεύσῃς ἐν τῇ καρδίᾳ σου ὅτι ὁ θεὸς αὐτὸν ἤγειρεν ἐκ νεκρῶν) will receive the salvation God bestows (σωθήσῃ).[18] Wallace notes that believing establishes the cause of salvation, while confessing provides the evidence of salvation.[19] Consequently, Paul reverses the sequence of believing and confessing to reflect the natural order in a summary statement that is carefully constructed in synonymous parallelism and brings together the key themes of "believing/faith," "righteousness," and "salvation" (10:10; cf. 1:16–17):

| For with the heart | a person believes | resulting in righteousness |
| and with the mouth | a person confesses | resulting in salvation.[20] |

3. Israel misunderstands the scope of righteousness based on faith (10:11–13).

Paul supports his exegesis with two Old Testament quotations proving that both believing (πιστεύω) and confessing (ὁμολογέω) are integral to the response God desires. Isaiah 28:16 uses the link-word "believe" (πᾶς ὁ πιστεύων ἐπ᾽ αὐτῷ), while Joel 2:32 uses the synonym "call upon" (ὃς ἂν ἐπικαλέσηται τὸ ὄνομα κυρίου). Both the wording of the quotations themselves (πᾶς in Isaiah; ὃς ἂν in Joel) and Paul's commentary on those quotations highlight the universal scope of righteousness by faith. First, it extends impartially to both Jew and Gentile (οὐ ἐστιν διασολὴ Ἰουδαίου τε καὶ Ἕλληνος). Second, it brings all into the same relationship with

---

17. Cranfield writes that the title κύριον Ἰησοῦν acknowledges that "Jesus shares the name and nature, the holiness, the authority, power, majesty, and eternity of the one true God" (*Romans*, 539).
18. Σωθήσῃ is a divine passive.
19. Wallace, *Grammar*, 686.
20. Moo correctly notes that it would be inappropriate to draw a fine distinction in this verse between "righteousness" and "salvation," because "Each expresses in a general way the new relationship with God that is the result of believing 'with the heart' and confessing 'with the mouth'" (*Romans*, 659).

Jesus as Lord (ὁ αὐτὸς κύριος πάντων). Third, it bestows the same spiritual wealth on all (πλουτῶν εἰς πάντας τοὺς ἐπικαλουμένους αὐτόν).[21] This universal scope is key to understanding Israel's lack of responsiveness—both their defiant disobedience (10:14–21) and how their current condition fits into God's plan of salvation (11:1–32).

Theology and Appropriation

In Romans 10:5, Paul quotes Leviticus 18:5 to explain the nature of "the righteousness that is based on the law." That statement echoes 2:13; 7:10; and 9:31, which all reflect the idea that the Law promises life/righteousness for obedience.[22] It also raises two issues: (1) how best to understand the phrase "the righteousness that is based on the law," and (2) whether Leviticus 18:5 actually teaches that the law promises righteous status to the person who keeps it.

Scholars have suggested multiple understandings of the phrase "the righteousness that is based on the law." Cranfield argues that it refers to the perfect obedience of Christ.[23] Howard concludes that it refers to the obedience that follows faith.[24] Dunn thinks it describes righteousness that is validated by faithfulness to ancestral customs.[25] The most likely understanding, however, is that it captures a traditional Jewish premise[26]—either that blessing is contingent on obedience to the law,[27] or that obedience to the law is a source of life.[28] Under either of the latter two understandings, Murray notes that Leviticus 18:5 offers "a watertight definition of the principle of legalism."[29] Paul then cites Deuteronomy 30:12–14 to demonstrate that such an interpretation of Leviticus 18:5 is incorrect (cf. Gal. 3:11–14).

It is important to note, however, that in context both Leviticus 18:5 and Deuteronomy 30:12–14 call Israel to obey the Mosaic law within

---

21. Ἐπικαλέω serves as a second link-word that anticipates the quotation from Joel and becomes the first link in the chain of 10:14–15.
22. In 2:13 he writes that the doers of the law will be justified; in 7:10 he writes that the law was to result in life; in 9:31 he refers to "the law of righteousness," which is best understood as "the law that promises righteousness" (objective genitive).
23. Cranfield, *Romans*, 521–22.
24. G. E. Howard, "Christ the End of the Law: The Meaning of Romans 10:4ff," *JBL* 88 (1969): 331–37.
25. Dunn, *Romans*, 612.
26. Jewett, *Romans*, 625.
27. Moo, *Romans*, 648.
28. See Schreiner, who has an extended discussion (*Romans*, 551–55).
29. Murray, *Romans*, 2:51.

the covenant.[30] In Leviticus 18:4 Moses commands Israel to "live in accordance with [God's judgments and statutes]." In Deuteronomy 30:8–9 Moses promises Israel that God "will prosper [them] abundantly" if they obey his commandments. In both instances, obedience is a response to grace received, not a requirement to receive grace. Both passages highlight the original intent of the law: to provide guidelines for living as God's people in response to his grace.[31]

Status as God's People	$\rightarrow$	Guidelines of the Law	$\rightarrow$	Walk of Obedience

Nomism: the original intent of the law

A legalistic approach, however, distorts the original intent of the law and makes keeping the regulations of the law the means of becoming God's people.

Regulations of the Law	$\rightarrow$	Works of Law	$\rightarrow$	Status as God's People

Legalism: the distorted use of the law

In Galatians 3:21–24, Paul articulates a different understanding of the law as a set of regulations. He writes that the law "has shut up all men and women under sin" (3:22) and serves as "our tutor to lead us to Christ, that we might be justified by faith" (3:24). This role of the law is sometimes called the "pedagogical use," while the original role of the law is sometimes called the "normative use." Paul seems to reflect the latter use of the law in Romans 13:8 and Galatians 5:14. If faith in Christ replaces works of law in the second diagram above, the pedagogical and normative uses of the law in Paul's letters may be represented in this way:

Regulations of the Law	$\rightarrow$	Faith in Christ	$\rightarrow$	Status as God's People	$\rightarrow$	Guidelines of the Law	$\rightarrow$	Walk of Obedience

The Pedagogical Use of the Law:	The Normative Use of the Law:
Point out sin and lead *to* Christ (Gal. 3:20; Rom. 3:20)	Provide norms for living *in* Christ (Gal. 5:14; Rom. 13:8)

---

30. Dunn describes this approach to the law as "covenantal nomism," that is, the righteous are those who confirm the covenant by performing acts of law-keeping (*Romans*, 601, 612).
31. In Leviticus the focus is on God's grace in redeeming Israel from bondage in Egypt; in Deuteronomy the focus is on God's grace in restoring Israel after future captivity.

When we were in Adam, the law fulfilled its pedagogical role of pointing out sin and leading us to faith in Christ. When we responded to the preached promise by believing and confessing Christ, God brought us into relationship with him as his people. Now that we are in Christ, the law assumes its normative role of providing guidelines for a walk of obedience.

Paul's primary purpose for including this passage at this point in his letter was to contrast the gospel's approach of righteousness by faith with Israel's approach of seeking to establish their own righteousness by law. With the original readers we need to realize that no amount of "doing" can ever make it possible for us to achieve right standing before God. The idea of doing something yourself provides a natural point of connection to the passage and is captured in the familiar saying, "If you want something done right, do it yourself." The passage corrects that idea by making it clear that no work, however extreme (e.g., bringing Christ down from heaven or bringing him up from the dead), is what God requires. As Paul has written in 8:3, "What the law could not do . . . God did." Instead, the passage commends a response of inward conviction and outward confession of faith in Christ. The objective in communicating this passage should be to help others understand that right standing before God is available to all who respond in faith to the preached word of the gospel so that they will reject all attempts to earn God's favor by what they do and embrace the simplicity of the gospel of righteousness based on faith.

ROMANS 10:14–21

Text and Translation

14 Therefore, how will they call upon *the one* in whom[1] they did not believe? And how will they believe *in the one* about whom[2] they did not hear? And how will they hear apart from *one who is* preaching?[3] **15** And how will they preach unless[4] they are sent? Just as it is written,

How timely are the feet[5] of the *ones who* are proclaiming[6] good things.

16 But not all obeyed the gospel.[7] For Isaiah says,

Lord, who believed our report?[8]

17 Therefore, faith *is* based on *the act of* hearing, and hearing comes through the word about Christ.[9] **18** But I am saying, they heard, didn't they?[10] Indeed,[11]

Their voice went out into all the earth,
and their words to the ends of the inhabited world.[12]

19 But I am saying, Israel knew, didn't they? Moses *is the* first *one who* says,

I will make you jealous because of[13] *those who are* not a nation;
because of a senseless nation I will make you angry.

20 And Isaiah is bold and says,

---

1. The relative pronoun includes an embedded demonstrative (twice).
2. The genitive regularly follows ἀκούω to denote the person who is heard.
3. Κηρύσσοντος is an anarthrous substantival participle.
4. Ἐὰν μή is idiomatic.
5. Πόδες is the shorter reading and is well supported ($\mathfrak{P}^{46}$, ℵ*, A, B, C).
6. Τῶν εὐαγγελιξομένων is a substantival participle.
7. Τῷ εὐαγγελίῳ is a dative of direct object.
8. Τῇ ἀκοῇ is a dative of direct object; ἡμῶν is a subjective genitive (cf. ESV, "what he has heard from us").
9. Χριστοῦ is an objective genitive. The reading ῥήματος Χριστοῦ ($\mathfrak{P}^{46}$, ℵ*, B, C, D*) is more difficult because it occurs only here in the New Testament, while ῥήματος θεοῦ (ℵ¹, A, D1, 33) is more common (cf. Luke 3:2; John 3:34; Eph. 6:17; Heb. 6:5; 11:3).
10. When μή introduces a question in which the verb is negated (οὐκ ἤκουσαν), the question expects a positive answer. See also verse 19.
11. In this context μενοῦνγε confirms (cf. GNB, "Of course they did").
12. Τῆς οἰκουμένης is a descriptive genitive.
13. Ἐκ + dative denotes cause.

I was found by[14] *the ones who* are not seeking me,[15]
  I became manifest to the ones who are not asking
  for me.
21 But concerning Israel[16] he says,
  All day long I stretched out my hands toward a disobedient[17] and defiant people.

Context and Structure

II. Letter Body (1:18–15:13)
  C. The Gospel as the Fulfillment of God's Plan (9:1–11:36)
    1. Paul's concern for Israel (9:1–5)
    2. The gospel fulfills God's plan to keep his word (9:6–29)
    3. The gospel fulfills God's plan to use Israel's unrespon-
        siveness (9:30–10:21)
      a. In pursuing a law of righteousness (9:30–10:4)
      b. In failing to embrace righteousness by faith
          (10:5–13)
      c. **In failing to believe the gospel (10:14–21)**
    4. The gospel fulfills God's plan to show mercy to all
        (11:1–32)
    5. Paul's doxology of praise to God for his working
        (11:33–36)

Paul concludes his explanation of Israel's unresponsiveness with a two-
part paragraph that incorporates six Old Testament quotations. The
first part uses a series of rhetorical questions to lead his readers to the
conclusion that faith comes from hearing and believing the message of
the gospel (10:14–17). The second part uses Old Testament proof from
the writings (Ps. 19:4), the law (Deut. 32:21), and the prophets (Isa.
65:1–2) to demonstrate conclusively that Israel has heard, known, and
rejected the gospel (10:18–21).

Basic Message and Exegetical Outline

*Although God has made known his message of salvation, Israel has not
responded to that message.*

---

14. Ἐν + dative denotes agency.
15. Τοῖς . . . ζητοῦσιν and τοῖς . . . ἐπερωτῶσιν are both substantival participles.
16. Πρός + accusative denotes reference.
17. Ἀπειθοῦντα and ἀντιλέγοντα are adjectival participles modifying λαόν.

Israel's Frustrating Disobedience (10:14–21)
1. God has made known his message of salvation (10:14–17)
   a. God sends preachers with the message of salvation (10:14–15)
   b. Not all obey the message (10:16)
   c. Salvation comes from hearing and believing the message (10:17)
2. Israel has not responded to God's message (10:18–21)
   a. Israel has heard the message (10:18)
   b. Israel has known about the message (10:19–20)
   c. Israel has rejected the message (10:21)

Explanation of the Text

1. God has made known his message of salvation (10:14–17).
If responding to God's message of salvation with inner conviction and outward confession is the requirement to receive God's righteousness (10:5–13), could Israel's problem be that they have never heard the message (cf. 10:18)? Paul begins the next step in his argument by establishing the connection between the ultimate human response of confessing Christ and the initial divine act of sending messengers. He does so by building a climax of rhetorical questions that traces the four steps in the process in reverse order: (1) calling upon the name of the Lord (ἐπικαλέσωνται) is the result of believing the message of the gospel (ἐπίστευσαν); (2) believing the message of the gospel (πιστεύσωσιν) is the result of hearing that message (ἤκουσαν); (3) hearing the message (ἀκούσωσιν) is the result of someone preaching it (κηρύσσοντος); (4) preaching of the message (κηρύξωσιν) is the result of someone being sent to preach it (ἀποσταλῶσιν). The sequence of actions, therefore, looks like this:

Sending → Preaching
          Preaching → Hearing
                      Hearing → Believing
                                Believing → Calling

Could the problem be that God has not sent anyone to preach to Israel? Paul has already identified himself and his coworkers as those who are preaching the message of the faith (cf. 10:8), and Isaiah 52:7 makes it clear that God has sent those who are proclaiming good news about good things (τῶν εὐαγγελιζομένων τὰ ἀγαθά). Israel's problem is not God's failure to send messengers; the problem is their own failure to obey the gospel (οὐ πάντες ὑπήκουσαν τῷ εὐαγγελίῳ).[18] In fact, the prophet suggests that believing the message might be the exception rather than the rule when he asks (Isa. 53:1), "Lord, who believed our report?" (κύριε, τίς ἐπίστευσεν τῇ ἀκοῇ ἡμῶν). The only logical conclusion (ἄρα) is that faith is based on the act of hearing (ἡ πίστις ἐξ ἀκοῆς), and hearing comes through the word about Christ (ἡ ἀκοὴ διὰ ῥήματος Χριστοῦ).

2. Israel has not responded to God's message (10:18–21).

Israel's problem is not that they have had no opportunity to hear God's message. Paul addresses that issue directly with a question of his own: "But I am saying, they heard, didn't they?" (ἀλλὰ λέγω μὴ, οὐκ ἤκουσαν). Psalm 19:4 makes it clear that "Of course they did!" (μενοῦνγε),[19] by asserting the global proclamation of God's revelation:

Their voice went out into all the earth,
and their words to the ends of the inhabited world.[20]

The words (τὰ ῥήματα αὐτῶν) to which David refers are the gospel message (ῥῆμα) that Paul and his coworkers preach (cf. 10:8) and that has reached the ends of the inhabited world (εἰς τὰ πέρατα τῆς οἰκουμένης). Since the gospel has gone out into all the earth (εἰς πᾶσαν τὴν γῆν), the Old Testament prophecies about those who will announce salvation to all the nations have been fulfilled (cf. Isa. 52:7–10), and Israel has certainly heard the message of the gospel.

Nor is Israel's problem that they did not know about the impact of the message: "But I am saying, Israel knew, didn't they?" (ἀλλὰ λέγω, μὴ Ἰσραὴλ ἔγνω). Both Moses and Isaiah make it clear that the Old Testament predicted exactly the circumstances Israel was experiencing. First in Deuteronomy 32:21 Moses predicted (πρῶτος Μωϋσῆς

---

18. "Obey" (ὑπακούω) is parallel to "believe" (πιστεύω) in verse 16 and creates a wordplay with both "report" (ἀκοή) in verses 17 and 18 and "hear" (ἀκούω) in verses 14 and 18. It also serves as a reminder that "the obedience of faith" is the goal of the gospel Paul preaches (cf. 1:5; 16:26).
19. GNB.
20. It is best to understand the quotation of Psalm 19:4 as extending beyond general revelation to include special revelation for three reasons. First, quoting a single Old Testament verse was often intended to invoke the entire context in which that verse occurs. In this instance, Psalm 19 describes both God's revelation in creation (Ps. 19:1–6) and his revelation in Scripture (Ps. 19:14). Second, Paul has used ῥῆμα to refer to the gospel (10:8, 17). Third, Paul's focus is on hearing and believing the gospel (10:17–18), not on responding to general revelation.

λέγει) that the response of the Gentiles to the gospel would provoke Israel to jealousy (cf. 11:11, 14):

I will make you jealous because of those who are not a nation; because of a senseless nation I will make you angry.

Then in Isaiah 65:1 the prophet boldly predicted ('Ησαΐας ἀποτολμᾷ καὶ λέγει) that the Gentiles would be found by God even though they were not pursuing him (cf. 9:30):

**I was found by the ones who are not seeking me,
I became manifest to the ones who are not asking for me.**

Israel's problem is neither a lack of an opportunity to hear the gospel nor a lack of knowledge about the impact of the gospel. Israel's problem is that they have not responded to the message of the gospel (Isa. 65:2):

All day long I stretched out my hands toward a disobedient and defiant people.

God has extended his hands to them in welcome (ἐξεπέτασα τὰς χεῖράς μου) without pause (ὅλην τὴν ἡμέραν). Yet, Israel's response has been widespread disobedience (ἀπειθοῦντα) and defiance (ἀντιλέγοντα).[21] Their problem does not stem from a lack of preaching, a lack of hearing, or a lack of knowing. Their problem stems from a lack of willingness to believe and obey the message about Christ.

Theology and Appropriation

In Romans 1:18–23, Paul explained the role of general revelation in making God known. That same explanation made it clear that general revelation is adequate to render men and women without excuse but inadequate to save. Romans 10:14–21 highlights the essential role of special revelation in the process of salvation, because "faith is based on the act of hearing, and hearing comes through the word about Christ" (10:17). That word about Christ, however, is neither new to Paul's preaching nor unique to the New Testament. As Paul has made clear, the righteousness that comes through faith has been witnessed by the law and the prophets (3:21–22) and is clearly seen when God counted Abraham's faith for righteousness (4:3, 9, 16–22).

Abraham's faith, however, had an object: God's promise. In fact, faith in God's promise always has been and always will be the basis for salvation. The centrality of God's promise may be traced throughout the Old Testament, especially in an overview of the biblical covenants. God's initial promise in the garden of Eden offered life for obedience (Gen. 2:16–17). After the fall, God promised a redeemer (Gen. 3:15) and, based on Eve's statement at Seth's birth (Gen. 4:25),

---

21. Cf. CSB.

it is fair to conclude that Adam and Eve understood and believed that promise. God promised preservation from future destruction by flood to Noah and his descendants (Gen. 9:8–17). God repeated his promise to Abraham of a land, a seed, and a blessing (Gen. 12:1–3) three times (Gen. 13; 15; 17), and Abraham's faith in that promise was paradigmatic for Paul. God then extended the same promise to Isaac (Gen. 26) and Jacob (Gen. 28). It is true that the Mosaic covenant brought law (Exod. 19–24), but it also brought the promise of God's presence with his redeemed people (Exod. 20:22–26). God's promise to David included a throne and a kingdom, while repeating earlier promises of a land and a seed (2 Sam. 7:8–17). Along with God's law written on hearts and a personal knowledge of God, the new covenant promised forgiveness of sins (Jer. 31:31–34). The common thread running through the Abrahamic, Mosaic, Davidic, and new covenants is the promise of a personal relationship with God as his people (Gen. 17:7; Exod. 6:7; 20:2; 2 Sam. 7:14; Jer. 31:33).

The fact that each of the biblical covenants points to Christ is clearly seen, for example, in Matthew's gospel as the following table documents:

Covenant	Scripture	Promise	Fulfillment in Christ
Adamic	Genesis 3	Redeemer	Matt. 1:18–25
Noahic	Genesis 9	Protection	Matt. 2:13–23
Abrahamic	Genesis 12	Blessing	Matt. 2:7–12; 12:18–21; 28:16–20
Mosaic	Exodus 19–24	Presence	Matt. 1:18–25; 28:16–20
Davidic	2 Samuel 7	King	Matt. 2:1–6; 21:1–11
New	Jeremiah 31	Forgiveness	Matt. 26:26–29

So, faith has always been based on the act of hearing, and hearing has always come through the word about Christ.

Paul's primary purpose for including this passage at this point in his letter was to help the Romans understand that Israel's failure was the result of their willful disobedience, not of a lack of hearing or of understanding. With the original readers we need to realize that we must subordinate our own knowledge, emotion, and will to God's truth regardless of our own natural inclination to turn away from that truth. The failure of individuals to believe what they hear or are told provides a natural point of connection to the passage, as does the concept of "selective hearing"—hearing what we want to hear while ignoring what we do not want to hear. This passage corrects attitudes of disobedience and defiance and reminds us that we ignore God's truth at our own risk. It commends a willingness to submit our minds, hearts, and wills to God's truth. The objective in communicating this passage should be to help others understand that the gospel message demands a response of faith demonstrated by humble obedience to truth so that they will submit themselves to God and his message about Christ.

ROMANS 11:1–10

Text and Translation

1 Therefore, I am saying, God did not reject his people,[1] did he? May it never be! For indeed[2] I myself[3] am an Israelite, out of the seed[4] of Abraham, of the tribe of Benjamin. **2** God did not reject his people whom he foreknew. Or are you not knowing what the Scripture says in *the section about* Elijah? How he intercedes to God against Israel,[5]

3   **Lord, they killed your prophets,**
        they destroyed your altars,
    and I alone[6] am left,
        and they are seeking my life.

4 But what is the divine answer to him saying?

    I left behind for myself seven thousand men,
        who did not bow a knee to Baal.

5 Therefore, in the same way also[7] there has been in the present time a remnant because of election characterized by grace;[8] **6** now if *it is* based on grace,[9] *it is* no longer based on works; for otherwise grace *is* no longer grace.[10] **7** What then? *That* which[11] Israel is seeking, this they did not achieve, but the election achieved it; but the rest were hardened, **8** just as it is written,

    God gave to them a sluggish spirit,[12]
        eyes so as not to see[13]
        and ears so as not to hear,
    until this very day.

---

1. The variant that substitutes τὴν κληρονομίαν ($\mathfrak{P}^{46)}$) for τὸν λαόν (א, A, B, C, D, 33) is most likely an assimilation to the LXX of Psalm 93:14.
2. Καί is adjunctive.
3. Ἐγώ is emphatic.
4. Both ἐκ σπέρματος Ἀβραάμ and φυλῆς Βενιαμείν denote source.
5. Κατά + accusative denotes opposition.
6. Μόνος is adjectival, modifying ἐγώ.
7. Καί is adjunctive.
8. Κατά + accusative denotes cause; χάριτος is a descriptive genitive.
9. Ἐκ + genitive denotes basis (twice).
10. Χάρις is the shorter reading and is well supported ($\mathfrak{P}^{46}$, א*, A, C, D). There would not appear to be a compelling reason to omit the additional words of the longer reading if it were original.
11. The relative pronoun includes an embedded demonstrative.
12. Κατανύξεως is an attributed genitive.
13. Τοῦ + infinitive denotes result (twice); see also verse 10.

9 And David is saying,

> **May their table be for a snare and for a trap
> and for a stumbling block and for a recompense to
> them.**
> **10   May their eyes be darkened so as not to see,
> and bend their backs continually.**

Context and Structure

> II. Letter Body (1:18–15:13)
>> C. The Gospel as the Fulfillment of God's Plan (9:1–11:36)
>>> 1. Paul's concern for Israel (9:1–5)
>>> 2. The gospel fulfills God's plan to keep his word (9:6–29)
>>> 3. The gospel fulfills God's plan to use Israel's unresponsiveness (9:30–10:21)
>>> 4. The gospel fulfills God's plan to show mercy to all (11:1–32)
>>>> a. **By preserving a Jewish remnant (11:1–10)**
>>>> b. By bringing salvation to the Gentiles (11:11–16)
>>>> c. By demonstrating his kindness and severity (11:17–24)
>>>> d. By restoring Israel (11:25–32)
>>> 5. Paul's doxology of praise to God for his working (11:33–36)

Paul uses yet another rhetorical question to raise the issue of whether Israel's unresponsiveness has resulted in God rejecting his people (11:1). Paul's explanation unfolds in two parts. On the one hand, God has preserved a remnant within Israel (11:2–6); on the other hand, God has hardened the rest of Israel (11:7–10). He again provides Old Testament proof for his argument from the law (Deut. 29:4), the prophets (Isa. 29:10), and the writings (Ps. 69:22–23).

Basic Message and Exegetical Outline

Rather than completely rejecting Israel for their unresponsiveness, God has graciously preserved some and justly hardened others.

> Rejected, Selected, or Hardened? (11:1–10)
>> 1. Paul himself is proof that God has not rejected Israel (11:1)

2. God has preserved a remnant of Israel (11:2–6)
   a. He did so in Elijah's time (11:2–4)
   b. He does so in the present time (11:5–6)
3. God has hardened the rest of Israel (11:7–10)
   a. He gave them a sluggish spirit (11:7–8)
   b. He caused their advantages to become liabilities (11:9–10)

Explanation of the Text

1. Paul himself is proof that God has not rejected Israel (11:1).

Israel's current situation does not reflect a failure of God's word (9:6–29). Instead, it reflects Israel's failure to believe that word (9:30–10:21). Could it be, therefore, that God has rejected his people? Paul raises that very issue with a rhetorical question (μὴ ἀπώσατο ὁ θεὸς τὸν λαὸν αὐτοῦ) and, characteristically, rejects it emphatically (μὴ γένοιτο). He then points to himself as proof that God has not rejected Israel: he is an Israelite (καὶ γὰρ ἐγὼ Ἰσραηλίτης) with his origin in Abraham's seed (ἐκ σπέρματος Ἀβραάμ) and Benjamin's tribe (φυλῆς Βενιαμείν). The mention of both national and tribal identities marks Paul as "a Hebrew of Hebrews" (cf. Phil. 3:5) and reinforces his claim that God has not rejected his chosen people.[14]

2. God has preserved a remnant of Israel (11:2–6).

By rewording his question as a statement without a connecting conjunction (οὐκ ἀπώσατο ὁ θεὸς τὸν λαὸν αὐτοῦ), Paul reinforces his premise. Before moving to his Old Testament proof, he adds a reminder that God "foreknew" Israel (ὃν προέγνω), which echoes 8:29–30 and "implies foreordination, with the emphasis being on God's covenantal love for his people."[15] As Paul notes later, God has not rescinded his sovereign calling of Israel (cf. 11:29).[16]

Paul's readers should already recognize (ἢ οὐκ οἴδατε) that the Old Testament section describing Elijah's experience (ἐν Ἠλίᾳ τί λέγει ἡ γραφή) demonstrates the point Paul wants to make. When Elijah appealed to God against Israel (ἐντυγχάνει τῷ θεῷ κατὰ τοῦ Ἰσραήλ), his accusation included four arguments (1 Kings 19:10): Israel had killed God's prophets (τοὺς προφήτας σου ἀπέκτειναν), Israel had destroyed

---

14. See Moo for a representative discussion of suggested reasons Paul might have included his Benjaminite background (*Romans*, 673n11).
15. Schreiner, *Romans*, 580.
16. See 9:6–13 for the earlier discussion of "calling."

God's altars (τὰ θυσιαστήριά σου κατέσκαψαν), only Elijah had remained faithful (κἀγὼ ὑπελείφθην μόνος), and his own life was in jeopardy (καὶ ζητοῦσιν τὴν ψυχὴν μου). The divine response to Elijah (λέγει αὐτῷ ὁ χρηματισμός), however, corrected the prophet's understanding by focusing on the third argument (1 Kings 19:18). God declared that he had preserved seven thousand men (κατέλιπον ἐμαυτῷ ἑπτακισχιλίους ἄνδρας), whose faithfulness was demonstrated by their refusal to worship Baal (οἵτινες οὐκ ἔκαμψαν γόνυ τῇ Βάαλ).

The conclusion (οὖν) Paul draws from Elijah's experience is that God continues to work in the same way (οὕτως καί) in the present time (ἐν τῷ νῦν καιρῷ). He has preserved a remnant (λεῖμμα . . . γέγονεν) because of his gracious election (κατ' ἐκλογήν χάριτος). This election must be on the basis of grace rather than works (χάριτι οὐκέτι ἐξ ἔργων); otherwise (ἐπεί), "grace would cease to be grace" (ἡ χάρις οὐκέτι γίνεται χάρις).[17] Rather than rejecting his people, God has acted graciously to preserve a remnant of Israel

3. God has hardened the rest of Israel (11:7–10).

In conclusion (τί οὖν), Paul adds a summary analysis of Israel's situation. Corporately, Israel has pursued righteousness in the wrong way and has not attained it (ὃ ἐπιζητεῖ Ἰσραήλ τοῦτο οὐκ ἐπέτυχεν). The exceptions are those whom God has chosen to attain righteousness (ἡ δὲ ἐκλογή ἐπέτυχεν). Those whom God has not chosen, however, he has made callous (οἱ δὲ λοιποὶ ἐπωρώθησαν) in accordance with the Old Testament witness (καθὼς γέγραπται). The composite quotation from Deuteronomy 29:4 and Isaiah 29:10[18] makes it clear that God has given Israel the "sluggish spirit" under which they labor (ἔδωκεν αὐτοῖς ὁ θεὸς πνεῦμα καρανύξεως), with the result that they can neither see nor hear properly (ὀφθαλμοὺς τοῦ μὴ βλέπειν καὶ ὦτα μὴ ἀκούειν). That situation persists even now (ἕως τῆς σήμερον ἡμέρας). The quotation from Psalm 69:22–23 reminds Paul's readers that God can and will turn the benefits he bestows into a source of stumbling and affliction if the recipients fail to recognize those benefits for what they are. Despite the benefits God has bestowed on them (9:1–5) and the patience with which he has borne with their waywardness (9:19–29), Israel has pursued the wrong goal in the wrong way (9:30–10:21). As a result—although he has preserved a remnant by his grace (11:1–6)—God has given the

---

17. NEB.
18. See Jewett for a detailed analysis of the form of the quotation (*Romans*, 662).

greater part of Israel a sluggish spirit and has turned their own advantages into liabilities that work against them (11:7–10).

Theology and Appropriation

Romans 11:8 is the third of four times in the letter that Paul refers to "hardening" (cf. 2:5; 9:18; 11:25). The Old Testament historical books highlight the hardening of non-Israelites such as Pharaoh (e.g., Exod. 7:13, 22; 8:15) and the Canaanites (e.g., Josh. 11:20). The prophetic books focus on the hardening of Israel. Their refusal to hear and repent (e.g., Jer. 5:1–3) leads to God's act of judgment (e.g., Isa. 6:10). Pharaoh's experience includes human responsibility and divine sovereignty, when Moses records that both Pharaoh (Exod. 8:32) and God (Exod. 9:12) hardened Pharaoh's heart.

The New Testament provides a more complete theological perspective on the topic. Hardness is a condition of the human heart (Matt. 19:8; Mark 3:5; Rom. 2:5) that men and women are responsible to reject (Heb. 3:8, 15; 4:7; cf. Ps. 95:8). The condition is brought about by sin (Heb. 3:13), is reflected in disobedience (Acts 19:9), and results in darkened understanding (Eph. 4:18). A hardened heart brings God's act of judgment (Rom. 2:5; 9:18). That judgment produces spiritual numbness (Rom. 11:8), which makes it increasingly difficult to comprehend God's message (cf. Mark 6:52; 8:17). Becker provides a helpful summary, "Hardening is the continually mounting refusal on the part of man to listen to God's command . . . [it] describes the inability to hear which renders a man liable to judgment."[19]

Paul's primary purpose for including this passage at this point in his letter was to help the Romans understand that although Israel's disobedience resulted in God's hardening the majority, he has graciously preserved a remnant for himself. With the original readers we need to realize that God remains faithful to his purposes for his people, even when they turn away from him. Possible points of connection to this passage include the acts of rejection and preservation, the example of a small group being selected from a larger group, and the experience of being unable to see or hear well. The passage corrects the ideas that God turns his back on those who are his or changes his plans based on our actions. It commends a sense of gratitude for God's gifts and his gracious preservation of a faithful remnant. The objective in communicating this passage should be to help others understand that God always preserves a faithful remnant so that they will make every effort to remain faithful and, so, be counted among that remnant.

---

19. U. Becker, "Hard, Harden" (*NIDNTT* 1.155–56).

ROMANS 11:11–16

Text and Translation

11 Therefore, I am saying, they did not stumble so that they might fall,[1] did they? May it never be! But because of their trespass[2] salvation *has come* to the Gentiles in order to make them jealous.[3] **12** Now if[4] *it is true that* their trespass *brings* riches to the world[5] and their failure *brings* riches to the Gentiles, much more indeed *will* their fullness *be*. **13** But I am speaking to you *who are* Gentiles; to the degree that in truth[6] I myself am[7] an apostle to the Gentiles,[8] I am glorifying my ministry, **14** if somehow[9] I will make jealous my flesh[10] and will save some of them.[11] **15** For if *it is true that* their falling away *brings* reconciliation to the world,[12] what *will* their acceptance *bring* except life from the dead? **16** Now if *it is true that* the firstfruits *are* holy, the lump *will be* also;[13] and if *it is true that* the root *is* holy, the branches *will be* also.

Context and Structure

II. Letter Body (1:18–15:13)
    C. The Gospel as the Fulfillment of God's Plan (9:1–11:36)
        1. Paul's concern for Israel (9:1–5)
        2. The gospel fulfills God's plan to keep his word (9:6–29)
        3. The gospel fulfills God's plan to use Israel's unresponsiveness (9:30–10:21)

---

1. Ἵνα + subjunctive denotes result.
2. Τῷ αὐτῶν παραπτώματι is a dative of cause.
3. Εἰς τὸ + infinitive denotes purpose.
4. Εἰ introduces a first-class condition; see also verses 14 and 16.
5. Κόσμου and ἐθνῶν are objective genitives.
6. Ἐφ᾽ ὅσον denotes degree; μὲν οὖν is idiomatic (cf. Longenecker, *Romans*, 887).
7. Ἐγὼ εἰμι is emphatic.
8. Ἐθνῶν is an objective genitive.
9. Although εἰ + the future indicative forms the protasis of a first-class condition (Wallace, *Grammar*, 707), πως introduces a sense of "hesitant expectation" (Moo, *Romans*, 692n46).
10. Μου τὴν σάρκα ("my flesh") is equivalent to τῶν συγγενῶν μου κατὰ σάρκα ("my kinsmen according to the flesh"; cf, 9:3).
11. Ἐξ αὐτῶν is partitive.
12. Κόσμου is an objective genitive.
13. Καί is adjunctive (twice).

4. The gospel fulfills God's plan to show mercy to all (11:1–32)
   a. By preserving a Jewish remnant (11:1–10)
   b. **By bringing salvation to the Gentiles (11:11–16)**
   c. By demonstrating his kindness and severity (11:17–24)
   d. By restoring Israel (11:25–32)
5. Paul's doxology of praise to God for his working (11:33–36)

An opening rhetorical question and emphatic response introduce the next step in Paul's argument (11:11): Israel's hardening has a purpose, because it brings salvation to the Gentiles. The rest of the paragraph uses a series of "if-then" constructions to reinforce the importance of Israel's role in God's plan (11:12, 14, 15, 16). Verses 13–14 form a parenthesis in which Paul explains his role in God's plan as apostle to the Gentiles.

Basic Message and Exegetical Outline

Israel's hardening brings salvation to the Gentiles, provokes the Jews to jealousy, and promises life to the world.

God's Purposes in Israel's Hardening (11:11–16)
1. Israel's trespass brings salvation to the Gentiles (11:11–12)
2. Paul's ministry provokes the Jews to jealousy and salvation (11:13–14)
3. Israel's falling away promises global reconciliation and life from the dead (11:15–16)

Explanation of the Text

1. Israel's trespass brings salvation to the Gentiles (11:11–12).
    Although God has preserved a faithful remnant (11:2–6), he has hardened the majority of Israel (11:7–10). Does that hardening mean Israel has fallen into "irreversible ruin" (μὴ ἔπταισαν ἵνα πέσωσιν)?[14] Once again, Paul rejects the suggestion emphatically (μὴ γένοιτο). Later, he will make it clear that the hardening is temporary (cf. 11:25–32). In this paragraph, however, his point is that God uses Israel's

---

14. Cranfield suggests this translation for πταίω (*Romans*, 555).

hardening to further his own purposes in three ways. First, because of Israel's trespass (τῷ αὐτῶν παραπτώματι), salvation has come to the Gentiles (ἡ σωτηρία τοῖς ἔθνεσιν). Second, the purpose of salvation coming to the Gentiles is to provoke the Jews to jealousy (εἰς τὸ παραζηλῶσαι αὐτοῖς). Paul articulates this dynamic with an eloquently structured three-line statement highlighted by the use of three nouns with the same ending and inverted word order in the third line that emphasizes the end result:

τὸ <u>παράπτωμα</u> αὐτῶν	πλοῦτος κόσμου
τὸ <u>ἥττημα</u> αὐτῶν	πλοῦτος ἐθνῶν
πόσῳ μᾶλλον	τὸ <u>πλήρωμα</u> αὐτῶν

Their trespass (τὸ παράπτωμα αὐτῶν) and their failure (τὸ ἥττημα αὐτῶν) already produce widespread spiritual gain (πλοῦτος κόσμου . . . πλοῦτος ἐθνῶν). The end result of Israel's disobedience, however, will be something even greater (πόσῳ μᾶλλον): the bringing in of their full number (τὸ πλήρωμα αὐτῶν).[15]

2. Paul's ministry provokes the Jews to jealousy and salvation (11:13–14).
Verses 13–14 form a parenthesis in which Paul addresses his Gentile readers directly (ὑμῖν λέγω τοῖς ἔθνεσιν) and uses his own ministry as a case study of the way God accomplishes his second purpose. Paul is zealous in pursuing his ministry (τὴν διακονίαν μου δοξάζω) as apostle to the Gentiles (εἰμι ἐγώ ἐθνῶν ἀπόστολος). He pursues that ministry in the hope that somehow (εἴ πως) he might provoke his fellow Israelites (παραζηλώσω μου τὴν σάρκα) and might convert some of them (καὶ σώσω τινὰς ἐξ αὐτῶν).

3. Israel's falling away promises global reconciliation and life from the dead (11:15–16).
God's third purpose in Israel's hardening is to use them to bring global reconciliation and life from the dead. Paul uses a carefully structured rhetorical question to make his point:

εἰ ἡ ἀποβολὴ αὐτῶν	καταλλαγὴ κόσμου
τίς ἡ πρόσλημψις	εἰ μὴ ζωὴ ἐκ νεκρῶν

---

15. In light of 11:25, the phrase τὸ πλήρωμα αὐτῶν is best understood as the full number of elect Israelites (cf. Harvey, *Romans*, 274).

The casting away of Israel (ἡ ἀποβολὴ αὐτῶν) brings reconciliation to the world now (καταλλαγὴ κόσμου). When they are restored to their relationship with God in the future (ἡ πρόσλημψις), however, the result will be the final resurrection (ζωὴ ἐκ νεκρῶν). God's plan, therefore, consists of three steps: (1) Israel's failure brings salvation and reconciliation to the Gentiles; (2) the Gentiles' salvation will provoke Israel to salvation; (3) Israel's salvation will bring final redemption to all of God's people (cf. 8:23–25). Paul summarizes this understanding of God's purposes in working with Israel in a proverbial couplet:

If the firstfruits (ἡ ἀπαρχή) are holy,	also the lump (τὸ φύραμα);
if the root (ἡ ῥίζα) is holy,	also the branches (οἱ κλάδοι).

Paul's point is clear: "God's promises to the patriarchs mean that Israel is still set apart in his sight."[16] The mention of root and branches in verse 16 anticipates the extended metaphor Paul develops in the next paragraph (11:17–24) to apply the truth he has just established.

Theology and Appropriation

God's promises to Israel have not failed (9:6). God has not rejected Israel (11:1). Israel's failure does not place them beyond hope (11:11). Paul has made each of these points in his argument from 9:5–11:16. Nor does Israel's failure mean that God has stopped working through or on behalf of Israel. Paul brings his argument to a conclusion in 11:25–32, but he sets out the basic contours of God's plan for salvation history in 11:11–16. Longenecker draws "four vitally important points" from those verses.[17] First, Israel has not fallen permanently or beyond recovery. Second, God has ordained Israel's rejection of Messiah as a means of bringing salvation to the Gentiles. Third, God has ordained the salvation of the Gentiles as a means of making Israel jealous. Fourth, Israel's future salvation will bring even greater blessing to the world. There is no basis in Paul's argument for concluding that all of God's words of promise have been transferred to the church, or that only God's words of judgment now apply to Israel.[18] Israel continues to have an essential place in God's present purposes and an important

---

16. Harvey, *Romans*, 275.
17. Longenecker, *Romans*, 884.
18. This suggested understanding is sometimes called "replacement theology" or "supersessionism." See "Theology and Appropriation" under 11:17–24 for further discussion.

place in God's future plan. In fact, Paul's intent in 11:11–16 is to inspire confidence in God's future plans for Israel.

Paul's primary purpose for including this passage at this point in his letter, therefore, was to help his Roman readers understand that Israel's present plight is not irreversible but, instead, is part of God's larger redemptive plan. With those original readers we need to realize that God has a plan and will accomplish his purposes—both for Israel and for us. Possible points of connection to this passage include the emotion or experience of jealousy and the idea of unexpected or unforeseen results. What God intends to result from Israel's failure is, most likely, different from what we might conclude or expect. The passage corrects the ideas that Israel's lack of responsiveness is permanent and that God has concluded his dealings with Israel. It commends confidence in both God's plan and the ultimate success of that plan. The objective in communicating this passage should be to help others understand that the outworking of God's plan will always accomplish his purposes so that they will renew their confidence in God's sovereign and providential working and will trust that working to produce results we cannot even imagine.

ROMANS 11:17–24

Text and Translation

17 Now if[1] *it is true that* some of the branches[2] were broken off, and you *who* are[3] a wild olive tree were grafted in among them and *you* became sharers in the root that produces the richness that comes from the olive tree,[4] **18** do not boast against the branches;[5] but if, *for the sake of argument*, you are boasting,[6] you are not bearing the root, but the root *is bearing* you. **19** Therefore, you are saying, "Branches were broken off in order that I[7] might be grafted in." **20** Well![8] They were broken off because of unbelief,[9] but you have been caused to stand[10] because of belief. Do not think highly *of yourselves*, but fear; **21** for if *it is true that* God did not spare the natural[11] branches, he will not spare you either.[12] **22** Therefore, behold God's[13] kindness and severity. On the one hand severity upon the *ones who* are falling,[14] on the other hand God's kindness upon you, if you remain[15] in kindness, for other-

---

1. Εἰ introduces the triple protasis of a first-class condition; the apodosis is in verse 18a.
2. Κλάδων is a partitive genitive.
3. Ὤν is an adjectival participle.
4. The combination τῆς ῥίζας τῆς πιότητος τῆς ἐλαίας is difficult. The best understanding is that τῆς ῥίζας is an objective genitive; τῆς πιότητος is a genitive of product; and τῆς ἐλαίας is a genitive of source. The combination is complicated by the existence of four textual variants. The UBS[5] reading (א*, B) is more difficult and best explains the others.
5. The genitive of κλάδων reflects that idea of opposition in the κατά- prefix of κατακαυχάομαι.
6. Εἰ κατακαυχᾶσαι is a first-class condition; the protasis is assumed to be true for the sake of argument.
7. Ἐγώ is emphatic.
8. Jewett decides that καλῶς accepts the point just made (*Romans*, 687).
9. Τῇ ἀπιστίᾳ is a dative of cause, as is τῇ πίστει.
10. Ἕστηκας is intransitive; the perfect tense is intensive.
11. Κατὰ φύσιν functions as an attributive modifier. See also verse 24.
12. Μὴ πως οὐδέ (𝔓46, D, 33) reflects typical Pauline phraseology, but οὐδέ is the shorter reading, has solid manuscript support (א, A, B, C), and is more likely original.
13. Θεοῦ is a genitive of source.
14. Τοὺς πεσόντας is a substantival participle.
15. Ἐὰν ἐπιμένῃς introduces a third class condition.

wise you also[16] will be cut off. **23** But those also, except they remain[17] in unbelief, will be grafted in; for God is able to graft them in again. **24** For if *it is true that* you were cut out[18] of your own[19] naturally wild olive tree and contrary to *your* nature were grafted into the cultivated olive tree, much more indeed these natural *branches* will be grafted into their own olive tree.

Context and Structure

II. Letter Body (1:18–15:13)
   C. The Gospel as the Fulfillment of God's Plan (9:1–11:36)
      1. Paul's concern for Israel (9:1–5)
      2. The gospel fulfills God's plan to keep his word (9:6–29)
      3. The gospel fulfills God's plan to use Israel's unresponsiveness (9:30–10:21)
      4. The gospel fulfills God's plan to show mercy to all (11:1–32)
         a. By preserving a Jewish remnant (11:1–10)
         b. By bringing salvation to the Gentiles (11:11–16)
         c. **By demonstrating his kindness and severity (11:17–24)**
         d. By restoring Israel (11:25–32)
      5. Paul's doxology of praise to God for his working (11:33–36)

Paul uses an extended metaphor to remind his Gentile readers that they must maintain a proper perspective on God's dealings with Israel. First, they must avoid boasting (11:16–18). Second, they must avoid pride (11:19–21). Finally, they must recognize that God is able to extend his kindness and severity to both Gentiles and Jews (11:22–24).

Basic Message and Exegetical Outline

Israel's hardening is not a reason for Gentile Christians to boast or be proud, because God extends his kindness and severity to both Gentiles and Jews.

---

16. Καί is adjunctive.
17. Ἐὰν μὴ ἐπιμένωσιν introduces a third class condition.
18. Εἰ . . . ἐξεκόπης introduces a first-class condition.
19. The definite article functions as a possessive pronoun.

Proper Perspective on Israel's Hardening (11:17–24)
1. Israel's hardening is not a reason for Gentile boasting (11:17–18)
   a. The Gentiles were grafted in (11:17)
   b. But they have no reason to boast (11:18)
2. Israel's hardening is not a reason for Gentile pride (11:19–21)
   a. The Gentiles stand by faith (11:19–20a)
   b. But they have no reason to be proud (11:20b–21)
3. Israel's hardening demonstrates God's kindness and severity (11:22–24)
   a. He currently extends kindness to persevering Gentiles (11:22)
   b. He is able to exercise kindness to repenting Jews (11:23–24)

Explanation of the Text

The mention of "root" and "branches" in 11:16 launches an extended horticultural metaphor that allows Paul to draw out the implications of the preceding paragraph for his Gentile readers. Although the details of the metaphor have generated considerable discussion,[20] the applications Paul makes are clear. The two parties represented in the metaphor are Israel and believing Gentiles. Paul refers to the former group as "root" (ῥίζα), "branches" (κλάδοι), and "cultivated olive tree" (καλλιέλαιος). He addresses the latter group as "you" (συ) and characterizes them as a "wild olive tree" (ἀγριέλαιος).[21] By using the second person singular to address a Gentile Christian in a representative sense, Paul enlivens and personalizes the application.

1. Israel's hardening is not a reason for Gentile boasting (11:17–18).
At the same time that God has broken off some of the branches of Israel's olive tree (τινες τῶν κλάδων ἐξεκλάσθησαν), he has also grafted in Gentile branches among those that remain (σὺ . . . ἐνεκεντρίσθης ἐν αὐτοῖς)—even though the Gentile branches come from a wild olive tree (ὢν ἀγριέλαιος). As a result, the Gentiles now participate in the root that produces the richness that comes from the olive tree (συγκοινωνὸς τῆς ῥίζης τῆς πιότητος τῆς ἐλαίας ἐγένου). As the branches, however,

---

20. See Longenecker for a concise analysis of Paul's imagery (*Romans*, 892–94).
21. Jewett notes that ἀγριέλαιος describes "a small scraggly bush that produces nothing useful" (*Romans*, 684).

they need to remember that they do not support the root (οὐ σὺ τὴν ῥίζαν βαστάζεις). Instead, the root makes their life possible (ἀλλὰ ἡ ῥίζα σέ). Because of God's gracious act in adding them to his people, the Gentiles now share the spiritual blessings originally promised to Israel. Nevertheless, Israel is still the source of those blessings. For that reason, the Gentiles have no grounds for arrogant boasting against Israel (μὴ κατακαυχῶ τῶν κλάδων).

2. Israel's hardening is not a reason for Gentile pride (11:19–21).

The Gentiles could legitimately say (ἐρεῖς οὖν . . . καλῶς) that God broke off Israelite branches for the purpose of grafting in Gentile branches (ἐξεκλάσθησαν κλάδοι ἵνα ἐγὼ ἐγκεντρισθῶ). Nevertheless, they need to remember that God broke off those Israelites because of their unbelief (τῇ ἀπιστίᾳ ἐξεκλάσθησαν), while the Gentiles enjoy their present status because of faith (σὺ δὲ τῇ πίστει ἕστηκας). God, however, is "the ultimate source of status assignment."[22] He did not spare the natural branches (ὁ θεὸς τῶν κατὰ κλάδων οὐκ ἐφείσατο); neither will he spare Gentile Christians (οὐδὲ σοῦ φείσεται) if they arrogantly consider themselves superior to Israel (μὴ ὑψηλὰ φρόνει). In the same way that he has reversed Israel's status and has turned their advantages into liabilities (cf. 11:7–11), God could do the same to the Gentiles. For that reason, the Gentiles "should adopt an attitude of profound respect for God and his working" (ἀλλὰ φοβοῦ).[23]

3. Israel's hardening demonstrates God's kindness and severity (11:22–24).

Paul concludes his argument (οὖν) by calling on his readers to "Pay attention!" (ἴδε) as they consider God's kindness (χρηστότης) and his severity (ἀποτομία).[24] He structures his concluding warning antithetically using an ABBABA sequence in which (A) addresses Israelite concerns, and (B) addresses Gentile concerns. His readers understand the current situation:

(A) Severity has come upon fallen Israel (ἐπὶ τοὺς πεσόντας ἀποτομία).

(B) Kindness has come upon believing Gentiles (ἐπὶ σὲ χρηστότης θεοῦ).

---

22. Jewett, *Romans*, 688.

23. Harvey, *Romans*, 278.

24. Dunn notes the etymological connection between ἀποτομία and the imagery of "cutting off" that Paul has used in his metaphor (*Romans*, 664).

The existing situation will change, however, if the underlying attitudes change:

(B) The Gentiles will continue to experience God's kindness if they continue living lives of dependence on him (ἐὰν ἐπιμένῃς τῇ χρηστότητι); otherwise, they will also be cut off (ἐπεὶ καὶ σὺ ἐκκοπήσῃ).

(A) The Israelites will be grafted in (κἀκεῖνοι ... ἐγκεντρισθήσονται), unless they continue in their lives of unbelief (ἐὰν μὴ ἐπιμένωσιν τῇ ἀπιστίᾳ), because God is able to graft them in again (δυνατὸς ἐστιν ὁ θεός πάλιν ἐγκεντρίσαι αὐτούς).

In fact, having already accomplished the more difficult task, God is also capable of accomplishing the easier task.

(B) He has cut Gentile branches out of a naturally wild olive tree (σὺ ἐκ τῆς κατὰ φύσιν ἐξεκόπης ἀγριελαίου) and—contrary to their own nature (παρὰ φύσιν)—has grafted them into a cultivated olive tree (ἐνεκεντρίσθης εἰς καλλιέλαιον).

(A) It will be even easier (πόσῳ μᾶλλον) for him to take natural (οὗτοι οἱ κατὰ φύσιν) Israelite branches that were broken off (cf. 11:17) and graft them back into their very own olive tree (ἐγκεντρισθήσονται τῇ ἰδίᾳ ἐλαίᾳ).

Just as God currently extends his kindness to persevering Gentiles, he is also able to extend his kindness to repenting Israelites. Conversely, just as God currently exercises his severity toward unbelieving Israel, he will also exercise his severity toward ungrateful Gentiles. The blessings the Gentiles currently enjoy are not grounds for boasting or pride; they are the result of God's grace bestowed in response to faith. Their attitude should be characterized by reverence and gratitude for God and his working.

Theology and Appropriation

Historically, Christians have understood the relationship between Israel and the church in one of three ways. The first understanding is that the church has replaced Israel as God's people and that the promises given to God's people now apply exclusively to the church.[25] The second understanding is that Israel and the church are different and that God works with the two entities in distinct ways.[26] Israel is a political entity, while the church is a spiritual entity; each is given different sets of promises. God has temporarily suspended his working with the

---

25. This understanding appeals to the reference in Galatians 6:16 to "the Israel of God." It is often called "replacement theology."
26. This understanding is reflected in dispensational theology.

nation of Israel. During the present time God gives his attention to the church, but in a future time his attention will return to Israel, and he will fulfill his promises to them. The third understanding is that believing Jews (Israel) and believing Gentiles (the church) form one people of God with whom God has worked and is working throughout redemption history.[27] Paul's discussion in Romans 11:1–24, especially the olive tree metaphor in 11:17–24, supports the third understanding.

The key points in Paul's argument are (1) that God has hardened/ broken off the majority of Israel because of unbelief (11:7–10, 17); (2) that God preserves a faithful remnant of Israel according to his election because of grace (11:5–7); (3) that God grafts in believing Gentiles because of his kindness (11:19, 22, 24); and (4) that God is able to graft in Israelites if they turn from their unbelief (11:23). Taken together, these points indicate that God works with Israel and the church in parallel rather than in sequence. He has neither replaced Israel nor suspended his working with them. He continues to harden the majority and to preserve a remnant who respond in faith. At the same time, he continues to save Gentiles who respond in faith and to darken the understanding of those who harden their hearts (cf. Eph. 4:17–19).

God has always had one people—those who respond to his promises with faith—and he has always been selective regarding those to whom he has extended his promises (cf. 9:6–13). In the Old Testament era, those who responded were predominantly Jews, although God also added Gentiles to his people. Rahab (Josh. 6:25), Ruth (Ruth 4:13–15), and Naaman (2 Kings 5:1–14) were prominent examples. In the New Testament era, those who respond are predominantly Gentiles, although God continues to add Israelites to his people (cf. Acts 2:41; 4:4; 6:7; 21:20). Paul himself is a prime example (11:1), and the list of Christians he greets in Romans 16 includes at least seven individuals of Jewish ethnicity and four he identifies explicitly as "my kinsmen." In the next paragraph, Paul points to a future increase in the number of Israelites who will be grafted into God's family tree.

Paul's primary purpose for including this passage at this point in his letter was to warn his believing Gentile readers against attitudes of pride and arrogance toward Israel. With those original readers we need to adopt an attitude of humility, gratitude, and respect for God and his gracious working. If the horticultural practices of pruning and grafting are not familiar to the audience, the idea of tracing a family tree probably is. Other possible points of connection to this passage include attitudes of pride and arrogance as well as the human inclination

---

27. This understanding is reflected in covenant theology.

to boast in status or accomplishments. The passage corrects any sense of superiority over other ethnic, cultural, or religious groups and any sense of pride or arrogance that might lead to boasting. It also corrects the idea that God can only work in one way or never alters the way in which he works with people groups. It commends humility before God, gratitude for his grace, and respect for his workings. The objective in communicating this passage should be to help others understand that God works sovereignly as he knows best to extend kindness in response to faith. God exercises severity in response to unbelief so that believers will adopt an attitude of humility, gratitude, and respect for God and his gracious working.

ROMANS 11:25–32

Text and Translation

25 For I do not want you to be ignorant, brothers, about this mystery, in order that you might not be wise with reference to yourselves,[1] that hardening has partially come upon Israel[2] until[3] the fullness of the Gentiles[4] comes in, **26** and in this way all Israel will be saved, just as it is written,

> The *one who* is delivering[5] will come out of Zion,[6]
>   he will turn away ungodliness from Jacob;[7]
> **27**   and this *will be* my[8] covenant with them,[9]
>   whenever I will take away their sins.

28 On the one hand with reference to the gospel[10] *they are* enemies for your sake,[11] on the other hand with reference to the election *they are* beloved because of the fathers; **29** for the gifts and calling God bestows[12] *are* irrevocable. **30** For as you once disobeyed God,[13] but now were shown mercy because of their disobedience,[14] **31** in the same way also these now disobeyed because of the mercy shown to you,[15] in order that they might also[16] now[17] be shown mercy. **32** For

---

1. Ἑαυτοῖς is a dative of reference. ℵ, C, D, and 33 support the insertion of παρ' before the pronoun, while A and B support the insertion of ἐν. The reading that omits a preposition (𝔓46), however, best explains the others and is most likely original (cf. Jewett, *Romans*, 694na).
2. Τῷ Ἰσραήλ is a dative of disadvantage.
3. Ἄχρις οὗ is adverbial of time.
4. Τῶν ἐωνῶν is a partitive genitive.
5. Ὁ ῥυόμενος is a substantival participle.
6. Ἐκ Σιών denotes origin.
7. Ἀπό + genitive denotes separation.
8. Παρ' ἐμοῦ functions as an attributive modifier.
9. Αὐτοῖς is an associative dative.
10. Κατά + accusative denotes reference (twice).
11. Δι' ὑμᾶς denotes advantage; διὰ τοὺς πατέρας denotes cause.
12. Τοῦ θεοῦ is a subjective genitive.
13. Τῷ θεῷ is a dative of indirect object.
14. Τῇ ἀπειθείᾳ is a dative of cause.
15. Τῇ ἐλέει is a dative of cause; ὑμετέρῳ is objective.
16. Καί is adjunctive.
17. The variants that either omit νῦν (P46, A, D2) or replace it with ὕστερον (33) resolve the exegetical problem related to the time when Israel will be shown mercy. The variant that includes νῦν, however, has early manuscript

God has shut up[18] all[19] in disobedience,[20] in order that he might show mercy to all.

Context and Structure

II. Letter Body (1:18–15:13)
    C. The Gospel as the Fulfillment of God's Plan (9:1–11:36)
        1. Paul's concern for Israel (9:1–5)
        2. The gospel fulfills God's plan to keep his word (9:6–29)
        3. The gospel fulfills God's plan to use Israel's unresponsiveness (9:30–10:21)
        4. The gospel fulfills God's plan to show mercy to all (11:1–32)
            a. By preserving a Jewish remnant (11:1–10)
            b. By bringing salvation to the Gentiles (11:11–16)
            c. By demonstrating his kindness and severity (11:17–24)
            d. **By restoring Israel (11:25–32)**
        5. Paul's doxology of praise to God for his working (11:33–36)

Paul concludes his discussion of Israel's situation by looking forward to their future restoration. He begins by disclosing the mystery that, although their hardening is partial and temporary, the Old Testament supports Israel's future salvation (11:25–27). He concludes by explaining the theological interaction between human unbelief and divine mercy as it relates to the Gentiles, to Israel, and to all humankind (11:28–32).

Basic Message and Exegetical Outline

God's plan is to reverse Israel's hardening in order to show mercy to all without distinction.

---

support ($\aleph$, B, D*), is the more difficult reading, and balances the presence of νῦν in the first half of the sentence.

18. Συνέκλεισεν is a consummative aorist.
19. Τοὺς πάντας has strong manuscript support ($\aleph$, A, B, D², 33) and parallels the presence of τοὺς πάντας in the second half of the sentence. The reading τὰ πάντα ($\mathfrak{P}^{46}$, D*) possibly reflects an assimilation to Galatians 3:22 (cf. Metzger, *Textual Commentary*, 465).
20. Εἰς + accusative denotes state.

The Mystery of Salvation History (11:25–32)
1. God's plan is to reverse Israel's hardening (11:25–27)
   a. Israel's hardening is partial and temporary (11:25)
   b. Israel's salvation is certain (11:26–27)
2. God's purpose is to show mercy to all (11:28–32)
   a. God's calling of Israel is irrevocable (11:28–29)
   b. God will show mercy to all despite their disobedience (11:30–32)

Explanation of the Text

1. God's plan is to reverse Israel's hardening (11:25–27).

Paul uses a disclosure formula (οὐ γὰρ θέλω ὑμᾶς ἀγνοεῖν, ἀδελφοί) to add special emphasis to his conclusion of both 11:1–24 and chapters 9–11 as a whole. What he has previously set out is a "mystery" (τὸ μυστήριον τοῦτο),[21] which he discloses for a specific purpose: that the Gentiles might not be "wise in their own conceits" (ἵνα μὴ ἦτε ἑαυτοῖς φρόνιμοι).[22] The content of the mystery that follows (ὅτι) recapitulates God's plan for the restoration of Israel (11:15–16), and the purpose clause (ἵνα) reinforces Paul's previous warning to the Gentiles (11:17–24).

God's plan for Israel includes three steps. First, hardening has partially come upon Israel (πώρωσις ἀπὸ μέρους τῷ Ἰσραὴλ γέγονεν).[23] Second, that hardening will continue until (ἄχρις οὗ) God brings in "the full number of the elect from among the Gentiles" (τὸ πλήρωμα τῶν ἐθνῶν εἰσέλθῃ).[24] Third (καὶ οὕτως), all Israel will be saved (πᾶς Ἰσραὴλ σωθήσεται).[25] Since the prophet Isaiah (Isa. 27:9; 50:10–11) has already predicted that third step of Israel's ultimate salvation (καθὼς

---

21. See Harvey (*Romans*, 283–84): "Μυστήριον, -ου, τό denotes a secret too profound for human ingenuity (BDAG 662b). Paul uses it elsewhere to describe the bodily change at the resurrection (1 Cor. 15:51), the principle of lawlessness embodied in antichrist (2 Thess. 2:7), the basic tenets of the Christian faith (1 Tim. 3:9, 16), unspecified divine secrets (1 Cor. 4:1; 13:2; 14:2), and the eternal council of God eschatologically fulfilled in Christ (1 Cor. 2:1; Eph. 1:9; 3:3–4, 9; 6:19; Col. 1:26–27; 2:2; 4:3). Here, it describes God's three-step plan for the restoration of Israel."
22. ESV. Jewett writes that the purpose clause implies "an unacceptable measure of arrogance" (*Romans*, 699).
23. Ἀπὸ μέρους is best understood as adverbial, modifying γέγονεν (cf. Harvey, *Romans*, 284).
24. Cranfield, *Romans*, 575.
25. See "Theology and Appropriation" below for suggested understandings of "all Israel."

γέγραπται), it should come as no surprise to Paul's readers. The deliverer who will come out of Zion (ἥξει ἐκ Σιὼν ὁ ῥυόμενος) is Christ (cf. 1 Thess. 1:10), and he will turn away ungodliness from Israel (ἀποστρέψει ἀσεβείας ἀπὸ Ἰακώβ). Further, in fulfillment of God's covenant with Israel (καὶ αὕτη αὐτοῖς ἡ παρ' ἐμοῦ διαθήκη), he will take away their sins (ἀφέλωμαι τὰς ἁμαρτίας αὐτῶν). Both the original context of the Old Testament quotation and the immediate context in which Paul uses it point to Christ's second coming as the timing of Israel's restoration.[26]

2. God's purpose is to show mercy to all (11:28–32).

God's plan to restore Israel is complex, but his purpose is clear. The complexity of the plan resides in Israel's dual roles. On the one hand (μέν), their failure to respond to the gospel works to the advantage of the Gentiles (cf. 11:11–12); on the other hand (δέ), God remains faithful to them because of his prior acts on their behalf that can be traced back to the patriarchs (cf. 9:1–5). Paul captures these dual roles using parallelism:

with reference to the gospel	they are enemies	for your sake
with reference to the election	they are beloved	because of the fathers

In particular, Paul reminds his Gentile readers that the gifts and calling God has bestowed on Israel (cf. 9:4–5) cause him no regrets (ἀμεταμέλητα τὰ χαρίσματα καὶ ἡ κλῆσις τοῦ θεοῦ).[27]

Paul makes the purpose of God's plan clear with a carefully constructed formulation that artistically weaves the ideas of disobedience (A) and mercy (B) into an ABABAB pattern that moves from the Gentiles (ὑμεῖς) to the Israelites (οὗτοι) to all humankind (τοὺς πάντας). Although the Gentiles previously disobeyed God (ὑμεῖς ποτε ἠπειθήσατε τῷ θεῷ), they now have been shown mercy because of Israel's disobedience (νῦν ἠλεήθητε τῇ τούτων ἀπειθείᾳ).

(A) The Gentiles disobeyed (ἠπειθήσατε).
(B) They have been shown mercy (ἠλεήθητε).

---

26. The promise of deliverance in Isaiah comes after Israel has been judged for their sin (Isa. 59:9–19), and the salvation of Israel in Paul comes after the full number of the Gentiles have come in (Rom. 11:25–26). Cf. Schreiner, *Romans*, 619–20.
27. Compare 2 Corinthians 7:10 for ἀμεταμέλητος. Jewett provides helpful background on the adjective (*Romans*, 708–9).

In the same way also (οὕτως καί) Israel now has disobeyed because of the mercy shown to the Gentiles (οὗτοι νῦν ἠπείθησαν τῷ ὑμετέρῳ ἐλέει), in order that they also might be shown mercy (ἵνα καὶ αὐτοὶ νῦν ἐλεηθῶσιν).

   (A)   Israel disobeyed (ἠπείθησαν).

   (B)   They will be shown mercy (ἐλεηθῶσιν).

In the end, God has imprisoned all (συνέκλεισεν ὁ θεὸς τοὺς πάντας)— both Gentile and Israelite—in the state of disobedience (εἰς ἀπείθειαν), in order that he might show mercy to all (ἵνα τοὺς πάντας ἐλεήσῃ).

   (A)   God has shut up all to disobedience (εἰς ἀπείθειαν).

   (B)   He will show mercy (ἐλεήσῃ) to all.

Israel's present unresponsiveness, therefore, is an integral part of God's overall redemptive purpose. Prior to Christ's coming, God extended mercy to Israel, but the Gentiles were disobedient (11:30a). With the preaching of the gospel, Israel became disobedient, but God extended mercy to the Gentiles (11:30b). Now Israel is disobedient, but God will again extend mercy to them (11:31). When he does so, he will have extended his mercy to all solely on the basis of his grace, despite their collective disobedience (11:32; cf. 3:23–24).

Theology and Appropriation

As might be expected, Paul's statement that "all Israel will be saved" has generated extensive discussion. Commentators have suggested at least six different understandings of "all Israel." The following table provides a summary.

Commentator	Interpretation of "all Israel"
Jewett *Romans*, 702	All Jews throughout history, including those who have been hardened
Cranfield *Romans*, 577	The nation of Israel as a whole, but not necessarily including every individual member
Moo *Romans*, 723	The corporate entity of the nation of Israel as it exists at a particular point in time
Calvin Noted by Schreiner, *Romans*, 614n7	"Spiritual Israel," consisting of all elect Jews and Gentiles throughout time
Ridderbos *Paul: An Outline of His Theology*, 358	All elect Jews throughout all time
Longenecker *Romans*, 897	A large number of elect ethnic Jews near the end of history

The sixth understanding is the most likely for four reasons. First, Paul has used "Israel" to refer to ethnic Israel throughout chapters 9–11. Second, the Old Testament use of "all Israel" supports the ethnic sense (e.g., 1 Sam. 25:1; 1 Kings 12:1; 2 Chron. 12:1; Isa. 45:25; Dan. 9:11). Third, Paul has emphasized God's gracious election throughout chapters 9–11. Fourth, the sequence of events Paul has outlined in 11:25–26 specifies an eschatological time frame for Israel's salvation. Further, the entire context of Romans 9–11 presupposes that this future salvation will come through faith in Christ rather than through some sort of "special way" unique to Israel.[28]

Paul's primary purpose for including this passage at this point in his letter was to summarize God's plan for Israel and explain how that plan furthers God's overall redemptive purpose. With the original readers we need to realize that God is still working to extend mercy to all. The passage offers multiple possible points of connection, including the concept of something that is mysterious, the account of someone being rescued or delivered, the attitude of disobedience, and the experience of mercy. The passage corrects the ideas that God's future plan for Israel is something uncertain and that he somehow "changes his mind" regarding his promises. It commends trust in God's plan, his purpose, and his commitment to following through on both. The objective in communicating this passage should be to help others understand that God continues to work out his plan of including all under sin/disobedience in order to extend mercy to all so that they will trust him to superintend events to accomplish his redemptive purpose.

---

28. See Moo (*Romans*, 725–62) and Schreiner (*Romans*, 616) for refutations of the "special way" suggestion, including the significance of the quotation from Isaiah 50:20 that follows.

ROMANS 11:33–36

Text and Translation

33 O, the depth of God's[1] riches and wisdom and knowledge!
How unsearchable *are* his judgments and untraceable *are* his ways.

34 **For who knew the mind of the Lord?**
Or who was his counselor?

35 **Or who gave to him in advance, and it will be repaid to him?**

36 Because from him[2] and through him[3] and to him[4] *are* all things.
To him *be* the glory forever. Amen.

Context and Structure

II. Letter Body (1:18–15:13)
   C. The Gospel as the Fulfillment of God's Plan (9:1–11:36)
      1. Paul's concern for Israel (9:1–5)
      2. The gospel fulfills God's plan to keep his word (9:6–29)
      3. The gospel fulfills God's plan to use Israel's unresponsiveness (9:30–10:21)
      4. The gospel fulfills God's plan to show mercy to all (11:1–32)
      5. **Paul's doxology of praise to God for his working (11:33–36)**

Paul closes the third major section of his letter (9:1–11:36) with a three-part expression of praise to God, each with three elements. He begins with an expression of amazement at God's goodness as reflected in three qualities (11:33a). He then moves to an affirmation that human beings cannot understand God's ways (11:33b), supported by three rhetorical questions from the Old Testament (11:34–35). He concludes with praise for God's sovereignty that includes three prepositional phrases (11:36).[5]

---

1. Θεοῦ is a subjective genitive; so also αὐτοῦ (twice).
2. Ἐκ + genitive denotes source.
3. Διά + genitive denotes agency.
4. Εἰς + accusative denotes goal.
5. Jewett suggests that Paul inserted the Old Testament quotations into a preexisting hymn (*Romans*, 713–14). Although there is no evidence to

Basic Message and Exegetical Outline

God deserves praise for his unfathomable goodness, his unsearchable ways, and his unparalleled sovereignty.

Paul's Praise to God (11:33–36)
1. God's goodness is unfathomable (11:33a)
2. God's ways are unsearchable (11:33b–35)
3. God's sovereignty is unparalleled (11:36)

Explanation of the Text

1. God's goodness is unfathomable (11:33a).

It is impossible to plumb the depths (βάθος) of God and his goodness.[6] Paul includes three qualities that highlight the relational nature of that goodness. "Riches" (πλοῦτος) echoes 11:12 (cf. 10:12), where the focus is on the blessing that comes to the Gentiles because of Israel's failure. In 1 Corinthians, Paul identifies Christ as God's "wisdom" (σοφία), previously hidden in a mystery but now revealed in the preaching of the gospel (1 Cor. 1:18–2:15). "Knowledge" (γνῶσις) echoes 11:2 (cf. 8:29–30), where the focus is on God's special knowledge of and love for his people.

2. God's ways are unsearchable (11:33b–35).

It is impossible for humans to search out (ἀνεξεραύνητα) the manner in which God executes his judgments (τὰ κρίματα αὐτοῦ). Similarly, it is impossible to trace (ἀνεξιχνίαστοι) the ways God takes in accomplishing his purposes (αἱ ὁδοὶ αὐτοῦ). Paul supports these truths with three rhetorical questions from the Old Testament.[7] The anticipated answer to each question is "no one." No one knows God's mind (τίς ἔγνω νοῦν κυρίου); no one gives him advice (τίς σύμβουλος

---

support such a hypothesis, his analysis that identifies the four primary lines (11:33a/11:33b/11:36a/11:36b) is helpful in understanding the main points of emphasis in the doxology.

6. Cranfield suggests that βάθος highlights God's "profundity and immensity" (*Romans*, 589).
7. The first two lines are a verbatim quotation of Isaiah 40:13, but it is difficult to determine the origin of the third and fourth lines. Jewett notes, "Although there is a broad consensus that Paul is citing Job 41:3, the differences are so great that caution is required" (*Romans*, 720).

αὐτοῦ ἐγένετο); he owes no one an explanation (τίς προέδωκεν αὐτῷ καὶ ἀνταποδοθήσεται αὐτῷ).

3. God's sovereignty is unparalleled (11:36).

Behind God's unfathomable goodness and unsearchable ways lies his unparalleled sovereignty. He is the source (ἐξ αὐτοῦ), the agent (δι' αὐτοῦ), and the goal (εἰς αὐτόν) of all things (τὰ πάντα). In the context of Romans 9–11, the plan for redemptive history begins with him; he is the one who implements that plan; his purposes are the goal toward which that plan moves. Israel's current situation is perfectly aligned with that plan. Our response should not be questioning (9:19–20), boasting (11:18), pride (11:20), or arrogance (11:25). Instead, God deserves everlasting glory (αὐτῷ ἡ δόξα εἰς τούς αἰῶνας).

Theology and Appropriation

Paul's doxology of praise touches on the doctrines of God's decrees and God's providence. The *Westminster Shorter Catechism* (Q7) defines God's decrees as "his eternal purpose, according to the counsel of his will, by which, for his own glory he has fore-ordained whatever comes to pass." It further explains (Q8) that "God executes his decrees in the works of creation and providence," (Q9) that "the work of creation is God's making all things of nothing, by the word of his power, in the space of six days, and all very good, and (Q11) that "God's works of providence are his most holy, wise, and powerful preserving and governing of all his creatures and their actions." God's sovereign supervision of his plan and purpose, therefore, consists of his sustaining care of all creation (i.e., his preservation; cf. Ps. 36:5–6) and his certain control of all events (i.e., his governance; cf. Isa. 46:10–11).

God's preservation extends to the cohesion and stability of the universe (Col. 1:17; Heb. 1:3a), to the operation of the laws and processes of nature (Ps. 104:14–15), and to all the phases of life (Acts 17:28). His governance includes such areas as physical nature (Ps. 148:8), plant life (Jonah 4:6), animal life (Jonah 1:17), the birth and careers of men and women (Esther 4:14), death (John 21:19), the provision of needs (Matt. 6:8), guidance (Prov. 3:5–6; 16:33), circumstances (Phil. 1:12–14), calamities (2 Sam. 24:15), national affairs (Ps. 65:6–7), and acts of evildoers (John 19:10–11).

He accomplishes his sovereign supervision through extraordinary means and ordinary means. The most common extraordinary means is miracles (e.g., Acts 12:5–11). More frequently, however, God works through ordinary means such as the laws and processes of nature (Ps. 148:8), the acts of free moral agents (Acts 3:12–18), human reason (Acts

6:2; 15:13–21), inner checks and restraints (Acts 16:6–8), and outward circumstances (1 Cor. 16:9). God uses his works of providence to achieve three ends: (1) the security, peace, and comfort of his people (Rom. 8:28), (2) the government of the universe (Acts 4:27–28), and (3) as, Paul writes in Romans 11:33–36, his own glory (cf. 9:17).

Paul's primary purpose for including this passage at this point in his letter was to call his readers to respond with praise to God's goodness and his sovereign working. With the original readers we need to realize that God is in control, and we do not need to know all the details of what he is doing. The passage offers multiple possible points of connection, including the concepts of wisdom and knowledge, the acts of seeking and/or giving counsel or advice, and trying to understand a complex plan. The passage corrects the ideas that God owes us an explanation for what he does and that we can figure out for ourselves what he is doing. It commends a response of praise to God's sovereign working. The objective in communicating this passage should be to help others understand that the only appropriate response to God's sovereign working is to give him everlasting glory so that they will embrace a continuing attitude of praise to and trust in him.

ROMANS 12:1–15:13

The Gospel as the Transformation of God's People

The body of Romans consists of four major parts, each of which unpacks one of the four topics Paul includes in his thematic statement of 1:16–17. The central topic of Romans 12:1–15:13 is **the transformation of God's people** by the gospel. Paul's argument makes it clear that God uses the gospel to transform the way his people live their lives (12:1–15:13) and to transform the way his people exercise their liberty (14:1–15:13).

II. Letter Body (1:18–15:13)
    D. The Gospel as the Transformation of God's People (12:1–15:13)
        1. The gospel transforms the way God's people live their lives (12:1–13:14)
            a. As they pursue total transformation (12:1–2)
            b. As they exercise their spiritual gifts (12:3–8)
            c. As they overcome evil with good (12:9–21)
            d. As they are subject to authorities (13:1–7)
            e. As they love one another (13:8–10)
            f. As they wait for Jesus's return (13:11–14)
        2. The gospel transforms the way God's people exercise their liberty (14:1–15:13)
            a. By not despising one another (14:1–12)
            b. By not judging one another (14:13–23)
            c. By seeking to please one another (15:1–6)
            d. By accepting one another (15:7–13)

ROMANS 12:1–2

Text and Translation

1 Therefore, I am exhorting you, brothers, based on the mercies God has shown you[1] to present your bodies *as* a sacrifice *that is*, living,[2] holy, *and* acceptable to God, *which is* your reasonable service.[3] **2** And stop allowing yourselves to be conformed[4] to *the standard of* this age,[5] but keep on allowing yourselves to be transformed by the renewing of your mind[6] in order for you to approve[7] what God's will is, *that which is* good and acceptable and perfect.[8]

Context and Structure

II. Letter Body (1:18–15:13)
    D. The Gospel as the Transformation of God's People (12:1–15:13)
        1. The gospel transforms the way God's people live their lives (12:1–13:14)
            a. **As they pursue total transformation (12:1–2)**
            b. As they exercise their spiritual gifts (12:3–8)
            c. As they overcome evil with good (12:9–21)
            d. As they are subject to authorities (13:1–7)
            e. As they love one another (13:8–10)
            f. As they wait for Jesus's return (13:11–14)

Paul introduces the final major section of the letter body with a request formula that calls his readers to action (cf. 15:30; 16:17).[9] He follows

---

1. Διὰ τῶν οἰτιρμῶν denotes the basis of Paul's appeal; τοῦ θεοῦ is a subjective genitive.
2. Ζῶσαν is an adjectival participle.
3. The noun phrase τὴν λογικὴν λατρεία ὑμῶν stands in apposition to the preceding infinitival phrase.
4. Συσχηματίζεσθε and μεταμορφοῦσθε are causative/permissive passives (cf. Wallace, *Grammar*, 441).
5. Τῷ αἰῶνι τούτῳ is a dative of rule.
6. Τῇ ἀνακαινώσει is an instrumental dative; τοῦ νοός is an objective genitive.
7. Εἰς τό + infinitive denotes purpose.
8. The three adjectives stand in apposition to θέλημα.
9. Paul uses παρακαλῶ formulas elsewhere both to introduce major sections of letters (1 Cor. 1:10; 2 Cor. 10:1; Eph. 4:1; 1 Thess. 4:1) and to address discrete topics (Rom. 15:30; 16:17; 1 Cor. 4:16; 16:15; Philem. 10; 1 Tim.

that call with two contrasting commands that set out the means for implementing it. As 1:16–17 serves as the thesis statement for the entire letter, 12:1–2 serves as the topic statement for 12:1–15:13.

Basic Message and Exegetical Outline

The reasonable response to God's mercies is to be sacrifices who are transformed by renewed minds and are able to affirm God's will.

Total Commitment to God (12:1–2)
1. Present yourselves as sacrifices (12:1)
   a. On the basis of God's mercies
   b. Because it is your reasonable service
2. Be transformed, not conformed (12:2)
   a. By renewing your mind
   b. In order to validate God's will

Explanation of the Text

1. Present yourselves as sacrifices (12:1).

Paul now begins to develop the implications (οὖν) of what he has written in the theological section of the letter body (1:18–11:36). As he used a disclosure formula (1:13) to introduce the body-opening (1:13–17), he uses a request formula to introduce the fourth major section of the letter body (12:1–15:13). The verb "exhort" (παρακαλῶ) highlights Paul's authority and adds urgency to his call to action; the direct address "brothers" (ἀδελφοί) highlights the family relationship Paul and his readers share in Christ; the infinitival command to "present your bodies"[10] (παραστῆναι τὰ σώματα ὑμῶν) echoes his earlier commands for the readers to present themselves and their members to God (6:13, 16, 19). The basis for Paul's exhortation is the mercy God has shown to them (διὰ τῶν οἰκτιρμῶν τοῦ θεοῦ).[11] Their sacrifice (θυσίαν) identifies them with God and demonstrates that their commitment is continuing

---

2:1). See C. J. Bjerkelund, *Parakalo: Form, Funktion und Sinn der parakalo-Satze in der paulinischen Briefen* (Oslo: Universitetsforlaget, 1967).

10. "Bodies" is a synecdoche for the entire person. In 12:9–21, Paul explores the implications of the exhortation for believers' reason, conscience, and volition.

11. Longenecker concludes that the plural (οἰκτιρμῶν) refers to all God's deeds of mercy connected with the proclamation of the gospel and presented throughout 1:18–11:36 (*Romans*, 920).

(ζῶσαν), set apart to him alone (ἁγίαν), and consistent with his will (εὐάρεστον τῷ θεῷ). Their act of worship (τὴν λατρείαν ὑμῶν) is the logical (λογικήν) response to God's mercy toward them.[12]

2. Be transformed, not conformed (12:2).

Paul sets out the means[13] for carrying out his exhortation in a pair of contrasting[14] present tense[15] imperatives using the permissive passive voice.[16] The first imperative is a negative prohibition that is best translated "stop allowing yourselves to be conformed" (μὴ συσχηματίζεσθε). The verb carries the sense of being formed according to a pattern or mold;[17] in this case, the standard of conduct to avoid is the one set by "this age" (τῷ αἰῶνι τούτῳ).[18] The second imperative is a positive command that is best translated "keep on allowing yourselves to be transformed" (μεταμορφοῦσθε). The verb carries the sense of an inward change in fundamental character or conduct.[19] That change is accomplished by renewing the mind (τῇ ἀνακαινώσει τοῦ νοός).[20] The purpose[21] of renewing the mind is a capacity to discern God's will (εἰς τὸ δοκιμάζειν ὑμᾶς τί τὸ θέλημα τοῦ θεοῦ). The verb carries the sense of drawing a conclusion about something on the basis of testing (cf. 1:28; 2:18; Eph. 5:10; Phil. 1:10).[22] When it is fully tested, the only conclusion that can be

---

12. See Cranfield for an extended discussion of the adjective λογικός, -ή, -όν (*Romans*, 602–5).
13. See Moo's analysis of καί as introducing means in this context (*Romans*, 754).
14. Μὴ . . . ἀλλά establishes a strong contrast.
15. The present tense highlights continuing action, which reinforces the continuing commitment implied by the participle ζῶσαν in the previous verse.
16. See Wallace, *Grammar*, 441.
17. BDAG 979.
18. "This age" regularly carries a negative connotation for Paul (e.g., 1 Cor. 1:20; 2:6, 8; 3:18; 2 Cor. 4:4).
19. BDAG 640.
20. Paul is the first author to use ἀνακαίνωσις and ἀνακαινόω, but he uses each word twice (Rom. 12:1; 2 Cor. 4:16; Col. 3:10; Titus 3:5; cf. ἀνανεόω in Eph. 4:23). The other uses suggest that the initial renewal takes place at regeneration (Col. 3:10; Titus 3:5), but that there is also a continuing process of renewal (2 Cor. 4:16; cf. Eph. 4:23). The renewing is the result of Christ's work (cf. Rom. 6:4) and is enabled by the Holy Spirit (cf. Rom. 7:6).
21. Εἰς τό + infinitive can denote either purpose or result (cf. Wallace, *Grammar*, 591, 593). In this verse, the construction could denote either or, possibly, both (purpose/result). The question is whether the intention, its sure accomplishment, or both is in view.
22. BDAG 255.

drawn is that God's will is of highest moral quality (ἀγαθόν), of highest ethical quality (εὐάρεστον), and of highest spiritual quality (τέλειον).[23]

Theology and Appropriation

Paul uses three word groups in discussing God's will: θέλημα/θέλω (27 times), βούλημα/βουλή (2 times), and πρόθεσις/προτίθεμαι (6 times).[24] Θέλημα, -τος, το is a general term that denotes desire or purpose (Rom. 1:10; 2:18; 12:2; 15:32).[25] Βούλημα, -τος, το is a more specific term that denotes resolve or decision (Rom. 9:19).[26] Πρόθεσις, -εως, ἡ denotes plan or design (Rom. 8:28; 9:11).[27] The relationship among them is best understood in this way: God's desire (θέλημα) is the source of his resolve (βούλημα) that results in his plan (πρόθεσις).

God's will encompasses everything (1 Thess. 5:18) and extends to such subjects as ministry roles (1 Cor. 1:1; 2 Cor. 1:1; Eph. 1:1), spiritual gifts (1 Cor. 12:11, 18), and travel plans (Rom. 1:10; 15:32; 1 Cor. 4:19). Believers are called to understand God's will (Eph. 5:17), know God's will (Col. 1:9), be assured in God's will (Col. 4:12), and do God's will (Eph. 6:6).[28] Murray labels the former "God's will of determinative purpose" and the latter "God's will of commandment." The latter is in view in Romans 12:2 and refers to our responsible activity in progressive sanctification. As God has made known the mystery of his will (Eph. 1:9; Col. 1:26–27), sanctification is one of two primary aspects explicitly identified (1 Thess. 4:3; cf. Phil. 2:13). The other is salvation (1 Tim. 2:4; cf. Gal. 1:4; Eph. 1:5, 11). The focus of God's will for believers, therefore, should be on living out his plan for their own sanctification and the world's redemption.

Paul's primary purpose for including this passage at this point in his letter was to help his readers understand that the logical response to what God has done for them is to give themselves wholly to him. With the original readers we need to realize that God deserves our total commitment. The passage offers multiple possible points of connection. One is the concept of sacrifice, whether it involves one individual

---

23. This threefold explanation has its roots in Jewett's analysis (*Romans*, 734–35).
24. All three words occur in Ephesians 1:11—"according to the purpose (κατὰ πρόθεσιν) of the one who is working all things according to the counsel (κατὰ τὴν βουλήν) of his will (τοῦ θελήματος αὐτοῦ)."
25. Cf. BDAG 447.
26. Cf. BDAG 182.
27. Cf. BDAG 869.
28. Murray, *Romans*, 2:115.

sacrificing his or her life for another or an individual being willing to forgo something desired in order to obtain something greater. Others include the experience of conforming something or someone to a standard or pattern or of seeing a "metamorphosis." The experience par excellence of the latter idea, of course, is Jesus's transfiguration. The passage corrects any idea that God's will is somehow unknowable, imperfect, or irrational. It commends wholehearted commitment to God and his purposes. The objective in communicating this passage should be to help others understand the magnitude of what God has done for them so that they will respond with sacrificial service, wholehearted worship, and consistent commitment to renewing their minds.

ROMANS 12:3–8

Text and Translation

3 For I am saying by virtue of the grace *that* was given[1] to me to everyone *who* is[2] among you, not to be thinking more highly *of yourself* than[3] it is necessary to be thinking, but be thinking in order to be thinking sensibly,[4] to each one as God has measured[5] a measure *that is* faith.[6] **4** For just as we are having many members in one body and all the members are not having the same function, **5** in this way we, the many, are one body in Christ and individually[7] *we are* members of one another. **6** Now because we are having[8] different grace gifts according to the grace that was given us, *let us exercise them*—whether prophecy according to the analogy *that is* faith, **7** or service in his[9] serving, or the one who is teaching[10] in his teaching, **8** or the one who is encouraging in his encouraging, the one who is sharing with generosity,[11] the one who is leading with diligence, the one who is having mercy with gladness.

Context and Structure

II. Letter Body (1:18–15:13)
- D. The Gospel as the Transformation of God's People (12:1–15:13)
  - 1. The gospel transforms the way God's people live their lives (12:1–13:14)
    - a. As they pursue total transformation (12:1–2)
    - b. **As they exercise their spiritual gifts (12:3–8)**
    - c. As they overcome evil with good (12:9–21)
    - d. As they are subject to authorities (13:1–7)

---

1. Τῆς δοθείσης is an adjectival participle modifying χάριτος; verse 6 is similar.
2. Τῷ ὄντι is a substantival participle.
3. Παρ' ὅ is comparative.
4. Εἰς τό + infinitive denotes purpose.
5. Ἐμέρισεν is a consummative aorist.
6. Πίστεως is a genitive of apposition; see also verse 4.
7. Καθ' εἷς is idiomatic (cf. BDAG 293b).
8. Ἔχοντες is an adverbial participle of cause.
9. The definite article functions as a possessive pronoun (three times).
10. Ὁ διδάσκων and the four participles that follow are substantival.
11. Ἐν + dative denotes manner (three times).

e. As they love one another (13:8–10)
f. As they wait for Jesus's return (13:11–14)

Paul uses a saying formula to introduce a three-sentence discussion of spiritual gifts. The first sentence calls for a proper attitude (12:3). The second sentence emphasizes the importance of unity and diversity (12:4–5). The third sentence highlights the aspect of diversity by listing seven different gifts and the manner in which each should be exercised (12:6–8).

Basic Message and Exegetical Outline

Spiritual gifts should be exercised with the proper attitude, with the proper understanding, and in the proper manner.

The Exercise of Spiritual Gifts (12:3–8)
1. You should think sensibly about yourselves (12:3)
    a. Do not think more highly than is proper
    b. But think sensibly as God has given faith
2. You should understand that you are members of one body (12:4–5)
    a. One body has many members with different functions
    b. Those in Christ are members of one another
3. You should exercise the gift God has given you (12:6–8)

Explanation of the Text

1. You should think sensibly about yourselves (12:3).
   Paul uses a saying formula (λέγω γάρ) to introduce the first concrete example of living a transformed life. He reinforces his instructions with a reference to the grace God has given to him (διὰ τῆς χάριτος τῆς δοθείσης μοι) and applies them to each of his readers (παντὶ τῷ ὄντι ἐν ὑμῖν). Incorporating a fourfold wordplay (ὑπερφρονεῖν–φρονεῖν–φρονεῖν–σωφρονεῖν) and strong contrast (μὴ . . . ἀλλά) into indirect discourse calls attention to the importance of pursuing a proper attitude:

   Do not <u>be thinking more highly</u>[12]
         than it is necessary to <u>be thinking,</u>

---

12. The first and third infinitives are imperatival. Ὑπερφρονέω describes an attitude that thinks highly of oneself (BDAG 1034), while σωφρονέω describes being prudent and self-controlled (BDAG 986).

but be thinking
    in order to be thinking sensibly.

"To each one" (ἑκάστῳ) echoes the first line and begins to apply Paul's instruction on pursuing a proper attitude to the discussion of unity in diversity that follows. That application begins with an understanding that God has "measured a measure that is faith" (ὡς ὁ θεὸς ἐμέρισεν μέτρον πίστεως) to each believer. The context suggests that "faith" refers to the unique gifts of faith God gives by his Spirit.[13]

2. You should understand that you are members of one body (12:4–5).
    To explain (γάρ) the theological truth of unity and diversity, Paul uses a familiar example as the basis for a comparison (καθάπερ). A human body has many members (ἐν ἑνὶ σώματι πολλὰ μέλη ἔχομεν), but all the members do not have the same function (τὰ μέλη πάντα οὐ τὴν αὐτὴν ἔχει πρᾶξιν). The same (οὕτως) holds true for the body of Christ. By our union with Christ (ἐν Χριστῷ) the many are one body (οἱ πολλοὶ ἓν σῶμα ἐσμεν), and individually (τὸ καθ᾽ εἷς) they are members of one another (ἀλλήλων μέλη).

3. You should exercise the gift God has given you (12:6–8).
    One practical application of the theological truth of unity and diversity relates to the exercise of spiritual gifts. Paul begins a sentence he leaves unfinished with the reminder that the different gifts believers possess (ἔχοντες χαρίσματα . . . διάφορα) are distributed according to God's grace (κατὰ χάριν τὴν δοθεῖσαν ἡμῖν).[14] He then lists seven gifts, giving special attention to how each is to be exercised.[15] Prophecy (προφητείαν), the gift of interpreting the divine will or purpose, should be exercised "in proportion to a person's faith" (κατὰ τὴν ἀναλογίαν τῆς πίστεως).[16] Service (διακονίαν), the gift of practical service to those in need, should be exercised in the sphere of serving (ἐν τῇ διακονίᾳ). The one who communicates the truth of the gospel by teaching (ὁ διδάσκων) should exercise that gift in the sphere of teaching (ἐν τῇ διδασκαλίᾳ).

---

13. See Dunn (*Romans*, 721–22), Jewett (*Romans*, 742), and Schreiner (*Romans*, 652–53); contra Cranfield (*Romans*, 613–16), and Moo (*Romans*, 761).
14. The adjective διάφορα modifies χαρίσματα; χαρίσματα . . . χάριν is a play on words.
15. Moo notes the seven gifts Paul mentioned in these verses do not correspond to those in other gift lists, although there might be overlap in function (*Romans*, 764).
16. NEB.

The one who applies the gospel by encouraging others in belief or action (ὁ παρακαλῶν) should exercise that gift in the sphere of encouragement (ἐν τῇ παρακλήσει). The one who shares what he or she possesses with others (ὁ μεταδιδούς) should exercise that gift "with generosity" (ἐν ἁπλότητι).[17] The one who leads as elders do (ὁ προϊστάμενος)[18] should exhibit an earnest commitment to the task (ἐν σπουδῇ). The one who extends mercy to others (ὁ ἐλεῶν) should do so with cheerfulness, even under stress (ἐν ἱλαρότητι). Schreiner summarizes well when he writes, "Paul's main point is that those who have such gifts should devote themselves to the gift that they have received."[19]

Theology and Appropriation

The term "body" (σῶμα) is common in the New Testament and occurs 145 times. Paul himself uses the term thirteen times in Romans and eighty times in his other letters. Eleven of the thirteen occurrences in Romans refer to the human body.[20] The two occurrences in Romans 12:4–5, however, reflect a meaning that is special to Paul, when he uses "body" to refer to "the essential character of the Christian church"[21] as the body of Christ (τὸ σῶμα τοῦ Χριστοῦ). His metaphor of the body and its members in those two verses captures a theme that occupies one-third of Paul's uses of the word.[22] The three primary elements of the metaphor in Romans 12 are (1) one body, (2) many members, and (3) different functions. Paul uses the metaphor to address a fourth element: (4) right attitudes within the body (12:3). These same elements appear in the other passages that use the metaphor.

In 1 Corinthians 12:12–27 Paul uses the body-members metaphor to address an attitude of pride that had arisen over the spiritual gift of speaking in tongues. He reminds the Corinthians that there are many members but one body (12:12–14, 20; cf. Rom. 12:4) and that they are all members of one another (12:27; cf. Rom. 12:5). God has placed the members as he desired (12:18, 29; cf. Rom. 12:3) and has given them different functions (12:26–30; cf. Rom. 12:4). As a result, there should be no sense of inferiority (12:15–16), superiority (12:21), or division (12:25) within the body.

---

17. The use of ἁπλότης, –ητος, ἡ in other contexts related to money suggests generosity (cf. 2 Cor. 8:2; 9:11, 13).
18. Cf. 1 Timothy 3:4, 5, 12; 5:17; 1 Thessalonians 5:12.
19. Schreiner, *Romans*, 657.
20. Romans 1:24; 4:19; 6:6, 12; 7:4, 24; 8:10, 11, 13, 23; 12:1.
21. Wibbing, "Body," *NIDNTT* 1.237.
22. Thirty-two of ninety-three occurrences.

Ephesians 4:1–16 furthers Paul's reflection on the church as Christ's body that is "the fullness of him who fills all in all" (1:23) and the result of Christ's reconciling work that brings Jew and Gentile together in one new man (2:11–22). That "one body" is unified (4:1–6), but it is also diverse, because God has given "to each one of us grace according to the measure of Christ's gift" (4:7; cf. Rom. 12:3, 6). As a result, all the members grow in unity and maturity as each individual member does its work (4:11–16). That maturity is demonstrated by an ability to speak the truth in love (4:15).

In Colossians, Paul was addressing false teaching that emphasized special knowledge and led some among the Colossians to become "inflated without cause in [the] fleshly mind" (2:16–19; cf. Rom. 12:3). Such individuals did not hold fast to the body of which Christ is the head (1:18) and which he holds together (2:19; cf. Eph. 4:16). Instead, Paul exhorts believers to remember that they are called to peace in one body (3:15) and, so, should adopt attitudes of compassion, kindness, humility, gentleness, patience, forbearance, forgiveness, and love (3:11–14).

Paul's primary purpose for including this passage at this point in his letter was to help his readers embrace the unity and diversity that exists in the church. In that sense, the passage anticipates the Jew-Gentile tension he addresses in his teaching on the weak and strong in 14:1–12. With his original readers we need to accept our roles within the body of Christ and devote ourselves to them with a proper attitude of humility. The passage offers multiple possible points of connection, including the metaphor of the human body, the idea of different roles and functions, and the concept of right and wrong thinking. The passage corrects any idea that some believers are more important than others along with any attitude of arrogance or conceit growing out of a sense that some gifts or roles are indicative of a special relationship with God. It commends humble service in the sphere of activity God has allocated to us. That service should grow from a proper perspective on ourselves and the grace God has given us as well as a proper appreciation for the way in which God has gifted others. The objective in communicating this passage should be to help others adopt a proper perspective on unity and diversity among believers and their place in the body of Christ so that they will accept their roles within that body and devote themselves to those roles with humility.

ROMANS 12:9–21

Text and Translation

9 Love[1] *must be* without pretense; abhor *that which is* evil; hold on to *that which is* good;[2] **10** *be* devoted to one another with reference to brotherly love;[3] esteem one another highly with reference to honor; **11** *do* not *be* lazy with reference to diligence; be set on fire[4] by the Spirit; serve the Lord;[5] **12** rejoice in hope;[6] endure in tribulation; be devoted to prayer;[7] **13** contribute to the needs[8] of the saints; pursue hospitality.

14 Bless *those who* are persecuting[9] *you*;[10] bless and do not curse. **15** Rejoice with the *ones who* are rejoicing;[11] weep with the *ones who* are weeping. **16** Think the same thing toward one another; do not think highly of yourself, but associate with the humble;[12] do not be wise in your own eyes.[13]

---

1. Of the thirty individual instructions in this paragraph, three use adjectives, seventeen use imperatival participles, two use imperatival infinitives, and eight use true imperatives. Where Paul uses adjectives, verbs are added; where he uses imperatival participles and infinitives, the forms are translated as commands. The divisions within the translation reflect changes in the predominant verbal form.
2. Κολλάομαι takes a dative direct object.
3. Τῇ φιλαδελφίᾳ . . . τῇ τιμῇ . . . τῇ σπουδῇ are datives of reference.
4. Ζέοντες may be either adjectival (compare ὀκνηροί, which precedes) or verbal (compare δουλεύοντες, which follows). In either case the participle functions as a command.
5. Δουλεύω takes a dative direct object. The substitution of καιρῷ (D*) is probably an error of sight; the omission of the participial phrase (1912) is probably the result of a similar error. The reading with κυρίῳ has good manuscript support ($\mathfrak{P}^{46}$, ℵ, A, B, D², 33).
6. Τῇ ἐλπίδι and τῇ θλίψει are locative.
7. Προσκαρτερέω takes a dative direct object.
8. Κοινωνέω takes a dative direct object.
9. Τοὺς διώκοντας is a substantival participle.
10. Manuscript evidence is divided over the inclusion (ℵ, A, 33) or omission ($\mathfrak{P}^{46}$, B) of ὑμᾶς. The decision makes little difference exegetically, because the sense is easily inferred if the object is omitted.
11. Χαιρόντων and κλαιόντων are substantival participles.
12. Τοῖς ταπεινοῖς is a dative of association.
13. Παρ' ἑαυτοῖς is locative.

17 Do not repay to anyone evil in return for evil;[14] give careful thought to good things in the presence of all people; **18** if—*assuming it is*—possible,[15] as far as it depends on you, be at peace with all people.[16] **19** Do not avenge yourselves, beloved, but give an opportunity with reference to *God's* wrath,[17] for it is written, **"'Vengeance is mine,**[18] **I will repay,' says the Lord." 20** But **"if** [19]**your opponent is hungry, feed him; if he is thirsty, give him something to drink; for by doing**[20] **this you will pile up fiery coals upon his head." 21** Do not be conquered by evil, but conquer evil by good.

Context and Structure

II. Letter Body (1:18–15:13)
    D. The Gospel as the Transformation of God's People (12:1–15:13)
        1. The gospel transforms the way God's people live their lives (12:1–13:14)
            a. As they pursue total transformation (12:1–2)
            b. As they exercise their spiritual gifts (12:3–8)
            c. **As they overcome evil with good (12:9–21)**
            d. As they are subject to authorities (13:1–7)
            e. As they love one another (13:8–10)
            f. As they wait for Jesus's return (13:11–14)

Paul continues his discussion of how the gospel transforms the way God's people live with a series of thirty loosely related instructions. Those instructions may be grouped into three general clusters appealing to reason (12:9–13), conscience (12:14–16), and volition (12:17–21).[21]

---

14. Ἀντί + genitive denotes exchange.
15. Ἐι introduces a first-class condition.
16. Μετά + genitive denotes association.
17. Τῇ ὀργῇ is a dative of reference.
18. Ἐμοί is a dative of possession.
19. Ἐάν introduces a third class condition (twice).
20. Ποιῶν is an adverbial participle of means.
21. See N. F. Miller, who argues that participles introduce appeals to reason, adjectives introduce appeals to emotion, infinitives introduce appeals to conscience, and imperatives introduce appeals to will ("The Imperativals of Romans 12," in *Essays in Discourse Analysis*, D. A. Black, K. Barnwell, S. Levinson, eds. [Nashville: Broadman, 1992], 162–82). Verses 9–13 include ten participles and three adjectives; verses 14–16 include four

Basic Message and Exegetical Outline

The gospel transforms our attitudes, our relationships, and our choices.

Total Transformation (12:9–21)
1. The gospel transforms our attitudes (12:9–13)
   a. We embrace sincere love and goodness (12:9)
   b. We embrace brotherly love and honor (12:10)
   c. We embrace diligent zeal and service (12:11)
   d. We embrace joyful endurance and prayer (12:12)
   e. We embrace active assistance and hospitality (12:13)
2. The gospel transforms our relationships (12:14–16)
   a. We deal graciously with those who oppose us (12:14)
   b. We identify with others' joy and sorrow (12:15)
   c. We live with others in harmony and humility (12:16)
3. The gospel transforms our choices (12:17–21)
   a. We choose to be at peace with others (12:17–18)
   b. We choose to trust in God's justice (12:19)
   c. We choose to do good to enemies (12:20)
   d. We choose to overcome evil with good (12:21)

Explanation of the Text

1. The gospel transforms our attitudes (12:9–13).

Thirteen brief commands use adjectives (three) and participles (ten) to promote attitudes that should characterize individuals who have transformed minds. They should love sincerely and without pretense (ἀνυπόκριτος), "hate violently" (ἀποστυγοῦντες)[22] anything that is evil or morally worthless (τὸ πονηρόν), and cling (κολλώμενοι) to anything that is good and noble (τῷ ἀγαθῷ). They should be devoted to one another (εἰς ἀλλήλους φιλόστοργοι) with respect to brotherly love (τῇ φιλαδελφίᾳ) and highly esteem one another (ἀλλήλους προηγούμενοι) with respect to honor (τῇ τιμῇ). They should never be lazy (μὴ ὀκνηροί) with regard to their commitment to any task (τῇ σπουδῇ), should be set on fire (ζέοντες) by the Holy Spirit (τῷ πνεύματι), and consistently

---

imperatives, two infinitives, and three participles; verses 17–21 include four participles and five imperatives.

22. Dunn, *Romans*, 740.

serve the Lord (τῷ κυρίῳ δουλεύοντες). They should continually rejoice in hope (τῇ ἐλπίδι χαίροντες), steadfastly maintain their beliefs or course of action (ὑπομένοντες) in the face of difficult circumstances (τῇ θλίψει), and consistently devote themselves to prayer (τῇ προσευχῇ προσκαρτεροῦντες). They should provide practical financial and material assistance (κοινωνοῦντες) to other believers who are in need (ταῖς χρείαις τῶν ἁγίων) and take the initiative in providing hospitality (τὴν φιλοξενίαν διώκοντες).

2. The gospel transforms our relationships (12:14–16).

A second cluster of eight brief commands uses imperatives (four), infinitives (two), and participles (three) to call readers to transform the way in which they relate to others in three ways. First, rather than calling on God to withhold his favor (μὴ καταρᾶσθε) from those who persecute them (τοὺς διώκοντας), they should deal graciously with them by calling on him to bestow a blessing instead (εὐλογεῖτε). Second, they should share the happiness of those who are rejoicing (χαίρειν μετὰ χαιρόντων) and share the sadness of those who are weeping (κλαίειν μετὰ κλαιόντων). Third, they should "live in harmony with one another" (τὸ αὐτὸ εἰς ἀλλήλους φρονοῦντες),[23] by not thinking too highly of themselves (μὴ τὰ ὑψηλὰ φρονοῦντες) or being wise in their own eyes (μὴ γίνεσθε φρόνιμοι παρ' ἑαυτοῖς) but, rather, identifying themselves with humble persons and tasks (ἀλλὰ τοῖς ταπεινοῖς συναπαγόμενοι).[24]

3. The gospel transforms our choices (12:17–21).

The third group of commands uses participles (four) and imperatives (five) to provide three examples of how the readers can choose to overcome evil by doing good, as Paul summarizes with antithetical parallelism in verse 21:[25]

---

23. NIV, ESV, NET. Literally, "be thinking the same thing toward one another" (cf. Rom. 15:5; 2 Cor. 13:11; Phil. 2:2; 4:2).

24. Commentators are divided on whether τοῖς ταπεινοῖς συναπαγόμενοι should be translated "associate with humble persons" (NIV) or "be carried away with humble tasks" (GNB). Moo argues that it is impossible to decide between the two options, because both have parallels elsewhere in the New Testament (*Romans*, 783). The strong contrast (μὴ . . . ἀλλά) between the attitudes of pride and humility, however, is clear.

25. The mention of good (ἀγαθός) and evil (κακός) in verse 21 forms an inclusion with verse 9 (πονηρός . . . ἀγαθός).

Do not be conquered (μὴ νικῶ)	by evil (ὑπὸ τοῦ κακοῦ),	
but conquer (ἀλλὰ νίκα)	by good (ἐν τῷ ἀγαθῷ)	evil (τὸ κανόν).

First, rather than responding in the same way to someone who has acted in a morally reprehensible manner (μηδενὶ κακὸν ἀντὶ κακοῦ ἀποδιδόντες), they should give careful attention to that which is morally pleasing in the sight of others (προνοούμενοι καλὰ ἐνώπιον πάντων ἀνθρώπων) and should seek to be at peace with everyone (μετὰ πάντων ἀνθρώπων εἰρηνεύοντες). Second, rather than seeking justice when they are wronged (μὴ ἑαυτοὺς ἐκδικοῦντες), they should leave the situation in God's hands (ἀλλὰ δότε τόπον τῇ ὀργῇ),[26] because Deuteronomy 32:35 makes it clear that he is the one who avenges injustice (ἐμοὶ ἐκδίκησις, ἐγὼ ἀνταποδώσω, λέγει κύριος). Finally, rather than simply refraining from seeking vengeance against someone who has wronged them (ὁ ἐχθρός σου), Paul invokes Proverbs 25:21–22 to call them to respond by doing good instead:

If he is hungry (ἐὰν πεινᾷ),	feed him (ψώμιζε αὐτόν);
if he is thirsty (ἐὰν διψᾷ),	give him something to drink (πότιζε αὐτόν).

By responding to evil with good (τοῦτο ποιῶν), they will allow God to exercise his role of avenging injustice (ἄνθρακας πυρὸς σωρεύσεις ἐπὶ τὴν κεφαλὴν αὐτοῦ),[27] and, so, will be victorious (νικάω) over evil.

Theology and Appropriation

It should come as no surprise that the image of piling fiery coals on the head of an enemy (Prov. 25:22) has raised questions. Jewett notes that it has been explained "as a mistaken metaphor due to ambiguities in the Hebrew text; as a metaphor for 'burning pangs of shame' felt by an adversary moved by the generosity of the persecuted; as a sophisticated form of revenge by increasing the guilt of the persecutor; and . . . a reference to an Egyptian ritual of a sinner carrying a dish of hot coals

---

26. In the command "Give place to wrath" (δότε τόπον τῇ ὀργῇ), τόπος describes the favorable circumstances for doing something (BDAG 1012), and the article with ὀργή marks the wrath as well known—that is, God's wrath (Harvey, *Romans*, 310). The ESV translates the command as "leave it to the wrath of God."
27. See the discussion of this statement under "Theology and Appropriation" below.

on the head to symbolize repentance."[28] Cranfield[29] and Moo[30] argue for pangs of shame and contrition; Longenecker argues for repentance.[31] Schreiner, however, notes that the Old Testament metaphor of "coals of fire" nearly always signifies God's judgment (e.g., Ps. 140:10; Prov. 6:27–29; Ezek. 24:11) and adds a parallel from 4 Ezra 16:53: "God will burn coals of fire on the head of everyone who says, 'I have not sinned before God and his glory.'"[32] The conjunction Paul uses at the beginning of verse 20 (ἀλλά) suggests that he is drawing a contract between two possible responses to someone who has wronged a follower of Jesus: seeking justice for oneself (12:19a) or doing good to the offender (12:20a). The rationale for rejecting one response and adopting the other, however, is the same: God can be trusted to act justly on behalf of the one who has been wronged (12:19b, 20b; cf. 2 Thess. 1:6–10).

The sources for Paul's ethic of selfless love that does good to enemies goes beyond the Old Testament support he offers (Deut. 32:35; Prov. 25:21–22). His instruction, "Do not repay to anyone evil in return for evil" (12:17) reflects Jesus's teaching in Matthew 5:39, "Do not resist him who is evil," and it is possible that at least Romans 12:17–21 has its roots in Jesus's teaching recorded in the Sermon on the Mount (Matt. 5:38–48; cf. Luke 6:27–36). Further, Paul's instruction, "Bless those who are persecuting you; bless and do not curse" (12:14) echoes Jesus's teaching in Matthew 5:44, "Love your enemies and pray for those who persecute you" (cf. Matt. 5:10–12). Other echoes of the Sermon on the Mount include compassion for those who experience sorrow (12:15; cf. Matt. 5:4; Luke 6:21) and the importance of pursuing peace with others (12:18; cf. Matt. 5:9). These echoes suggest that Paul not only knew but also based his ethical instruction on the tradition stemming from Jesus and his teaching.

Paul's primary purpose for including this passage at this point in his letter was to lay a foundation of ethical instruction for those who have experienced God's mercies and choose to be transformed by renewing their minds. With his original readers we need to realize that following Jesus involves the total transformation of the way we think, relate to others, and choose to respond when we encounter hostility.

---

28. Jewett, *Romans*, 777. He goes on to suggest that Paul is talking about the impact of showing hospitality to strangers (12:13) and being at peace with everyone (12:18). Dunn's conclusion is similar (*Romans*, 751).
29. Cranfield, *Romans*, 649.
30. Moo, *Romans*, 788–89.
31. Longenecker, *Romans*, 941.
32. Schreiner, *Romans*, 675.

The passage offers multiple possible points of connection, including love, joy, sorrow, the human desire to see justice done, and the human tendency to retaliate or seek revenge when wronged. The passage corrects the natural inclinations to strike back when wronged and to seek redress for injustice. It commends hospitality, peace, care, and compassion toward those in need, and adopting a commitment to responding to evil with good. The objective in communicating this passage should be to help others understand that following Jesus goes far beyond our objective standing before God to embrace the subjective areas of our reason, our conscience, and our will, so that they will adopt lifestyles of selfless love that seek the good of others.

ROMANS 13:1–7

Text and Translation

1 Every soul must be subject to the governing[1] authorities.[2] For there is no authority except *it is appointed* by God, and the *ones who* are[3] have been appointed[4] by God. **2** So then, the one who is setting himself against the authority[5] has resisted[6] the ordinance God established,[7] and the ones who have resisted[8] will receive judgment on themselves.[9] **3** For the rulers are not a *cause for* fear with reference to good but to evil.[10] Now if you are wishing not to fear *the one in* authority,[11] do good and you will have praise from him; **4** for he is God's minister to you for the *purpose of* good.[12] But if you do evil,[13] fear; for he is not carrying the sword to no purpose; for God's servant is an avenger for wrath[14] against the *one who* is practicing[15] evil. **5** Therefore, *it is* necessary to be subject, not only because of wrath[16] but also because of your[17] conscience. **6** For because of this you are also[18] paying tribute; for they are ministers

---

1. Ὑπερεχούσαις is an adjectival participle modifying ἐξουσίαις.
2. UBS[5] adopts the reading with a third person command because of its stronger manuscript support (ℵ, A, B, D[2,] 33); it also marks a change in topic. The alternate second person command has primarily Western support (P[46], D*) and might reflect an attempt to avoid the Semitic idiom. The meaning of the command is not significantly affected by either reading.
3. Αἱ οὖσαι is a substantival participle.
4. Τεταγμέναι εἰσίν is a periphrastic participle; the perfect tense is intensive.
5. Ὁ ἀντιτασσόμενος is a substantival participle; the middle voice is a direct middle; τῇ ἐξουσίᾳ is a dative of disadvantage.
6. Ἀνθέστηκεν is an intensive perfect.
7. Τοῦ θεοῦ is a subjective genitive.
8. Οἱ ἀνθεστηκότες is a substantival participle.
9. Ἑαυτοῖς is a dative of disadvantage.
10. Τῷ ἔργῳ and τῷ κακῷ are datives of reference.
11. Τὴν ἐξουσίαν refers to the individual in authority; the translation that follows reflects that understanding.
12. Εἰς + accusative denotes purpose.
13. Ἐάν ... ποιῇς introduces a third class condition.
14. Εἰς + accusative denotes purpose.
15. Τῷ ... πράσσοντι is a substantival participle; the dative denotes disadvantage.
16. Διά + accusative denotes cause (twice).
17. The definite article functions as a possessive pronoun.
18. Καί is adjunctive.

to God[19] *who are* devoted[20] to this very thing. **7** Repay to everyone *that which is* due: to the *one to whom* tribute *is due*, tribute; to the *one to whom* tax *is due*, tax; to the *one to whom* respect *is due*, respect; to the *one to whom* honor is *due*, honor.

Context and Structure

    II. Letter Body (1:18–15:13)
        D. The Gospel as the Transformation of God's People (12:1–15:13)
            1. The gospel transforms the way God's people live their lives (12:1–13:14)
                a. As they pursue total transformation (12:1–2)
                b. As they exercise their spiritual gifts (12:3–8)
                c. As they overcome evil with good (12:9–21)
                d. **As they are subject to authorities (13:1–7)**
                e. As they love one another (13:8–10)
                f. As they wait for Jesus's return (13:11–14)

Paul next turns to the believer's relationship to governing authorities. He begins with a command supported with two reasons (13:1–4). He then provides a concluding summary followed by four specific obligations (13:5–7).

Basic Message and Exegetical Outline

Believers must be subject to governing authorities, because God has appointed them to serve him by doing his work in the pursuit of good.

    The Christian and Government (13:1–7)
        1. The governing authorities are appointed by God (13:1–4)
            a. They are ordained by God (13:1–2)
            b. They reward good and punish evil (13:3–4)
        2. The governing authorities carry out service to God (13:5–7)
            a. They are God's devoted ministers (13:6)
            b. They are due tribute, tax, respect, and honor (13:7)

---

19. Θεοῦ is an objective genitive.
20. Προσκαρτεροῦντες is an adjectival participle modifying λειτουργοί.

Explanation of the Text

1. The governing authorities are appointed by God (13:1–4).

Paul begins his third example of living a transformed life by omitting a connecting conjunction (asyndeton) and shifting to the third person. His thesis statement for the paragraph is a command: "every soul" (πᾶσα ψυχή) must recognize and accept their subordinate relationship (ὑποτασσέσθω) to those individuals who hold positions of authority in governmental hierarchies (ἐξουσίαις ὑπερεχούσαις). The discussion that follows suggests Paul has in mind both national and local authorities (cf. 13:6–7). The remainder of verses 1–4 provides two reasons (γάρ) in support of his initial command. First, governing authorities are divinely ordained (13:1b–2). They have been appointed by God (ὑπὸ θεοῦ τεταγμέναι), and apart from his appointment (εἰ μή ὑπὸ θεοῦ), there is no authority (οὐ ἔστιν ἐξουσία). As a consequence (ὥστε) resistance to those in authority (ὁ ἀντιτασσόμενοι τῇ ἐξουσίᾳ) is actually resistance to God's ordinance (τῇ τοῦ θεοῦ διαταγῇ ἀνθέστηκεν), and those who have resolved to resist God (οἱ ἀνθεστηκότες) will bring judgment on themselves (ἑαυτοῖς κρίμα λήμψονται).[21] Second, governing authorities maintain social order by rewarding good and avenging evil (13:3–4). The authorities should arouse no fear (οἱ ἄρχοντες οὐκ εἰσὶν φόβος) with reference to good works (τῷ ἀγαθῷ ἔργῳ), only with reference to evil works (ἀλλὰ τῷ κακῷ). The way to live without fear of the one in authority (μὴ φοβεῖσθαι τήν ἐξουσίαν) is to do good (τὸ ἀγαθὸν ποίει). The result will be praise from that very authority figure (ἕξεις ἔπαινον ἐξ αὐτῆς), who is God's minister (θεοῦ διάκονός ἐστιν) and is working for the purpose of bringing about good (εἰς τὸ ἀγαθόν). On the other hand, the person who does evil should fear (ἐὰν τὸ κακὸν ποιῇς φοβοῦ), because those in authority hold the power of punishment (τὴν μάχαιραν φορεῖ) and enforce justice (ἔκδοκος εἰς ὀργήν) against the one who practices evil (τῷ τὸ κακὸν πράσσοντι).

2. The governing authorities carry out service to God (13:5–7).

Paul summarizes (διό) verses 1–4 by reminding his readers that it is necessary (ἀνάγκη) to be subject (ὑποτάσσεσθαι) to governing authorities for two reasons. "Because of wrath" (διὰ τὴν ὀργήν) summarizes verses 3–4 and the state's role as God's minister that exercises its authority

---

21. Commentators are divided on whether Paul is referring to temporal judgment inflicted by human authorities (Schreiner, *Romans*, 683) or to eschatological judgment inflicted by God (Moo, *Romans*, 799). It is possible that Paul is thinking of both.

to reward good and punish evil. "Because of your conscience" (διὰ τὴν συνείδησιν) summarizes verses 1b–2 and the state's status as divinely ordained.[22] For these reasons (διὰ τοῦτο), God's people fulfill (τελεῖτε) their civic obligations.[23] Paul repeats the second reason by describing individuals engaged in public service as those who minister to God (λειτουργοὶ θεοῦ) and are consistently devoted (προσκαρτεροῦντες) to that very task (εἰς αὐτὸ τοῦτο). A summary command to repay to everyone that which is due (ἀπόδοτε πᾶσιν τὰς ὀφειλάς) introduces four specific examples of civic obligation. "Tribute" (φόρος) and "tax" (τέλος) describe fiscal obligations and most likely refer to direct taxes and indirect tariffs.[24]

"Respect" (φόβος) and "honor" (τιμή) describe moral obligations and most likely refer to proper attitudes toward imperial and local authorities.[25] Stott concludes, "Christians should accept their tax liability with good grace, paying their dues in full, both national and local, direct and indirect, and also giving proper esteem to the officials who collect and apply them."[26]

Theology and Appropriation

Stott summarizes the four main historical models of understanding the relationship between church and state. In Erastianism the state controls the church. In a theocracy, the church controls the state. Constantinianism is a compromise in which the state favors the church while the church accommodates to the state. In a partnership, church and state collaborate to recognize and encourage each other's God-given responsibilities. He concludes that "the fourth seems to accord best with Paul's teaching in Romans 13."[27]

Some scholars have suggested that Paul views government positively in Romans 13 because he wrote the letter during the first half of Nero's reign (A.D. 54–62) when the provinces experienced sound government and good order. Paul articulates the same view during the second

---

22. Schreiner defines "conscience" (συνείδησις) as "a sense of moral responsibility and obligation to conform to what is required" (*Romans*, 685).
23. See verse 7 for φορός ("tribute") as one of four specific obligations.
24. Schreiner concludes that "tribute" refers to direct tax paid by subject nations, and "tax" refers to indirect tariff levied on goods and services (*Romans*, 686).
25. It is possible that "respect" acknowledges the jurisdiction of the emperor (Jewett, *Romans*, 803), and "honor" refers to local officials (cf. Longenecker, *Romans*, 966).
26. Stott, *Romans*, 346.
27. Stott, *Romans*, 339.

half of Nero's reign, however, when he writes in 1 Timothy 2:1–2, "First of all, then, I urge that entreaties and prayer, petitions and thanksgiving be made on behalf of all men, for kings and for all who are in authority, in order that we may lead a tranquil and quiet life in all godliness and dignity" and in Titus 3:1, "Remind them to be subject to the rulers, to authorities, to be obedient, to be ready for every good deed."[28] Since both Tacitus (*Annals* 13.50–51) and Seutonius (*Lives* 6.10.1) record unhappiness over high taxes and the practices of tax collectors, it seems likely that historical context informs Paul's instructions in Romans 13:6–7. The literary context continues to be Paul's exhortation in 12:1–2 that believers are to place themselves fully at God's service in light of the mercies he has shown them. Other scholars have argued that the "authorities" Paul has in mind are angelic (cf. 1 Cor. 15:29; Eph. 1:21; 2:2; 3:10; 6:12; Col. 1:16; 2:10, 15), but Schreiner notes that such an understanding runs counter to Colossians 2:8–15, where Paul explicitly prohibits Christians from being subservient to angelic powers.[29] Given Jesus's instruction to "Render to Caesar the things that are Caesar's, and to God the things that are God's" (Matt. 22:15–22; Mark 12:13–17; Luke 20:20–26), a reference to human authorities seems more natural. Specifically, Paul instructs believers to respect three aspects of human government. First, they should respect its origin, because government is established by God (13:1–2, 5b). Second, they should respect its operation, because government is responsible to reward good and punish evil (13:3–4, 5a). Third, they should respect its ordinances and representatives, because those representatives are serving God (13:6–7). Although Acts 4:19 and 5:29 make it clear that Christians should obey God rather than human authorities, and although Revelation 13:1–18 presents human government as an ally of Satan rather than a servant of God, Paul's focus is on "the normal and usual relationship between believers and ruling powers."[30] That is, because human government is ordained by God, it deserves proper respect and submission.[31]

Paul's primary purpose for including this passage at this point in his letter was to help his readers adopt the proper perspective on the Christian's relationship to governmental authorities. With his original

---

28. Both letters are commonly dated to A.D. 63–65.
29. Schreiner, *Romans*, 682. He also notes that it is impossible to pay taxes to angels (cf. 13:6–7).
30. Schreiner, *Romans*, 686.
31. As such, Paul's instructions in Romans align with Peter's in his first letter (1 Peter 2:13–17).

readers we need to realize the divinely ordained origin and purpose for national, state, and local government agencies and their representatives. The passage offers multiple possible points of connection. The most natural is the experience of interacting with government agencies and officials. Other possible points of connection include taxes, conscience, honor, and respect. The passage corrects any suggestion that it is acceptable for a person or group to reject or oppose legally constituted government authority at any level simply because that person or group disagrees with the authority or its policies. It commends proper respect and support for government, its representatives, and its ordinances. The objective in communicating this passage should be to help others understand the biblical teaching on human government so that they will fulfill their civic, fiscal, and moral responsibilities.

ROMANS 13:8–10

Text and Translation

8 Owe nothing to anyone, except to be loving one another; for the *one who* is loving[1] the other has fulfilled the law. **9** For the[2] *commandments that say* **"You shall not commit adultery; you shall not murder; you shall not steal; you shall not covet,"**[3] and if—*assuming there is*—any other commandment,[4] it has been summed up[5] by this word,[6] **"You shall love your neighbor as yourself."** **10** Love is not working evil against the neighbor; therefore, love *is* the fulfillment of the law.[7]

Context and Structure

    II. Letter Body (1:18–15:13)
        D. The Gospel as the Transformation of God's People
           (12:1–15:13)
            1. The gospel transforms the way God's people live their
               lives (12:1–13:14)
                a. As they pursue total transformation (12:1–2)
                b. As they exercise their spiritual gifts (12:3–8)
                c. As they overcome evil with good (12:9–21)
                d. As they are subject to authorities (13:1–7)
                e. **As they love one another (13:8–10)**
                f. As they wait for Jesus's return (13:11–14)

In a brief three-sentence paragraph, Paul explains the role of the Mosaic law in lives that have been transformed by the gospel. He begins with a command and supporting reason (13:8), continues with further explanation that incorporates Old Testament evidence (13:9), and concludes with a summary statement (13:10).

---

1. Ὁ ἀγαπῶν is a substantival participle.
2. The definite article introduces the Old Testament quotations.
3. The addition of οὐ ψευδομαρτυρήσεις between οὐ κλέψεις and οὐ ἐπιθυμήσεις (א) is most likely a secondary addition to complete the list of commandments (cf. Deut. 5:19–21).
4. Εἰ introduces a first-class condition.
5. Ἀνακεφαλαιοῦται is a perfective present.
6. Ἐν τῷ λόγῳ τούτῳ denotes impersonal means.
7. Νόμου is an objective genitive (cf. verse 8).

Basic Message and Exegetical Outline

We fulfill the law by loving our neighbor.

Love and the Law (13:8–10)
1. We are obligated to love our neighbor (13:8)
2. The command to love our neighbor summarizes the Old Testament law (13:9)
3. Because love does no evil to our neighbor, it fulfills the law (13:10)

Explanation of the Text

1. We are obligated to love our neighbor (13:8).

The idea of obligation connects Paul's previous discussion of civil responsibilities (τὰς ὀφειλάς in 13:7) to a new discussion of moral responsibilities (ὀφείλετε in 13:8), as Paul moves to his fourth example of living a transformed life. His thesis statement for the brief paragraph is, again, a command: Christians must not be morally indebted to anyone in any way (μηδενὶ μηδὲν ὀφείλετε) other than the obligation to love them (εἰ μὴ τὸ ἀλλήλους ἀφαπᾶν). The reason undergirding Paul's command (γάρ) is that the person who loves his or her neighbor (ὁ ἀγαπῶν τὸν ἕτερον)[8] demonstrates that he or she has performed the Mosaic law perfectly (νόμον πεπλήρωκεν).[9] Paul proves the accuracy of his reasoning in verses 9–10.

2. The command to love our neighbor summarizes the Old Testament law (13:9).

Paul explains (γάρ) his reasoning by bringing together quotations from Exodus 20:13–17 and Leviticus 19:18. He lists four commandments from the second tablet of the Decalogue: "you shall not commit adultery" (οὐ μοιχεύσεις); "you shall not murder" (οὐ φονεύσεις); "you shall not steal" (οὐ κλέψεις); "you shall not covet" (οὐ ἐπιθυμήσεις) and adds a further qualifier—"and if—assuming there is—any other commandment" (καὶ εἴ τις ἑτέρα ἐντολή)—making the scope of his argument

---

8. Τὸν ἕτερον ("the neighbor") is equivalent to τὸν πλησίον ("the neighbor") in verses 9 and 10. The definite article particularizes the substantival adjective, and Dunn suggests "each man whom God presents as one's neighbor" (*Romans*, 776).

9. The list of commandments in verse 9 makes it clear that Paul is referring to the Mosaic law.

all-embracing. All of these commandments are "summed up completely" (ἀνακεφαλαιοῦται)[10] by the single statement (ἐν τῷ λογῷ τουτῷ) of Leviticus 19:18: "You shall love your neighbor as yourself" (ἀγαπήσεις τὸν πλησίον σου ὡς σεαυτόν).

3. Because love does no evil to our neighbor, it fulfills the law (13:10).

The representative commandments cited from Exodus prohibit harming others in some way. Love accomplishes the same end: it works no evil against a person's neighbor (ἡ ἀγάπη τῷ πλησίον κακὸν οὐκ ἐργάζεται). It is only logical to conclude (οὖν) that loving others fully accomplishes the intent of the Mosaic law (πλήρωμα νόμου ἡ ἀγάπη). Paul's logic may be set out as a syllogism.

Major premise:	The intent of the law is to prevent harm to others.
Minor premise:	Love does no harm to others.
Conclusion:	Therefore, love accomplishes the intent of the law.

Theology and Appropriation

As Dunn notes, Paul's discussion of the law earlier in Romans "was bound to raise the question of its continuing role as norm for personal and social ethics in the redefined people of God."[11] Although Paul has written that Christ is the termination of the law as a way of pursing righteousness (cf.10:4), he understands that the law is still central to the ethical teaching of the gospel. It is logical, therefore, that he would address the way in which the law relates to those whose lives have been transformed by that gospel. The connection is love, which "fulfills the law." As Stott writes, "Love and law need each other. Love needs law for its direction, while law needs love for its inspiration."[12]

There is little doubt that Paul knew and based his teaching on that of Jesus, who set out three fundamental commandments. First, Jesus taught that Deuteronomy 6:5 proclaims the "foremost" commandment: "You shall love the Lord your God with all your heart and with all your soul and with all your mind" (Matt. 22:37; Mark 12:30; Luke 10:27a). Second, he taught that Leviticus 19:18 proclaims the "royal" commandment: "You shall love your neighbor as yourself" (Matt. 22:39; Mark 12:31; Luke 10:27b; James 2:8). Together, these two laws cover both of

---

10. BDAG 65.
11. Dunn, *Romans*, 775. See also "Theology and Appropriation" under 10:5–13.
12. Stott, *Romans*, 350.

the tablets of the Decalogue; commandments 1–4 focus on loving God, while commandments 5–10 focus on loving others.[13] Third, he gave his followers the "new" commandment to "Love one another" (John 13:34–35). Although Paul bases his explanation in 13:9 on the royal commandment, it is clear that he also has the new commandment in mind when he writes, "Owe nothing to anyone, except to be loving one another" (13:8).[14] Paul's ethical teaching, therefore, aligns perfectly with that of his Lord.

Paul's primary purpose for including this passage at this point in his letter was to clarify the relationship of the law to living a transformed life in Christ. With his original readers we need to recognize that the mandate to love (i.e., do good to) others is central to Scripture's ethical teaching. The most natural point of connection to the passage is the concept of love. An old Beatles' song could be used to help capture the main point of the passage, because in order to fulfill the law "all you need is love." The idea of being a good neighbor also provides a point of connection, with the insurance company slogan "like a good neighbor . . ." as a possible illustration. The passage corrects the idea that the purpose of the law is to punish evil, when, in fact, its purpose is to promote good. It also corrects the theory that the law has no significance for a believer's walk with Christ. The passage commends a commitment to doing good to others, or as Jesus teaches, "However you want people to treat you, so treat them, for this is the law and the prophets" (Matt. 7:12). The objective in communicating this passage should be to help others understand the centrality of love to the Christian walk, so that they will fulfill God's law by doing good to others.

---

13. The same two-part schema, of course, occurs in Jesus's model prayer, where the first three petitions relate to God and the second three petitions relate to others (Matt. 6:9–14).

14. Jesus's teaching on the new commandment includes new subjects: other believers (cf. John 13:34a); a new standard: as Jesus loved (cf. John 13:34b); and new significance: proof of discipleship (cf. John 13:35).

ROMANS 13:11–14

Text and Translation

11 And this,[1] because you know[2] the time, that *it is* already the hour for you[3] to be raised from sleep; for now your salvation *is* nearer than[4] when you believed. **12** The night advanced, and the day is drawing near.[5] Therefore, let us lay aside[6] the works that are characteristic of the darkness,[7] and let us put on the weapons that are characteristic of the light. **13** Let us walk decently as in the day, not in carousing[8] and drunkenness, not in sexual impurity and excess, not in strife and jealousy; **14** but put on the Lord Jesus Christ, and do not make provision for the flesh[9] for the purpose of *obeying* its lusts. [10]

Context and Structure

II. Letter Body (1:18–15:13)
   D. The Gospel as the Transformation of God's People (12:1–15:13)
      1. The gospel transforms the way God's people live their lives (12:1–13:14)
         a. As they pursue total transformation (12:1–2)
         b. As they exercise their spiritual gifts (12:3–8)

---

1. Καὶ τοῦτο ("And this") is best understood as adverbial "heightening the force of what has been said" (Cranfield, *Romans*, 680). Wallace suggests the translation "And especially" (*Grammar*, 335).
2. Εἰδότες is an adverbial participle of cause; the perfect tense has present force.
3. The vowel exchange between ὑμᾶς (א*, A, B, C) and ἡμᾶς (𝔓⁴⁶, א², D) is common. Most commentators view ἡμᾶς as a change to parallel ἡμῶν in the second half of the sentence (e.g., Schreiner, *Romans*, 701).
4. Ἤ is comparative after ἐγγύτερον.
5. Ἤγγικεν is a perfect tense with present force.
6. Although ἀποθώμεθα (𝔓⁴⁶, D*) occurs nowhere else in Paul and is, therefore, the more difficult reading, ἀποθώμεθα has strong manuscript support (א, A, B, C, D², 33) and better fits Paul's style (cf. Eph. 4:22, 25; Col. 3:8). The middle voice is indirect, as is also the case with ἐνδυσώμωεθα in this verse and ἐνδύσασθε in verse 14.
7. Τοῦ σκότους and τοῦ φωτός are descriptive genitives.
8. The datives of the six nouns in this sequence denote manner.
9. Τῆς σαρκός is an objective genitive.
10. Εἰς ἐπιθυμίας denotes purpose.

    c. As they overcome evil with good (12:9–21)
    d. As they are subject to authorities (13:1–7)
    e. As they love one another (13:8–10)
    f. **As they wait for Jesus's return (13:11–14)**

The context for the transforming work of the gospel is the impending day of salvation. The nearness of that day should challenge Paul's readers to action (13:11). They should respond with three specific actions: put on the instruments of light (13:12), walk in the light (13:13), and make no provision for the flesh and its lusts (13:14).

Basic Message and Exegetical Outline

Because the day of salvation is near, we should rise from sleep, walk in the light, and reject the lusts of the flesh.

    Waiting for the Day of the Lord (13:11–14)
       1. Salvation is near (13:11)
       2. We should respond accordingly (13:12–14)
          a. By putting on the instruments of light (13:12)
          b. By walking as in the day (13:13)
          c. By making no provision for the flesh (13:14)

Explanation of the Text

1. Salvation is near (13:11).
    Paul introduces the fifth facet of living a transformed life with a call to action in light of the time of crisis (καὶ τοῦτο εἰδότες τὸν καιρόν).[11] Specifically, his readers should "get up" from their sleep (ὅτι ὥρα ἤδη ὑμᾶς ἐξ ὕπνου ἐγερθῆναι) and be ready for action (cf. Eph. 5:14: 1 Thess. 5:6–8). The reason (γάρ) for them to act is the imminence of their final salvation, which is nearer in time than when they initially believed (νῦν ἐγγύτερον ἡμῶν ἡ σωτηρία ἢ ὅτε ἐπίστευσαν).

2. We should respond accordingly (13:12–14).
    The night of the present age "is nearly over" (ἡ νὺξ προέκοψεν),[12]

---

11. Καιρός ("time") refers to the period of crisis associated with the last days (BDAG 498; cf. Rom. 3:26; 8:18). Elsewhere in the New Testament, ὥρα ("hour") is eschatological (cf. John 4:13; 5:25; 12:34; 1 John 2:18; Rev. 3:3, 10), as is ἡμέρα ("day") in Paul's writings (13:12; e.g., Rom. 2:5, 16).
12. NIV.

and the dawn of the age to come has drawn near (ἡ ἡμέρα ἤγγικεν).[13] The nearness of the coming age calls for three responses (οὖν). First, followers of Christ should "lay aside" any conduct that might be associated with the present age (ἀποθώμεθα τὰ ἔργα τοῦ σκότους) and "put on" only conduct that is appropriate to the new age (ἐνδυσώμεθα τὰ ὅπλα τοῦ φωτός). Second, they should live decent, proper, and presentable lives as though the new age were already present (ὡς ἐν ἡμέρᾳ εὐσχημόνως περιπατήσωμεν). Specifically, they should reject uncontrolled drink (κώμοις καὶ μέθαις), unrestrained sex (κοίταις καὶ ἀσελγαίαις), and unkind social interaction (ἔριδι καὶ ζήλῳ).[14] Third, they should clothe themselves with Christ (ἐνδύσασθε τὸν κύριον Ἰησοῦν Χριστόν)[15] and allow no opportunity for the driving force that dominates life in the present age (σάρξ) to exercise its desires (τῆς σαρκὸς πρόνοιαν μὴ ποιεῖσθε εἰς ἐπιθυμίας).

Theology and Appropriation

The background for Paul's understanding of the eschatological "day" is the Old Testament day of Yahweh's appearing to judge evil and inaugurate a future age of peace and blessing (e.g., Isa. 24:1–3; Joel 2:28–32; Amos 5:18–20). Paul uses several phrases to refer to the event of Jesus's return: "the day" (1 Cor. 3:13), "that day" (2 Tim. 1:12, 18; 4:8), "the day of Christ" (Phil. 1:6, 10; 2:16), and "the day of the Lord" (1 Cor. 1:8; 5:5; 2 Cor. 1:14; 1 Thess. 5:2; 2 Thess. 2:2). Throughout his letters three repeated words capture different aspects of the same idea. "Revealing" (ἀποκάλυψις) refers to the disclosure of Christ's power and glory (1 Cor. 1:7; 2 Thess. 1:7); "appearing" (ἐπιφάνεια) refers to Christ's glorious entrance to establish his kingdom (2 Thess. 2:8; 1 Tim. 6:14; 2 Tim. 4:1, 8; Titus 2:13); "presence" (παρουσία) describes the manifestation of Christ in his glory (1 Cor. 15:22–23; 1 Thess. 2:19; 3:13; 4:15; 5:23; 2 Thess. 2:1, 8). On "that day," Paul teaches that the dead will be raised (1 Cor. 15:23); God's people will be gathered to him (2 Thess. 2:3); evil will be destroyed (2 Thess. 2:8); everything will be made subject to Christ (1 Cor. 15:25; Eph. 1:20–23; Phil. 2:9–11); creation will be set free from the corruption caused by sin (Rom. 8:19–23); and those who have not obeyed the gospel will experience God's wrath and will

---

13. Compare the contrast between night and day in 2 Corinthians 6:14; Ephesians 5:8; 1 Thessalonians 5:4–5.
14. See Dunn for the suggestion that these three pairs of nouns represent three examples of hendiadys (*Romans*, 768).
15. Moo suggests that the idea is to "embrace Christ in such a way that his character is manifest in all we say and do" (*Romans*, 825).

be excluded from God's presence (Rom. 2:5, 8; Phil. 3:19; 5:9; 2 Thess. 1:9; 2:10). The nearness of "that day" provides motivation for Christ's followers to take seriously Paul's call to live a transformed life.

Paul's primary purpose for including this passage at this point in his letter was to help his readers understand the implications of Christ's return for living transformed lives. With his original readers we need to realize that our citizenship in the age to come should affect the way we live in the present age. The passage offers several possible points of connection, including darkness and light, night and day, and putting off/on garments. The passage corrects the idea that someone who follows Christ can continue in previous patterns of conduct. The passage commends a commitment to adopting a lifestyle consistent with citizenship in the age to come. The objective in communicating this passage should be to help others understand the nearness of the day of their ultimate salvation so that they will live today as though Christ were coming tomorrow.

ROMANS 14:1–12

Text and Translation

1 Now receive the *one who* is weak[1] with reference to the faith,[2] not for the purpose of disputing over opinions.[3] **2** One person is believing *it is acceptable* to eat all things; but the *one who* is weak[4] is eating vegetables. **3** The *one who* is eating[5] must not despise the *one who* is not eating, and the *one who* is not eating must not judge the *one who* is eating, for God received him. **4** Who are you, the *one who* is judging[6] *the members of* another's household? With reference to his own lord[7] he is standing or falling; and he will stand,[8] for his[9] lord[10] is making him able to stand. **5** For[11] one person is judging a day more than *another* day;[12] another person is judging all days *to be the same*; each one must be fully convinced in his own mind. **6** The *one who* is being concerned[13] about the day is being concerned with reference to the Lord;[14] and the *one who* is eating is eating with reference to the Lord, for he is giving thanks to God;[15] and the one *who is* not eating is not eating with reference to the Lord, and he is giving thanks to God. **7** For no one of us is living with reference to himself, and no one is dying with reference to himself; **8** for if we are living,[16] we are living with reference to the Lord; if we are dying, we are dying with reference to the Lord; therefore,

---

1. Τὸν ἀσθενοῦντα is a substantival participle.
2. Τῇ πίστει is a dative of reference.
3. Εἰς διακρίσεως denotes purpose; διαλογισμῶν is an objective genitive.
4. Ὁ ἀσθενῶν is a substantival participle.
5. Ὁ ἐσθίων is the first of four substantival participles.
6. Ὁ κρίνων depends on and defines the emphatic personal pronoun σύ.
7. Τῷ ἰδίῳ κυρίῳ is a dative of reference.
8. Σταθήσεται is intransitive; the passive form has an active meaning.
9. The definite article functions as a possessive pronoun.
10. Κύριος has strong manuscript support ($\mathfrak{P}^{46}$, ℵ, A, B, C), while θεός (D, 33) is most likely influenced by verse 3.
11. Manuscript evidence for omitting γάρ (P46, ℵᶜ, B, D, 33) is stronger than for including it (ℵ*, A). Including the conjunction, though, is the more difficult reading, because a causal/explanatory relationship between verse 4 and verse 5 is not readily evident (cf. Schreiner, *Romans*, 724).
12. Παρά + acccusative denotes comparison.
13. Ὁ φρονῶν is the first of three substantival participles.
14. Κυρίῳ is the first of seven datives of reference.
15. The dative regularly follows εὐχαριστέω (twice).
16. Ἐάν . . . ζῶμεν is the first of four third class conditions.

whether we are living or dying, we are the Lord's. **9** For to this *very purpose*[17] Christ has died[18] and became alive, in order that he might be Lord over both *the* dead and *the* living. **10** But why are you judging your brother? Or why are you also despising your brother? For all will stand before God's judgment seat,[19] **11** for it is written,

> ***As* I live, says the Lord, that to me[20] every knee will bend and every tongue will praise God.**

12 Consequently, each of us[21] will give account concerning himself[22] to God.[23]

Context and Structure

    II. Letter Body (1:18–15:13)
        D. The Gospel as the Transformation of God's People (12:1–15:13)
            1. The gospel transforms the way God's people live their lives (12:1–13:14)
            2. The gospel transforms the way God's people exercise their liberty (14:1–15:13)
                a. **By not despising one another (14:1–12)**
                b. By not judging one another (14:13–23)
                c. By seeking to please one another (15:1–6)
                d. By accepting one another (15:7–13)

The transforming power of the gospel affects the believer's practice of Christian liberty (14:1–15:13). The opening paragraph of the section follows an A-B-A' structure in which the verbs ἐξουθενέω and κρίνω link the first and third panels. An inclusion using προσλαμβάνω frames the first panel, which establishes the basic theme of the paragraph (14:1–3). The central panel sets out four guiding principles for accepting one

---

17. Εἰς τοῦτο denotes purpose.
18. Ἀπέθανεν is a consummative aorist; ἔζησεν is an ingressive aorist.
19. Τῷ βήματι is a local dative; τοῦ θεοῦ is a possessive genitive. Θεοῦ (ℵ*, A, B, C*, D) is the more likely original reading; the variant Χριστοῦ (ℵ², C²) is most likely an assimilation to 2 Corinthians 5:10.
20. Ἐμοί is a dative of advantage.
21. Ἡμῶν is a partitive genitive.
22. Περί + genitive denotes reference.
23. Τῷ θεῷ has strong manuscript support (ℵ, A, B, C* D, 33), but the reading that omits it (B) is shorter and more difficult. The decision makes little difference exegetically, because the sense is easily inferred if the object is omitted.

another (14:4–9). The third panel draws a conclusion that incorporates Old Testament support (14:10–12).

Basic Message and Exegetical Outline

We are to accept others' positions on nonessentials, because God has accepted them, Christ has died for them, and God will evaluate them.

> To Eat or Not to Eat, Part 1 (14:1–12)
> 1. Accept others, because God has accepted them (14:1–3)
>   a. Avoid disputes over nonessentials (14:1–2)
>   b. Do not despise or condemn those whom God has accepted (14:3)
> 2. Respect others, because Christ has died for them (14:4–9)
>   a. Each is responsible to his/her master (14:4)
>   b. Each must be assured in his/her mind (14:5)
>   c. Each gives thanks to God (14:6)
>   d. Each lives or dies to Christ (14:7–9)
> 3. Do not evaluate others, because God will evaluate them (14:10–12)
>   a. Do not despise or condemn your brother (14:10)
>   b. All will stand before God's judgment seat (14:11)

Explanation of the Text

1. Accept others, because God has accepted them (14:1–3).

Paul establishes the primary focus of his next topic by issuing a command to "receive the one who is weak with reference to the faith" (τὸν ἀσθενοῦντα τῇ πίστει προσλαμβάνεσθε). The "weak" and the "strong" describe two parties who held opposing positions on "the literal obedience of the ceremonial law [as] an integral element of their response of faith to Jesus Christ."[24] It seems likely that the "weak" are the Jewish

---

24. Cranfield, *Romans*, 697; see his extended discussion in pages 690–98. Jewett suggests that "weak" describes individuals who are "excessively observant in a religion" (*Romans*, 834). It is worth noting that "weak" only occurs three times in these chapters (14:1, 2; 15:1), while "strong" never occurs. The terms describe two groups of individuals who held different convictions on dietary practices (14:2–3), observing special days (14:5), and possibly abstaining from strong drink (14:21).

minority in the Roman church and the "strong" are the Gentile ma-jority.[25] Paul's command to the latter group, therefore, is that they welcome (προσλαμβάνεσθε) their Jewish brothers and sisters into their circle of fellowship despite differences in the way they express their faith (τῇ πίστει). Further, they should not engage those brothers and sisters in "disputes over opinions" (μὴ εἰς διακρίσεις διαλογισμῶν).[26]

An example of specific differences relates to dietary practices. One group—the strong—believes eating all things is permissible (ὃς μὲν πιστεύει φαγεῖν πάντα); another group—the weak—eats only vegeta-bles (ὁ δὲ ἀσθενῶν λάχανα ἐσθίει). The two groups have reciprocal re-sponsibilities. Those who eat all things must never view those who limit their diets as having no merit or worth (ὁ ἐσθίων τὸν μὴ ἐσθίοντα μὴ ἐξουθενείτω). Those who eat only vegetables must never condemn those who eat meat (ὁ δὲ μὴ ἐσθίων τὸν ἐσθίοντα μὴ κρινέτω). In either case, the reason to accept rather than despise or condemn is that God has accepted both groups (ὁ θεὸς γὰρ αὐτὸν προσελάβετο).[27]

2. Respect others, because Christ has died for them (14:4–9).

Paul sets out four principles that should guide us in relating to those who express their faith in ways that differ from our own. First, each believer is responsible to his/her master, Christ.[28] Paul explains this principle by using the example of members of a household. In such a household the individual members are responsible to the master of the household. [29] It would be inappropriate, therefore, for someone out-side that household to stand in judgment of any of its members (σὺ τίς εἶ ὁ κρινῶν ἀλλότριον οἰκέτην), because the members of that house-hold are held to the standard established by their own master (τῷ ἰδίῳ κυρίῳ στήκει ἢ πίπτει). Ultimately, each member of Christ's household

---

25. Moo specifically identifies the "weak" as Jewish members of the Roman church and the "strong" as Gentile members (*Romans*, 826–33).

26. Jewett, *Romans*, 836. Dunn writes that "newcomers should not be sub-jected to demanding discussion about their common faith and its out-working . . . and . . . the majority should not seek to impose their views and practices" (*Romans*, 798).

27. Αὐτόν ("him") is best understood as referring to individual representatives of each group (cf. Jewett, *Romans*, 841). Προσελάβετο forms an inclusio with verse 1.

28. In verse 4, both ἀλλότριος and κύριος refer to Christ.

29. Οἰκέτης describes "all persons in a typical Greco-Roman household who are dependent on the master of the house, including children, house slaves, freed persons, clients, and spouses" (Jewett, *Romans*, 842).

will receive approval from Christ (σταθήσεται δέ, δυνατεῖ γὰρ ὁ κύριος στῆσαι αὐτόν)—"whether [that member] has ours or not."[30]

Second, each believer must be fully convinced that his/her practice is one that Christ approves. Paul explains this principle by using the example of observing special days. One person might consider one day more sacred than another (ὃς μὲν γὰρ κρίνει ἡμέραν παρ᾽ ἡμέραν).[31] Another person might consider all days to be the same (ὃς δὲ κρίνει πᾶσαν ἡμέραν). The precise practice is not important; being fully convinced of the conclusion each person reaches is (ἕκαστος ἐν τῷ ἰδίῳ νοῒ πληροφορείσθω).[32]

Third, each believer should be focused on Christ and motivated by thanksgiving. The individual who is concerned about observing sacred days (ὁ φρονῶν τὴν ἡμέραν) should do so out of a concern for Christ (κυρίῳ φρονεῖ). The individual who eats more than vegetables (ὁ ἐσθίων) should do so out of respect for Christ (κυρίῳ ἐσθίει) and should be motivated by the opportunity to give thanks to God (εὐχαριστεῖ γὰρ τῷ θεῷ), while the individual who does not eat meat (ὁ μὴ ἐσθίων) should also do so out of respect for Christ (κυρίῳ οὐκ ἐσθίει) and should also be motivated by the opportunity to give thanks to God (εὐχαριστεῖ τῷ θεῷ).

Fourth, each believer should consciously seek to please Christ. The aim in expressing personal faith in Christ, whether in life or in death, is never self-interest (οὐδεὶς ἡμῶν ἑαυτῷ ζῆ, καὶ οὐδεὶς ἑαυτῷ ἀποθνήσκει).[33] Instead, our aim should always be to live for Christ (τῷ κυρίῳ ζῶμεν) and to die for him (τῷ κυρίῳ ἀποθνήσκομεν), because we belong to him (τοῦ κυρίου ἐσμέν).[34] In fact, it was for this very purpose (εἰς

---

30. Stott, *Romans*, 361.

31. Commentators are divided on the identity of the "day" in question (e.g., Cranfield, *Romans*, 705; Schreiner, *Romans*, 715), but the difference in practice is clear.

32. Jewett notes that νοῦς refers to "the constellation of thoughts and assumptions that a person holds" and that Paul's statement highlights "extraordinary confidence in the power and appropriateness of individual conviction" (*Romans*, 845).

33. Dunn notes that to "live for oneself" is to live selfishly (*Romans*, 807).

34. Schreiner comments, "In all of life and even at the hour of death the believer's aim is to please the Lord, to bring praise and honor to his name. Even at death believers resign themselves to God's will, and endeavor to please him in the way they die. This conscious submission to the Lord is based on the lordship of Christ. Both life and death are not under our control but are in the hands of the Lord, who is sovereign over both" (*Romans*, 721).

τοῦτο) that Christ both died and rose (Χριστὸς ἀπέθανεν καὶ ἔζησεν):[35] that he might exercise lordship over both the dead and the living (ἵνα καὶ νεκρῶν καὶ ζώντων κυριεύσῃ). Because he is our Lord who died for us, our aim should be to seek to please him in whatever we do.

3. Do not evaluate others, because God will evaluate them (14:10–12).

Each of the preceding principles highlights the believer's personal relationship with and accountability to Christ. It is inappropriate, therefore, for members of the weak party to evaluate and judge fellow believers who practice their piety differently (σὺ τί κρίνεις τὸν ἀδελφόν σου), just as it is inappropriate for members of the strong party to evaluate and despise fellow believers who practice their piety differently (σὺ τί ἐξουθενεῖς τὸν ἀδελφόν σου). Rather, they all should be concerned about God's evaluation of them when they stand before his judgment seat (πάντες γὰρ παραστησόμεθα τῷ βήματι τοῦ θεοῦ). As Isaiah 49:18 makes clear, God has decreed (ζῶ ἐγώ, λέγει κύριος) that every knee will bow to him (ἐμοὶ κάμψει πᾶν γόνυ) and every tongue will praise him (πᾶσα γλῶσσα ἐξομολογήσεται τῷ θεῷ).[36] We should, therefore, accept one another (14:1) because each of us (ἕκαστος ἡμῶν) will give a formal accounting to God (λόγον δώσει τῷ θεῷ) concerning our own lives (περὶ ἑαυτοῦ).

Theology and Appropriation

Later in this section of the letter (14:1–15:13), Paul identifies with the "strong" (14:14, 20; 15:1). Elsewhere in his letters, he speaks strongly against typically Jewish ceremonial observances. For example, he rejects circumcision in Galatians (5:1–15) and Philippians (3:1–16); he speaks against the observance of special days in Galatians (4:8–11) and Colossians (2:16–23); he argues that eating meat offered to idols should not be a concern for believers in 1 Corinthians (8:1–13; 10:14–33). It was Paul and Barnabas who raised concerns over Judaizers who had arrived in Antioch, and they were the messengers who brought the issue to the Jerusalem Council for discussion (Acts 15:1–35). If he

---

35. Ἔζησεν is an ingressive aorist ("began to live"). Both the sequence here and Paul's use of ζάω in Romans 5:10 and 2 Corinthians 4:10 support Murray's understanding that the verb refers to Christ's resurrection (*Romans*, 2:182).

36. The verb ἐξομολογέω usually carries the sense of "acknowledge/confess," but with the dative following (e.g., 2 Sam. 22:50; 1 Chron. 29:13; Ps. 85:12), it is better translated "praise" (cf. Moo, *Romans*, 847n106).

consistently opposed the imposition of Jewish ceremonial observances elsewhere, how can he be so tolerant in what he writes to the Romans?

The answer lies in the different concern within the Roman congregations, where the issue is one of piety not of salvation. In other letters, Paul was combatting Judaizers who taught that circumcision, for example, was a requirement for salvation. Three pieces of information set off his discussion in Romans as different. First, Paul commands the "strong" to accept the "weak" rather than reject them (14:1, 3; 15:7). The issue is not one of a "different gospel." Second, in regard to dietary restrictions, the "weak" in Rome refrained from eating meat entirely; they ate only vegetables (14:2).[37] The issue in Rome, therefore, is different from the issue in Corinth, where the focus was on eating meat sacrificed to idols (1 Cor. 8:1–13; 10:14–33). Third, Paul's use of "common/unclean" (κοινός) in 14:14 and "clean" (κάθαρος) in 14:20 points to a focus on the observance of Jewish dietary laws (cf. Mark 7:2, 5; Acts 10:14). Moo suggests that this last piece of evidence reflects situations in which "scrupulous Jews would sometimes avoid all meat in environments where they could not be sure that the meat had been prepared in a 'kosher' manner."[38] It is logical to conclude that the issue in Rome is related to differences in the way in which the two groups practiced their piety. This new issue introduces an important contribution to Paul's ethical teaching: the role of individual conviction and accountability.[39] In matters that are neither required of Christians nor prohibited to them (*adiaphora*), believers are free to follow their personal conviction (14:5). They are, however, also accountable to Christ for their actions (14:4, 6, 10–12) because of their personal relationship to him as the Lord who lived and died for them (14:7–9). Paul continues to explore this topic throughout 14:13–15:13.

Paul's primary purpose for including this passage at this point in his letter was to address tensions within the Roman congregations over practices of personal piety. With his original readers we need to learn to respect and accept the convictions of others regarding nonessential beliefs and practices. The passage offers several possible points of connection, including dietary restrictions (both voluntary and imposed), the observance of certain holy days and seasons, and convictions or

---

37. Although Paul mentions both food and drink in 14:17 and 14:21, it is likely that the combination βρῶσις καὶ πόσις is a conventional phrase (Wallace, *Grammar*, 419). He mentions special days only in 14:5–6.
38. Moo (*Romans*, 831); he notes Daniel as an example. His extended discussion of the issue in Romans 14:1–15:13 is helpful (827–33).
39. The aspect of conviction is sometimes discussed under the term "conscience."

preferences that we might hold on certain issues. The passage corrects the idea that we may impose on others our own convictions regarding nonessentials as well as any tendency we might have to view the convictions of others as somehow inferior. The passage commends respect and acceptance of other believers and recognition of others' responsibility to Christ for their beliefs and actions. The objective in communicating this passage should be to help others understand the liberty and responsibility that come from belonging to Christ so that they will accept fellow believers whose beliefs and practices differ from their own.

ROMANS 14:13–23

Text and Translation

13 Therefore, let us no longer be judging one another; but judge this instead: not to put an offense or stumbling block before your brother.[1] **14** For I know and have been persuaded in the Lord Jesus that nothing *is* unclean in itself,[2] except to the *one who* is considering[3] something to be unclean, to that one *it is* unclean. **15** For if *it is true that* your brother is being grieved by food,[4] you are no longer walking governed by love;[5] do not destroy because of your food[6] that one on behalf of whom[7] Christ has died.[8] **16** Therefore, you must not allow your good to be blasphemed.[9] **17** For God's kingdom is not eating and drinking but righteousness and peace and joy by the Holy Spirit;[10] **18** for the *one who* is serving[11] Christ in this *is* pleasing to God and esteemed by people.[12] **19** Consequently, let us be pursuing[13] the things *that make for* peace and the things *that make for* the edification of one another.[14]

---

1. Τῷ ἀδελφῷ is a locative dative; the definite article functions as a possessive pronoun.
2. Διά + genitive denotes location/sphere.
3. Τῷ λογιζομένῳ is a substantival participle.
4. Εἰ ... λυπεῖται introduces a first-class condition; διὰ βρῶμα denotes agency.
5. Κατά + accusative denotes conduct (Harris, *Prepositions*, 134).
6. Τῷ βρώματι is causal.
7. Ὑπέρ + genitive denotes representation.
8. Ἀπέθανεν is a consummative aorist.
9. Βλασφημείσθω is a permissive passive.
10. Ἐν πνεύματι ἁγίῳ denotes agency.
11. Ὁ δουλεύων is a substantival participle; δουλεύω takes a dative direct object.
12. Τοῖς ἀνθρώποις is a dative of agency.
13. There are three variant readings of the verb; present subjunctive, present indicative, and present imperative. Manuscript support for the imperative is minimal. The rest of that evidence reflects the frequent interchange between o and ω, with somewhat stronger support for the indicative διώκομεν (ℵ, A, B) than for the subjunctive διώκωμεν (C, D, 33). On the basis of internal considerations, therefore, Dunn (*Romans*, 816nf) and Jewett (*Romans*, 853ng) prefer the indicative, while Cranfield (*Romans*, 721), Moo (*Romans*, 849n1), and Schreiner (*Romans*, 743) prefer the subjunctive. The translation above follows UBS[5], which gives the subjunctive a [D] rating.
14. Τῆς εἰς ἀλλήλους functions adjectivally to modify τῆς οἰκοδομῆς; εἰς + accusative denotes advantage.

20 Do not destroy the work God accomplishes[15] because of food. On the one hand, all things *are* clean, but *eating is* evil to the person *who* is eating[16] in a way that causes stumbling.[17] **21** *It is* good not to eat meat and not to drink wine and not *to do anything* by which[18] your brother is stumbling.[19] **22** The faith that[20] you are having, have it with reference to yourself[21] before God. Blessed *is* the *one who* is not judging[22] himself with reference to *that* which[23] he is approving; **23** but the *one who* is doubting[24] if he eats[25] has been condemned, because *it is* not on the basis of faith;[26] and everything *that* is not on the basis of faith is sin.[27]

Context and Structure

II. Letter Body (1:18–15:13)
  D. The Gospel as the Transformation of God's People (12:1–15:13)
    1. The gospel transforms the way God's people live their lives (12:1–13:14)
    2. The gospel transforms the way God's people exercise their liberty (14:1–15:13)
      a. By not despising one another (14:1–12)
      b. **By not judging one another (14:13–23)**
      c. By seeking to please one another (15:1–6)
      d. By accepting one another (15:7–13)

---

15. Θεοῦ is a subjective genitive.
16. Τῷ ἀνθρώπῳ is a dative of disadvantage; ἐσθίοντι is an adjectival participle modifying ἀνθρώπῳ.
17. Διά + accusative denotes cause.
18. Ἐν + dative is instrumental.
19. Προσκόπτει (א¹, A, C) is one of two shorter readings; the other, λυπεῖται (א*), is an assimilation to verse 15. The longer readings should be considered secondary.
20. The reading that includes the relative pronoun has good manuscript support (א, A, B, C). A scribe would be more likely to omit the pronoun in order to smooth the syntax than add it.
21. Κατά + accusative denotes reference.
22. Ὁ μὴ κρίνων is a substantival participle.
23. Ἐν ᾧ denotes reference; the relative includes an embedded demonstrative.
24. Ὁ διακρινόμενος is a substantival participle.
25. Ἐὰν φάγῃ introduces a third class condition.
26. Ἐκ + genitive denotes basis (twice).
27. See the Introduction for a discussion of the doxology that appears in different manuscripts after 14:23, after 15:33, or after 16:23.

Paul moves from the principles of the preceding discussion to the implications that logically follow. The paragraph divides into four generally equal parts (14:13–15, 16–18, 19–21, 22–23), each introduced by an exhortation, prohibition, or command.

Basic Message and Exegetical Outline

We practice Christian liberty by avoiding anything that causes others to stumble, by not forcing our convictions on others, and by pursuing peace and edification with others, while maintaining our own convictions before God.

To Eat or Not to Eat, Part 2 (14:13–23)
1. Determine not to cause stumbling (14:13–15)
    a. Nothing is unclean in itself except to the one who considers it to be (14:14)
    b. Grieving another destroys Christ's work (14:15)
2. Your good must not be blasphemed (14:16–18)
    a. The kingdom of God is not eating or drinking (14:17)
    b. Obedience is pleasing to God and respected by others (14:18)
3. Pursue peace and edification (14:19–21)
    a. All things are good except to the one who eats with stumbling (14:20b)
    b. Abstaining is good if it forestalls stumbling (14:21)
4. Maintain your convictions before God (14:22–23)
    a. The one who does not judge himself is blessed (14:22b)
    b. The one who doubts is condemned because what is not of faith is sin (14:23)

Explanation of the Text

1. Determine not to cause stumbling (14:13–15).

The logical conclusion to draw from Paul's teaching in the preceding paragraph (οὖν) is that believers should no longer judge one another (μηκέτι ἀλλήλους κρίνωμεν) when they practice their piety in different ways.[28] Instead (μᾶλλον), they should "make up their

---

28. Interestingly, Paul chooses to address the weak who tend to judge others (cf. 14:3), but it is logical to conclude that a similar injunction applies to the strong who tend to despise others (cf. Jewett, *Romans*, 857).

mind"[29] (τοῦτο κρίνατε) not to place an offense or a stumbling block before a brother (τὸ μὴ τιθέναι πρόσκομμα τῷ ἀδελφῷ ἢ σκάνδαλον). In other words—to anticipate 15:1–6—they should place the welfare of others ahead of their own preferences. Although Paul is absolutely convinced (οἶδα καὶ πέπεισμαι) on the basis of the authority of the Lord Jesus (ἐν κυρίῳ Ἰησοῦ)[30] that nothing is ceremonially impure[31] (ὅτι οὐδὲν κρονόν) in itself (δι' ἑαυτοῦ), his concern is with the faith of others. If someone considers something to be unclean (τῷ λογιζομένῳ το κοινὸν εἶναι), it is unclean to that person (ἐκείνῳ κοινόν). If that brother or sister is grieved[32] (ὁ ἀδελφός σου λυπεῖται) by our approach to food (διὰ βρῶμα), our conduct is no longer governed by love (οὐκέτι κατὰ ἀγάπην περιπατεῖς) as 13:8–11 commands. We must, at any cost, avoid putting the faith of others in jeopardy. Insisting on our own approach to a nonessential practice (τῷ βρώματι σου) runs the risk of bringing eschatological destruction[33] (ἀπόλλυε) upon that one on whose behalf Christ died (ἐκαῖνον ὑπὲρ οὗ Χριστὸς ἀπέθανεν).[34]

2. Your good must not be blasphemed (14:16–18).

Because insisting on our own approach to a nonessential practice can lead to the ruin of our brother or sister (14:15), we should realize (οὖν) that we must not allow "what we regard as good"[35] (ὑμῶν τὸ ἀγαθόν) to become an object of censure (μὴ βλασφημείσθω). The key principle to remember is that the kingdom of God is not characterized by practices we prefer or prescribe (οὐ ἐστιν ἡ βασιλεία τοῦ θεοῦ βρῶσις καὶ πόσις); rather, it is characterized by qualities the Holy Spirit

---

29. NIV.
30. Paul's statement might refer to direct revelation by the risen Christ or to teaching by the historical Jesus (cf. Moo, *Romans*, 852–53). The use of the personal name, Jesus, is at least suggestive of the latter understanding (cf. Mark 7:19).
31. BDAG 552.
32. *EDNT* suggests "terrible worry and fearful distress" (2:363); Dunn suggests grievous hurt in which the integrity of a person's faith is destroyed (*Romans*, 820).
33. See Dunn (*Romans*, 821), Moo (*Romans*, 854n28), and Schreiner (*Romans*, 734).
34. This prepositional phrase echoes Paul's argument in the previous paragraph that Christ both died and rose in order to exercise his lordship over each of his followers (cf. 14:7–9). In this paragraph Christ's death on behalf of believers highlights their value to him.
35. GNB. It is probably best to understand the phrase as referring to the particular practice we consider to be a good thing.

produces: righteousness, peace, and joy (ἀλλὰ δικαιοσύνη καὶ εἰρήνη καὶ χαρά ἐν πνεύματι ἁγίῳ). Those qualities should be our focus. When we serve Christ in this way (ὁ ἐν τούτῳ δουλεύων τῷ Χριστῷ), it produces a double benefit. First and foremost, we please God (εὐάρεστος τῷ θεῷ). Second, others respect us (δόκιμος τοῖς ἀνθρώποις).

3. Pursue peace and edification (14:19–21).

Paul concludes his argument (ἄρα οὖν)[36] with an exhortation to pursue practices that result in peace with other believers (τὰ τῆς εἰρήνης διώκωμεν) and strengthen the church as a whole (καὶ τὰ τῆς οἰκοδομῆς τῆς εἰς ἀλλήλους). Such an approach is the corrective to practices that tear down God's work in the congregation[37] by focusing on nonessentials (μὴ ἕνεκεν βρώματος κατάλυε τὸ ἔργον τοῦ θεοῦ). Although all practices are ceremonially pure and fit for use (πάντα καθαρά),[38] they are evil if they cause another believer to stumble when he or she practices them (ἀλλὰ κακὸν τῷ ἀνθρώπῳ τῷ διὰ προκόμματος ἐσθίοντι).[39] The only morally advantageous approach that is pleasing to God (καλόν)[40] is to abstain from any practice that causes another to stumble (τὸ μὴ φαγεῖν κρέα μηδὲ πιεῖν οἶνον μηδὲ ἐν ᾧ ὁ ἀδελφός σου προσκόπτει).

4. Maintain your convictions before God (14:22–23).

Paul drives home his instruction by applying it to each member of the Roman church (σύ).[41] They should practice the faith they have (πίστιν ἣν ἔχεις) with reference to themselves (κατὰ σεαυτὸν) as if they were in God's presence (ἐνώπιον τοῦ θεοῦ). The basic idea is the same as in 14:4–9; that is, their primary accountability is to God whom they are seeking to please (cf. 14:18a). In his eyes, they are "blessed" (μακάριος) if they practice what they have determined is proper (ἐν ᾧ δοκιμάζει) without

---

36. Elsewhere in the letter, Paul uses the combination ἄρα οὖν to conclude a portion of his argument (cf. 5:18; 7:3, 25; 8:12; 9:16, 18). "Consequently" is a reasonable translation.
37. Cf. Jewett, *Romans*, 866.
38. The first clause echoes Jesus's teaching in Luke 11:41. See BDAG 489 for καθαρός.
39. Paul uses the particular example of dietary practices, but the implications extend to other nonessentials.
40. BDAG 505.
41. Both the absence of a coordinating conjunction (asyndeton) and the emphatic personal pronoun highlight the content of Paul's command. Moo suggests "As for you . . ." (*Romans, 861*).

self-condemnation (ὁ μὴ κρίνων ἑαυτόν).[42] If, however, their conscience is not clear (ὁ διακρινόμενος ἐὰν φάγῃ), they will stand condemned by God (κατακέκριται),[43] because they are not acting in accordance with their conviction (ὅτι οὐκ ἐκ πίστεως). In fact, any practice that is not based on faith (πᾶν ὃ οὐκ ἐκ πίστεως) is an act of sin (ἁμαρτία ἐστίν). Cranfield provides a helpful summary of the two contrasting approaches: the one who doubts in verse 23 is "the Christian who does a particular action in spite of the fact that he has not received the inner freedom to do it," and the one who has faith in verse 22 is "the Christian who does possess the inner freedom to do that which he does."[44]

Theology and Appropriation

As Paul continues his instruction on the practice of Christian liberty, he sets out a number of principles that should guide our conduct in regard to nonessentials (*adiaphora*). His teaching in these paragraphs fits within the larger framework of his overall practical theology for ethical living. Paul makes it clear (a) that there are certain virtues every follower of Christ should cultivate, and (b) that there are certain vices from which every follower of Christ should abstain. Among other passages, he sets out lists of virtues in Galatians 5:22–23; Ephesians 4:32; and Colossians 3:12–17.[45] Contrasting lists of vices appear in Galatians 5:19–21, Ephesians 4:25–31, and Colossians 3:5–10.[46]

Such lists, however, leave many issues unaddressed. In instances of such nonessentials, Paul expects believers to exercise discernment (Phil. 1:9–11; 1 Thess. 5:21). First Corinthians 8–10 and Romans 14–15 represent his longest sets of instruction on how to exercise discernment. In 1 Corinthians, Paul identifies three primary guidelines: (1) the practice must edify others (8:1–13); (2) the practice must promote the spread of the gospel (9:19–23); and (3) the practice must bring glory to God (10:23–33). Romans 14 sets out eight additional guidelines:

---

42. Note the triple wordplay in 14:22–23 (κρίνων ... διακρινόμενος ... κατακέκριται) that echoes the double wordplay in 14:13 (κρίνωμεν ... κρίνατε) and frames the paragraph.
43. Κατακέκριται is a divine passive.
44. Cranfield, *Romans*, 729.
45. A partial list of such virtues includes love, joy, peace, patience, kindness, goodness, faithfulness, gentleness, self-control.
46. A partial list of such vices includes immorality, impurity, sensuality, idolatry, sorcery, enmity, strife, jealousy, anger.

1. The practice must be done with full conviction (14:5).
2. The practice must be done with thanksgiving to God (14:6).
3. The practice must be done "to the Lord" (14:7–9).
4. The practice must not cause others to stumble (14:13–15, 20–21).
5. The practice must be done according to love (14:15).
6. The practice must advance God's kingdom purposes (14:16–18).
7. The practice must lead to peace and edification (14:19–21).
8. The practice must be based on faith (14:22–23).

In Romans 15:1–13, Paul will add a ninth guideline: the practice must follow Christ's example.

Paul's teaching on Christian liberty, therefore, balances personal conviction (i.e., faith; cf. 14:5, 22) with concern for the welfare of others (i.e., love; cf. 14:15). Stott offers the following summary, "In fundamentals, then, faith is primary, and we may not appeal to love as an excuse to deny essential faith. In non-fundamentals, however, love is primary, and we may not appeal to zeal for faith as an excuse for failures in love. Faith instructs our own conscience; love respects the conscience of others. Faith gives liberty; love limits its exercise."[47]

Paul's primary purpose for including this passage at this point in his letter was to challenge his Roman readers to put the spiritual welfare of others ahead of their own personal preferences. With his original readers we need to be willing to subordinate our own liberty for the spiritual good of others. The passage offers several possible points of connection, including judging others, giving offense to others, and receiving respect from others. The passage corrects at least three ideas: (1) that the sole focus of the Christian life is on how we practice our faith, (2) that our actions have no impact on others, and (3) that there can be a disconnect between personal conviction and ethical practice. The passage commends attitudes and actions that put others first and seek their edification. The objective in communicating this passage should be to help others understand the potential damage that can result from imposing our personal preferences and practices on others so that they will be willing to subordinate their own liberty for the spiritual welfare of other believers.

---

47. Stott, *Romans*, 375.

ROMANS 15:1-6

Text and Translation

1 Now we, the *ones who are* able, ought to be bearing with the weaknesses of the *ones who are* not able, and not to be pleasing ourselves. **2** Each one of us[1] must please his neighbor[2] for his good[3] with a view to edification.[4] **3** For even[5] Christ did not please himself, but just as it is written. **"The reproaches of the *ones who* are reproaching[6] you fell upon me."** **4** For as many things as were written previously, were written for the purpose of our teaching,[7] in order that by the perseverance[8] and encouragement that come from the Scriptures[9] we might be having hope. **5** And may the God who produces perseverance and encouragement[10] give you to be thinking the same thing among one another in accordance with Christ Jesus,[11] **6** in order that with one mind *and* with one voice you might glorify the God and Father of our Lord Jesus Christ.[12]

Context and Structure

   II. Letter Body (1:18–15:13)
     D. The Gospel as the Transformation of God's People (12:1–15:13)
        1. The gospel transforms the way God's people live their lives (12:1–13:14)
        2. The gospel transforms the way God's people exercise their liberty (14:1–15:13)

---

1. Ἡμῶν is a partitive genitive.
2. Ἀρέσκω takes a dative direct object; the definite article functions as a possessive pronoun.
3. Εἰς + accusative denotes purpose; the definite article functions as a possessive pronoun.
4. Πρός + accusative denotes purpose.
5. Καί is ascensive.
6. Τῶν ὀνειδιζόντων is a substantival participle; the genitive case is objective.
7. Εἰς + accusative denotes purpose.
8. Διά + genitive is instrumental (twice).
9. Τῶν γραφῶν is a genitive of source.
10. Τῆς ὑπομονῆς and τῆς παρακλήσεως are genitives of product.
11. Κατά + accusative denotes standard.
12. Τοῦ κυρίου is a genitive of relationship; Ἰησοῦ Χριστοῦ is a genitive of apposition.

    a. By not despising one another (14:1–12)
    b. By not judging one another (14:13–23)
    c. **By seeking to please one another (15:1–6)**
    d. By accepting one another (15:7–13)

Paul's third paragraph on Christian liberty consists of three parts. The first highlights the importance of bearing with others' weaknesses (15:1–2). The second uses Christ's example and an Old Testament quotation as theological rationale for the preceding admonitions (15:3–4). The third is a prayer-wish for God to provide the readers with the enabling they need to apply the teaching (15:5–6).

Basic Message and Exegetical Outline

Bearing with others' weaknesses promotes edification, follows Christ's example, and brings glory to God.

      Put Your Brother/Sister First (15:1–6)
        1. We should bear with others' weaknesses (15:1–2)
           a. By pleasing our neighbor (15:1)
           b. For the purpose of edification (15:2)
        2. We should follow Christ's example (15:3–4)
           a. Who did not please himself (15:3)
           b. Whose example gives us instruction and hope (15:4)
        3. God will help us think the same way together (15:5–6)
           a. According to the standard Christ set (15:5)
           b. In order to glorify God together (15:6)

Explanation of the Text

1. We should bear with others' weaknesses (15:1–2).
    Paul shifts his perspective to align himself with the "strong" (ἡμεῖς οἱ δυνατοί) and drive home his point. He reminds them of their moral obligation (ὀφείλομεν) to carry the burdens (βαστάζειν) that are the "conscientious scruples" (τὰ ἀσθενήματα)[13] of the "weak" (τῶν ἀδυνάτων) and, so, to put the welfare of others ahead of their self-interest (καὶ μὴ ἑαυτοῖς ἀρέσκειν). Putting the welfare of others first cuts both ways, however, as Paul makes clear by commanding "each one of us" (ἕκαστος ἡμῶν)—that is, both strong and weak—to put his/her neighbor first

---

13. BDAG 142.

(τῷ πλησίον ἀρεσκέτω) with the purpose of doing what is good (εἰς τὸ ἀγαθόν) which, in turn, leads to the building up of the congregation (πρὸς οἰκοδομήν).

2. We should follow Christ's example (15:3–4).

The reason to put others first (γάρ) is the example Christ provides: he did not put himself first (ὁ Χριστὸς οὐχ ἑαυτῷ ἤρεσεν). Instead, as Psalm 68:10 testifies (ἀλλὰ καθὼς γέγραπται), he bore the humiliating verbal abuse that was intended for us (οἱ ὀνειδισμοὶ τῶν ὀνειδιζόντων σε ἐπέπεσαν ἐπ’ ἐμέ). In fact, those words that David wrote in the Old Testament (ὅσα προεγράφη) were specifically intended to instruct us (εἰς τὴν ἡμετέραν διδασκαλίαν ἐγράφη) in order that (ἵνα) we might have the confident expectation (τὴν ἐλπίδα ἔχωμεν) through the perseverance and encouragement (διὰ τῆς ὑπομονῆς καὶ δια τῆς παρακλήσεως) that comes from Scripture (τῶν γραφῶν).

3. God will help us think the same way together (15:5–6).

The very God of Scripture who produces that perseverance and encouragement in us (ὁ θεὸς τῆς ὑπομονῆς καὶ τῆς παρακλήσεως) will also give to us (δώῃ ὑμῖν) the ability to have the same corporate point of view (τὸ αὐτὸ φρονεῖν ἐν ἀλλήλους),[14] a point of view that is "modeled on and obedient to" the standard set by Christ Jesus (κατὰ Χριστὸν Ἰησοῦν).[15] The purpose (ἵνα) of having the same point of view is that, with one mind (ὁμοθυμαδόν) and with one voice (ἐν ἑνὶ στόματι), we might glorify the God who is also the Father of our Lord Jesus Christ (δοξάζητε τὸν θεὸν καὶ πατέρα τοῦ κυρίου ὑμῶν Ἰησοῦ Χριστοῦ).

Theology and Appropriation

Christ and his work are central to Paul's theology (e.g., Rom. 5:6–11). It is, however, interesting to note that Paul rarely refers to Christ's teaching (e.g., Rom. 13:7 is most likely an allusion to Matt. 22:15–22; Mark 12:13–17; Luke 20:20–26) and only seldom uses Christ as an example for ethical living.[16] In this passage (Rom. 15:3–4), he uses Christ's example of not pleasing himself to challenge his readers to put the interests of others first. In 1 Corinthians 11:1, Paul alludes to his

---

14. GNB.
15. Cf. Dunn, *Romans*, 840.
16. Elsewhere in the New Testament letters, Christ as an example for ethical living occurs only twice, both times in 1 Peter. Peter cites Christ's example of trust rather than verbal retaliation in response to persecution (1 Peter 2:21–25) and his example of resisting sin (1 Peter 4:1–6).

own imitation of Christ to reinforce his willingness to limit his liberty for the good of the gospel. In Ephesians 5:1–2, he uses the example of Christ's sacrificial love to challenge his readers to act lovingly toward others. In Ephesians 5:25–28, he uses the example of Christ's willingness to love and give himself for the church as the model for the way in which husbands should care for their wives. The emphasis on unity (Phil. 2:1–4) in the context of the well-known hymn of Philippians 2:5–11 brings that passage closest to Romans 15:1–6. Christ's example of humility should lead the Philippians to "regard one another as more important than himself" (2:3) and to "look out . . . for the interests of others" (2:4). What these passages have in common is the emphasis on being willing to pursue the spiritual well-being of others.

Paul's primary purpose for including this passage at this point in his letter was to challenge his Roman readers to promote unity in nonessential matters by seeking to please others with whom they disagreed. With his original readers we need to place the spiritual well-being of others ahead of our own self-interests. The passage offers several possible points of connection, including the idea of seeking to please others and the virtues of perseverance and encouragement. The passage corrects the often-expressed advice that we should "look out for number one," and "if you don't look out for yourself, no one else will." The passage commends a willingness to forgo individual liberty in order to pursue corporate unity and edification.[17] The objective in communicating this passage should be to help others understand the importance of promoting corporate unity so that they will give priority to actions that edify and encourage fellow believers.

---

17. "Think the same thing among one another" (15:5) and "with one mind and with one voice" (15:6) highlight Paul's emphasis on unity.

ROMANS 15:7–13

Text and Translation

7 Therefore, accept one another, just as also[1] Christ accepted you[2] in order for God to receive glory.[3] **8** For I am saying *that* Christ has become a minister[4] to the circumcision[5] for the sake of God's truthfulness,[6] in order to confirm[7] the promises given to the fathers,[8] **9** and in order for the Gentiles to glorify God because of *his* mercy,[9] just as it is written,

> **Because of this I will confess you among the Gentiles,**
> **and I will sing praise to your name.**

10 And again it says,

> **Rejoice, Gentiles, with his people.**[10]

11 And again,

> **Praise the Lord, all the Gentiles,**
> **and all the peoples must celebrate him.**

12 And again Isaiah says,

> **There will be a root *who comes* from Jesse,**[11]
> **and the one who is arising to be ruling the Gentiles;**[12]
> **in him the Gentiles will hope.**

---

1. Καί is adjunctive.
2. Ὑμᾶς (ℵ, A, C, D², 33) has stronger manuscript support than ἡμᾶς (B, D*). It is also preferable on internal grounds because it includes both the strong and the weak, while ἡμᾶς would refer only to one of the groups.
3. Εἰς + accusative denotes purpose; τοῦ θεοῦ is an objective genitive.
4. Χριστὸν διάκονον γεγενῆσθαι is indirect discourse.
5. Περιτομῆς is an objective genitive; the noun is a metonymy for the Jewish people.
6. Ὑπέρ + genitive denotes motive; θεοῦ is a subjective genitive.
7. Εἰς τό + infinitive denotes purpose; δοξάσθαι in verse 8 adds a second infinitive of purpose.
8. Τῶν πατέρων is an objective genitive.
9. Ὑπέρ + genitive denotes cause.
10. Μετά + genitive denotes association.
11. Τοῦ Ἰεσσαί is a genitive of relationship.
12. Ὁ ἀνιστάμενος is a substantival participle; ἄρχειν is an infinitive of purpose; ἐθνῶν is a genitive of direct object.

13 And may the God who produces peace[13] fill you with all joy and peace while *you are* believing,[14] so that you might abound[15] with reference to hope[16] by the power the Holy Spirit gives.[17]

Context and Structure

    II. Letter Body (1:18–15:13)
        D. The Gospel as the Transformation of God's People (12:1–15:13)
            1. The gospel transforms the way God's people live their lives (12:1–13:14)
            2. The gospel transforms the way God's people exercise their liberty (14:1–15:13)
                a. By not despising one another (14:1–12)
                b. By not judging one another (14:13–23)
                c. By seeking to please one another (15:1–6)
                d. **By accepting one another (15:7–13)**

Paul concludes his discussion of Christian liberty by pointing to Christ's example of acceptance. An initial command to accept one another connects back to the beginning of Paul's argument (15:8; cf. 14:1–3). An extended reflection on Christ's example confirms God's purpose for the Gentiles (15:9–12) and provides proof from the writings (Pss. 18:49; 117:1), the law (Deut. 32:43), and the prophets (Isa. 11:10). Paul closes the paragraph with a prayer-wish (15:13).

Basic Message and Exegetical Outline

Following Christ's example of acceptance brings glory to God and results in hope, joy, and peace.

    Christ's Example of Acceptance (15:7–13)
        1. We should accept one another (15:7)
            a. As Christ accepted us (15:7)
            b. For God's glory (15:7)
        2. Christ's ministry unites Jews and Gentiles (15:8–12)

---

13. Ἐλπίδος is a genitive of product.
14. Ἐν τῷ + present tense infinitive denotes contemporaneous time.
15. Εἰς τό + infinitive denotes result.
16. Τῇ ἐλπίδι is a dative of reference.
17. Ἐν δυνάμει is instrumental; πνεύματος ἁγίου is a subjective genitive.

      a. To confirm the promises to the fathers (15:8)
      b. To allow the Gentiles to praise God (15:9–12)
    3. God will fill us with joy and peace, resulting in hope
       (15:13)

Explanation of the Text

1. We should accept one another (15:7).

As Paul began his extended discussion with a command to receive others in 14:1 (τὸν ἀσθενοῦντα τῇ πίστει προσλαμβάνεθε), he concludes the discussion with a command to receive one another (προσλαμβάνεσθε ἀλλήλους).[18] His command is the logical implication (διό) that follows from the immediately preceding paragraph where he introduced Christ's example (15:3–4). To reinforce the command, Paul adds two qualifiers. First, we are to receive one another in the same way that Christ also received us (καθὼς καὶ ὁ Χριστὸς προσελάβετο ὑμᾶς).[19] Second, when we do, "God will be given the glory" (εἰς δόξαν τοῦ θεοῦ).[20] Rather than engaging in "disputes over opinions" about nonessentials (cf. 14:1), therefore, we should focus on what really matters: following Christ's example and promoting God's glory.

2. Christ's ministry unites Jews and Gentiles (15:8–12).

The central section of the paragraph provides an explanation (γάρ) of the way in which Christ's work brings together groups that historically are at odds—specifically, Jews and Gentiles.[21] Paul's statement that "Christ has become a minister to the circumcision" (Χριστὸν διάκονον γεγενῆσθαι περιτομῆς)[22] reflects Jesus's own sense of his calling to the lost sheep of the house of Israel (Matt. 15:24), and the qualifier "on behalf of God's truthfulness" (ὑπὲρ ἀληθείας θεοῦ) highlights God's

---

18. Jewett notes that the use of ἀλλήλους includes both the "strong" and the "weak" (*Romans*, 888).

19. Ὁ Χριστός is best understood as a title: "The Messiah" (cf. Moo, *Romans*, 875n10).

20. GNB. Εἰς + accusative denotes purpose; τοῦ θεοῦ is an objective genitive.

21. Moo provides the helpful comment that "the barrier between 'strong' and 'weak' is at root the barrier between Jew and Gentile" (*Romans*, 875), which explains the connection between the preceding discussion and the current explanation.

22. Γεγενῆσθαι is an intensive perfect "that emphasizes continuing result beyond Jesus's earthly life and ministry" (Harvey, *Romans*, 352). Περιτομῆς is an objective genitive; the noun is a metonymy for the Jewish people.

covenant faithfulness. To the Jews, Christ confirmed God's promises to the fathers (βεβαιῶσαι τὰς ἐπαγγελίας τῶν πατέρων). To the Gentiles, Christ extended mercy so that they would glorify God (τὰ ἔθνη ὑπὲρ ἐλέους δοξάσαι τὸν θεόν). Both groups now stand on equal footing before God with equal responsibility before him (cf. 14:10–12) and to one another (15:1–2, 7).

Paul supports his explanation with quotations from each of the three major portions of the Old Testament: the law (Deut. 32:43), the prophets (Isa. 11:10), and the writings (Pss. 18:49; 117:1). Each quotation highlights the inclusion of the Gentiles in God's plan. Psalm 18:49 reflects God's intent that he would be confessed among the Gentiles (ἐξομολογήσομαί σοι ἐν ἔθνεσιν). Deuteronomy 32:43 calls the Gentiles to join the Jews in praising God (εὐφράνθητε, ἔθνη, μετὰ τοῦ λαοῦ αὐτοῦ). Psalm 117:1 "stresses the fact that no people is to be excluded from this common praise" (αἰνεῖτε, πάντα τὰ ἔθνη, τὸν κύριου . . . ἐπαινεσάτωσαν αὐτὸν πάντες οἱ λαοί).[23] Isaiah 11:10 predicts the coming of the "root of Jesse" (ἔσται ἡ ῥιξα τοῦ Ἰεσσαί), who will rule the Gentiles (ἄρχειν ἐθνῶν) and give them an object of hope (ἐπ᾽ αὐτῷ ἔθνη ἐλπιοῦσιν).

3. God will fill us with joy and peace, resulting in hope (15:13).

Paul's wish for his readers is that, as they follow Christ's example by receiving one another, the God of hope (ὁ θεὸς τῆς ἐλπίδος) might fill them (πλψρώσαι ὑμᾶς) with all joy and peace (πάσης χαρᾶς καὶ εἰρήνης) as they respond in faith (ἐν τῷ πιστεύειν) to his instruction. The end result is that they will abound with reference to hope (εἰς τὸ περισσεύειν ὑμᾶς ἐν τῇ ἐλπίδι) as the Holy Spirit gives them power (ἐν δυνάμει πνεύματος ἁγίου). This prayer-wish concludes the paragraph (15:7–13), the extended discussion of Christian liberty (14:1–15:13), and the letter body as a whole (1:18–15:13).

Theology and Appropriation

The Old Testament establishes the truth that God does not show partiality (Deut. 10:19; 2 Chron. 19:7), and Peter affirmed it for the early church (Acts 10:34; cf. 1 Peter 1:17). Paul also affirms God's impartiality (Rom. 2:11; cf. Gal. 2:6; Eph. 6:9; Col. 3:25) and is particularly concerned to establish that there is no distinction between Jew and Greek (Rom. 10:12–13; Gal. 3:28; Col. 3:10–11). It is true that the Jews have priority in God's plan—"to the Jew first then to the Greek" (Rom. 1:16; 2:9)—but both stand on the same footing before God. Both Jew and Greek are under sin (Rom. 3:9); God is the God of both (Rom. 3:29); members of the

---

23. Cranfield, *Romans*, 746.

body are called from both Jews and Greeks (1 Cor. 1:24); all are baptized into one body, whether Jews or Greek (1 Cor. 12:13).

Ephesians 2:11–22, in particular, develops the unity Christ has created between Jew and Gentile. Apart from Christ, the Gentiles were separated, excluded, without hope, and without God (vv. 11–12). Christ's work, however, brought them near (vv. 13–15a), so that Jews and Gentiles are now "one new man" (vv. 15b–18), fellow-citizens, and members of God's household (vv. 19–22). The author of *Preaching of Peter* summarized this new reality by writing that "we who worship God in a new way, as the third race, are Christians."[24] As members of this new race, therefore, both Jewish and Gentile believers join in glorifying God by confessing him among the nations, rejoicing in him, praising him, and celebrating him (Rom. 15:9–11).

Paul's primary purpose for including this passage at this point in his letter was to conclude his instruction on Christian liberty by reminding his readers that Christ has accepted both Jewish and Gentile members of the Roman congregations on the basis of his work for them. With his original readers, we need to accept one another regardless of ethnic and cultural differences or concerns over nonessential matters. One significant point of connection to this passage is contemporary awareness of globalization that encourages us to welcome/accept "all peoples" from "all nations." The passage corrects any inclination toward ethnocentricity or exclusivity within the body of Christ. The passage commends a willingness to embrace others in Christ's body on the basis of his work on their behalf. The objective in communicating this passage should be to help others understand that Christ's work unites them in a way that transcends differences of ethnicity, theology, or personal piety, so that they will focus on their oneness in Christ that glorifies God rather than on comparatively minor differences that lead to disputes and conflicts.

---

24. Quoted in Clement of Alexandria, *Strom.* 6.5.41.6. Cf. *Epistle of Diognetus* 1.

ROMANS 15:14–16:27
Letter Closing

Since Paul's extended argument ends at 15:13, it seems most natural to view the remainder of the letter as the closing. Doing so aligns with a rhetorical analysis of the letter, which identifies 15:14–16:27 as the *Peroratio* (conclusion). There are eight distinct sections within the letter closing of Romans: an overview of Paul's mission (15:14–21), a preview of Paul's travel plans (15:22–29), a prayer request for Paul's upcoming visit to Jerusalem (15:30–33), a commendation of Phoebe (16:1–2), greetings from Paul (16:3–16), closing advice (16:17–20), greetings from others (16:21–24), and a doxology (16:25–27).

The parallels between the letter opening and the letter closing are noteworthy:

1:2	διὰ τῶν προφητῶν αὐτοῦ ἐν γραφαῖς ἁγίαις	16:26	διά γραφῶν προφητικῶν
1:5	δι' οὗ ἐλάβομεν χάριν	15:15	διὰ τὴν χάριν τὴν δοθεῖσάν μοι
1:5	εἰς ὑπακοὴν πίστεως	15:18	εἰς ὑπακοὴν ἐθνῶν
1:5	ἐν πᾶσιν τοῖς ἔθνεσιν	15:16	εἰς τὰ ἔθνη
1:9	ᾧ λατρεύω . . . τῷ εὐαγγελίῳ	15:16	λειτουργὸν . . . τὸ εὐαγγέλιον
1:10	ἐπὶ τῶν προσευχῶν μου	15:30	ἐν ταῖς προσευχαῖς ὑπὲρ ἐμοῦ
1:10	ἐν τῷ θελήματι τοῦ θεοῦ	15:32	διὰ θελήματος θεοῦ
1:11	ἐπιποθῶ γὰρ ἰδεῖν ὑμᾶς	15:23	ἐπιποθίαν . . . τοῦ ἐλθεῖν πρὸς ὑμᾶς
1:11	εἰς τὸ στηριχθῆναι ὑμᾶς	16:25	τῷ δυναμένῳ ὑμᾶς στηρίξαι
1:14	ὀφειλέτης εἰμί	15:27	ὀφείλουσιν
1:15	εὐαγγελίσασθαι	15:20	εὐαγγελίζεσθαι

These parallels serve to bracket the content expounded in the body of the letter. Because the opening and closing of letters serve rhetorically to establish and/or maintain personal relations between the writer and the reader, Paul returns to themes and ideas first introduced in 1:1–17 in order to reinforce his purpose(s) in writing. The discussion of his mission, travel plans, and prayer request (15:14–33) highlights his apostolic authority and ministry (cf. 1:1–7). The commendation, greetings, and closing advice (16:1–24) highlight the inclusiveness and effectiveness of the gospel he preaches (cf. 1:8–15). The doxology (16:25–27) highlights both the wisdom of God and the richness and depth of the gospel (cf. 1:16–17).

III. Letter Closing (15:14–16:27)
    A. Paul's Mission (15:14–21)
    B. Paul's Travel Plans (15:22–29)
    C. Paul's Prayer Request (15:30–33)
    D. Commendation of Phoebe (16:1–2)
    E. Greetings from Paul (16:3–16)
    F. Closing Advice (16:17–20)
    G. Greetings from Others (16:21–24)
    H. Doxology (16:25–27)

ROMANS 15:14-21

Text and Translation

14 Now I am persuaded, my brothers, even[1] I myself[2] concerning you,[3] that you yourselves[4] also[5] are full of goodness,[6] having been filled[7] with all knowledge, being able also[8] to be admonishing one another. **15** But I wrote more boldly to you on some points,[9] so as to cause you to remember[10] because of the grace[11] *that* was given[12] to me by God, **16** in order for me to be[13] a minister of Christ Jesus to the Gentiles *who is* serving[14] the gospel of God as a priest, in order that the offering that is the Gentiles[15] might be acceptable, sanctified[16] by the Holy Spirit.[17] **17** Therefore, I am having this[18] boasting about Christ Jesus[19] with reference to the things concerning God;[20] **18** for I will not dare to be speaking anything about those things that[21] Christ accomplished through me resulting in the obedience by the Gentiles,[22] by word and by work,[23] **19** by power that

---

1. Καί is ascensive.
2. Ἀυτὸς ἐγώ is emphatic.
3. Περί + genitive denotes reference.
4. Αὐτοί is emphatic.
5. Καί is adjunctive.
6. Ἀγαθωσύνης is a genitive of content following μεστοί; so also γνώσεως following πεπληρωμένοι.
7. Πεπληρωμένοι is an adjectival participle; it functions as a second predicate adjective that is parallel to ἀγαθωσύνης.
8. Καί is adjunctive.
9. Elsewhere, ἀπὸ μέρους carries the sense of "partially" (cf. 11:25; 15:24).
10. Ἐπαναμιμνήσκων is an adverbial participle; ὡς indicates purpose.
11. Διά + accusative denotes purpose.
12. Τὴν δοθεῖσαν is an adjectival participle modifying χάριν.
13. Εἴς το + infinitive denotes purpose.
14. Ἰερουργοῦντα is an adjectival participle modifying λειτουργόν.
15. Τῶν ἐθνῶν is a genitive of apposition.
16. Ἡγιασμένη is an adjectival participle modifying προσφορά.
17. Ἐν + dative is instrumental.
18. The definite article functions as a demonstrative adjective.
19. Ἐν + dative identifies the object of boasting (cf. Harris, *Prepositions*, 133).
20. Πρός + accusative denotes reference.
21. Ὧν includes an embedded demonstrative and is equivalent to ἐκείνων ἅ οὐ (cf. Cranfield, *Romans*, 758).
22. Εἰς + accusative denotes result; τῶν ἐθνῶν is a subjective genitive.
23. Both λόγῳ and ἔργῳ are datives of means; ἐν δυνάμει that follows also denotes means (twice).

produces signs[24] and wonders, by the power from God's Spirit;[25] so that[26] from Jerusalem[27] and around[28] as far as Illyricum I have fulfilled the gospel about Christ,[29] **20** but *I have done it* in this way:[30] by making it my aim[31] to preach not where Christ is named, in order that I might not build on another's foundation, **21** but just as it is written,

To whom it was not announced concerning him,[32] they will see,

And the *ones who* had not heard,[33] they will understand.

Context and Structure

III. Letter Closing (15:14–16:27)
  A. **Paul's Mission (15:14–21)**
  B. Paul's Travel Plans (15:22–29)
  C. Paul's Prayer Request (15:30–33)
  D. Commendation of Phoebe (16:1–2)
  E. Greetings from Paul (16:3–16)
  F. Closing Advice (16:17–20)
  G. Greetings from Others (16:21–24)
  H. Doxology (16:25–27)

Paul begins the letter closing with an overview of his mission. He includes a similar overview (the "apostolic apologia") in six of his other letters (2 Cor. 1:12–24; Gal. 1:11–2:10; Eph. 3:1–13; Phil. 1:12–26; Col.

---

24. Σημείων and τεράτων are both genitives of product.
25. Πνεύματος is a genitive of source. Although πνεύματος is the shortest reading, it has the weakest manuscript support (B). Πνεύματος ἁγίου (A, D*, 33) occurs five other times in Paul's letters (Rom. 5:5; 15:13; 1 Thess. 1:6; 2 Tim. 1:14; Titus 3:5) and is most likely an assimilation to 15:13. Πνεύματος θεοῦ ($\mathfrak{P}^{46}$, ℵ, D¹) occurs nowhere else in Paul's letters and, therefore, is the more difficult reading.
26. Ὥστε . . . πεπληρωκέναι is adverbial of result.
27. Ἀπό . . . μέχρι establishes the easternmost (Jerusalem) and westernmost (Illyricum) extents of Paul's preaching.
28. The adverb κύκλῳ describes the completing of a circuit.
29. Τοῦ Χρισστοῦ is an objective genitive.
30. Οὕτως points forward to the means by which Paul has carried his preaching of the gospel.
31. Φιλοτιμούμενον is an adverbial participle of means.
32. Περί + genitive denotes reference.
33. Οἳ οὐκ ἀκηκόασιν is a substantival participle.

1:24–29; 1 Thess. 2:1–12).[34] The paragraph consists of three parts. Paul begins by expressing his confidence in the Romans' character (15:14). He then explains his apostolic authority (15:15–16). He concludes by describing the nature, scope, and strategy of his ministry (15:17–21).

Basic Message and Exegetical Outline

Paul writes to the Romans because he has confidence in their character, has received apostolic authority, and has fulfilled his ministry in the East.

Paul's Motivation for Writing to the Romans (15:14–21)
1. Paul has confidence in the Romans' character (15:14)
   a. They are full of goodness and knowledge (15:14b)
   b. They are able to admonish one another (15:14c)
2. Paul has received apostolic authority (15:15–16)
   a. To be a priestly minister of Christ Jesus to the Gentiles (15:16a)
   b. To serve the gospel as a priest (15:16b)
   c. To present a well-pleasing offering (15:16c)
3. Paul has fulfilled his ministry in the East (15:17–21)
   a. Empowered by Christ's working and the Spirit's power (15:17–19a)
   b. From Jerusalem to Illyricum (15:19b)
   c. By focusing on pioneer preaching (15:20–21)

Explanation of the Text

1. Paul has confidence in the Romans' character (15:14).

As he prepares to explain his apostolic mission (15:15–21) and sketch his travel plans (15:22–29), Paul uses a statement of confidence (πέπεισμαι; cf. 8:38; 14:14) to highlight the character of his Roman readers and secure their support for his upcoming activities. Adding "my brothers" (ἀδελφοί μου) adds warmth; including "even I myself" (καὶ αὐτὸς ἐγώ) emphasizes his personal concern for them (περὶ ὑμῶν). In particular, Paul highlights three aspects of their character. First,

---

34. Jervis, following Funk, includes this paragraph in the apostolic parousia as the "writing unit" (*Purpose of Romans*, 111). The writing unit, however, is the least represented portion of the apostolic parousia, occurring in only four of the eleven letters other than Romans, and each of the other sections is far shorter. Romans 15:14–21 seems more naturally related to the "apologia" sections that occur in other letters.

they are "full of goodness" (μεστοί ἐστε ἀγαθωσύνης); that is, they are characterized by an interest in the welfare of others.[35] This quality stands in strong contrast to sinful humankind, who have been previously described as "full of" (μεστούς) envy, murder, strife, deceit, and meanness (cf. 1:29). Second, they are "filled with all knowledge" (πεπληρωμένοι πάσης τῆς γνώσεως); that is, they have comprehensive insight into God's saving purposes.[36] This quality also stands in contrast to sinful humankind, who have been previously described as "filled" (πεπληρωμένους) with all unrighteousness, wickedness, covetousness, and evil (cf. 1:29). Third, they are "able also to admonish one another" (δυνάμεμοι καὶ ἀλλήλους νουθετεῖν); that is, they have the concern for others and the spiritual insight they need in order to counsel each other regarding potentially improper conduct.[37] By affirming that they are able to instruct one another, Paul acknowledges that they need no further instruction from him.

2. Paul has received apostolic authority (15:15–16).

Nevertheless (δέ), Paul has been "rather bold" (τολμηρότερον) in writing to them (ἔγραψα ὑμῖν) "on some points" (ἀπὸ μέρους) with the purpose of causing them to remember (ὡς ἐπαναμιμνῄσκων ὑμᾶς) what they already know and believe.[38] He has authority to write, however, because of the grace God gave him (διὰ τὴν χάριν τὴν δοθεῖσάν μοι ὑπὸ τοῦ θεοῦ). The purpose of this gift of grace was that Paul might be a priestly minister[39] of Christ Jesus to the Gentiles (εἰς τὸ εἶναι με λειτορυργὸν Χριστοῦ Ἰησοῦ εἰς τὰ ἔθνη). The fact that Gentile Christians comprise

---

35. BDAG 4.
36. Dunn, *Romans*, 858.
37. BDAG 679. Cranfield writes, "What is denoted is the earnest attempt by words spoken (or written) to correct what is wrong in another, to encourage him to do what is right and to refrain from what is evil" (*Romans*, 753n3). Although Jewett connects this phrase to Paul's instructions in 14:1–15:13 regarding the "strong" and "weak" (*Romans*, 905), it is not clear Paul has that particular issue in mind.
38. Moo suggests that ". . . the things he has taught them and exhorted them to do all derive from the faith that they hold in common with Paul. In his letter Paul has done nothing but to explicate, for them in their circumstances, the implications of the gospel" (*Romans*, 889).
39. Although Paul uses λειτουργός in 13:7 to refer to the ministry of civil authorities, the cultic terms that follow in the immediate context (ἱερουγοῦντα, προσφορά, εὐπρόσδεκτος, ἡγιασμένη) support a priestly understanding (cf. Schreiner, *Romans*, 766). Jewett notes further connections to 1:9 and 12:1 (*Romans*, 907).

the majority of the members in the Roman congregations brings his readers into Paul's sphere of activity as one who "serves the gospel of God as a priest" (ἱερουγοῦντα τὸ εὐαγγέλιον τοῦ θεοῦ). As a priest, his calling is to present the Gentiles as a voluntary offering that God finds acceptable (ἵνα γένηται ἡ προσφορὰ τῶν ἐθνῶν εὐπρόσδεκτος)[40] because the Holy Spirit has set him apart (ἡγιασμένη ἐν πνεύματι ἁγίῳ).

3. Paul has fulfilled his ministry in the East (15:17–21).

Paul's description of his apostolic ministry follows logically (οὖν) from the role God has given him. Any reason Paul might have to claim that his offering of the Gentiles is acceptable to God and set apart by the Holy Spirit (τὴν καύχησιν)[41] must be qualified in two ways. It is "about all Christ Jesus has done" (ἐν Χριστῷ Ἰησοῦ),[42] and it is with reference to what God has called him to do (τὰ πρὸς τὸν θεόν). He continues by explaining (γάρ) that he would not even dare to talk about anything (οὐ τολμήσω τι λαλεῖν) other than what Christ has accomplished through him (ὧν οὐ κατειργάσατο Χριστὸς δι' ἐμοῦ). The result Christ has brought about is the obedient response of faith by the Gentiles (εἰς ὑπακοὴν ἐθνῶν; cf. 1:5). The means Christ has used include speech (λόγῳ), action (ἔργῳ), and power that produces signs and wonders (ἐν δυνάμει σημείων καὶ τεράτων; cf. 2 Cor. 12:12). All of these means have been empowered by the Holy Spirit (ἐν δυνάμει πνεύματος θεοῦ).

The ultimate outcome of Paul's ministry (ὥστε) is that he has fully completed (με . . . πεπληρωκέναι) his preaching of "the good news about Christ" (τὸ εὐαγγέλιον τοῦ Χριστοῦ)[43] from one end of the Eastern Empire (ἀπὸ Ἰερουσαλήμ) to the other (μέχρι τοῦ Ἰλλυρικοῦ). That preaching has consistently had unreached people groups as its aim (οὕτως φιλοτιμούμενον εὐαγγελίζεσθαι οὐχ ὅπου ὠνομάσθη Χριστός).[44] Throughout his pioneer church-planting work, Paul has been intentional about not building on foundations laid by others (ἵνα μὴ ἐπ'

---

40. Schreiner notes a likely connection to Isaiah 66:18–20, where the prophet describes God gathering the nations to Jerusalem as a grain offering (*Romans*, 767).

41. "This boasting" (τὴν καύχησιν) is best understood as referring back to verse 16.

42. NLT.

43. GNB.

44. If, as Cranfield suggests, ὠνομάσθη carries the sense of "be named in worship" (*Romans*, 764), Piper's statement, "Missions exists because worship doesn't" is a fitting reminder (*Let the Nations be Glad: The Supremacy of God in Missions*, 2nd ed. [Grand Rapids: Baker, 2003], 17).

ἀλλότριον θεμέλιον οἰκοδομῶ).[45] Rather (ἀλλά) he has followed an Old Testament pattern from Isaiah 52:15 (καθὼς γέγραπται) of focusing his efforts on those to whom Christ has not been proclaimed (οἷς οὐκ ἀνηγγέλη) and who, consequently, have not heard (οἳ οὐκ ἀκηκόασιν). In so doing, Paul has also helped fulfill the prophecy of the same verse that "many nations" will marvel over God's Servant (LXX, οὕτως θαυμάσονται ἔθνη πολλὰ ἐπ᾽ αὐτῷ).

Theology and Appropriation

Although little formal study has been done in comparing passages in which Paul defends his ministry, there are at least seven such passages in his letters. In those passages, he presents his credentials and defends his ministry. In its fullest form, such a passage includes five elements: (a) a reference to the source of Paul's authority, (b) a self-designation, (c) a description of the nature of his ministry, (d) a reference to the source of his enabling for ministry, and (e) the objective of his ministry. As the following table shows, not every passage necessarily includes every element. Romans 15:14–21, Ephesians 3:1–13, and Colossians 1:24–29 are the most complete. It is interesting to note that Romans and Colossians were written to congregations Paul had not planted, while Ephesians might possibly have been intended for other congregations in the province of Asia that might have come into existence as a result of Paul's extended ministry in that city (cf. Acts 19:10).

	Source of Authority	Self-Designation	Nature of Ministry	Source of Enabling	Objective
Romans 15:14–21	God's grace (15:15)	Minister of Christ Jesus to Gentiles (15:16)	Minister as a priest of the gospel (15:16)	Christ and the Holy Spirit (15:17–19)	Present acceptable offering of Gentiles (15:16)
2 Corinthians 1:12–24	God's grace; anointing (1:12, 21)	Coworker (1:20)	Preach Christ Jesus (1:19)	Sealed by the Holy Spirit (1:22)	--

---

45. See 1 Corinthians 3:10–12 for the imagery of laying and building on a foundation.

	Source of Authority	Self-Designation	Nature of Ministry	Source of Enabling	Objective
Galatians 1:11–2:10	Revelation; God's grace (1:11–12, 15)	Apostle (1:17)	Preach Christ among Gentiles (1:16, 23; 2:2)	--	--
Ephesians 3:1–13	God's grace; revelation (3:1–3)	Minister of the gospel (3:6–7)	Preach riches of Christ to Gentiles (3:8–10)	Holy Spirit (3:5)	Make known the manifold wisdom of God (3:10)
Philippians 1:12–26	--	--	Defend the gospel (1:16)	Holy Spirit (1:19)	Promote progress and joy in the faith (1:25)
Colossians 1:24–29	Stewardship from God (1:25)	Minister of the church (1:24–25)	Preach mystery of Christ among Gentiles (1:25–28)	Christ's power (1:29)	Present others complete in Christ (1:28–29)
1 Thessalonians 2:1–12	Approved by God (2:4)	Apostle (2:6)	Proclaim the gospel of God (2:8–9)	--	Encourage to walk worthy of God (2:12)

The value of a comparative study of similar passages in Paul's letters resides in identifying the differences and considering how those differences relate to the argument of the letters in which they occur. In the case of Romans 15:14–21, the primary differences are (a) the threefold mention of the Gentiles (15:16 [twice], 18) plus the use of Isaiah 52:15, (b) the self-designation as a "minister of Messiah Jesus" (15:16), (c) the use of cultic language (15:16), and (d) the reference to both Christ and the Holy Spirit as the sources of enabling for ministry (15:17–19a). The repeated mention of the Gentiles reinforces the target audience of Paul's ministry and brings his Roman readers into the scope of that ministry. The use of "Messiah Jesus" reflects Paul's titular use of Χριστός earlier in the letter (e.g., 7:4; 8:35; 9:3, 5; 14:18;

15:3, 7, 20; 16:16)[46] as the fulfillment of the Old Testament promises. The cultic language Paul uses in describing his ministry would logically resonate with the Jewish members of the Roman congregations. Including the Holy Spirit as a source of his enabling for ministry reflects the emphasis on the Spirit throughout the letter, particularly in Romans 8. Each of these ideas echoes an important theme in the letter.

Paul's primary purpose for including this passage at this point in his letter was to establish his apostolic authority for writing to the Roman congregations even though he had not been involved in their founding. With his original readers, we need to understand and embrace the source, nature, scope, and purpose of the task God has given us as well as the truth that we cannot fulfill that task apart from the enabling God provides for it. The most natural point of connection to this passage is the idea of being given a task to accomplish. Other possible points of connection include the experience of reminding others of information they already know and a sense of confidence in others based on their reputation. The passage corrects the idea that any success we experience in ministry is the result of our own talent, skill, or ability. The passage commends obedience to and dependence on God in fulfilling any ministry task we might be given. It also commends a commitment to reaching the unreached with the gospel. The objective in communicating this passage should be to help others understand the nature of Christian ministry, so that they will approach ministry as priestly service to God that is focused on taking the gospel to those who have never heard it.

---

46. See also the frequent use of Χριστὸς Ἰησοῦς (1:1; 2:16; 3:24; 6:3, 11; 8:1, 2, 34, 39; 16:3).

ROMANS 15:22–29

Text and Translation

22 Therefore also,[1] I was often[2] being hindered from coming[3] to you; **23** but now because I am no longer having[4] an opportunity in these regions and because I am having a longing to come[5] to you for many years,[6] **24** whenever I am going to Spain[7]—for I am hoping to see you when I am passing through[8] and by you to be sent on my way there, if[9] first I might enjoy your company[10] for a time[11]— **25** But now I am going to Jerusalem in order to be ministering[12] to the saints. **26** For Macedonia and Achaia were pleased to make some contribution for the poor among the saints[13] *who are* in Jerusalem. **27** For they were pleased, and they owe them a debt;[14] for if *it is true that* the Gentiles shared[15] in the sphere of spiritual things,[16] they are also[17] obligated to serve them[18] in the sphere of material things. **28** Therefore, after I have completed[19] this *task* and have sealed this fruit to them, I will

---

1. Καί is adjunctive.
2. Τὰ πολλά is an adverbial accusative of time.
3. Τοῦ ἐλθεῖν has an ablative sense.
4. Ἔχων is an adverbial participle of cause (twice).
5. Τοῦ ἐλθείν is a substantival infinitive in apposition to ἐποποθίαν.
6. Ἀπὸ πολλῶν ἐτῶν is equivalent to an accusative of extent.
7. Σπανίαν is the shorter reading, has strong manuscript support ($\mathfrak{P}^{46}$, ℵ*, A, B, C, D), and is the more likely original reading. The longer variant was probably added to address the anacoluthon that exists without it (cf. Schreiner, *Romans*, 779).
8. Διαπορευόμενος is an adverbial participle of time.
9. Ἐὰν . . . ἐμπλησθῶ is a third class condition.
10. BDAG 324a; literally, "I might be filled by you." Ὑμῶν is a genitive of source.
11. Ἀπὸ μέρους is temporal.
12. Διακνοῶν is an adverbial participle of purpose.
13. Εἰς τούς πτωχούς denotes advantage; τῶν ἀγίων is a partitive genitive.
14. The genitive (αὐτῶν) with ὀφειλέται (debtors) identifies those to whom the debt is owed.
15. Εἰ . . . ἐκοινώνησαν is a first-class condition.
16. Πνευματικοῖς is a dative of sphere; so also ἐν τοῖς σαρκικοῖς.
17. Καί is adjunctive.
18. Αὐτοῖς is the object of the infinitive, specifying to whom service is rendered.
19. Both ἐπιτελέσας and σπραγισάμενος are adverbial participles of time; the aorist tenses are consummative.

depart through you to Spain. **29** And I know that when I am coming[20] to you, I will come with the full blessing that comes from Christ.[21]

Context and Structure

   III. Letter Closing (15:14–16:27)
      A. Paul's Mission (15:14–21)
      B. **Paul's Travel Plans (15:22–29)**
      C. Paul's Prayer Request (15:30–33)
      D. Commendation of Phoebe (16:1–2)
      E. Greetings from Paul (16:3–16)
      F. Closing Advice (16:17–20)
      G. Greetings from Others (16:21–24)
      H. Doxology (16:25–27)

Next, Paul explains his travel plans. He includes a similar section (the "apostolic parousia") in ten of his other letters (1 Cor. 4:19–21; 2 Cor. 13:1–10; Eph. 6:20–22; Phil. 2:19–24; Col. 4:7–9; 1 Thess. 2:17–3:10; 1 Tim. 3:14–15; 2 Tim. 4:9–13; Titus 3:12–13; Philem. 21–22). The paragraph consists of three parts: Paul's longing to visit Rome (15:22–24), his need to visit Jerusalem (15:25–27), and his plans to visit Spain (15:28–29).

Basic Message and Exegetical Outline

Paul will fulfill his longing to visit Rome by stopping to see his readers when he travels from Jerusalem to Spain.

   Paul's Travel Plans (15:22–29)
      1. Paul longs to visit Rome (15:22–24)
         a. Because he has been hindered previously (15:22)
         b. Because his work in the East is complete (15:23–24a)
         c. Because he hopes for their help (15:24b)
      2. Paul needs to visit Jerusalem (15:25–27)
         a. To minister to the saints (15:25)

---

20. Ἐρχόμενος is an adverbial participle of time.
21. Εὐλογίας is an attributed genitive; Χριστοῦ is a genitive of source. The shorter reading (Χριστοῦ) has strong manuscript support ($\mathfrak{P}^{46}$, ℵ*, A, B, C, D) and is most likely original.

b. Because of Macedonia's and Achaia's contribution (15:26–27)
3. Paul plans to visit Spain (15:28–29)
   a. By way of Rome (15:28)
   b. With the full blessing of Christ (15:29)

Explanation of the Text

1. Paul longs to visit Rome (15:22–24).

The success of Paul's church-planting ministry in the east (15:19b–21) has had an additional effect (διὸ καί): it regularly hindered him from visiting his Roman readers (ἐνεκοπτόμην τὰ πολλὰ τοῦ ἐλθεῖν πρὸς ὑμᾶς).[22] At the time of writing, however, the conclusion of (νυνὶ δέ) that ministry means Paul no longer has opportunities for pioneer work (μηκέτι τόπον ἔχων) in the regions where he has been traveling (ἐν τοῖς κλίμασι τούτοις). An important further consideration (δέ) is that Paul has longed to visit them (ἐπιποθίαν ἔχων τοῦ ἐλθεῖν πρὸς ὑμᾶς) "for many years" (ἀπὸ πολλῶν ἐτῶν), whenever he might be going to Spain (ὡς ἂν πορεύομαι εἰς τὴν Σπανίαν).

This first mention of his planned Spanish mission leads Paul to interject a further explanation (γάρ) for his visit to Rome. His initial explanation (1:11–12) highlighted the spiritual benefit; this explanation adds the logistical benefit.[23] When he will be passing through Rome (διαπορευόμενος), Paul hopes that he will see them (ἐλπίζω θεάσασθαι ὑμᾶς) and they will be moved to provide support for him as he travels on to Spain (καὶ ὑφ' ὑμῶν προπεμφθῆναι ἐκεῖ).[24] That decision, of course, will only be made after he has "first enjoyed [their] company for a while" (ἐὰν ὑμῶν πρῶτον ἀπὸ μέρους ἐμπλησθῶ).[25] Jewett notes that adding the conditional clause "makes clear that the discussion of logistics will not

---

22. Although Jewett thinks Paul "was hindered" (ἐνεκοπτόμην) by Satan (*Romans*, 922), most commentators believe it was the work God had for him in the east (cf. Harvey, *Romans*, 363).

23. Schreiner suggests that "Paul wanted the Roman church to support his mission to Spain financially, in prayer, and possibly also with personnel" (*Romans*, 774).

24. Προπέμπω ("send on one's way") describes the act of assisting someone in making a journey (BDAG 873). Elsewhere in the New Testament, it refers to providing missionary support (Acts 15:3; 20:38; 21:5; 1 Cor. 16:6; 2 Cor. 1:16; Titus 3:13). Ἐκεῖ ("there") most naturally refers to Spain.

25. CSB.

occur until a personal relationship is established between Paul and the Roman congregations."[26]

2. Paul needs to visit Jerusalem (15:25–27).

At the time of writing, however, (νυνὶ δέ) Paul will soon be traveling to Jerusalem (πορεύομαι εἰς Ἰερουσαλήμ) in order to minister to the saints there (διακονῶν τοῖς ἁγίοις) by delivering the collection he has gathered from the Gentile churches he has planted. In particular, he highlights the participation of the churches in Macedonia and Achaia (Μακεδονία καὶ Ἀχαΐα), which have "considered it a good and worthy choice" (ηὐδόκησαν)[27] to make a contribution (κοινωνίαν τινὰ ποιήσασθαι) to the poor among the saints who live in Jerusalem (εἰς τοὺς πτωχοὺς τῶν ἁγίων τῶν ἐν Ἰερουσαλήμ). The voluntary decision of those congregations is based on (γάρ) the moral debt they owe to the Jerusalem church (ὀφειλέται εἰσὶν αὐτῶν).[28] The Gentiles have shared (ἐκοινώνησαν τὰ ἔθνη) the spiritual blessings that originated with the Jerusalem church (τοῖς πνευματικοῖς αὐτῶν). The Gentiles are also obligated (ὀφείλουσιν καί), therefore, to serve the Jerusalem church (λειτουργῆσαι αὐτοῖς) with "their material possessions" (ἐν τοῖς σαρκικοῖς).[29]

3. Paul plans to visit Spain (15:28–29).

In summary, then (οὖν), once he brings the collection to a conclusion (τοῦτο ἐπιτελέσας)[30] and confirms its integrity to the Jerusalem church (καὶ σφραγισάμενος αὐτοῖς τὸν καρπὸν τοῦτον),[31] Paul will depart for Spain (ἀπελεύσομαι ... εἰς Σπανίαν) by way of Rome (δι᾽ ὑμῶν). He is confident (οἶδα δέ) that when he comes to Rome (ὅτι ἐρχόμενος πρὸς ὑμᾶς), he will come (ἐλεύσομαι) "with the full blessing that comes from Christ" (ἐν πληρώματι εὐλογίας Χιρστοῦ). In keeping with his previously stated dependence on Christ's enabling (15:18–19), Paul's future plans are not based on "his own calling or his apostolic powers," but on the blessing Christ bestows and "the gospel that Paul's letter and travel aim to advance."[32]

---

26. Jewett, *Romans*, 926.
27. BDAG 404.
28. Schreiner concludes that ὀφειλέτης carries the nuance of moral debt (*Romans*, 778).
29. NCV.
30. Τοῦτο refers back to verses 25–27.
31. Cf. Cranfield, *Romans*, 774–75.
32. Jewett, *Romans*, 933, 934.

Theology and Appropriation

As Jewett notes, "Jerusalem is hardly on the route between Corinth and Rome,"[33] and the natural question for Paul's Roman readers to ask would be "Why visit Jerusalem first?" Paul addresses that question briefly in 15:25–27: he is going to make the detour in order to "minister to the saints among the poor who are in Jerusalem." That phrase refers to his task of delivering the Jerusalem collection. There is no single passage that describes that task in detail, but there are mentions of it in three of Paul's letters. The precedent lies in the famine relief visit described in Acts 11:27–30, where the church in Antioch sent a contribution for the relief of the Christians living in Judea in response to a widespread severe famine. It is likely that Paul's conversation with James, Peter, and John regarding the scope of his ministry also took place during that visit (Gal. 2:1–10).[34] As part of that conversation Paul affirmed his eagerness to "remember the poor" (Gal. 2:10).

Early in his travels, Paul had given the churches in Galatia directions regarding the collection (1 Cor. 16:1). He subsequently gave similar instructions to the churches in Achaia (1 Cor. 16:2–4) and to the churches in Macedonia (2 Cor. 8:1–5). Those instructions included at least four guiding principles: (1) the process of gathering the funds should be orderly (1 Cor. 16:1–4), (2) the goal of the process should promote equality among churches in areas that were experiencing abundance and those that were experiencing scarcity (2 Cor. 8:13–15), (3) the administration of the process should be honorable (2 Cor. 8:18–21), and (4) the process should be characterized by an attitude of generosity (2 Cor. 9:6–7). The overall purpose of the process was to demonstrate the unity of the church as a whole, whether the congregations involved were primarily Jewish or Gentile (Rom. 15:27). Schreiner suggests that Paul saw the gifts he would convey to Jerusalem as fulfilling Old Testament prophecies that the nations would bring their wealth to Jerusalem (e.g., Isa. 60:5–17).

By the time Paul wrote to the Romans from Corinth, the collection was complete, and he was ready to depart for Jerusalem. His original plan to sail from Corinth was disrupted by a plot against him by Jewish opponents (Acts 20:3a). As a result, he revised his plans and traveled overland through Macedonia to Philippi and then by boat to Troas, where he was joined by a group of traveling companions who represented the churches from various regions of his church-planting

---

33. Jewett, *Romans*, 926.
34. For a discussion of the relationship between Paul's letters and his visits to Jerusalem, see Harvey, *Pauline Letters*, 64–66.

efforts (Acts 20:3b–6).[35] Although his visit to Jerusalem met with a mixed response (Acts 20:17–26),[36] Paul's continuing commitment to the collection highlights at least four lessons. First, the power of the gospel transcends ethnic lines. Second, the unity of the church transcends geographic borders. Third, the church has a responsibility to care for the poor, both locally and globally. Fourth, the church owes its spiritual heritage to the Jews. Contemporary congregations that ignore these lessons fall short of the model Paul's ministry offers.

Paul's primary purpose for including this passage at this point in his letter was to communicate the details of and rationale for his upcoming travel plans. With his original readers, we need to realize the obligation we owe to the global church of Christ. The passage offers multiple possible points of connection, including wanting to visit someone but being hindered from doing so, caring for those in need, and being under obligation to another individual or group. The passage corrects the idea that local congregations operate in isolation from one another and from the global church. There can be no "Lone Ranger" attitude toward how a group of believers functions; each group is under obligation to assist other groups as the need arises. The passage commends an attitude of cooperation among congregations that promotes the material welfare of others and the advancement of the gospel. The objective in communicating this passage should be to help others understand the trans-local nature of the church, so that they will actively cooperate with other congregations across local, regional, and global boundaries for the worldwide advancement of the gospel.

---

35. Sopater was from Berea (Macedonia); Aristarchus and Secundus were from Thessalonica (Macedonia); Gaius and Timothy were from Derbe (Galatia); Tychicus and Trophimus were from Ephesus (Asia).
36. Paul's own uncertainty over his reception is reflected in the prayer requests that follow in 15:30–33.

Text and Translation

30 Now I am exhorting you, brothers, for the sake of our Lord Jesus Christ[1] and based on the love that comes from the Spirit,[2] to contend along with me in your[3] prayers to God on my behalf,[4] **31** in order that I might be delivered from the unbelievers[5] in Judea and my service[6] which is for Jerusalem[7] might be acceptable to the saints, **32**[8] *and* in order that when I come[9] to you joyfully[10] by God's will[11] I might be refreshed with you.[12] **33** Now *may* the God who produces peace[13] *be* with all of you. Amen.[14]

Context and Structure

    III. Letter Closing (15:14–16:27)
        A. Paul's Mission (15:14–21)
        B. Paul's Travel Plans (15:22–29)

---

1. Διά + genitive denotes the basis of Paul's appeal (twice).
2. Τοῦ πνεύματος is a genitive of source.
3. The definite article functions as a possessive pronoun.
4. Ὑπέρ + genitive denotes advantage.
5. Τῶν ἀπειθούντων is a substantival participle.
6. The fact that δωροφορία (B, D*) occurs nowhere else in the New Testament makes it the more difficult reading, but Jewett concludes that it is a correction for ecclesiastical purposes (*Romans*, 920nt). Διακονία has good manuscript support (𝔓46, ℵ, A, D2, 33).
7. Εἰς + accusative denotes advantage.
8. There are five variant readings for this verse. Since Paul always speaks of the will of God rather than the will of Christ Jesus or the will of Jesus Christ (Metzger, *Textual Commentary*, 474), there are three variants to consider. Of those three readings, the two that include the subjunctive ἔλθω are easier than the one that includes the participle ἐλθών. The UBS5 reading, therefore, is most likely the original.
9. Ἐλθών is an adverbial participle of time.
10. Ἐν + accusative denotes manner.
11. Ἐκ + genitive denotes intermediate agency.
12. Ὑμῖν is an associative dative.
13. Εἰρήνης is a genitive of product.
14. Although the readings that omit ἀμήν (𝔓46, A) are shorter and might have tempted scribes to add it, the reading that includes ἀμήν has stronger manuscript support (ℵ, B, D, 33). The omission most likely arises from the versions of the letter that add 16:25–27 at this point.

C. **Paul's Prayer Request (15:30–33)**
D. Commendation of Phoebe (16:1–2)
E. Greetings from Paul (16:3–16)
F. Closing Advice (16:17–20)
G. Greetings from Others (16:21–24)
H. Doxology (16:25–27)

Paul's travel plans lead him to request prayer from his readers. A request formula (cf. 12:1) introduces two petitions (15:30–32). He closes with his own prayer-wish for the Romans (15:33).

Basic Message and Exegetical Outline

Paul asks the Romans to pray that his visit to Jerusalem might be successful and that his visit to Rome might be profitable.

Paul's Prayer Request (15:30–33)
1. Paul requests urgent prayer from the Romans (15:30–32)
   a. That his visit to Jerusalem might be successful (15:31)
   b. That his visit to Rome might be profitable (15:32)
2. Paul prays for the Romans (15:33)

Explanation of the Text

1. Paul requests urgent prayer from the Romans (15:30–32).

Having set out his travel plans, Paul continues (δέ) by seeking to enlist his readers' prayer support for those travels (παρακαλῶ ὑμᾶς, ἀδελφοί). He highlights the urgency of his request by including two grounds: the cause of the Lord Jesus Christ whom he serves (διὰ τοῦ κυρίου Ἰησοῦ Χριστοῦ) and the love the Spirit produces in them (διὰ τῆς ἀγάπης τοῦ πνεύματος). He asks that they might "contend along with me" (συναγωνίσασθαί μοι) in their prayers (ἐν ταῖς προσευχαῖς) to God (πρὸς τὸν θεόν) on his behalf (ὑπὲρ ἐμοῦ). Jewett suggests that the verb describes an "urgent need for assistance,"[15] while Longenecker describes it as "combat in company with another person."[16] Clearly, Paul viewed the Romans' prayers as crucial to the outcome of his travel plans.

Paul asks them to focus their prayers on the first two stops on

---

15. Jewett, *Romans*, 934.
16. Longenecker, *Romans*, 1098.

his itinerary. The most pressing need relates to his upcoming visit to Jerusalem and involves two items. First, he expects to meet opposition from nonbelieving Jews and asks prayer that God might rescue him from any opponents he might encounter in Judea (ῥυσθῶ ἀπὸ τῶν ἀπειθούντων ἐν τῇ Ἰουδαίᾳ).[17] Second, he hopes to meet acceptance from believing Jews and asks prayer that they will be pleased with the monetary gifts he will deliver in Jerusalem (ἡ διακονία μου ἡ εἰς Ἰερουσαλὴμ εὐπρόσδεκτος τοῖς ἁγίοις γένηται). His "ministry" refers to the collection he previously mentioned in verse 25, and "acceptable" echoes his hope for the result of his priestly service in verse 16.

The outcome (ἵνα) of a successful visit to Jerusalem will allow Paul to continue his travels and visit Rome. When he arrives (ἐλθὼν πρὸς ὑμᾶς), it will be a cause for rejoicing (ἐν χαρᾷ) that God's will makes possible (διὰ θελήματος θεοῦ; cf. 1:10). He will then be able to engage in the mutual encouragement (cf. 1:12), relationship building (cf. 15:24), and refreshment (συναναπαύσωμαι ὑμῖν) he has anticipated for so many years (cf. 15:23). Their prayers for him, therefore, will work out to their own advantage as well as to the advantage of Paul and the progress of the gospel.

2. Paul prays for the Romans (15:33).

Paul offers wishes of peace before he closes others letters (cf. 1 Cor. 16:23; Phil. 4:9; 1 Thess. 5:23; 2 Thess. 3:16). In Romans, Paul states that God is the source of peace (ὁ θεὸς τῆς εἰρήνης; cf. 1:7; 15:33; 16:20), which he gives both in terms of individuals' relationships with him (2:10; 5:1; 8:6) and in terms of their relationships with one another (14:17, 19; 15:13).[18] The all-inclusive scope of this prayer at the end of the letter (μετὰ πάντων ὑμῶν) echoes a similar note in the salutation at the beginning of the letter (cf. 1:7). Although Paul's prayer for peace is appropriate in light of the tensions within the Roman church (14:1–15:13),[19] it is probably best not to limit the prayer only to that aspect.[20] Ἀμήν ("so be it") invites the readers to respond by "confirm[ing] God's peace as uniting both the Roman believers and their fellow members from various ethnic traditions throughout the world."[21]

---

17. Ῥύομαι describes deliverance from serious danger; the passive voice is a divine passive that points to God as the source of deliverance.
18. It is worth noting the combination of love (15:30), joy (15:32), and peace (15:33) in this brief section.
19. Schreiner, *Romans*, 783.
20. Moo, *Romans*, 911.
21. Jewett, *Romans*, 940.

Theology and Appropriation

Paul clearly placed a high value on prayer. He mentions prayer explicitly forty-four times in twelve of his thirteen letters.[22] Scattered throughout those occurrences are five principles that should guide prayer: (1) prayer demands commitment and devotion (Rom. 12:12; 1 Cor. 7:5; Col. 4:2; 1 Tim. 5:5); (2) prayer should be constant and consistent (Eph. 6:18; 1 Thess. 5:17); (3) prayer should be peaceful and united (1 Tim. 2:8); (4) prayer should be offered with thanksgiving (Phil. 4:6; Col. 4:2); (5) ultimately, prayer must be enabled by the Holy Spirit (Rom. 8:26; Eph. 6:18; cf. Rom. 8:15; Gal. 4:6).

Paul prayed regularly for those churches and individuals to whom he wrote. Perhaps the best-known prayer passages are those in the introductions of Paul's letters, where he incorporates prayer reports into eight thanksgiving sections (Rom. 1:8–12; Eph. 1:15–23; Phil. 1:3–11; Col. 1:3–12; 1 Thess. 1:2–10; 2 Thess. 1:3–12; 2 Tim. 1:3–5; Philem. 4–7).[23] In those passages, Paul is particularly concerned with the spiritual welfare and growth of others. He praises God for their faith (Eph. 1:15; Col. 1:4; 1 Thess. 1:3, 8; 2 Thess. 1:3; 2 Tim. 1:5; Philem. 5), for their love (Col. 1:4; 1 Thess. 1:3; 2 Thess. 1:3; Philem. 5), for their hope (1 Thess. 1:3), for their participation in the gospel (Phil. 1:5), and for the way in which they became examples to others (1 Thess. 1:7–9; 2:13–14). He prays that they might be established and encouraged (Rom. 1:11–12), that they might more fully understand the riches that are theirs in Christ (Eph. 1:16–19), that their love might grow in knowledge and discernment (Phil. 1:9–11), that they might understand God's will and walk worthy of their calling (Col. 1:9–12), that God would count them worthy of their calling and fulfill their every desire (2 Thess. 1:11), that Christ would be glorified in them (2 Thess. 1:12), and that the fellowship of their faith might grow (Philem. 6).

---

22. The exception is Paul's letter to Titus. Προσεύχομαι and προσευχή occur thirty-one times; δέομαι and δέησις occur seventeen times, although four occurrences of δέομαι relate to making requests to other believers (2 Cor. 5:20; 8:4; 10:2; Gal. 4:12). There do not appear to be major distinctions between the two word groups. One suggestion is that προσεύχομαι/προσευχή refers to prayer in general, while δέομαι/δέησις describes spoken requests and/or intercession on behalf of another (*NIDNTT* 2.855).

23. The first comprehensive studies of prayer in Paul's letters were D. M. Stanley, *Boasting in the Lord: The Phenomenon of Prayer in Saint Paul* (New York: Paulist, 1974) and G. P. Wiles, *Paul's Intercessory Prayers* (Cambridge: Cambridge University Press, 1974).

Paul also occasionally requested prayer for himself. Those requests focused on his ministry and its effectiveness. He was particularly concerned that God would provide open doors for the gospel (Col. 4:3) so that the word of God might spread (2 Thess. 3:1). Even his requests that God might deliver him from danger (Rom. 15:31; Phil. 1:19) related to the continuing progress of the gospel. His requests that God might allow him to visit certain churches and individuals (Rom. 1:9–10; 1 Thess. 3:10; Philem. 22) involved a desire to promote their spiritual growth and participation in the gospel. Combined with his regular prayer for others, Paul's requests for himself provide a powerful example for the contemporary church. Rather than focusing prayer on personal needs, individuals and congregations should focus their prayer on the spiritual growth of others and on the continuing worldwide advance of the gospel.

Paul's primary purpose for including this passage at this point in his letter was to involve his readers in his ministry activities by calling them to prayer. With his Roman readers, we need to recognize the importance of corporate involvement in supporting the ministry of the gospel. The passage offers multiple possible points of connection, including urgency in seeking help and support from others, opposition that might arise while seeking to fulfill a task, and being refreshed and encouraged by spending time with others who share similar interests and concerns. The passage corrects the idea that prayer is an activity for which we have no responsibility and/or an activity that is conveniently relegated to others (e.g., the midweek prayer group). The passage commends commitment to united corporate prayer for ministry plans and activities as well as trust in God's will to accomplish his purposes. The objective in communicating this passage should be to help others understand the importance of prayer in advancing God's kingdom purposes so that they will commit to praying regularly for the spiritual growth of others and the global progress of the gospel.

ROMANS 16:1–2

Text and Translation

1 Now I am commending to you Phoebe, our sister, *who* is also[1] a minister over the church[2] *that* is in Cenchrea, **2** in order that you might receive her as belonging to the Lord[3] worthily of the saints[4] and might stand by to help her[5] with reference to whatever task[6] she might need from you;[7] for indeed[8] she was a helper to many[9] and especially to me.[10]

Context and Structure

This paragraph follows the basic structure of other recommendations in Paul's letters (1 Cor. 16:5–18; Phil. 4:2–3; 1 Thess. 5:12–13a; Philem. 10–17): introduction (16:1a), credentials (16:1b), and request (16:2a–b). Paul also adds rationale to support the request (16:2c).

Basic Message and Exegetical Outline

The church in Rome should welcome and assist Phoebe because of her work in the church in Cenchrea, and because she has helped Paul and others.

---

1. Οὖσαν is an adjectival participle modifying Φοίβην; καί is adjunctive.
2. Τῆς ἐκκλησίας is a genitive of subordination.
3. Ἐν κυρίῳ highlights personal relationship.
4. A genitive (here, τῶν ἁγίων) regularly follows the adverb ἀξίως.
5. Αὐτῇ denotes the person helped.
6. Ἐν + dative denotes reference.
7. Ὑμῶν is equivalent to a dative of source.
8. Καί is ascensive.
9. Πολλῶν and ἐμοῦ are objective genitives.
10. Αὐτοῦ is intensive.

Commendation of Phoebe (16:1–2)
1. Paul commends Phoebe as a leader in the church in Cenchrea (16:1)
2. The church should welcome and assist Phoebe (16:2a–b)
3. Phoebe has helped Paul and others (16:2c)

Explanation of the Text

1. Paul commends Phoebe as a leader in the church in Cenchrea (16:1).

It is likely that Phoebe served as the messenger who carried Paul's letter to Rome.[11] Her name suggests that she was a Gentile and a freed slave.[12] Because the Romans did not know her, Paul includes a brief note of recommendation for her (συνίστημι ὑμῖν Φοίβην). She is "our sister" (τὴν ἀδελφὴν ἡμῶν) and, therefore, a member of the Christian fellowship. It is also important for the Romans to know that she is either a "deacon" or a prominent "minister" of the church in Cenchrea (οὖσαν καὶ διάκονον τῆς ἐκκλησίας τῆς ἐν Κεγχρεαῖς), which was the eastern port for Corinth (cf. Acts 18:18) and the venue from which Paul was writing (cf. Acts 20:2).

2. The church should welcome and assist Phoebe (16:2a–b).

Paul commends Pheobe with two purposes in mind (ἵνα). First, he wants the Romans to receive her favorably (προσδέξησθε αὐτήν). They are to welcome her because she shares with them a personal relationship to Christ (ἐν κυρίῳ) and because she is worthy of their respect (ἀξίως τῶν ἁγίων).[13] Second, Paul wants the Romans to stand ready to assist her (παραστῆτε αὐτῇ). He does not specify her need but leaves the details for her arrival in Rome (ἐν ᾧ ἂν ὑμῶν χρῄζῃ πράγματι). Their response to whatever need she might have would demonstrate their solidarity with Phoebe and with Paul in the work of the gospel.

---

11. Dunn, *Romans*, 866. In a number of his other letters, Paul includes an "emissary unit" that introduces the messenger who will carry the letter (1 Cor. 4:17; Eph. 6:21–22; Phil. 2:19–23; Col. 4:7–9; 1 Thess. 3:1–8).
12. Cranfield, *Romans*, 780.
13. For ἐν κυρίῳ, see Harris, *Prepositions*, 128–30. Jewett suggests that Pheobe's role in the church in Cenchrea, her previous contribution to the gospel ministry, and her role in the project Paul wants to introduce to the Romans make her worthy of special honor (*Romans*, 945). NIRV translates the phrases as "as one who belongs to the Lord . . . in the way God's people should."

3. Phoebe has helped Paul and others (16:2c).

Specific rationale (γάρ) for the Romans welcoming and assisting Phoebe is her role as a patroness of many (αὐτὴ προστάτις πολλῶν ἐγενήθη), including Paul himself (καὶ ἐμοῦ αὐτοῦ). Commentators have suggested several possible understandings of Paul's description. Moo's conclusion is most natural and provides a logical explanation for the reason Paul left Phoebe's need unspecified: "A 'patron' was one who came to the aid of others, especially foreigners, by providing housing and financial aid and by representing their interests before local authorities, . . . Phoebe, then, was probably a woman of high social standing and some wealth, who put her status, resources, and time at the services of traveling Christians, like Paul, who needed help and support."[14] Paul now asks the Roman congregations to do the same for her, whatever specific need(s) she might have.

Theology and Appropriation

Phoebe is one of fifteen women Paul mentions by name in his letters when he writes about ministry activities.[15] Paul refers to them using a variety of designations that give us insight into the roles they played in the congregations to which he wrote.[16] Phoebe is described as a "sister," a "minister," and a "patroness." In ministry contexts, sister (ἀδελφή) and brother describe a worker in a local congregation (cf. Rom. 16:23; Eph. 6:23–24; Phil. 4:21–22; Col. 4:15); Apphia is also a "sister" (Philem. 2). Minister (διακονος) describes an associate who preaches and teaches, both in local congregations and on missionary travels, and who is worthy of pay. Elsewhere, Paul uses the same term to describe himself and Apollos (1 Cor. 3:5), Tychicus (Eph. 6:21; Col. 4:7), leaders in the Philippian church (Phil. 1:1), and Epaphras (Col. 1:7). Patroness (προστάτις) describes an individual who puts her status, resources, and time at the services of traveling Christians. It is likely that the same designation could be applied to Prisca (Acts 18:1–4, 18–19, 24–28; Rom. 16:3–5; cf. 1 Cor. 16:19; 2 Tim. 4:19;) and to Rufus's mother (Rom. 16:13).[17]

---

14. Moo, *Romans*, 916.
15. Paul mentions eleven women in Romans (Phoebe, Prisca, Mary, Junia, Tryphaena, Tryphosa, Persis, Rufus's mother, Julia, Nereus's sister, and Olympas), one in 1 Corinthians (Chloe), two in Philippians (Euodia and Syntyche), one in Philemon (Apphia). In 2 Timothy 1:5, he also mentions Eunice and Lois, but the context is Timothy's upbringing rather than Paul's ministry.
16. Ellis's entry, "Paul and His Coworkers" provides a concise but helpful discussion (*DPL*, 183–89).
17. Lydia of Philippi is another example (Acts 16:14–15).

Prisca is a "coworker" (συνεργός), which describes an itinerant or local worker with a right to pay or support. Euodia and Syntyche are also coworkers who shared in Paul's struggle for the gospel (Phil. 4:2–3).[18] Junia is an "apostle" (ἀπόστολος) which, in this context, describes a missionary church planter (e.g., Acts 14:4, 14; 1 Cor. 12:28; Eph. 4:11; 1 Thess. 2:6) rather than one of the Twelve.[19] Mary (16:6), Tryphaena (16:12), Tryphosa (16:12), and Persis (16:12) are "laborers" (ὁ κοπιῶν), which refers to itinerant or local workers with a right to pay or support. Paul uses the term elsewhere to describe his own ministry (1 Cor. 15:10; Col. 1:29), the work of those who have charge over a local congregation (1 Thess. 5:12), and the ministries of those who labor in teaching and preaching (1 Tim. 5:17). Although Julia, Nereus's sister, and Olympas (Rom. 16:15) have no specific designation, the context in which Paul mentions them suggests that they are members of house church leadership teams; Chloe (1 Cor. 1:11) and Apphia (Philem. 2) probably have similar roles.[20] The ways in which Paul mentions women in his letters makes it clear they had varied and active roles in first-century congregations and mission teams.

Paul's primary purpose for including this passage at this point in his letter was to commend Phoebe to the Roman congregations for her prominent role in the gospel ministry. With his original readers, we need to give due honor to those who serve Christ's cause well. The passage offers multiple possible points of connection, including providing letters of reference or recommendation, the role of a patron or a patroness (e.g., "a patron of the arts"), and the need for assistance when arriving in a new city. The passage corrects any idea that women have no significant roles in the ministry activities of local congregations. The passage commends recognition of and respect for those individuals who have played significant roles in the ministry of the gospel, whether locally or cross-culturally. The objective in communicating this passage should be to help others understand that those who labor faithfully in the cause of Christ are worthy of special honor, so that they will be intentional about honoring those individuals for their contribution to the gospel ministry.

---

18. Paul describes at least ten men as "coworkers," including Urbanus (Rom. 16:9), Timothy (Rom. 16:21; 1 Thess. 3:2), Epaphras (Phil. 2:25), Barnabas (Gal. 2:9), Jesus Justus (Col. 4:11), Philemon (Philem. 1), Demas (Philem. 24), Luke (Philem. 24), Mark (Philem. 24), and Aristarchus (Philem. 24). The activities of these men provide insight into the role of Paul's "coworkers."
19. For a discussion of Junia's gender and role, see the discussion of 16:7.
20. Alternately, Chloe might be a patroness.

ROMANS 16:3–16

Text and Translation

3   Greet Priscilla and Aquila, my coworkers in *the service of* Christ Jesus,[1] **4** who risked their own necks in the interest of my life,[2] for whom not only I but also all the Gentile churches[3] give thanks, **5** and the church *that is* in their house.[4]
Greet Epaenetus my beloved, who is the firstfruits from Asia for Christ.[5]

6   Greet Mary, who labored with reference to many things[6] for you.

7   Greet Andronicus and Junia,[7] my kinsmen and my fellow-prisoners, who are outstanding among the apostles, who also[8] have been Christians[9] before me.

8   Greet Ampliatus my beloved Christian *friend.*

9   Greet Urbanus, our co-worker in *the service of* Christ, and Stachys my beloved.

10   Greet Apelles, the *one who is* approved by Christ.[10]
Greet those who are from the *household of* Aristobulus.[11]

11   Greet Herodion, my kinsman.
Greet those who are from the *household of* Narcissus who are[12] Christians.

---

1. Ἐν + dative denotes sphere; see also verses 9, 12, 13.
2. Ὑπέρ + genitive denotes advantage.
3. Τῶν ἐθνῶν is an attributive genitive.
4. Κατά + accusative is local.
5. Τῆς Ἀσίας is a partitive genitive. Εἰς Χριστόν is equivalent to a dative of advantage; so also εἰς ὑμας in verse 6.
6. Πολλά is an accusative of reference.
7. Apart from accenting—which was not originally present— ℵ, A, B, D, and 33 all support Ἰουνιαν, which can be either masculine (Ἰουνιᾶν) or feminine (Ἰουνιᾶν). Jewett notes that the masculine is not found elsewhere (*Romans,* 950nh), and Moo notes that commentators before the thirteenth century unanimously understood the individual's identity as feminine (*Romans,* 922).
8. Καί is adjunctive.
9. Ἐν Χριστῷ denotes sphere of reference; see also verses 8, 11.
10. Ἐν Χριστῷ denotes agency; see also verse 13.
11. Ἐκ τῶν Ἀριστοβούλου is partitive; so also ἐκ τῶν Ναρκίσσου in verse 11.
12. Τοὶς ὄντας is a substantival participle standing in apposition to the preceding phrase.

12   Greet Tryphaena and Tryphosa, the *ones* who labored[13] in *the service of* the Lord.

           Greet Persis, the beloved, who labored with respect to many things[14] in *the service of* the Lord.

13   Greet Rufus, the *one who is* chosen by the Lord, and his mother and mine.

14   Greet Asyncritus, Phlegon, Hermes, Patrobas, Hermas, and the brothers *who are* with them.

15   Greet Philologus and Julia,[15] Nereus and his sister, and Olympas and all the saints *who are* with them.

16   Greet one another by means of a holy kiss.[16]

           All the churches of Christ are greeting you.

Context and Structure

     III. Letter Closing (15:14–16:27)
         A.   Paul's Mission (15:14–21)
         B.   Paul's Travel Plans (15:22–29)
         C.   Paul's Prayer Request (15:30–33)
         D.   Commendation of Phoebe (16:1–2)
         E.   **Greetings from Paul (16:3–16)**
         F.   Closing Advice (16:17–20)
         G.   Greetings from Others (16:21–24)
         H.   Doxology (16:25–27)

By greeting twenty-six individuals, Paul seeks a positive reception for his letter. The first fifteen sentences use a conventional greeting form and may be loosely grouped into two sections: greetings to individuals associated with Paul's mission (16:3–7) and greetings to other friends and acquaintances (16:8–15). The final two sentences call the Romans to greet one another and offer greetings from "all the churches of Christ" (16:16).

---

13. Tὰς κοπιώσας is a substantival participle in apposition to the preceding names.
14. Πολλά is an accusative of reference.
15. The manuscript support for Ἰουλίαν is strong (ℵ, A, B, D, 33); the variant Ἰουνιαν (C*) is most likely an assimilation to verse 7.
16. Ἐν + dative denotes instrumentality.

Basic Message and Exegetical Outline

Paul's greetings validate his apostolic credentials, provide witnesses to the content of his gospel, encourage the Romans to pursue unity with one another, and challenge them to mission.

> Greetings from Paul (16:3–16)
> 1. Paul greets those who have worked with him (16:3–7)
>   a. Priscilla and Aquila, and the church in their house (16:3–5a)
>   b. Epaenetus (16:5b)
>   c. Mary (16:6)
>   d. Andonicus and Junia (16:7)
> 2. Paul greets those who know him (16:8–15)
>   a. Ampliatus (16:8)
>   b. Urbanus and Stachys (16:9)
>   c. Apelles (16:10a)
>   d. Those from the household of Aristobulus (16:10b)
>   e. Herodion (16:11a)
>   f. Those from the household of Narcissus (16:11b)
>   g. Tryphaena and Tryphosa (16:12a)
>   h. Persis (16:12b)
>   i. Rufus and his mother (16:13)
>   j. Asyncritus, Phlegon, Hermes, Patrobas, Hermas, and the brothers with them (16:14)
>   k. Philologus and Julia, Nereus and his sister, Olympas, and the saints with them (16:15)
> 3. Paul greets the whole church (16:16)

Explanation of the Text

1. Paul greets those who have worked with him (16:3–7).

Paul begins his extended greeting list by addressing six individuals who are identified with his mission. They can, therefore, provide firsthand testimony to the effectiveness of his work in the east. The husband and wife team of Prisca and Aquila heads the list.

> Prisca (Priscilla) and Aquila were a married couple (Acts 18:2), who were leatherworkers (Acts 18:3) and are mentioned elsewhere in connection with Corinth (Acts 18:1–4, 18) and Ephesus (Acts 18:19, 24–28; 1 Cor. 16:19; 2 Tim. 4:19). . . . Although both names were Latin, Acts 18:2 identifies Aquila as

a Jew from Pontus; Prisca was most likely also Jewish. Aquila was a freed slave while Prisca was born free, which would give her a higher social status in Rome and might explain why she is mentioned first.[17]

Paul describes them as his coworkers (τούς συνεργοὺς μου) in Christ (ἐν Χριστῷ Ἰησοῦ), which establishes them as missionary colleagues engaged in ministry for Christ. They had "risked their own necks" (τὸν ἑυατῶν τράχηλον ἐπέθηκαν) on Paul's behalf (ὑπὲρ τῆς ψυχῆς μου), perhaps during the riot in Ephesus (Acts 19:23–40). They are well known enough that all the Gentile churches Paul had planted (πᾶσαι αἱ ἐκκλησίαι τῶν ἐθνῶν) join Paul in thanking God for them (οἷς οὐκ ἐγὼ μόνος εὐχαριστῶ). As was true in Ephesus (1 Cor. 16:19), they hosted a house church in Rome (καὶ τὴν κατ᾽ οἶκον αὐτῶν ἐκκλησίαν).

Epaenetus was a Greek freedman for whom Paul expresses particular affection and personal attachment (τὸν ἀγαπητόν μου). He is one of Paul's first converts in the province of Asia (ὅς ἐστιν ἀπαρχὴ τῆς Ἀσίας εἰς Χριστόν). Mary was most likely Jewish and came from a slave background.[18] Paul describes her as someone who exerted herself spiritually in many tasks (πολλὰ ἐκοπίασεν) on behalf of the Romans (εἰς ὑμᾶς). Elsewhere, Paul refers to those who "labor" (κοπιάω) in leadership (1 Thess. 5:12) and preaching/teaching roles (1 Tim. 5:17) and, therefore, have rights to pay or support.

Andronicus and Junia were a second husband and wife team, who were most likely Hellenized Jews with slave origins.[19] The manuscript support for "Junia/Junias" is considerably stronger than the support for the variant, "Julian"; the masculine name is not found elsewhere; and no commentators understood the name as masculine before the thirteenth century.[20] They were fellow Jews (τοὺς συγγενεῖς μου), a term Ellis suggests more narrowly refers to Paul's relatives who are also missionaries from local churches,[21] as well as Paul's fellow-prisoners (καὶ συναιχμαλώτους μου). The latter term might describe either being imprisoned with Paul or sharing the experience of being imprisoned for Christ.[22] They were Christians before Paul's conversion (οἳ πρὸ ἐμοῦ γέγονεν ἐν Χριστῷ), and they were apostles in the same sense that Paul was.

---

17. Harvey, *Romans*, 377.
18. Jewett, *Romans*, 961.
19. Dunn, *Romans*, 894.
20. See Harvey, *Romans*, 379.
21. *DPL*, 186.
22. Jewett, *Romans*, 923n37.

There is considerable discussion over how best to understand the phrase "outstanding among the apostles" (ἐπίσημοι ἐν τοῖς ἀποστόλοις). Most English versions (e.g., NASB, NIV, NLT) understand the combination as local: "outstanding *among* the apostles." A few English versions (e.g., CSB, ESV, NET) translate the phrase as idiomatic: "well-known *to* the apostles." The former seems the more natural understanding of ἐν + dative.[23]

2. Paul greets those who know him (16:8–15).

Next, Paul sends greetings to a wide-ranging collection of individuals and groups, who are either friends or acquaintances. They can testify to the content of the gospel Paul preaches and has set out in the body of his letter. Ampliatus and Urbanus were common Roman slave names. Paul describes Ampliatus as his "beloved Christian friend" (τὸν ἀγαπητόν μου ἐν Χριστῷ), which highlights his close relationship to both Paul and Christ. As was true of Prisca and Aquila, Urbanus is "our coworker in the service of Christ" (τὸν συνεργὸν ἡμῶν ἐν Χριστῷ). Cranfield suggests that the use of "coworker" indicates that Paul knew Urbanus more by his reputation for missionary service than from personal contact.[24] Stachys and Apelles were both Greeks of uncertain social status. "My beloved" (τὸν ἀγαπητόν μου) suggests Paul's personal connection to Stachys, while his description of Apelles (τὸν δόκιμον ἐν Χριστῷ) identifies him as one "whom Christ approves."[25]

"Those who are from the household of Aristobulus" (τοὺς τῶν Ἀριστοβούλου) describes members of a house church, most likely composed primarily of slaves.[26] Moo argues that the mention of Herodion immediately after Aristobulus connects both to the family of Herod.[27] If so, Aristobulus was most likely the grandson of Herod the Great, who had lived in Rome and died in A.D. 48 or 49. Although Herodion was a Greek name, the fact that Paul calls him "my kinsman" (τὸν συγγενῆ μου) identifies him as Jewish, perhaps a slave or freedman in the service of the extended family of Herod.[28] Moo notes that Narcissus was

---

23. Harvey, *Romans*, 380. For a detailed defense of the minority position, see M. Burer, "ΕΠΙΣΗΜΟΙ ΈΝ ΤΟΙΣ ἈΠΟΣΤΟΛΟΙΣ in Romans 16:7 as 'Well-Known to the Apostles': Further Defense and New Evidence," *JETS* 58 (2015): 731–55.
24. Cranfield, *Romans*, 791.
25. NLT.
26. Jewett, *Romans*, 966.
27. Moo, *Romans*, 925.
28. Dunn, *Romans*, 896.

"the name of a well known freedman who served the Emperor Claudius and who committed suicide just before Paul wrote Romans."[29] Paul greets the members of a Christian congregation consisting of individuals from that household (τοὺς ἐκ τῶν Ναρκίσσου τοὺς ὄντας ἐν κυρίῳ).

Tryphaena, Tryphosa, and Persis share the common designation of "laborers in the the service of the Lord" (τὰς κοπιώσας ἐν κυρίῳ; ἥτις πολλὰ ἐκοπίασεν ἐν κυρίῳ; cf. 16:6). All three names are Greek. Tryphaena and Tryphosa were most likely sisters and freedwomen with some degree of independence.[30] Persis was probably a slave captured in "Persia" and named for that region. Paul also describes her as "the beloved" (τὴν ἀγαπητήν; cf. 16:5, 8, 9). Rufus and his mother were freeborn Romans, possibly with considerable means.[31] He was well-known for the way in which the Lord chose him (τὸν ἐκλεκτὸν ἐν κυρίῳ); she had previously cared for and/or supported Paul in the same way that a mother might (τὴν μητέρα αὐτοῦ καὶ ἐμοῦ).

Paul concludes his list of specific greetings by addressing individuals who, most likely, comprised the leadership teams of two congregations.[32] Asyncritus, Phlegon, Hermes, Patrobas, Hermas, are all Greek names usually given to slaves or freedmen.[33] The fact that Paul adds no qualifiers to their names suggests that he knew of the congregation only by reputation. It might, however, have been a fairly large group, since it consisted of these five named individuals and "the brothers who are with them" (τοὺς σὺν αὐτοῖς ἀδελφούς). Another group of five named individuals probably comprised the leadership team of a different congregation:

> Philologus, Julia, Nereus, Nereus's sister, and Olympas. Philologus and Julia were a third husband and wife team; three of the five are women. Although Julia is a Roman name, the other four names are all Greek and were common for slaves and freedmen. This congregation might also have been fairly large, since Paul also greets "all the saints who are with them" (τοὺς σὺν αὐτοῖς πάντας ἁγίους).

---

29. Moo, *Romans*, 925.
30. Dunn, *Romans*, 897.
31. Jewett, *Romans*, 969.
32. Jewett suggests the nomenclature "tenement churches" for congregations without a patron or patroness. He describes them as "meeting in one of the multistoried dwellings where slaves and lower-class handworkers and laborers lived in rented spaces in the upper floors" (Jewett, *Romans*, 971).
33. Dunn, *Romans*, 898.

3. Paul greets the whole church (16:16).

Paul closes the section with a command and a general greeting. The command is to "greet one another by means of a holy kiss" (ἀσπάσασθε ἀλλήλους ἐν φιλήματι ἁγίῳ). Paul includes the same command at the end of three other letters (1 Cor. 16:20; 2 Cor. 13:12; 1 Thess. 5:26), and Peter concludes his first letter with a similar command (1 Peter 5:14). The kiss was a common form of greeting in the ancient world (cf. Gen. 29:11; Exod. 4:27; 2 Sam. 20:9; Luke 7:45; 15:20). Paul, however, adds the adjective "holy." Weima comments that "the reference to a 'holy' (ἅγιος) kiss suggests that the apostle wants to distinguish the greeting kiss of believers (ἅγιοι) from that practiced outside the faith . . . among Christians it assumed a deeper meaning . . . the kiss expressed not merely friendship and love, but more specifically reconciliation and peace."[34]

Paul also extends a greeting from "all the churches of Christ" (αἱ ἐκκλησίαι πᾶσαι τοῦ Χριστοῦ), which probably refers to the churches he had planted. By adding this final greeting, Paul "presents himself to the Romans as one who has the official backing of all the churches in Achaia, Macedonia, Asia, Galatian, Syria, and elsewhere in the eastern part of the empire."[35] He also provides evidence that "his gospel has taken root over the whole world and invites the Romans to be part of his mission."[36] Paul's extended greeting list, therefore, testifies to the effectiveness of his apostolic ministry (16:3–7), testifies to the orthodoxy of the gospel he preaches (16:8–15), calls the Romans to unity with one another (16:16a), and challenges them to be involved in Christ's global enterprise (16:16b).

Theology and Appropriation

It is incorrect to think of "the church in Rome" as though it were either a single homogeneous entity or a megachurch. It is better to speak of the "congregations in Rome," similar to the way Paul writes to "the churches in Galatia" (Gal. 1:2; cf. 1 Cor. 16:1). Galatia, of course, refers to a region in the same way that Paul refers to the congregations in "Macedonia and Achaia" (Rom. 15:26; cf. 2 Cor. 8:1). Nevertheless, the greetings in Paul's letter to Rome make it clear that his addressees were far from a single homogeneous group. In fact, they represented multiple ethnic (Jewish, Greek, Latin) and social (freeborn, freed,

---

34. Weima, *Neglected Endings*, 113.
35. Weima, *Neglected Endings*, 227.
36. Schreiner, *Romans*, 798.

slave) backgrounds. The following table groups the individuals who are named by both categories.[37]

	Freeborn (3)	Freed (6)	Slave (17)
Jewish (6)	Prisca	Aquila	Mary Andronicus Junia Herodion
Greek (15)		Epaenetus Apelles Tryphaena Tryphosa	Stachys Asyncritus Persis Phlegon Philologus Hermes Nereus Patrobas Nereus's sister Hermas Olympas
Latin (5)	Rufus Rufus's mother	Urbanus	Ampliatus Julia

Paul mentions at least five distinct congregations. Asyncritus, Phlegon, Hermes, Patrobas, and Hermas (16:14) appear to comprise the leadership team of a predominantly Greek congregation composed of slaves. The same appears to be true of a congregation led by Philologus, Julia, Nereus, Nereus's sister, and Olympas (16:15), although Julia's ethnic background was Latin. It is more difficult to draw any conclusions about the church composed of members of Narcissus's household (16:11). If the individuals named after the mention of that group (Tryphaena, Tryphosa, Persis, Rufus, Rufus's mother) were part of the congregation, it might have been more heterogeneous both ethnically (Greek

---

37. Longenecker's suggestion that "all those mentioned in this list were probably Jewish believers in Jesus (or those considered by Roman authorities to be related to Jewish Christians) who had left Rome because of the edict of Claudius in A.D. 49 but had, after the repeal of the edict of expulsion . . . either (1) returned to the capital city for family or economic reasons or (2) migrated there for these and other quite personal reasons" seems unlikely (*Romans*, 1066).

and Latin) and socially (freeborn, freed, and slave).[38] The members of the congregation from Aristobulus's household (16:10) were most likely Jewish slaves of whom Herodion was the best known. The congregation that met in the house of Prisca and Aquila (16:5) might have been more Jewish and of higher social status, especially if Epaenetus (freed Gentile) and Mary (Jewish slave) were part of that group. Regardless, it is clear that those individuals who knew Paul's ministry and his gospel crossed ethnic, social, and geographic boundaries.

Paul's primary purpose for including this passage at this point in his letter was to provide a wide range of witnesses to the effectiveness of his ministry and the orthodoxy of his gospel. With his original readers, we need to welcome and support proven workers in Christ's service. The passage offers multiple possible points of connection, including greeting old friends, making new acquaintances, and establishing a network of contacts in a new city. The passage corrects the idea that the New Testament church as a whole was a homogeneous entity. The passage commends an attitude that seeks to work with others of different ethnic, cultural, socioeconomic, and ministry backgrounds for the progress of the gospel. The objective in communicating this passage should be to help others understand the importance of acknowledging what God might be doing through those "outside their group," so that they will catch a vision for Christ's manifold wisdom and grace (cf. Eph. 3:10; 1 Peter 4:10).

---

38. Grouping those names together as members of a single congregation is tenuous, although most commentators follow a similar approach in grouping together the names in verse 15, in connecting Herodion with the household of Aristobulus (16:10–11), and in connecting Epaenetus with the church in Prisca and Aquila's house (16:5).

ROMANS 16:17–20

Text and Translation

17 Now I am exhorting you, brothers, to pay careful attention to the *ones who* are creating[1] dissensions and stumbling blocks contrary to the teaching[2] that you learned, and turn away from them. **18** For those of such kind are not serving our Lord, Christ,[3] but their own stomachs, and by smooth speech and fine words[4] they are leading astray the hearts of the unsuspecting. **19** For your obedience reaches to all; therefore, we are rejoicing because of you,[5] but I am wishing that you be wise with reference to that *which is* good[6] but innocent with reference to that *which is* evil. **20** And the God who produces peace[7] will crush Satan under your feet soon.[8] *May* the grace our Lord Jesus[9] bestows[10] *be* with you.

Context and Structure

III. Letter Closing (15:14–16:27)
- A. Paul's Mission (15:14–21)
- B. Paul's Travel Plans (15:22–29)
- C. Paul's Prayer Request (15:30–33)
- D. Commendation of Phoebe (16:1–2)
- E. Greetings from Paul (16:3–16)
- F. **Closing Advice (16:17–20)**
- G. Greetings from Others (16:21–24)
- H. Doxology (16:25–27)

---

1. Τοὶς ... ποιοῦντας is a substantival participle.
2. Παρά + accusative denotes opposition.
3. Τῷ κυρίῳ is a dative of direct object; so also τῇ κιολίᾳ; Χριστῷ stands in apposition to κυρίῳ.
4. Διά+ genitive denotes means.
5. Ἐπί + dative denotes cause.
6. Εἰς + accusative denotes reference (twice).
7. Εἰρήνης is a dative of product.
8. Ἐν τάχει is temporal.
9. The variant that omits the benediction has limited manuscript support (D). Of the two variants that include the benediction Ἰησοῦ (𝔓⁴⁶, ℵ, B) is shorter than Ἰησοῦ Χριστοῦ (A, 33), and a scribe would have been more likely to add Χριστοῦ than to omit it.
10. Τοῦ κυρίου is a genitive of source.

Paul includes closing advice in other letters (e.g., 2 Cor. 13:5–10; Eph. 6:10–20; Phil. 4:4–9; 1 Thess. 5:12–22); he also drafts brief paragraphs in his own hand (1 Cor. 16:21–24; Gal. 6:11–18; Col. 4:18; 2 Thess. 3:17). It is likely that this paragraph reflects both practices. To the Romans, he combines a warning about false teachers (16:17–18) with a commendation for their obedience (16:19–20). He closes with a grace benediction (16:20b).

Basic Message and Exegetical Outline

Paul's closing words to the Romans warn them about false teachers and commend them for their obedience.

> Paul's Closing Advice (16:17–20)
> 1. Paul warns the Romans to avoid false teachers (16:17–18)
>   a. They sow dissension and doubt, which are contrary to sound doctrine (16:17)
>   b. They use smooth speech and fine words to lead astray the unsuspecting (16:18)
> 2. Paul commends the Romans for their obedience (16:19–20)
>   a. It is known by all and brings joy to Paul (16:19)
>   b. It anticipates ultimate victory (16:20)

Explanation of the Text

1. Paul warns the Romans to avoid false teachers (16:17–18).

Paul uses a request formula (παρακαλῶ δὲ ὑμᾶς, ἀδελφοί) to mark a shift in subject matter (cf. 12:1; 15:30). The request involves a double warning that some commentators view as introducing a non-Pauline interpolation.[11] Moo, however, suggests that his concluding greeting from "all the churches of Christ" (16:16b) leads Paul to warn the Roman congregations against the doctrinal threats those other churches have encountered.[12] The first warning is that they should "mark so as to avoid" (σκοπεῖν)[13] anyone who might create (τοὺς ... ποιοῦντας) dissensions (τὰς διχοστασίας) and raise causes for stumbling (τὰ σκάνδαλα)

---

11. See Jewett, *Romans,* 986–88, but Schreiner ably refutes the interpolation theory (*Romans,* 801).
12. Moo, *Romans,* 929.
13. Cranfield, *Romans,* 798.

that are contrary to the teaching they have learned (παρὰ τὴν διδαχήν ἣν ὑμεῖς ἐμάθετε). The teaching the Romans have known from the beginning, therefore, aligns fully with the gospel Paul has set out earlier in the letter. Since Schreiner notes that "the σκάνδαλον word group typically occurs in contexts featuring the danger of abandoning the Christian faith,"[14] any deviation from the teaching they know and the gospel Paul preaches is a grave departure from the truth. Having marked any disruptive influences they might encounter, the Romans should "steer clear of them" (ἐκκλίνετε ἀπ᾽ αὐτῶν).[15]

It is impossible to identify these particular false teachers with any certainty, and Paul is probably warning about the character of false teachers in general rather than about specific false teachings. Regardless, he offers two reasons (γάρ) to steer clear of such people (οἱ τοιοῦτοι). First, they are serving their own interests (τῇ ἑαυτῶν κοιλίᾳ)[16] rather than the interests of Christ, whom they should serve as their Lord (τῷ κυρίῳ Χριστῷ οὐ δουλεύουσιν). Second, they lead astray (ἐξαπατῶσιν) the hearts of those who are innocent/without evil (τὰς καρδίας τῶν ἀκάκων). The means they use are plausible speech (χρηστολογίας) and words that are well chosen but untrue (εὐλογίας). Schreiner writes, "The Romans must be on guard because the opponents are urbane, witty, and sophisticated. They will not be unattractive boors."[17]

2. Paul commends the Romans for their obedience (16:19–20).

The reason (γάρ) for Paul's warning is the Romans' reputation for obedience, which is well-known throughout the eastern empire (ἡ ὑμῶν ὑπακοὴ εἰς πάντας ἀφίκετο).[18] Their obedience gives Paul a reason for rejoicing about them (ἐφ᾽ ὑμῖν χαίρω), but (δέ) he also wants to make certain they are growing in their ability to discern between good and evil. Most likely echoing Jesus's statement in Matthew 10:16, Paul writes that he wants them "to be wise with reference to that which is good" (σοφοὺς εἶναι εἰς τὸ ἀγαθόν) but "innocent with reference to that

---

14. Schreiner, *Romans*, 802.
15. Jewett, *Romans*, 990.
16. See Philippians 3:19 for a similar instance where "belly" (κοιλία) refers figuratively to self-interest rather than literally to the stomach (cf. Moo, *Romans*, 931n29).
17. Schreiner, *Romans*, 804.
18. Schreiner suggests that their reputation would make the Romans a special target for false teachers who would want to undermine their obedience (*Romans*, 804).

which is evil" (ἀκεραίους εἰς τὸ κακόν).[19] Stott puts it this way: "To be wise in regard to good is to recognize it, love it, and follow it. With regard to evil, however, he wants them to be unsophisticated, even guileless, so completely [that] they shy away from any experience of it."[20] Growing in their discernment will sustain them in their obedience and help them steer clear of false teachers.

The anticipation of their ultimate victory should also sustain them. Alluding to the "proto-evangelium" of Genesis 3:15, Paul encourages them with the promise that the God who bestows peace (ὁ θεὸς τῆς εἰρήνης; cf. 15:33) will give them peace as he "completely subdues"[21] Satan under their feet (συντρίψει τὸν Σατανᾶν ὑπὸ τοὺς πόδας ὑμῶν) and will do so "soon" (ἐν τάχει). Paul's promise probably includes both future victory over Satan and present victory over the false teachers against whom he was been warning them.[22] Since victory would be impossible without God's grace, Paul ends this section of closing advice with a grace-benediction: "May the grace our Lord Jesus bestows be with you" (ἡ χάρις τοῦ κυρίου ἡμῶν Ἰησοῦ μεθ' ὑμῶν).[23]

Theology and Appropriation

Although 16:20 is the only mention of Satan in Romans, supernatural beings are prominent in Paul's letters. Some serve God and are friendly to humankind (1 Cor. 4:9; 11:10; 2 Thess. 1:7; 1 Tim. 3:16; 5:21). Others are hostile to God and humankind (Rom. 8:38; Eph. 6:11–16). This age is dominated by evil supernatural forces (Eph. 2:2). The ruler of these forces is the devil, or Satan, who seeks to frustrate God's redemptive purposes (2 Cor. 4:4), but whose ultimate end is destruction.

Paul mentions Satan (ὁ Σατανᾶς) ten times, using a transliteration of the Hebrew word that means adversary or wicked opponent.[24] He mentions the devil (ὁ διάβολος) five times, using the LXX translation for Satan.[25] Βελιάρ (2 Cor. 6:15) appears frequently in the Qumran

---

19. It is worth noting the wordplay of "without evil/innocent" (ἀκάκων) . . . "innocent" (ἀκραίους) . . . "evil" (κακόν).
20. Stott, *Romans*, 400.
21. BDAG 976.
22. Cf. Moo, *Romans*, 933.
23. Paul includes grace benedictions at the ends of seven other letters (1 Cor. 16:23; 2 Cor. 13:14; Gal. 6:18; Phil. 4:23; Col. 4:18; 1 Thess. 5:28; 2 Thess. 3:18).
24. Romans 16:20; 1 Corinthians 5:5; 7:5; 2 Corinthians 2:11; 11:14; 12:7; 1 Thessalonians 2:18; 2 Thessalonians 2:9; 1 Timothy 1:20; 5:15.
25. Ephesians 4:27; 6:11; 1 Timothy 3:6, 7; 2 Timothy 2:26.

texts as the name of the evil spirit who lives in the hearts of "the sons of darkness."[26] The latter name possibly lies behind Paul's references to "the rule of the authority of the air" (ὁ ἄρχων τῆς ἐξουσίας τοῦ ἀέρος) in Ephesians 2:2 and "the god of this age" (ὁ θεὸς τοῦ αἰῶνος τούτου) in 2 Corinthians 4:4.[27] Other names are "the tempter" (ὁ πειράζων) and "the evil one" (ὁ πονηρός).[28]

At times, Satan is the agent of divine discipline (1 Cor. 5:5; 1 Tim. 1:20). Primarily, however, Satan is the ruler of the air (Eph. 2:2), who is wily and deceitful (Eph. 6:11) and disguises himself as an angel of light (2 Cor. 11:14). He takes advantage of openings (Eph. 4:27) to blind (2 Cor. 4:4), to tempt (1 Cor. 7:5; 2 Cor. 2:11; 1 Thess. 3:5; 1 Tim. 6:9), to trap (1 Tim. 3:7; 2 Tim. 2:26), to oppose God's purposes (2 Cor. 12:7; 1 Thess. 2:18), to attack (Eph. 6:16), and to lead into condemnation (1 Tim. 3:6). During the period prior to Christ's return, Satan will send and empower the antichrist (2 Thess. 2:9). Throughout Satan's attacks, however, God protects his people from the evil one (2 Thess. 3:3) and ultimately crushes him under their feet (Rom. 16:20).

Paul's primary purpose for including this passage at this point in his letter was to offer closing advice that will help his Roman readers remain faithful to the gospel they have learned and he preaches. With his original readers, we need to understand the character and strategy of false teachers so that we can steer clear of them and continue in our obedience to Christ. The passage offers multiple possible points of connection, including dissension, self-interest, eloquent speech, and having a good reputation. The passage corrects any sense of spiritual complacency that suggests it is possible to rely on past obedience to face future tests. The passage commends faithful obedience that is vigilant to discern good from evil and truth from error. The objective in communicating this passage should be to help others understand the character and strategy of false teachers so that they will be diligent to discern good from evil and truth from error.

---

26. Paul never mentions Βεελζεβούλ, a name that occurs seven times in the Synoptic gospels.
27. Both of these names are similar to Jesus's references to "the ruler of this age" (ὁ ἄρχων τοῦ κόσμου τούτου) in John 12:31; 14:30; 16:11).
28. "The evil one" is common in John's writings (1 John 2:13, 14; 3:12; 5:18).

ROMANS 16:21–23

Text and Translation

21   Timothy, my co-worker, is greeting you, and Lucius and Jason and Sosipater, my kinsmen.
22   I, Tertius who wrote[1] this[2] letter, am greeting you as a Christian.[3]
23   Gaius, my host, and *the host* of the whole church is greeting you. Erastus, the steward over the city,[4] and Quartus our brother[5] are greeting you.[6]

Context and Structure

III. Letter Closing (15:14–16:27)
    A. Paul's Mission (15:14–21)
    B. Paul's Travel Plans (15:22–29)
    C. Paul's Prayer Request (15:30–33)
    D. Commendation of Phoebe (16:1–2)
    E. Greetings from Paul (16:3–16)
    F. Closing Advice (16:17–20)
    G. **Greetings from Others (16:21–24)**
    H. Doxology (16:25–27)

Paul includes greetings from others elsewhere in his letters (1 Cor. 16:19–20a; 2 Cor. 13:13; Phil. 4:22; Col. 4:10–14; Titus 3:15a; Philem. 23–24). This brief list includes four of Paul's teammates (16:21), Paul's amanuensis (16:22), and three members of the church in Corinth (16:23).

Basic Message and Exegetical Outline

Greetings from teammates and members of the church in Corinth reinforce the inclusive nature of Paul's ministry.

---

1. Ὁ γράψας is a substantival participle in apposition to Τέρτιυς.
2. The definite article is deictic. Wallace suggests "the letter you have in your hands" (*Grammar*, 221).
3. Ἐν κυρίῳ denotes sphere of reference.
4. Τῆς πόλεως is a genitive of subordination.
5. The definite article with ἀδελφός functions as a possessive pronoun.
6. 𝔓⁴⁶, ℵ, A, and B omit the benediction of 16:24, and UBS⁵ gives the omission an [A] rating.

Greetings from Others (16:21–23)
1. Paul's Jewish teammates greet the Romans (16:21)
    a. Timothy (16:21a)
    b. Lucius, Jason, and Sosipater (16:21b)
2. Tertius greets the Romans (16:22)
3. Members of the Gentile church in Corinth greet the Romans (16:23)
    a. Gaius (16:23a)
    b. Erastus and Quartus (16:23b)

Explanation of the Text

1. Paul's Jewish teammates greet the Romans (16:21).

Longenecker suggests that some of Paul's associates and friends had gathered in Corinth to hear Paul's letter read before he dispatched it to Rome with Phoebe. After it was read, those associates and friends asked to add their own greetings to lend support to what Paul had written.[7] First, four teammates who had arrived in Corinth with the Macedonian contribution to the collection for Jerusalem offer their greetings.[8] Timothy heads the list. Paul designates him as "my co-worker" (ὁ συνεργός μου), the same term he used to refer to Prisca and Aquila (16:3) as well as Urbanus (16:9).[9]

> Timothy was from Lystra in Asia Minor, the son of a Jewish mother and a Greek father (Acts 16:1–2). He was co-author of 2 Corinthians (1:1), Philippians (1:1), 1 Thessalonians (1:1), 2 Thessalonians (1:1), Colossians (1:1), and Philemon (1) and the addressee of 1–2 Timothy. He traveled between Thessalonica (Acts 17:14–15), Corinth (Acts 18:5; 20:4), Macedonia (Acts 19:22), and Ephesus (1 Tim. 1:3) and is mentioned elsewhere in Paul's letters (1 Cor. 4:17; 16:10–11; 2 Cor. 1:19; Phil. 2:19–24; 1 Thess. 3:2, 6).[10]

Paul calls Lucius, Jason, and Sosipater "my kinsmen" (οἱ συγγενεῖς μου), the same term he used to refer to Andronicus and Junia (16:7) as well

---

7. Longenecker, *Romans*, 1079.
8. Jewett, *Romans*, 978.
9. Elsewhere, Paul refers to eight other men and two other women as "co-workers." (See the discussion under 16:1–2.)
10. Harvey, *Romans*, 392.

as Herodion (16:11). Despite their Latin and Greek names, they were Jewish converts who represented the Pauline churches in Macedonia.

> Although Lucius had a Latin name, he was most likely a Jewish convert and a representative from one of the Pauline churches. Jason was most likely Paul's host in Thessalonica (cf. Acts 17:5–9) and a Jewish convert. Sosipater is a longer version of the Greek name Sopater (cf. Acts 20:4) and most likely was a Jewish convert from Berea.[11]

2. Tertius greets the Romans (16:22).

Tertius adds his own greetings and identifies himself as the one "who wrote this letter" (ὁ γράψας τὴν ἐπιστολήν).

> The fact that Tertius inserts his own greetings as the one who wrote the letter (16:22) lends credence to the idea that Paul used secretaries when he wrote, as do references elsewhere to writing "in [his] own hand" (cf. 1 Cor. 16:21; Gal. 6:11; Col. 4:18; 2 Thess. 3:17; Philem. 19). The latter references also have led some scholars to identify possible autograph sections in Paul's letters. Harry Gamble, for example, has proposed that Romans 16:1–20 comprises such a section, while Weima argues for 16:16–20.[12]

Jewett suggests that Tertius was a scribe, who was a member of Phoebe's household and whom she had put at Paul's disposal as part of her patronage.[13] He was most likely an educated slave; the fact that he speaks for himself as "a Christian" (ἐν κυρίῳ) highlights the socioeconomic equality that characterized the early church.

3. Members of the Gentile church in Corinth greet the Romans (16:23).

Finally, three members of the church in Corinth—all with Latin names—offer their greetings, beginning with Gaius, who was Paul's current host (ὁ ξένος μου).

---

11. Harvey, *Romans*, 393.
12. Harvey, *Pauline Letters*, 32. For discussions of Paul's use of secretaries, see R. N. Longenecker, "Ancient Amanuenses and the Pauline Epistles" (*New Dimensions in New Testament Study*, ed. R. N. Longenecker and M. C. Tenney [Grand Rapids: Eerdmans], 218–97) and E. R. Richards, *Paul and First-Century Letter Writing: Secretaries, Composition, and Collection* (Downers Grove, IL: InterVarsity, 2004).
13. Jewett, *Romans*, 979.

Gaius's Latin name suggests that he was a noble or a freedman and a Roman citizen. His full name was most likely Gaius Titius Justus, which would identify him as a leader in the church in Corinth (Acts 18:7; 1 Cor. 1:14).[14]

A "host" was someone who extended hospitality and treated strangers as guests.[15] The addition "and the host of the whole church" (καὶ ὅλης τῆς ἐκκλασίας) suggests that Gaius's hospitality extended to others from the worldwide church who might also pass through Corinth.[16] Erastus was a financial official, perhaps the city treasurer (ὁ οἰκονόμος τῆς πόλεως).[17] The fact that Paul designates Quartus as "our brother" (ὁ ἀδελφός) suggests that he was a worker in the Corinthian church and might have been known to at least some of Paul's readers. Together, the greetings from these three prominent individuals with Roman backgrounds help endorse Paul and his ministry to the Roman congregations he hoped to visit soon.

Theology and Appropriation
Far from being an afterthought, including greetings from his associates and friends provides a fitting conclusion to Paul's letter, especially as it relates to his missiological purpose of seeking support for his proposed work in Spain. Taken with 16:1–20, these greetings highlight the inclusiveness and effectiveness of Paul's gospel ministry. Phoebe was a freed slave of Greek background who provided hospitality and support for Paul and his work (16:1–2). The long list of greetings from Paul highlights the personal connection the gospel creates, a connection that crosses cultural (Jewish, Greek, Latin) and social (slave, freed, freeborn) boundaries and embraces "all the churches of Christ" (16:3–16). Paul's closing advice reminds the Romans of the common gospel followers of Christ share as well as the fact that their reputation for obedience to that gospel extends beyond their own city and region (16:17–20).

In closing, the greetings Paul includes from his associates and friends reinforce his ministry that has made an impact on Jews (Timothy, Lucius, Jason, Sosipater) and Gentiles (Tertius, Gaius, Erastus. Quartus) alike. It has made an impact in Galatia (Timothy), Macedonia (Jason, Sosipater), and Achaia (Tertius, Gaius, Erastus,

---

14. Harvey, *Romans*, 393.
15. BDAG 684.
16. Cf. Moo, *Romans*, 935.
17. Literally, "the steward/manager/administrator over the city."

Quartus). It has penetrated every level of society, including slaves (Tertius), freed (Quartus), Roman citizens (Gaius), and public officials (Erastus). In fact, Jewett concludes that Phoebe and Erastus form a rhetorical inclusio around the final sections of the letter: "The sponsorship of the rich patroness Phoebe at the beginning of chapter 16 and the support of the influential . . . Erastus . . . at the end of the letter are the rhetorical trump cards that finally render Paul's project politically plausible."[18] How can the Romans fail to accept Paul and support his proposed work in Spain when the impact of his ministry is so inclusive and effective?

Paul's primary purpose for including this passage at this point in his letter was to allow his associates from the east and his friends from Corinth to voice their support for him and his ministry. With his original readers, we need to give serious attention to the testimony of others regarding what God is doing around the world. The passage offers multiple possible points of connection, including coworkers and associates, relatives and fellow-countrymen, and extending hospitality to others. The passage corrects any idea that local congregations have no responsibility for ministry activities outside their city or region. Along with 15:22–29, the passage commends cooperation across cultural, social, and geographic boundaries. The objective in communicating this passage should be to help others understand their connectedness to the global spread of the gospel, so that they will commit to supporting and being engaged in that work.

---

18. Jewett, *Romans*, 984.

ROMANS 16:25–27

Text and Translation

25 Now to the *one who* is able[1] to strengthen you according to my
gospel,[2] that is,[3] the preaching about Jesus Christ,[4]
based on the revelation[5] of the mystery[6]
  which has been kept secret[7] for eternal ages[8]
26   but now has been made manifest[9]
      and has been made known[10]
        by the prophetic Scriptures[11]
        because of the command[12] from the eternal God[13]
        for the obedience[14] that comes from faith[15]
        to all the Gentiles,
27 to *the* only wise God,
      through Jesus Christ,
to whom *be* the glory to the ages.[16] Amen.

---

1. Τῷ δυναμένῳ is a substantival participle.
2. Κατά + accusative denotes standard.
3. Καί is epexegetic.
4. Ἰησοῦ Χριστοῦ is an objective genitive.
5. Κατά + accusative denotes basis.
6. Μυστηρίου is an objective genitive.
7. Σεσιγημένου is an adjectival participle modifying μυστηρίου.
8. Χρόνοις αἰωνίοις is a temporal dative indicating duration.
9. Φανερωθέντος is an adjectival participle modifying μυστηρίου; the aorist tense is consummative.
10. Γνωρισθέντος is an adjectival participle modifying μυστηρίου; the aorist tense is consummative. Although the participle stands at the end of verse 26 in the Greek text, it has been brought forward so that it is parallel with the other two adjectival participles and the prepositional phrases that modify it read more naturally in the translation.
11. Διά + genitive is instrumental.
12. Κατά + accusative denotes cause.
13. Τοῦ αἰωνίου Θεοῦ is a subjective genitive.
14. Εἰς + accusative denotes purpose.
15. Πίστεως is a subjective genitive.
16. Εἰς + accusative is temporal, denoting duration. Manuscript evidence is divided between the shorter αἰῶνας (𝔓⁴⁶, B, 33) and the longer αἰῶνας τῶν αἰώνων (ℵ, A, D). A scribe would have been more likely to conform the shorter reading to the more common longer reading (cf. Gal. 1:5; Phil. 4:20; 1 Tim. 1:17; 2 Tim. 4:18).

Context and Structure

III. Letter Closing (15:14–16:27)
   A. Paul's Mission (15:14–21)
   B. Paul's Travel Plans (15:22–29)
   C. Paul's Prayer Request (15:30–33)
   D. Commendation of Phoebe (16:1–2)
   E. Greetings from Paul (16:3–16)
   F. Closing Advice (16:17–20)
   G. Greetings from Others (16:21–24)
   H. **Doxology (16:25–27)**

Since Paul elsewhere ends his letters with a grace-benediction (cf. 16:20b), the closing doxology of Romans is unique (compare other doxologies in Rom. 11:33–36; Eph. 3:20–21; Phil. 4:20; 1 Tim. 1:17). It consists of three datives referring to God (16:25a, 27a, 27c), which frame an extended summary of the gospel (16:25b–26), in which three participial phrases explain the nature of God's revealed mystery.

Basic Message and Exegetical Outline
The only wise God deserves eternal glory because he is able to strengthen us according to the gospel of Jesus Christ.

Why God Deserves Eternal Glory (16:26–27)
   1. God is able to strengthen us (16:25a)
   2. God has revealed the mystery of the gospel (16:25b–26)
   3. God is the only wise one (16:27)

Explanation of the Text
1. God is able to strengthen us (16:25a).

   In a doxology focused on God the Father, Paul begins with the first of three datives (δυναμένῳ) that frame the section. The one Paul is describing is not yet named but is characterized by his ability to strengthen believers (ὑμᾶς στηρίξαι). The verb δύναμαι echoes the power that raised Jesus from the dead (1:4) and the power of God for salvation (1:16); the verb στηρίζω echoes the strengthening Paul hopes to offer the Romans (1:11). That strengthening is possible only by God's enabling and enables them to be "firm, strong, and stable, whether in their faith (against error), in their holiness (against temptation), or in their courage (against persecution)."[17]

---

17. Stott, *Romans*, 403. As support, Stott notes 1 Corinthians 1:8; 2 Corinthians 1:21; Colossians 2:7; 1 Thessalonians 3:2, 13; 2 Thessalonians 2:17.

2. God has revealed the mystery of the gospel (16:25b–26).

The standard and means by which God will strengthen the Romans is Paul's gospel (κατὰ τὸ εὐαγγέλιον μου) that he preaches about Jesus Christ (τὸ κήρυγμα Ἰησοῦ Χριστοῦ). Τὸ εὐαγγέλιον is the gospel for which God has set Paul apart (1:1), which focuses on God's son (1:9), and which embodies God's saving power (1:16). This gospel is a revealed mystery (ἀποκάλυψιν μυστηρίου)[18] that God has kept secret (σεσιγημένου)[19] "for long ages" (χρόνοις αἰωνίοις)[20] but now has made known (φανερωθέντος δὲ νῦν). The instrument God has used to make known the gospel is the Old Testament, which Paul characterizes as "the prophetic Scriptures" (διὰ γραφῶν προφητικῶν), a description that echoes the agency (διὰ τῶν προφητῶν) and instrumentality (ἐν γραφαῖς ἁγίαις) with which Paul initially introduced the gospel (1:2). The basis of the revelation is "the command from the eternal God" (κατ᾽ ἐπιταγὴν τοῦ αἰωνίου θεοῦ). The objective of that revelation is "the obedience that comes from faith" (εἰς ὑπακοὴν πίστεως), which echoes the same phrase in the salutation (1:5) and is best understood as describing "obedience to the call of faith that results in a lifestyle of faithful obedience."[21] The audience of the revealed mystery is "all the Gentiles" (εἰς πάντα τὰ ἔθνη), which is the focus of Paul's apostleship (1:5) and includes his Roman readers (1:13).

3. God is the only wise one (16:27).

The second dative phrase (μόνῳ σοφῷ θεῷ) stands in apposition to the first (16:25a) and specifies God the Father as the one to whom Paul is referring. He is the "only-wise" one, whose wisdom is unfathomable, whose ways are unsearchable, and whose sovereignty is unparalleled (11:33–36). He is also the one to whom glory is due (ᾧ ἡ δόξα) as the incorruptible God (1:23) in whose glory we hope (5:2). Jesus Christ is the agent through whom the Father receives glory (διὰ Ἰησοῦ Χριστοῦ) "to the ages" (εἰς τοὺς αἰῶνας; cf. 9:5; 11:36). The God who is able to strengthen believers is also the God whose wise plan is revealed in the gospel and who receives the glory through Jesus Christ.

Theology and Appropriation

Of the doxology, Stott writes, "It is fair then to say that the major themes of Paul's letter are encapsulated in the doxology: the power of God

---

18. For μυστηρίου see the note 21 on page 288.
19. The adjectival participles σεσιγημένου, φανερωθέντος, and γνωρισθέντος are all divine passives.
20. ESV.
21. See the note on 1:5.

to save and to establish; the gospel and the mystery, once hidden and now revealed, which are Christ crucified and risen; the Christ-centred witness of the Old Testament Scripture; the commission of God to make the good news universally known; the summons to all the nations to respond with the obedience of faith; and the saving wisdom of God, to whom all glory is due for ever."[22] In particular, Paul focuses on the gospel, which provides the overall theme that encompasses the various topics of the letter,[23] and brackets that focus with three attributes of God.

"God" (θεός) occurs 153 times in the letter; "gospel" (εὐαγγέλιον) occurs nine times.[24] In the three verses of the doxology, Paul reminds us that God is powerful (16:25a), eternal (16:26b), and wise (16:27a). He is able to bring to completion the gospel he planned and unfolded throughout history. Elsewhere in the letter, Paul makes it clear that the gospel is from God (1:1; 15:16), is about God's Son (1:9; 15:19), and is God's power for salvation (1:16). In the doxology he highlights five truths about the gospel: (1) it is Christocentric (16:25a, 27b; cf. 1:3–4, 9); (2) it was hidden but now has been revealed (16:25b–26a; cf. 1:17); (3) it is prophetic and, therefore, authoritative (16:26b; cf. 1:2); (4) it is universal (16:26c; cf. 1:5, 16); and it is effectual (16:26c; cf. 1:16).

Paul's primary purpose for including this passage at this point in his letter was to call his Roman readers to give God glory for his gift of the gospel. With his original readers, we need to adopt an attitude of awe at God's wisdom and trust in his working. The passage offers multiple possible points of connection, including mysteries that are hidden and, then, uncovered as well as the ideas of giving commands, being wise, and ascribing "glory" to individuals for doing something special. The passage corrects the ideas that God is somehow limited in what he knows or what he does, that he somehow works haphazardly or arbitrarily, and that the truth of the gospel is something we can work out by using our own reasoning. The passage commends an attitude of praise to God for his wisdom, his plan, and his gospel, all of which are made known through his Son. The objective in communicating this passage should be to help others understand the richness and depth of the gospel so that they will view living out and sharing the gospel as an act of worship to the only wise God who is its source.

---

22. Stott, *Romans*, 406.
23. See the Introduction, page 21
24. A textual variant in 15:29 also includes εὐαγγέλιον; the verb εὐαγγελίζω occurs three times (1:15; 10:15; 15:20).